THE FRENCH NAVY
IN
WORLD WAR II

The

FRENCH NAVY

in

WORLD WAR II

by

Rear Admiral Paul Auphan, French Navy (Retired)

and

Jacques Mordal

Translated by

Captain A. C. J. Sabalot, U. S. Navy (Retired)

UNITED STATES NAVAL INSTITUTE

Annapolis, Maryland

Naval Institute Press
291 Wood Road
Annapolis, MD 21402

First Naval Institute Press paperback edition published in 2016.
ISBN: 978-1-59114-566-0 (paperback)
ISBN: 978-1-68247-060-2 (eBook)

Library of Congress Catalogue No. 59-8595

♾ Print editions meet the requirements of ANSI/NISO z39.48-1992 (Permanence of Paper).
Printed in the United States of America.

24 23 22 21 20 19 18   9 8 7 6 5 4 3 2

Foreword

Seldom in the history of a great nation has the fate of a Navy been so tragically involved in political events as in France during the course of the Second World War.

Heir to a past which dates back to the Crusades, the French Navy had previously experienced many painful vicissitudes. Not one was to equal that of 1939-1945.

After having efficiently contributed to the rescue of the French Army at Dunkirk and removed from reach of the enemy everything that floated in the Atlantic harbors, the Navy, like all Frenchmen, had its heart crushed by the tragedy of defeat. The causes of it were complex. The only chance to recover was to remain united. Faithful to its traditions, the Navy remained in the ways of discipline consistent with the promise it had given the Allies. While waiting for the day when the United States of America could come to the assistance of Europe, it maintained the empire welded to the mother country, revictualled the unhappy French and safeguarded—often under very difficult conditions—the French heritage overseas. That long martyrdom led to the scuttling of the French Fleet at Toulon on the 27th of November, 1942. On thus scuttling half of its Fleet, the Navy amputated one of its limbs, but saved its soul. No matter the separate ways they had pursued under the shock of events, all of its seamen could now, in a spirit of unanimity, return to the fight. They participated in the final victory to the best of their abilities. It is not their fault if their heroic actions did not end in unity.

Such is the story, not well known, even in France, and often misunderstood, that Admiral Auphan and Jacques Mordal narrate in this book. Few men could tell the story so well because each of them, after having actively participated in the war at sea, continued under the German occupation to oppose themselves to the Germanization of our country.

I do not forget the services rendered by Admiral Auphan, Deputy Chief of Staff of the French Admiralty, when he proceeded to Dover, somewhat at my request, to organize the revictualling and later the evacuation of the French divisions at Dunkirk, or each time an occasion presented itself to the Navy, during the Battle of France, to come to the aid of the Army. Neither do I forget the assistance he gave me after the armistice, when I did my utmost to reconstitute, in secrecy, the Army of Africa. Before being arrested by the Gestapo, in November, 1942, I was a witness to his efforts, as Minister of the Navy, to save the Fleet. Nobody is more qualified to express the state of mind of the Navy during the entire tragedy than Admiral Auphan himself.

His collaborator, Jacques Mordal, was blown up on a mine at the time of the evacuation of Dunkirk and was seriously wounded. He has been mentioned several times in dispatches, once for work in the Resistance. He has now dedicated himself to the study of history, in particular that of the Second World War. His books speak with authority. Their objectivity and their accuracy have never been questioned either in France or abroad.

I must compliment the United States Naval Institute for publishing a work indispensable to whoever wishes to understand, without a preconceived idea or made-up mind, the history of the six years which shook the world. But I know the two authors well enough to be certain that in stating merely the truth, they have aimed at a better thing yet—to strengthen the traditional bonds of friendship which unite us with the United States of America and to promote an understanding between the two shores of the Atlantic, the better to defend civilization.

Paris
November 10, 1957

MAXIME WEYGAND
General, French Army
Member of the French Academy

Preface

The Second World War has probably been the most trying period in the history of the French Navy. Aside from the material hardships, it was the unhappy outcome of the 1940 campaign, the armistice, the occupation of the homeland, and the war that continued which brought the Navy's corps of officers face to face with tragic problems of conscience. Their behavior in these times of crisis gave rise to hasty judgments, which were the result of exaggerated propaganda, and which history is already in the process of revising.

It was not in order to defend a particular attitude that we undertook to write this book. We did so, rather with the conviction that only a strict presentation of the facts could explain the different stands taken, clear up misunderstandings, and reconcile divergent opinions.

Perhaps it would have been desirable for such an account to come from a historian who had no part in the tragedy, whereas both of us were deeply involved in it. But, apart from the fact that events are often incomprehensible to those who have not lived through them, we do not believe that our having stayed with the majority in the path of discipline prevents us from understanding those who, under very difficult circumstances, elected to do otherwise.

One of the authors having been chosen by destiny to hold high positions in the Government, a respect for the truth has constrained us not to conceal either the deed or the thought. We have endeavored to write objectively, with the serenity allowed by the passage of time, and without giving our book the appearance of pleading a cause or of justifying it.

The facts which we report have been assembled and verified during the course of long years of research, reading, and thought. If at times our experiences have permitted us to add our personal testimony, we have not stated anything that cannot readily be documented. We could have increased, ad infinitum, the number of footnote references. We purposely limited these in order to make the book more readable by avoiding frequent interruptions in the thread of the story. Beyond our personal recollections, one or the other of us was able to have long discussions with most of the leaders who were directly involved in the events related. These discussions have clarified and filled out the picture of events resulting from a study of official records. Such discussions, checked against the innumerable personal accounts published in France and abroad, in Allied as well as in enemy countries, have brought us special advantages which other less favored authors might not have been in a position to obtain.

We realize that, in explaining events and in evaluating their effects, one may well arrive at opinions different from those we have reached. We believe that, as with all human endeavors, this one is not perfect and perhaps constitutes only a step toward an understanding of what took place. At least we are certain that we have never knowingly distorted the truth, and we hope that, by supplying the reader with facts he might not have known, our book will enable him to appraise at its high worth the service record, so often misunderstood, of the French Navy during World War II.

PAUL AUPHAN
Rear Admiral, French Navy (Retired)

JACQUES MORDAL

Villefranche de Rouergue—Paris
October 15, 1957

Introduction

The collapse of France in 1940 was a tragedy, not only for the nation, but for the Navy, the personnel of which—particularly those outside of France—were faced with the necessity of making agonizing decisions. No matter what course they took, or whether or not we agreed with them at the time, I feel that the majority of French naval officers and men must be given credit for pursuing what they felt to be their duty. It is hard to put one's self in their shoes. Our own Civil War was the cause of great sectional bitterness, which has been long in dying out. Even greater, in my opinion, have been the schisms and divergences of opinion produced in France by the unfortunate events of the last war—rifts which not only continue but which have had much to do with the difficult position in which France now finds herself.

The French Navy in World War II is believed to be the first complete account of French naval activities during the Second World War. It should constitute a valuable historical record, revealing many facts never before published. It covers the story of the French Navy before the Armistice, the Free French Naval Forces, the Vichy French Navy, the new "National Navy" formed under the Provisional Government in North Africa after the Allied landings in 1942, and the activities of the French naval personnel who remained in France after the total occupation of that country in November 1942.

The authors, Rear Admiral Paul Auphan, F.N. (Ret.), and Jacques Mordal, were of the category of those who were in France at the time of the North African landings, and perforce remained there, as a result of the Nazi occupation. Admiral Auphan, in the early days of the war, was Plans Officer on the staff of the then Chief of Naval Operations, Admiral Darlan. After the Franco-German Armistice, he became the Director of the Merchant Marine, at Vichy. Thereafter, as Admiral Darlan moved up, Admiral Auphan succeeded him as Chief of Naval Operations and Minister of Marine. Jacques Mordal was Admiral Auphan's confidential assistant in the latter post. Accordingly, both were in unique positions to observe at first hand many of the events described in this book. Each of them is a recognized historian of first rank, with many books behind him, and this work, as a whole, is the result of exhaustive research covering all of the material available to them.

Shortly before the scuttling of the Fleet at Toulon, Admiral Auphan resigned in protest at Laval's policies and retired to his home, there to engage in underground activities against the Germans. At the same time, Jacques Mordal got himself assigned as Medical Officer to the personnel of the

French merchant and fishing fleets operating out of English Channel and North Sea ports, and utilized that position as convenient cover for manifold intelligence activities.

Impartial as I feel sure the authors intend to be, it is almost impossible for a person to avoid some personal attitude toward persons and things with which he has been intimately connected. The understanding reader will bear this in mind. One can agree with many of the opinions expressed herein without agreeing with them all.

For one thing, however much one may disapprove of *some* of General de Gaulle's actions, and of those of the Provisional Government under his administration, one cannot fail to honor him and his followers for the courage with which they adhered to their convictions, for their loyalty to the cause which they believed to be right, and for the sacrifices they made in behalf of that cause. But, respect should also be accorded to those others who, conscientiously, felt themselves duty bound to obey the orders of the Vichy Government, and thus, under tragic circumstances, found themselves opposed to their erstwhile allies and to many of their fellow countrymen.

I understand the regret of the authors that the British and ourselves did not rely on Darlan's word that the French Fleet would never be surrendered intact to the Axis. But I do not agree with their view. That Darlan would have been true to his promise, I now firmly believe. The authors' statements in this respect are strikingly supported by the testimony of other French naval friends, close to Darlan, in whom I have the utmost confidence. Unfortunately, however, conditions at the time were not such as to inspire confidence on the part of the British, nor, later, of their American ally. With an aging Marshal Pétain at the head of the Government and such men as Laval wielding political power, who could be sure that Darlan, even were he determined not to give up the Fleet, would remain in power? And, for that matter, Darlan himself was suspect, owing to his apparent dealings with the Nazis—dealings which, it is now revealed, had the aim of securing the best possible bargain for France without sacrificing her Navy.

With respect to the seizure of French ships under their control at the time of the Franco-German Armistice, and the regrettable events at Mers-el-Kebir and Dakar, it must be remembered that, from the British side, there was much to justify their actions. A desperate Britain, left alone, but under an unconquerable leader, was courageously fighting for her national existence. She could take no chance whatever of losing her naval supremacy by permitting Axis acquisition of the French men-of-war at Mers-el-Kabir (or Alexandria). As to Dakar, a glance at the map indicates all too clearly what the seizure of that port by the Axis, and its employment as a U-boat base, would have meant. We ourselves, in the Atlantic Amphibious Force, were directed in the spring of 1942 to study plans for the possible seizure of Dakar, in order to deny it to the enemy.

The authors do not conceal their regret that the Anglo-American allies did not see fit to take the French leaders into their confidence with respect to the landings in North Africa, but they themselves recognize that this was not possible. Such a course would have been highly desirable, could it have been determined with certainty just *which* leaders to trust. But secrecy was *vital* to success. Had our objectives leaked to the enemy, concentrations of enemy submarines at the points of landing would certainly have resulted in tragic losses, *if not in complete failure.*

I know that many of our French friends believe that at Casablanca it was the American forces who opened fire first. But, as commander of the Western Naval Task Force, I can state authoritatively that this was not the case. Our orders, to take no hostile action unless resistance *was* encountered, were positive, and each of our task groups had definite orders to do no firing unless fired upon. As our first boat wave approached the beach at Fedhala, I saw to my delight a searchlight beam go vertical, the signal prescribed in our advance plans that we would be welcome. But shortly the searchlight beam dropped to horizontal and hostile machinegun fire was opened on our boats. Only when I received word from all our task forces that they were being fired upon, did I reluctantly give the code signal, "Play ball!" to our forces to open fire.

As to our attack on the French submarines in Casablanca harbor, these constituted the greatest menace to us of all the French forces. Even so, these were not attacked until their movements after daylight seemed to evidence hostile intent. It is my great regret that it was not possible to prevent the resulting tragic loss of life in combat between traditional friends and allies.

The spirit of the majority of the French Navy after the North African landings is well personified by the attitude and actions of Admiral Michelier, who so determinedly contested us until the receipt from Algiers of Admiral Darlan's declaration of an armistice. When I met him at Fedhala on November 11 (the anniversary of the World War I armistice), I offered him my hand and expressed my regret at having had to fire on the tricolor, the flag of a nation we always had considered as a friend. He took the proffered hand and said, "Admiral, you had *your* orders, and you carried them out. I had *mine,* and I carried *them* out. Now, I am ready to cooperate with you in every possible way." And cooperate he did, heartily and effectively, until months later, when he was removed from his command by the French Provisional Government—despite, it may be said, U. S. naval protest to the Supreme Allied Command. He remains, I am glad to say, a friend to this day—he and many other French naval leaders with whom it was my pleasure to be associated.

The French Navy is one of centuries-old traditions. It has prided itself, as a *"corps d'élite"*, on its morale, its aloofness from politics, and its allegiance to what it considered to be the legally constituted government of France. From personal association with it in Morocco, in the Mediterranean, and, later, in France, I can testify to its *esprit,* its *élan,* and its efficiency, even under the most adverse of circumstances.

Let us hope that the proud French Navy will ever remain our friend and ally, and that it will never again be called upon to undergo a travail such as that of 1940-1944.

H. Kent Hewitt
ADMIRAL, U. S. NAVY (RET.)

Orwell, Vermont
May, 1958

Table of Contents

List of Illustrations

Jean Bart at Casablanca on November 11, 1942—Undamaged gun battery at Casablanca—General Eisenhower, Admiral Darlan, and Admiral A. B. Cunningham at Tomb of the Unknown Soldier at Algiers—Damaged *Dunkerque* at Toulon

French troops disembarking in Corsica—*Gloire* with French troops aboard entering Naples harbor—The French Navy returns to Toulon

List of Charts and Diagrams

THE FRENCH NAVY
IN
WORLD WAR II

CHAPTER 1

The Naval Tradition of France

Geographers compare France to a hexagon, three sides of which front on the land and three on the sea. All the drama in French history derives from this dualism.

Having harbors on four seaways—the Mediterranean, the Atlantic, the English Channel, and the North Sea—France might have devoted greater effort to maritime development had she not found herself engaged in almost ceaseless struggles on the continent either to establish her sovereignty or to maintain it. Compelled to defend herself against hostile incursions on the line of the Rhine, the Alps, and the Pyrenees, France perforce turned her attention from the sea to the land, and so developed as a military land power rather than a sea power. Her Navy, never the first concern of her kings, was too often neglected, despite its patriotic spirit and the invaluable logistic support it gave to the land campaigns of the Army.

To understand this martial spirit, it must be remembered that the first Admiral of France, Florent de Varenne, was appointed to command the Crusader's Fleet by Saint Louis, the king, in 1270 to stem the tide of Moslem conquest which threatened to sweep over the entire Mediterranean. The spirit of the Crusade—that is to say, the disinterested devotion to an ideal for which one is willing to give his life—thus became an attribute of the mariners of France. The fleet of Saint Louis contained few ships that were really French. It was only at the beginning of the 17th century, after the Middle Ages and the wars of religion, that the French Navy truly began to exist as a national organization.

In France, at that period, only the nobility were granted the honor of wearing the sword, either on the land or on the sea. And the nobles of the day were distinguished more for their fighting qualities than for any administrative or organizational talents. On the other hand, the higher ranks of the clergy—men of peace rather than of war, though there were notable exceptions—possessed family connections and a general culture that fitted them well for administrative, political, or diplomatic positions. Thus it is understandable that Louis XIII had as prime minister a bishop of the Roman Catholic Church—the Cardinal de Richelieu.

To Richelieu the Navy seemed such an important factor in the destiny of the nation that he undertook its administration personally, and kept it under his immediate supervision from 1628 until his death in 1643. Richelieu breathed into the nascent naval establishment much of the realism and energy and solid commonsense that led him to write: "To command ships, I prefer the substantial seamen, brought up on the sea and the bottle, to the curled and perfumed cavaliers of the court."

Richelieu had on his staff an intelligent and hard-working assistant named Jean Baptiste Colbert, who succeeded the great cardinal as Minister of the Navy. Colbert and his son, the Marquis de Seignelay, between them administered the powerful Navy of Louis XIV for twenty-nine years. (The Ministers, it can be seen, did not change as often then as they do today!) The first organic regulations of the French Navy—analogous to the *King's Regulations* of Great Britain—date from Colbert. And certain expressions, certain customs on board ship, even certain installations still in existence in the dockyards of Brest and Toulon, are attributable to this great successor of Richelieu.

Thus the French Navy is inevitably an institution steeped in tradition—something which constitutes both a weakness and a strength. It is a weakness in that tradition has fostered in it a tendency to be conservative in technical progress; a strength in that it has inspired both officers and men to follow the precepts of an honorable past. Fidelity to traditional moral values is one of the characteristics of the French naval establishment—a fact which must never be forgotten in any study of the Navy of France during the Second World War.

Another characteristic of that navy is that, differently from many others, it was not created for mercenary gain or for the protection of private commercial interests. Genoa and Venice, for instance, were essentially merchant maritime republics. The northern powers, like the Dutch and the Hanseatic League, had as commanders men who were ship owners even before they were admirals. And the Royal Navy of Great Britain was built primarily to insure safe passage throughout the world of its merchant fleet as indispensable to the economic life of the nation.

Such was not the case—at least in the beginning—with the French Navy. In France, in the days of the monarchy, any nobleman who engaged in commerce acted beneath his station and forfeited his rank in the nobility. In the social framework of that period, the nobles were the heirs to the chivalry of the Middle Ages, with no function other than to bear arms for the defense of the nation. Therein lay their honor—and, in principle, their only occupation. No matter how often even Richelieu decreed that colonial commerce was an exception, the French nobles never quite acceded to his viewpoint.

Hence, in its inception the Navy of France was solely a political instrument, a disinterested weapon under the orders of the chief of state. Far from coming from commercial circles, many officers in the early days of the French Navy were Knights of Malta—that is, they belonged to an international order, semireligious, semimilitary, which since the days of the Crusades had had as its mission the checking of the Moslem corsairs in the Mediterranean. In an era when there were no naval schools, this order constituted an excellent training medium for the future officers of the Navy, who, from the age of thirteen or fourteen, fought on board the galleys of the order in the Mediterranean.

Throughout nearly all of its long history the French Navy had had one principal opponent—England. To conclude from this, however, that its present day officers are Anglophobes would be as erroneous as crediting them with still wearing the wigs and knee breeches of their forebears of the 18th century.

Excluding the so-called Hundred Years' War, which France fought partly to eliminate English colonial enclaves in her home territory, Franco-British naval competition lasted just about two centuries. The rivalry began when the expansionist ideologies of Louis XIV collided with the equally imperialistic ideas of William III of England. Faced with the problem of fighting the armed forces of practically all Europe on land at the same time that she fought the combined British and Dutch navies on the sea, France lost the opening round in 1713 despite such outstanding victories as Beachy Head, Barfleur, and Vélez-Málaga. Moreover the conflict quickly spread to the distant possessions of both major powers, particularly the East and West Indies and the North American colonies.

The French colonies in those days were administered by the Navy Department, just as if they were distant ships permanently at anchor. In America the French had established a sort of protectorate the whole length of the Mississippi basin, from Acadia and Canada in the north to Louisiana in the south, thus setting up a barrier to the westward expansion of the British colonies along the Atlantic Coast. But even with a colonial population in North America ten times that of the French, the British perhaps would not have conquered Canada so quickly if the French Navy, which provided the sole link with the home country, had not been completely crushed by the end of the Seven Years' War, in 1763. For in Europe the

French Army, which had absorbed the lion's share of the national man-power and the national budget, had fought its way to the heart of Europe—without ever realizing, perhaps, that at that very time France was losing an empire overseas.

A defeat, when correctly analyzed, is always productive of reform. Courageously the French Navy reformed, rebuilt, and refitted—and waited for a chance to retaliate. The opportunity came in 1775, when Britain's North American colonies revolted and asked for French aid. Without the help of the French squadrons which were sent across, the colonies would have experienced a great deal more difficulty in winning their independence; in fact, as the American historian Samuel E. Morison wrote recently, it would not have been Lord Cornwallis but General George Washington who would have had to surrender at Yorktown.[1]

In the War of American Independence, French diplomats for once avoided the pitfalls of European politics, and through fifty months of war the French fleets, though outnumbered everywhere, held the British at bay. Their single setback was at the Battle of Saints Passage in 1782, where the French with 2,300 guns faced the British fleet with 3,000 cannon.

In 1789, on the eve of the French Revolution, the seaborne commerce of France nearly equaled that of England, and her Navy was at its peak. Not until 1939 would the French Navy again be so closely knit, so confident, and so comparable in strength to its opponents.

But the French Revolution began the downfall of the naval establishment. Confusion led to disorder, and disorder to mutinies. Many of its officers—*le grand corps*—were summarily dismissed; others went to the guillotine. Antirevolutionary political groups even assisted the English enemy to "peacefully" occupy the port and naval arsenal of Toulon, thereby confronting the French naval officers with the same problems of conscience that were to torment their counterparts in World War II.

True, Napoleon Bonaparte did try to rebuild the Navy to its former power, but he failed for lack of time. With what remained of ships and former commanders he attempted to gain control of the English Channel—"were it only for twenty-four hours," in his words—in order to land his Boulogne army on the English coast. Such an amphibious landing, in the miscellaneous assortment of lighters and barges he had assembled, would have been as ambitious an undertaking for that day as the Anglo-American landings in Normandy in June 1944. But Napoleon tried to maneuver his squadrons as he would so many troops of cavalry, without ever taking into account the ocean spaces, the contrary winds, the lack of properly trained

---

[1] Samuel E. Morison, "The Battle That Set Us Free," in the *Saturday Evening Post,* July 7, 1956.

crews, and all the other factors which enter into naval tactics and strategy.

Against the brave but untrained crews of the French fleets the British threw superbly manned ships of overwhelming firepower, and crushed the French, first at Aboukir and then at Trafalgar.

At Trafalgar, furthermore, the French and Spanish combined fleet fought more to satisfy honor than with any sound tactical plan in mind. Having had his courage questioned by Napoleon, the French commander in chief, Admiral Pierre de Villeneuve, was resolved to prove that the officers of the Navy could fight, even against a Nelson. And when he failed in his effort to die in battle, he later committed suicide to wipe out what he felt was the shame of defeat.

The course of the French Navy, as has been aptly said, has often been more dolorous than glorious.

After Trafalgar the Napoleonic hegemony eventually crumbled—not because of the failure of Marshal Emmanuel de Grouchy to arrive on the field of Waterloo, as claimed by some, but because seapower little by little strangled "Fortress Europe," as Hitler's similar creation was to be called some hundred years later.

Unfortunately the mass of the French people, dazzled with the victories won by their armies on the continent, failed to appreciate the significance of the operations at sea. This difference in the nation's impressions of the contributions of the two services is one of the reasons why, in France, the Navy has a different outlook from the rest of the country.

In addition to marking the end of the Napoleonic empire, 1815 marked the end of Franco-British naval competition as well—and to the advantage of England. Because the sea makes one a realist, however, and because its past exploits were sufficiently glorious to inspire its corps of officers, the French Navy harbored no feeling of bitterness. Instead, it devoted itself during the 19th century to winning for France a new colonial empire overseas—an accomplishment of which the public, however, was at times completely unaware. Rivaling in élan the officers of the British Navy, the French often cooperated with them in maintaining world peace in a spirit already "European." In such manner French and British squadrons fought side by side against the Egyptian Fleet at Navarino, against the Russians in the Crimea, and against the Boxers, the Chinese Nationalists of the 19th Century. Notwithstanding several political crises stemming from colonial disagreements—at Tahiti, at Fashoda, and elsewhere—the two navies came to appreciate each other in a way that prepared them for the Grand Alliance of 1914.

Before that time, however, the French Navy had to undergo the frustrating experiences of the Franco-Prussian War of 1870. The drama of that period strikingly forecast the events of 1940. In both cases all-out hostilities between the two regular armies lasted only a few weeks. In each case the French homeland was deeply invaded. If in 1870 the seaports such as Cherbourg and Brest were not taken by the enemy, it was because the armies of those days still marched on foot and not by mechanized transport. Finally, in both cases the fighting was followed by a prolonged occupation of a part of France by the German enemy.

At sea, the French Navy of 1870 was actually the second most powerful fleet in the world, not far behind the British, while the German Navy was almost insignificant. But except for blockading the enemy's coast—a blockade too short to have any effect—the French Navy had no opportunity to exploit its supremacy once the frontier defenses had been breached and the Germans were besieging Paris. A number of ships were demobilized in order to rush 10,000 sailors to help man the defenses of the capital, but this could not alter the course of events. With striking similarity, in 1940 the French Navy was again obliged to look on almost helplessly as the fate of the nation was settled by the battling of the armies ashore.

And in 1871, after the return of peace, the French people remembered only that their Navy had been of no help to them in the disastrous conflict. With habitual shortsightedness they believed the Navy had functioned poorly. Consequently, after the war naval budgets were reduced by the politicians. And since the Navy had to use much of its funds for meeting the colonial responsibilities with which it was entrusted, construction of new combatant ships was sadly neglected. Relegated to a little world all its own, the Navy vegetated. It required the extraordinary growth of the German Navy at the beginning of the 20th century, with its threat of a new conflict, to restore the French Navy to a point where the Entente Cordiale (France and Great Britain) could equal the seapower of the Triple Alliance (Germany, Austro-Hungary, and Italy.)

The First World War found the French Navy ready and eager to fulfill its obligations in the Entente by engaging the combined Austrian and Italian Mediterranean squadrons in a classical fleet action. But Italy declared her neutrality, and later became an ally, and the Austrian Fleet never came out of its harbors at all. All the French Fleet could do was to maintain a tedious watch at the entrance of the Adriatic for an Austrian sortie that never took place, and join the British in the ill-fated Dardanelles operation.

During this time France was again invaded by land. One of the authors of this book, at that time a young ensign, remembers a night in August 1914, when the landing party of his cruiser was rushed posthaste to Paris with its two machineguns—strong firepower for those days. Unlike the outcome in 1870, however, this time the capital was saved, by the victory on the Marne. The sailors rushed to the capital's defense stayed on to constitute the famous marine brigade *(Brigade des Fusiliers Marins)* which distinguished itself for four years in some of the most hard-fought engagements of the entire land campaign. The same was true of a regiment of naval gunners which had been formed to man the 305-mm. (12-inch) naval guns mounted on railway carriages. One of the moving spirits in that naval railway battery was Lieutenant François Darlan—later to be Admiral of the Fleet.

At sea the war took on an entirely unanticipated aspect. The appearance of German submarines off the Pas-de-Calais, a hundred miles from their bases, seemed quite an event to the sailors of 1914. And at the beginning there was no effective weapon to combat these surprising undersea menaces. The man-of-war which saw a periscope—or thought it saw one—had no choice but to try to ram, or to grapple for the submerged U-boat with its anchors!

Despite the land armament again getting the lion's share of the military budget, the French Navy, like the other allied navies, put forth an enormous effort in the manning and arming of more than a thousand patrol vessels and minesweepers, in addition to the regular men-of-war already in commission at the beginning of hostilities. Starting from zero, her naval air arm grew to a force of more than 2,000 planes by the end of the war—a war in which the French Navy lost 500 officers and 11,000 seamen killed or missing.

But escorting convoys and patrolling the sealanes, although arduous work, is not glamorous in the eyes of the civilians ashore. When peace returned, the Navy had the uncomfortable impression that its role in the national defense was again misunderstood and unappreciated by the general public.

It is true that had it not been for the heroic stand of the Army, the frontlines would have been broken—just as was to happen in 1940—and the war would soon have ended disastrously for France. But it is equally true that without the support of the innumerable men and the invaluable supplies safely transported from overseas to the European battleground, Germany could not have been checked, and ultimately defeated.

Displaying an understandable partiality, our allies from across the seas—England and the United States—were particularly concerned with the effective employment of the naval forces; to the French, the armies protecting their frontiers were of first importance. French naval officers accorded equal weight to land and sea—but for that very reason, their countrymen ashore saw them as a caste apart.

With the conclusion of hostilities, public opinion moved toward international limitation of arms. A conference was convened in Washington for the purpose of implementing Article 231 of the Treaty of Versailles, which had partially disarmed Germany as precursor to parallel disarmament by the victors.

The French Government was successful in obtaining a decision that land and air armaments would not be discussed—arms in which France at that time had superiority. On the other hand, England and the United States, which were withdrawing more and more into their own spheres, one into its commonwealth and the other into the American hemisphere, were interested primarily in naval armaments. So doing, they were abandoning Europe more or less to French influence.

It is very difficult to reduce armaments, particularly through the establishment of an hierarchy between nations, if disarmament is not wholeheartedly desired by all.

Both England and the United States had seen that submarines constituted a threat to the usual control of the seas by the larger naval powers, and they proposed that their construction and use be prohibited. This met opposition from the second-rank naval powers, for whom the submarine was an instrument of pressure and thus a means toward equalization. France for one refused to do away with the submarine, thereby drawing sharp rejoinders from the British. And partly as a consequence, France found herself, along with Italy, forced to accept a capital ships tonnage ratio of 1.75 to 3 for Japan and 5 for the United States and Great Britain.

Justifiable or not, in time of peace the political power of a nation, and hence her influence in world affairs, is often measured by the relative strength of her naval forces. With this limitation on her battleship tonnage, the measure of naval might at that time, France was deeply humiliated by the ratios of the Washington Treaty.

True, these ratios were fairly in accord with the relative strengths of the various navies at the end of the war. But during the war, with the French Army given industrial priority, the construction of capital ships in France had been suspended; in other countries, which had not been invaded, naval construction had been expedited. Moreover, parity with Italy failed to accord with tradition, or with the respective obligations of the two navies, or with the relative political power of the two countries. Nevertheless the French Government accepted the Washington Treaty ratios for capital ships —designedly offensive weapons—though it refused to limit cruisers and lighter craft, which were generally considered defensive weapons.

In actuality the capital ship limitation did not injure the French Navy, for the naval funds allotted from the war-exhausted treasury would not have permitted much more construction than was actually undertaken. But the blow to French naval pride—a blow for which they held the British responsible—caused ill feeling that lingered on until 1938 and Munich, with its ominous shadow of World War II.

In the opinion of one of the French Ministers, why should the French Navy build new combatant ships, anyway, since there would never be another war? Accordingly some twenty submarines and torpedo boats taken from the Germans, plus some dozen torpedo boats built in Japan and a few English sloops and several American dispatch boats, were amalgamated with what remained of the French Fleet to form the postwar French Navy. It was a navy of highly irregular composition and appearance, to say the least. And while there were enough ships to conduct a training program for officers, there were not enough to interest them in naval careers. The naval academy consisted of nothing more than temporary barracks. Pay schedules were not adjusted to compensate for devaluation of currency. Many officers left the service, and there was a constant shortage of personnel.

Within that decrepit body, however, the soul of the Navy persisted, the survivor of many trials and of more misunderstandings, sacrifices, and unmerited criticisms than glorious victories. But adversity had deeply impressed its officers with the conviction that despite its checkered history, the French Navy had served as an elite corps—few in numbers but of homogeneous organization, aloof from politics, always an example of efficiency and devotion in the critical hours of the destiny of France.

CHAPTER 2

The Navy on the Eve of the Second World War

In 1914 the French Navy consisted of 690,000 tons of combatant ships in commission, with an additional 257,000 tons under construction. At the time of the Washington Treaty of 1922, the combat fleet totalled only 485,000 tons in commission and a mere 25,000 tons under construction—an obvious indication that even obsolete ships were not being replaced. All of the other principal naval powers had emerged from the conflict larger and more modern. The French Navy lost forty per cent of its fighting strength, and the remaining Fleet units were ill assorted and decrepit. Morale was low. Neither the Government nor the public seemed to have any interest in naval affairs.

Nevertheless the Navy proved faithful to its trust. The funds which were allocated were spent wisely and in accordance with a carefully planned program. By comparison with other Government departments it revealed a constructive doctrine and an integrity that impressed even the members of Parliament. The Ministers of the Navy, who invariably entered office with prejudices against the seagoing service, became strong supporters. Among the best can be mentioned François Pietri, who served more than two years, and Georges Leygues, who died in his post in 1933 after having served as Naval Minister for more than seven years and through eight different changes of Government. It was Leygues who remarked to Lieutenant Commander Paul Auphan, "I served for fifteen or twenty years in practically every Ministry of the Republic before coming to the Navy. I found competent people everywhere. But here one is completely astounded to find his staff working indefatigably without demanding the Legion of Honor at the end of a month or a promotion at the end of three. What is most heart warming is the Navy's discipline, loyalty, and absolutely unselfish devotion to duty!"

As his principal adviser and private secretary (Chef de Cabinet), Leygues, who was a deputy from the Department of Lot-et-Garonne, chose his godson and compatriot, François Darlan, at that time a commander. Darlan was the son of an influential member of Parliament who had been a Minister and Keeper of the Seals under the Third Republic. In spite of some shortcomings and a timidity which he hid under a brusque manner

10

Darlan had a thorough knowledge of his profession, along with good commonsense and a quick mind. With his family connections he was naturally well known in political circles—something that is rarely a handicap in any country. With a mischievous sense of humor young Darlan would often introduce himself as "the naval officer with the greatest backing." Be that as it may, Darlan's position in the office of the Minister of the Navy insured that that service would at least receive a sympathetic hearing in Government circles—something which it had often lacked. So this teamwork of Darlan and Leygues, furthered by a succession of able Chiefs of the Navy General Staff—Admirals Louis Violette, Georges Durand-Viel, and, later, Darlan himself—achieved wonders in the revival of the Navy.

For instance, the Navy had long wanted the enactment of a law establishing the strength of the fighting fleet—personnel as well as ships—on which to base an orderly, year by year program of ship building.[1] The Navy would then have had a solid base on which to negotiate at future disarmament conferences. The Navy failed to secure the enactment of such a law; the Army succeeded. The Navy had to content itself with empirical programs, established annually, and always subject to the hazards of parliamentary debate. In this manner, the Navy managed to obtain, between wars, the assent of ever-changing Parliaments for sixteen yearly programs for new combat construction and ten supplementary ones for auxiliaries—a total of 705,000 tons of combatant ships, plus 126 auxiliary craft.

Naturally all these ships were not completed by 1939, for the more important programs were the latest ones. However, by 1939 the Navy was approaching that strength which its officers considered the minimum necessary to insure the nation's independence in time of peace and its security in time of war. This goal was not reached without critical struggles, not only with the politicians of their own country but of other countries as well.

For, as has been said, it is utopian indeed to hope to establish international disarmament if one country looks upon the armaments of its neighbors more critically than it looks at its own. And that was the story of the disarmament efforts of the later 1920's and the 1930's. On the one hand the charter of the League of Nations, to which most of the naval powers belonged, provided for a reduction of armaments, "taking into account the geographical position and the particular problems of each State." On the other hand the United States was not a member of the League of Nations, so the naval powers which were signatories to the Wash-

---

[1] In 1924 the Navy presented to Parliament a program calling for 175,000 tons of battleships, 60,000 tons of aircraft carriers, 360,000 tons of light craft, and 96,000 tons of submarines—a total of 691,000 tons of combatant ships (the same tonnage as in 1914, excluding auxiliaries). The program never passed.

ington Treaty were obliged to hold separate discussions on the only question which interested the Americans: that of naval armaments considered independently from land and air armaments.

In 1924 the "Preparatory Commission" which the League of Nations had established met at Geneva to study questions relating to disarmament. The English advocated limitation by specific categories—heavy cruisers, light cruisers, destroyers, etc.—which would automatically have insured control of the seas for the British by establishing their supremacy in each class. The French, on the contrary, advocated global limitation, which would permit complete freedom of action and leave the door wide open for "surprises."[2]

The discussions were deadlocked for three years. The French Navy offered a compromise plan, but the British refused to budge.

Then the United States intervened with an invitation to a naval conference with the view of extending the ratios of the Washington Treaty to all categories of ships. The French refused to be caught twice in the same trap, and Italy also declined the invitation. In 1927 the three remaining powers— Japan, Britain, and the United States—met, but could arrive at no agreement. The United States Navy, which had a greater need than Great Britain for heavy cruisers, refused the proposal of Britain in that category, whereupon the British began to veer around to the French point of view. In March, 1928, a British-French compromise plan began to take shape, which, however, required the acquiesence of all the powers. The United States not only rejected it, but to emphasize the rejection the U.S. Congress passed a building program providing for fifteen 10,000-ton cruisers. The whole attempt at arms limitation ended with the utopian but impractical Briand-Kellogg Pact, signed at Paris, by which all the great powers "renounced war"—but without any of them renouncing the right to arm.

The next conference of the five major naval powers assembled at London, in 1930. Again the Americans, though having no part in the League of Nations, wished to extend the ratios of the Washington Treaty to all navies and to all types of ships. Even if the French had been willing to discuss such a ratio in relation to the United States and British Navies, her interests in the Mediterranean were such that she could never have accepted parity with the still greatly inferior Italian Navy. The new construction program had now been in effect for eight years, and public opinion and the Government were behind the growing French Navy.

In 1932 the scene shifted to Geneva, where the General Disarmament Conference of the League of Nations met after eight years of preparation.

---

[2] By "surprises" is meant new inventions, new ship designs, or development of entirely new classes which would outmode existing ships possessed in superior numbers by another power.

The conference was dominated by the question of what rights were to be accorded Germany. That nation, noting that the victorious powers had not yet disarmed, as prescribed in the Versailles Treaty, asked for either disarmament all around or equality of armament for Germany. When this was refused, Hitler promptly withdrew from the conference. Later he decreed universal military service in Germany without anyone contesting it, since it was naval armaments alone that interested Great Britain at that time. The final result of the Geneva Conference was that the League of Nations no longer engaged itself with matters of naval armaments.

However, behind the scenes, the French and Italian naval experts carried on their own negotiations. It was to the interest of both countries to reduce expenditures. Unofficially they agreed on a formula of limited scope which would preserve the existing naval ratios of the two countries, without any commitment for the future. The French Minister of Foreign Affairs reluctantly accepted the Navy's recommendation, but the British, informed of the unofficial agreement, still pressed for parity for the Italian Navy with the French Navy. Encouraged, in 1934 Mussolini announced the laying of the keels of two 35,000-ton battleships in the near future. The French Navy, which had only the *Dunkerque* under construction, immediately obtained funds for the construction of the *Strasbourg* as a makeweight.

In 1934 Japan gave the required two-year notice that she would not renew the Washington Treaty, which, as a matter of fact, she had already been secretly violating. France sent out a similar notice in order to emphasize once and for all that she would not accept naval parity with Italy. Though the diametrically opposed points of view of the various nations had been recognized for a long time, nevertheless a call was sent out for a new conference to be held in 1936 to work out some sort of substitute for the Washington Treaty.

While France was preparing for the new conference with the hope that the threatening German rearmaments might also be taken under consideration, the British Government took the initiative by negotiating directly with Hitler. In June, 1935, following a visit to Berlin by Anthony Eden, she conceded to Germany the right to a Navy thirty-five per cent the strength of the Royal Navy, and the possibility of increasing this ratio to forty-five per cent in the case of submarines.

France was thus confronted with a *fait accompli*. The German Navy, which had already laid down two capital ships of 26,000 tons each, plus 12 heavy cruisers, 16 destroyers, and 28 submarines, would now be in a position to build up a global tonnage of 420,000 tons instead of the mere 100,000 tons she was permitted under the Treaty of Versailles.

Looking back after the intervening years, one can understand the cold logic of Great Britain in officially recognizing German naval rearmament and agreeing to a limit, even a very large one, rather than having no agreed limit at all. It would have been commonsense if the French too had been just as realistic and had jettisoned the ineffectual legalisms of the Versailles Treaty to which she still clung. At that time, however, the French Navy could not avoid the feeling of being abandoned—left alone and misunderstood in a world of increasing menace. Accordingly the French Navy that year obtained authorization for the construction of two more battleships, to be named respectively the *Richelieu* and the *Jean Bart*. With such additions the Navy was confident that, even without the British Navy as an ally, it could cope successfully with the combined German and Italian Navies.

And international peace in Europe was becoming steadily more precarious. More exasperated than hurt by the sanctions imposed on her for the Abyssinian campaign, Italy intensified her rapprochement with the German Reich. Germany reoccupied the left bank of the Rhine without the slightest reaction to this flagrant violation of one of the most important clauses of the Treaty of Versailles. And an ideological civil war broke out in Spain, where the German-Italian fascists on one side faced the democrats, anarchists, and Soviet communists on the other.

Part of the French naval forces were called upon to cruise for many months off the Spanish coasts in order to protect or evacuate French nationals. In 1937, French ships escorted an average of 500 merchantmen each month around the Iberian Peninsula. In the harbors, the Navy saved the lives of many nationals, even Spanish. It had no part, however, in delivering the shipments of arms which the Socialist-dominated government of France was sending to Republican Spain at the expense of the French Army's own stockpile. Convinced from their contacts with the officers of other navies that another European war was inevitable, the French Navy vigorously prepared for it.

For the London Conference of 1936 had been a complete fiasco. Japan had appeared merely to announce that she would no longer participate, and that she reserved complete freedom of action in the future. Neither Germany nor Russia was represented at all. Italy sent word that she would not know how to negotiate with nations which had just previously applied sanctions against her. All that Britain, the United States, and France could do was to establish qualitative limits (tonnage, size of guns) for each type of ship, to bind themselves not to exceed them, and to make known their building programs in advance to each other. This last was a needless clause since in every democratic country building programs only came into being after long hours of public debate. These agreements were pretty fairly observed, yet since no controls were provided, compliance depended entirely upon the good faith of the nations themselves.

In France, while the masses were engrossed in the social reforms with

ADMIRAL DARLAN *decorates the defenders of Dunkirk at French Admiralty Headquarters, Maintenon, June 1940. In the foreground, left to right, are Admiral Abrial and Admiral Darlan (with sword). Rear Admiral Platon (partially hidden) and Rear Admiral Leclerc appear just behind Admiral Darlan.*

FRENCH 10,000-TON CRUISERS *on maneuvers in* 1937. *Left to right:* FOCH, COLBERT, SUFFREN, *and* DUQUESNE *as seen from the* DUPLEIX.

which they were being appeased, the Navy, ever vigilant, vigorously pressed its reorganization. The regulations were modernized; training was intensified; construction of a new naval base at Mers-el-Kebir was begun. To insure fuel oil for the Fleet, the Navy encouraged the establishment of refineries and of commercial petroleum stocks in the homeland. Moreover it stocked approximately 3,000,000 tons of petroleum products in tanks in the vicinity of its navy yards. By 1939, reservoirs with a total capacity of 1,200,000 tons—most of them underground—had been completed. In a country where the civilian work week had been reduced to five days, naval personnel worked six days a week, and an extra hour each day. This expansion all had to be done despite only a minor share of the defense budget, the Air Force being allotted twenty-seven per cent and the Army fifty-two per cent against the Navy's twenty-one.

In 1938 the Navy obtained funds for the construction of two aircraft carriers, but unfortunately these ships were barely under construction when the war began. Following the Munich incident, it hastily increased its building program by two battleships, two cruisers, two super-destroyers, eighteen regular destroyers, and eighteen submarines, but only a few of these ships reached the stage of being given a name.

The result of the Navy's dogged perseverance was that at the beginning of the war France possessed a strong, modern, homogenous fleet, the composition of which is shown in Appendix A. Not counting the old battleships—though these too saw action during the war—there was not one combat ship over 13 years old. The ships were well built and dependable; their gunnery was excellent. The new super-destroyers—actually small cruisers—proved themselves the fastest ships in the world. Modern communications, including ship-to-ship voice radio, had been installed. The listening devices were good, but the submarine detection gear, of the asdic type, was still in the research stage. All the ships had been trained in day and night squadron maneuvers.

One major defect existed—a weakness in aviation striking power and also a weakness in air cover, owing to the lack of aircraft carriers and to the inadequate antiaircraft batteries. Perhaps because of lack of imagination, perhaps because of conservatism, the French Navy had concentrated more on building battleships than it had on aircraft carriers. One reason for this was undoubtedly the controversy that had arisen since World War I between the Air Ministry and that of the Navy. The Navy had had its air arm transferred to the newborn Air Ministry and had only regained shipboard aviation in 1932. During those years the aviation personnel were tossed from one Ministry to the other, and the two services devoted more time to squabbling than they did to working together on the problems of the future. Politically the Air Ministry was backed by the progressive parties, while the

Navy gained its support mostly from the ranks of the moderates. These rivalries between the services did not disappear until the very advent of war.

Notwithstanding all this, French naval aviation in 1939 consisted of approximately 350 combat planes, manned by picked personnel. At the same time large plane orders, some placed with American industry, were building up the air arm at a rapid rate. The squadrons underwent intensive training, especially in reconnaissance and search, illumination, sea patrol, and anti-submarine warfare.

Theoretically the provision of air cover to the fleet operating at sea and of air strikes on enemy forces was partially the responsibility of the Air Force. Actually the very opposite occurred in 1940. At the time of the German invasion then, the combat air squadrons of the Navy were the only ones in existence in France—and these were placed at the Army's disposal for service on the Oise River front.

The Navy also had some very good anti-aircraft weapons (75-mm., 90-mm., and even 130-mm. on the *Dunkerque*), but these were sadly handicapped by lack of radar. Except for this lack, the naval base at Toulon, some 200 kilometers from the Italian front, was one of the best defended against air attacks. In 1940 the 90-mm. batteries of the Navy were called upon to defend Paris, as the Army had nothing equivalent to them. The main weakness in the Navy's anti-aircraft defense—other than lack of radar—was an insufficiency of machineguns and light guns of 25-mm. or 40-mm., for use against low-flying planes and dive bombers. The need of such weapons would be bitterly felt in the Norwegian expedition and later off the northern coast of France. One difficulty was that the Navy was dependent upon the Army, which was charged with furnishing her with light automatic guns. And the complete lack of divebombing and low-flying attack planes in the French Air Force was not conducive to impressing the Army with the critical need for an adequate number of short-range anti-aircraft weapons.

Time will not be taken here to relate the Navy's struggle even to retain its status as a distinct service. Sometimes proposals were made to incorporate the Navy into a super-ministry of National Defense, which, of course, would be completely dominated by the Army. Again the proposal was to subordinate the Navy High Command to an over-all Commander of the Armed Forces. Only the stubborn intelligence of the Navy frustrated these attempts.

Only when there is unity of strategic aim should there be a single command. But the problem of France in case of war with the Axis powers was twofold, with each part having no relation to the other. It was the Army's mission to prevent the invasion of the country, and, if possible, to carry the war to the enemy. The Navy, on the other hand, had the mission of keeping the sealanes and the seaports open so that the country and its fighting men could receive the supplies they needed. Only at places where sea and land fronts joined was there any problem requiring single command.

Such a place was Dunkirk in 1940, when a single command was set up there at the time of the evacuation by the French and the British.

As for the rest, all that was needed was coordination and cooperation between the services, and the Navy considered this sufficiently well taken care of by the Committee of the Chiefs of Staff (*Comité des Chefs d 'Etat-Major*). In 1939 the presiding officer of this Committee was General Maurice Gamelin, Commander in Chief-designate of the Army, who was assisted by a staff made up of officers from all three services. General Gamelin held the title of Chief of Staff of the National Defense, which made him the principal military adviser of the Government. In this connection he, of course, had the benefit of the advice of his colleagues. But the conduct of naval operations remained entirely outside his jurisdiction.

These operations fell within the province of the Chief of the Navy General Staff who, merely a collaborator of the Navy Minister in time of peace, assumed the title of Comander in Chief of the French Naval Forces in time of war. In 1939 the Chief was Admiral Darlan.

Experience had vastly matured this officer. Among other assignments he had commanded the Atlantic Squadron with brilliance. Chief of the Navy General Staff at the time, he had attended the coronation of King George VI, as did the chiefs of all the foreign navies. But he did not appreciate the protocol which, as he said, placed him during the coronation service "behind a pillar and after the Chinese admiral."

At that time the two highest permanent grades in the French Navy were vice admiral and rear admiral. Although wearing an extra star as Chief of the Navy General Staff, Darlan's permanent rank was only vice admiral, which ranked him after all regular four-star admirals, be they Chinese or Panamanian. Darlan came to the conclusion that there was only one step to take, so upon his return to Paris he had himself elevated to the rank and dignity of Admiral of the Fleet, equivalent to the Royal Navy rank of that name. Thenceforth when Darlan spoke at international meetings in the name of France, he had insured himself an equal footing with anyone else present.

Later on, the French naval officers of that time were reproached with being individualistic, aloof from the rest of the country. Some politicians even accused the Navy of being hostile to the political institutions of the day.

This may partly be attributed to the conflicting attitudes the French were to take at the time of the armistice and during the German occupation. The truth of the matter was that the Navy of those days was a tightly knit and homogenous group of dedicated officers and men—a Navy in which all were proud to serve and in which everyone obeyed without question the orders of their superiors, and these superiors in turn unhesitatingly carried out the directives of the Government, regardless of the political party which might for the moment be in power. Differently from the Army, whose strength lay mostly in mobilized reservists, eighty-six per cent of the Navy's personnel was made up of volunteers, reenlistments, and career petty officers. If the Navy seemed aloof from the general public, it was mainly because they did not engage in politics, and because, as professional seamen, their viewpoints were on a worldwide basis rather than confined to the limited horizons of the average Frenchman.

The French Navy of 1939 may best be described by the four words which for over a century have been lettered in gold above the quarterdecks of all French men-of-war. On one side of the panel there appears the motto "Honor and Country," and on the other side, facing it, the words "Valor and Discipline." Not one of those four virtues but would be needed by the seamen of France in the ordeal to come.

CHAPTER *3*

The Opening of Hostilities

Regardless of how much they may have been anticipated, and plans made for all foreseeable eventualities, wars frequently break out in an unexpected manner. In 1870 a cleverly worded—and therefore misinterpreted—news dispatch, the famous Ems dispatch, so inflamed French public opinion that the national cry was, "On to Berlin!" In 1914 it was the assassination of the Archduke of Austria at Sarajevo that set up a chain of reactions which a month later provoked the First World War. In 1939 it was for remote Danzig that the Western democracies were willing to go to war. But for years the cause of peace in Europe had deteriorated.

In 1935 Mussolini's invasion of Ethiopia had roused Britain's opposition to the extent that the entire British Fleet had been concentrated between Gilbraltar, Alexandria, Haifa, and the Red Sea. Concerned over the threat of the Italian Fleet and Air Force to her naval forces in the constricted Mediterranean, Britain had asked the French Navy to guarantee her free use of the naval bases at Toulon and Bizerte. This accord was quickly given, and although hostilities between the powers did not then materialize, technical contacts had been established between the two navies which would bear fruit. Furthermore the British thereafter made no further attempts to limit French naval power.

When, in March, 1936, German troops entered the Rhineland in flagrant violation of treaty agreements, the contacts between the two navies were quickly reestablished. Neither the French Government, nor the British— especially the latter—desired or dared to react with force. Furthermore the bulk of the British Fleet was still in the Mediterranean, and British public opinion would not have supported even a token stand against Hitler. However, further military conversations took place not only between the Navies but between the General Staffs of the Armies and Air Forces as well. The Belgians also attended these conferences. The British promised the French that in case of German aggression, two divisions would be ready to embark in British ports within fourteen days after mobilization. The problem of transporting and escorting these troops was one of the main things discussed, and this joint staff work laid the foundation for joint effort in 1939.

On both these occasions, 1935 and 1936, the French Navy discreetly

19

called back to service, by individual postcards, a few reserve specialists for "a period of training." When, in 1938, Hitler's annexation of the Sudetenland brought on another crisis, the precautionary measures taken by the French Navy were much greater in scope. As early as September all hands on leave were recalled and all ships brought up to full complement. Wartime commands were activated, and even a few preliminary mobilization measures were ordered. The cruiser schoolship *Jeanne d'Arc,* about to leave Brest on a round-the-world training cruise, took aboard combat ammunition over one side, and, over the other, it took on board cases of fine wines to be served at international receptions. No one knew which would go off first, the guns or the champagne corks! Then came the settlement at Munich, and peace—though for how long, no one had any idea.

These crises, as well as the Spanish Civil War, accustomed officers and crews to living in a constant warlike atmosphere. Flaws which had been revealed in the semimobilizations were promptly corrected—something which brought its reward in 1939, when mobilization was effected without a hitch. The Navy looked upon Munich as being nothing more than a temporary respite, and it vigorously speeded up its programs.

In March, 1939, came the next great crisis when Hitler marched his troops into Prague and "peacefully" annexed Czechoslovakia. This little country had an army 35 divisions strong, and would have provided worthwhile bases for Allied aviation. But its main defenses had been dismantled six months earlier when the statesmen of the West had withdrawn their support—partly because they considered Czechoslovakia indefensible.

Strategically this decision was prudent and wise—perhaps too wise. But such logic did not continue to prevail, for on March 31 Britain and France officially guaranteed the defense of Poland, a country much more remote and more difficult to defend. Thereupon Hitler immediately put forward new claims—on Danzig, this time—and war again seemed inevitable.

Joint British and French staff conferences were held at London on March 31, April 27, and May 3, 1939. The French delegation was headed by Vice Admiral Jean Odend'hal, who later was to represent the French High Command at the British Admiralty throughout the war.

Today, the officers of the North Atlantic Treaty Organization have daily staff conferences to work toward a common concept. In 1939 no such procedure was in existence, and these prewar Allied planning conferences were indispensable in deciding upon the general disposition of each fleet in time of war, as well as in establishing liaisons, and coordinating areas of command and establishing convoy routes and escort procedures. The Franco-British naval entente had been effected cordially and without mental reservations.

But Poland, trusting in the Allied guarantee, was beginning to inquire urgently what plans were being made to protect her in case of aggression. The British Navy declared—and justifiably—that circumstances did not lend themselves to operations in the Baltic; all that England contemplated was a few bombing raids over Germany. The French default was of the same order. The Army declared that all it could do, as a diversionary measure, was to hurl itself against the powerful fortifications of the German Siegfried line, without much hope of breaching it. The Air Force promised to contribute sixty Amiot type-143 bombers—planes which barely had flying range sufficient to make the trip across Germany to Poland's westernmost airfields. As these airfields were captured by the Germans on the first day of hostilities, the gesture never had to be carried out.

Regardless of the Allies' admission of helplessness, and perhaps suffering under the fatuous delusion that Hitler would be deterred by the mere paper guarantee of France and Britain, Poland refused to compromise. A Franco-British military and naval mission hurried to Moscow in an attempt to obtain the support of the Russians, but the Poles did not trust the Russians, did not want them on their territory. And then on August 21 Stalin closed the door in the face of the Allies by concluding a treaty of nonaggression and economic cooperation with Germany, with whom he also had a secret understanding for the partition of Poland.

In the French Navy, as odd as it may seem today, the pact between Stalin and Hitler was welcomed with relief. If French sailors had to fight, they would prefer not to have the Communists as allies.

Morale in the Navy was high. All leaves were cancelled and men ordered to report back to their ships immediately. On August 23 the Reservists were called up. Lookout and antiaircraft defenses were manned. Exchange of liaison officers was arranged: French officers to Malta, Gibraltar, Plymouth, Dover; British to Bizerte, Toulon, Brest, Dunkirk. Sizable naval missions were established in Paris and London. On August 25 a Franco-British signal code, prepared in great secrecy, was taken out of the security vaults and put into effect. Central Mediterranean trade was suspended; merchant ships and fishermen were advised to depart from German or Italian waters as speedily as possible. Even before mobilization a few trawlers were being obtained from willing owners for conversion to minesweepers. On the 30th the convoy and routing sections charged with the wartime dispatching of merchant shipping set up offices in the principal ports.

Little by little, the various wartime commands were activated. At the summit were Admiral of the Fleet François Darlan, Chief of the General Staff of the French Naval Forces, and General Gamelin, the Commander in Chief of the Army, each of them answerable only to the Government. The Minister of the Navy retained only the responsibility of operating the navy yards and maintaining the ships of the Fleet. The Commander in Chief,

Darlan, had under his direct control the commanders of the various theaters of naval operations, each one responsible to Darlan for the conduct of all routine operations in his respective zone—convoys, escorts, air reconnaissance, antisubmarine warfare, etc.—as well as for special operations, for which the necessary ships were assigned to them. Under these theater commanders, in turn, were the commandants of the naval districts, who were responsible for the coastal defenses. As a rule the Commander in Chief reserved to himself the operational control of the high seas forces, the most powerful of which would be the Raiding Force *(Force de Raid),* under Admiral Marcel Gensoul. This force, to be set up on mobilization, consisted of the battleships *Dunkerque* and *Strasbourg,* the aircraft carrier *Béarn,* and some ten cruisers or super-destroyers.

In accordance with the war plan, the principal subordinates of the Commander in Chief were as follows: in the Mediterranean, Admiral, South (Admiral Jean Pierre Esteva), with headquarters at Toulon—or, in case of war with Italy, at Bizerte; in the North Atlantic, Admiral, West (Admiral Jean de Laborde), with headquarters at Brest; in the English Channel and North Sea, Admiral, North (Admiral Raoul Castex at first, and later Admiral Jean Abrial), with headquarters at Dunkirk; in the Far East, Admiral, French Naval Forces, Far East (Admiral Jean Decoux), with headquarters on board the *Lamotte-Picquet,* usually at Saigon; in the Caribbean Sea, Admiral, Antilles (Admiral George Robert), with headquarters at Martinique. Early in the war another theater commander, Admiral, Africa (Admiral Emmanuel Ollive), was established, with headquarters at Casablanca and with an operational zone reaching from Gibraltar to Dakar, and extending westward to include the Azores, Madeira, the Canaries, and the Cape Verde Islands.

Such was the worldwide extent of the French naval establishment, yet the organization was simple, adaptable, and efficient. It relieved the Commander in Chief of routine chores, it gave him time to think, and it allowed him to devote his attention to the global concept of a war at sea.

All tourists familiar with Paris know the Ministry of the Navy, that beautiful colonnaded building which borders the Place de la Concorde to the east of the Rue Royale. Its ornate facade dates back to Louis XV, and even before the Revolution it had the aspects of a museum. Except for a forest of antennas on the roof, the edifice in 1939 was externally much as it had been for 150 years. But the Navy had constructed a gastight underground air raid shelter there of reinforced concrete, designed to provide a safe working place for all the personnel in the building. It was at Rue Royale, center of information from all over the world, that the decision was made in August, 1939, to place the Navy on a war footing. And it was there that the final fatal information was received that plunged France into the chaos of another world conflict.

At daybreak on the 1st of September, following a so-called refusal on the part of the Warsaw Government to discuss the latest unacceptable proposals from Hitler, the German Army invaded Poland. In Berlin the British and French ambassadors solemnly warned Hitler that their countries would honor their commitments to Poland if this aggression was not halted immediately. In France general mobilization was decreed.

With the Navy's personnel now up to strength of about 160,000,[1] the Navy's forces took their initial stations as planned in case of war with Germany and Italy. On the assumption that there would be a German raid toward the Moroccan coast, a barrier line of large submarines was posted off Vigo and the Portuguese coast. Other submarines were stationed in the Mediterranean.

However, during the day Italy declared herself provisionally neutral. Accordingly orders were issued immediately to all French ships and planes that Italian shipping was to be approached with the utmost caution and provoking incidents were to be carefully avoided.

The 2nd of September was a day of suspense, with frantic diplomatic negotiations proceeding in all the capitals. The French Parliament voted the military credits asked for by the Government, but not once was the word "war" mentioned. The navy yards began ship conversions according to program.

That same day the Navy Ministry received information indicating that the German Fleet had sortied in force from its bases two or three days previously, but, upon being questioned, the British confessed that they had no information of its whereabouts. Remembering the bombardments of Bône and Philippeville which had marked the beginning of World War I, the French now feared a similar raid on the Moroccan ports. Accordingly the Raiding Force was ordered to proceed at high speed from Brest toward Casablanca, and the minelaying cruiser *Pluton* to lay a protective minefield off the Moroccan coast. However, these emergency measures were countermanded when later intelligence rendered them unnecessary. Even though there was no fighting, however, the French suffered their first naval casualty of the war, for the *Pluton* was destroyed on September 13 by an explosion while her mines were being disarmed prior to off-loading. The French Navy lost 215 officers and men killed or missing in the explosion.

The 3rd of September was the day when the question of war or peace would be decided. Unfortunately the diplomats of France and Britain had

---

[1] Regulars—91,093, of which 5,486 were officers; Reserves—69,243, of which 4,820 were officers.

not coordinated their efforts, for the British ultimatum to Germany expired at 11 a.m., while the French ultimatum did not expire until 5 p.m. Consequently the Royal Navy's liaison officers already working beside their counterparts in the French Naval Ministry had some anguished hours while they faced the possibility, however unlikely, that they might find themselves alone in the conflict. However, 5 o'clock came, with no reply from Hitler, and the hours of peace in Europe had run out.

General Gamelin, speaking for the Army, advised the Navy that he would not undertake any operations until 5 o'clock the next morning, the 4th of September. With the authorization of the Premier, however, the Navy sent out a plain language radio message to all its ships and stations notifying them of a state of war.

Within two days Paris had its first air raid alarm. At the Navy Ministry, a beehive of activity, all hands grabbed gas masks and rushed to the armored shelter underground. The alarm proved to be false, but it confirmed one thing: the shelter was far too small, and it was unbearably hot. At the "all clear" the exhausted, perspiring officers and men climbed from the enclosure and stretched themselves out, panting, on the floors and desks, without regard to rank or station. And Admiral Darlan decided that he and his staff would move immediately to the "standby" headquarters, established several years earlier at Maintenon as an emergency command post outside the capital.

In modern war a bird's-eye view of the field of battle is no longer an essential to the military leader. The primary functions of a naval commander in chief are the coordination and analysis of information, and, in conjunction with the Ministries of the government and with the other services, the determination of a program of action, which is then transmitted to the various subordinate commanders for actual implementation. To fulfill these functions, it was not necessary for the Chief of Staff of the French Naval Forces to locate his headquarters either on board ship or in the Naval Ministry at the capital. The most important requirement for a headquarters location is that it provide an adequate communication and liaison network.

The Navy had pondered this problem for some time, and originally it had selected as headquarters several casemates of the old fort of Vincennes, an edifice erected by the kings of France in the 14th century, and located in the immediate suburbs of Paris. But the accommodations were clearly inadequate, and in addition the location was too close to the capital with all its intrigues, indiscretions, and political interference.

The Navy's preference, Maintenon, was a charming village seventy kilometers west of Paris. Excellent national and international telegraphic and telephonic communications were assured by cutting in the Navy's headquarters directly on telephone and telegraph trunklines laid underground to the capital. The radio network was equally satisfactory. High speed tele-printers provided permanent liaison with subcommanders. There was an airfield nearby. And finally, while the capital was reasonably near, it was not uncomfortably so.

In effect, life at Maintenon was very like life aboard ship. Personnel were forbidden to have their families in the village, and everyone had to obtain special permission before "going ashore," as it were. The offices of the staff were a group of huts ranged under the trees of a beautiful park, though a circle of sentries surrounded all.

It was there that Admiral of the Fleet Darlan, Commander in Chief of the Naval Forces, and his staff would reside until the spring of 1940. To distinguish this command post or headquarters from the Ministry of the Navy, which would remain at Rue Royale in Paris, Maintenon was designated the "French Admiralty." The three or four hundred people attached to the command were under the orders of the Chief of Staff (Rear Admiral Maurice Le Luc) and the Deputy Chiefs of Staff (Captain Paul Auphan and Jean Négadele). These three worked at the same table, to which was routed all incoming information and from which all outgoing orders emanated. In his free moments Admiral Darlan would join the group and watch his staff at work while he smoked his beloved pipe.

As correspondent at Paris the French Admiralty had a man who today would be called a "sage"—Professor Henry Moysset, who for twenty years had lectured at the Naval War College and who also had been the chief private secretary of Navy Minister Georges Leygues. Professor Moysset[2] was intimately acquainted with Germany and the Germans, and his wide international contacts constituted precious sources of information.

In establishing his headquarters at Maintenon, on the opposite side of Paris from the battlefront, Admiral Darlan felt certain that he would never be forced to evacuate them, even though the frontlines should waver.

But the Admiral's confidence was short-lived, for by June, 1940, the German invasion threatened to engulf it, and the French Navy's head-quarters moved to Montbazon, near Tours. Then, during the tragic days of the armistice, it moved successively to Dulamont, near Bordeaux, then to Nérac, and, finally, to Vichy.

---

[2] In 1941 Moysset became Minister without Portfolio to Marshal Philippe Pétain.

CHAPTER 4

Protecting the Sea Lanes

In September, 1939, the combined British-French naval forces were far superior to the German Navy. Outside of the North Sea, a zone of contact, all they expected to meet on the high seas were German submarines or occasional lone surface raiders. However, merchant shipping was as vitally important to France as it was to Great Britain, and the French Navy was determined to guard it well.

Ordinarily France received almost three-fourths of her imports by sea, mainly through Atlantic ports. War requirements would greatly increase French overseas purchases, particularly in America, where, without waiting for mobilization, she had placed large orders. On the side toward Germany, the frontier of course was already closed to traffic. Imports over the other land frontiers had never been very large. From an economic point of view France was almost an island like England. Her heavy industry was smaller than that of Germany, and her agriculture was seriously affected by the calling up of so many of the farmhands to the colors. The sea alone could assure the necessary food, arms, ammunition, petroleum, and other materials needed to supply the armed forces and civilian inhabitants, and to carry on the war.

Moreover France had to maintain close liaison with North Africa and the various colonies of the empire everywhere. It was not merely a matter of administering the colonial governments but also of transporting to Europe the immense resources of men and raw materials which these overseas possessions could contribute. All Navy men remembered that during the First World War the colonies sent to the assistance of the mother country some 500,000 fighting men and 200,000 workers. The lines of communication with Africa were as important to France as the great commercial shipping routes which brought the products of America.

Finally, transporting the British Expeditionary Force to France, along with the supplies necessary to maintain it, required the establishment of a convoy system linking Britain with French ports on the Channel or the Atlantic.

Strategically, France was the bridgehead of the Allies on the European continent—a fact brought home to the democracies, including the United States, in 1944 when the bridgehead no longer existed and had to be regained by a tremendous amphibious effort.

The problem of utilizing their merchant shipping to maximum benefit had been discussed between the two countries in the London meetings before the war. At that time the two navies had expected to have to face the Italian Navy as well as the German, and it had appeared necessary to have all the French light forces stationed in the Mediterranean in order to protect traffic with North Africa. Even then the ships available for escort would have been fewer than needed. Accordingly the French Admiralty had decided to permit its ordinary merchant ships in the Mediterranean to proceed unescorted, with routing varied according to circumstances, and to convoy only the troop transports and vessels with unusually valuable cargoes. In the Atlantic, French ships would join up with convoys which the British intended to form at regular intervals at Freetown (Sierra Leone), Kingston (Jamaica), and Halifax (Canada) for passage to the British Isles and return. The French Navy would participate in escorting certain convoys across the Channel.

Such were the plans of the French Naval High Command at the time hostilities began.

On the 1st of September, the French Admiralty, as a matter of precaution, had prohibited the sailing of any merchant ship from its ports. The following day this embargo was lifted—except for Atlantic traffic—as soon as Italy's declaration of nonbelligerency permitted Mediterranean and coastal traffic to proceed almost normally. The Navy waited for positive information as to the whereabouts of the German Fleet before authorizing the resumption of transatlantic traffic, which it did on September 5.

One of the problems of the moment was what disposition to make of the *Normandie*. This magnificent liner of 80,000 tons, the pride of the French merchant marine, was in New York, scheduled to sail for Europe toward the end of August. Too large to be of immediate use as a transport, she would have to be put in a caretaker status either in France or in New York. The decision was to leave her in New York. Those who made that decision—including one of the authors of this book—could not then guess the destiny which fate held out for this beautiful vessel.[1]

Within weeks after mobilization began, French maritime traffic increased to a point it had never reached before. To the approximately 3,000,000 tons which made up the French merchant marine, there were progressively

---

[1] Taken over by the American Maritime Commission shortly after Pearl Harbor, the *Normandie* was rechristened the USS *Lafayette* (AP 52). While undergoing conversion to a troop transport, she took fire from a workman's blowtorch, and, after burning for hours, capsized. A total loss, she was raised, only to be scrapped.

added 2,000,000 tons of ships—Greek, Danish, Norwegian, Swedish, Dutch —which were chartered for French account by a mission with headquarters in London. This entire fleet was administered by the State. Singly or in convoys, the ships followed the routes and schedules laid down in each port by the routing officers responsible to the Admiralty.

On the very day that war was declared, the British passenger ship *Athenia* was torpedoed and sunk in British waters, but it was two or three weeks later before French ships were likewise attacked—a discrimination made, it is now known, by direct order of Hitler to the Kriegsmarine, the German Navy.

At the end of September an important convoy which included several large tankers left the Caribbean Sea for Britain and France. In its Atlantic crossing, up to the point where it was to be met in European waters by a British escort, it was convoyed by the large French submarine *Surcouf*, which was armed with two 203-mm. (8-inch) guns. But bad weather and machinery breakdowns on several ships resulted in the convoy scattering and the *Surcouf* losing contact. In this state the dispersed ships were attacked with torpedoes and gunfire by several German submarines. Between October 12 and 15, seven ships were sunk, including four French vessels: the tanker *Emile-Miguet,* the freighters *Louisiane* and *Vermont,* and the passenger ship *Bretagne.* French light units and seaplanes from Brest joined British ships in searching for the U-boats, and the British succeeded in rescuing 300 passengers from the *Bretagne.*

This was only the beginning. While the land front was settling down to a war of patrols and limited objective raids, the sea front was aflame with daily torpedoings and sinkings. If Germany had waited until she had had more submarines and, especially, more magnetic mines in order to unmask all her weapons simultaneously, she could have obtained more important—even decisive—results. The German Naval High Command was to recognize that fact later. But it requires great strength of character to sit back patiently and delay the employment of a new weapon when one is at war, particularly when there are tempting opportunities to use it. In fact Germany plunged immediately into a form of war based upon that of 1918, which obliged the Franco-British allies to convoy almost all of their commercial shipping, just as in World War I. Fortunately the abstention of Italy facilitated the task.

For some time the explosions of the new German magnetic mines were taken for the work of torpedoes or else ordinary mines equipped with some sort of effective antisweep mechanism. The technical experts of the two navies were at their wits' end. Finally on the 23rd of November the mystery was solved. One of the magnetic mines, dropped from a German mine-laying plane, fell in shallow water in the Thames estuary, where it was discovered and pulled ashore. Then two British officers disassembled it and discovered its secret—a feat of daring and technical skill which received the admiring accolade of all French officers.

Nevertheless the tempo of war—and especially mine warfare—increased with each passing day. To counter the new menace, the French Navy requisitioned in France, and purchased in Belgium, all the wooden-hulled fishing boats it could find, and equipped them with electric sweeps. These boats were mostly old and worn out, and their decrepit engines could not buck the current in many areas. However, no means could be neglected. At the end of a few weeks there were eight pairs of magnetic sweepers working in the channels off Dunkirk, four at Le Havre, and as many at Cherbourg. They exploded quite a number of magnetic mines, but they were to prove even more useful later in the evacuation of the northern ports as the German armies swept to the sea.[2]

Another measure for insuring the safety of the coastal shipping lanes and the Dunkirk roadstead was the laying of twin electric cables at the bottom, in the center of the ship channel. When electric current was sent through these cables in the proper manner, they were capable of blowing up any magnetic mine in the near vicinity.

Finally all men-of-war and merchant ships sailing the Atlantic, the Channel, or the North Sea were immunized or demagnetized by the system known as degaussing, a method discovered in the nick of time. When the waters of the northern ports became infested with magnetic mines upon the approach of the German armies, not a single ship degaussed in the Cherbourg navy yard was lost to them during the entire evacuation.

During the first four months of the war forty per cent of Allied ship losses resulted from magnetic mines; after that, the percentage of losses dropped by half. On the whole, while magnetic mines constituted an added hazard to navigation and a source of mental anxiety to the High Command, they caused less actual losses than might have been expected. In fact they proved less deadly than the more conventional weapons, such as submarines or surface raiders.

At the very beginning, however, the situation was at times so alarming that Winston Churchill, accompanied by Admiral of the Fleet Sir Dudley Pound, made a special trip to Maintenon to ask the French Navy for assistance.

Admiral Darlan, who, like General Gamelin, had a special train at his personal disposal, sent it to Cherbourg to pick up the distinguished guests.

---

[2] If Dunkirk was little plagued with magnetic mines during the evacuations of May-June, 1940, Le Havre on the other hand was the target of a very heavy mine drop during which several of our minesweepers destroyed as many as eight mines each in a single day.

The French naval stewards who manned the dining car were ordered to make certain that there would be no lack of champagne and other spirituous refreshments. Consequently the atmosphere of the meeting was particularly cordial. The conference took place under the trees of the Parc de Noailles, a setting which somewhat astonished the English. But the exchange of views which took place was straightforward and without ulterior motive, for both sides had in mind the one objective of winning the war. Curiously enough, when one reflects on events which were to follow, Mr. Churchill declared to Admiral Darlan that he had complete confidence in the Admiral and his officers—but he would prefer that the French Navy Minister and the French politicians not be kept too well informed on operating plans as he, Mr. Churchill, did not consider them capable of keeping a secret!

The British were particularly interested in the large new French battleships. To meet German battleship and cruiser raids they had only battleships that were too slow or battle cruisers that were too thinly armored. Until the time the new *Prince of Wales* would be ready in 1941, the British were counting a great deal on the *Dunkerque* and the *Strasbourg,* as well as on the *Richelieu,* then nearing completion, and on the *Jean Bart,* under construction, which they asked be completed at the earliest possible moment.

French industry was to perform miracles in this respect; the British were far ahead in submarine detection gear, and they promised to provide the French Navy with a class of trawlers equipped with asdic.

Returning to London after his conference with the French Admiralty, Mr. Churchill informed the House of Commons on November 8, "I wish to point out to you the remarkable contribution of the French Navy, which has never been, for many generations, as powerful and effective as it is now." Later, he was to write in his memoirs that French assistance "exceeded by a great deal all the promises made or engagements entered into before the war."

A few days after the conference, and in the same spirit of fellowship, the British Admiralty asked for the assistance of French submarines in escorting the transatlantic convoys being formed at Halifax. To defend against German surface ships that might possibly be encountered, the convoy escort generally included one British battleship or cruiser and one submarine steaming in the midst of the merchant ship group. From November, 1939, to May, 1940, except for the middle of the winter, French submarines of 1,500 tons alternated with British submarines in escorting eight Halifax convoys. On the African coast, likewise, the British often requested French assistance in escorting British convoys for Sierra Leone and Cape Town.

With their resources strained by the transatlantic convoys, the Royal Navy no longer had enough ships to escort their important shipping which traversed the Suez Canal and the Mediterranean unguarded, but which had to be convoyed from Gibraltar to England. The French Navy agreed to take turns with the British Navy in escort duty on that essential route, and from October, 1939, to May, 1940, French destroyers, torpedo boats, and sloops provided the escort for 29 convoys in one direction and 27 in the other. Ships thus escorted totalled 2,100, of which 89 per cent were British or British-chartered vessels. Out of the 56 convoys, only four ships were lost—three British and one Greek.

These large convoys, sometimes numbering as many as 60 ships, were too unwieldy to burden them further by adding French ships bound from the Mediterranean or Morocco to French Atlantic ports. Moreover many of the older French merchant ships could not make the minimum required speed of nine knots to keep up with the English convoys. Consequently the French Admiralty was forced to sail its ships in small groups from Oran and Casablanca, and then form them into one convoy off Gibraltar for the run north; on the return voyage, the procedure was reversed. From October, 1939, to May, 1940, the Navy thus escorted almost 200 small convoys between the Bay of Biscay and Gibraltar. These convoys totalled 1,532 French or French-chartered ships, of which only seven were sunk by the enemy.

The greatest deficiency of the French Navy in antisubmarine warfare was in submarine detection devices. Rarely was a U-boat found on the surface where well-aimed guns would quickly eradicate it, and the only way to reach it down below was by depth bombs. Differently from the gun crews, for whom target practice was frequently held, there had been no practice at depth bombing with live charges. Consequently the ships too often mistook the great surface upheaval resulting from the explosion of the depth bomb as sure evidence of a "kill." To reduce such erroneous reports to a minimum, the French Admiralty distributed a film on depth charging which showed the true crescent-shaped eddies formed on the surface by a series of explosions. Still, in order not to discourage the attackers, the Admiralty was quite liberal in giving credits to those who had pressed home an attack vigorously.

Up to May, 1940, the French Navy had recorded more than fifty attacks on submarines in the western theater, not counting numerous ineffectual searches. In the eastern end of the Channel, German submarine activity was practically zero, thanks to the effective Allied Pas-de-Calais minefield barrier, in which three U-boats were sunk during the month of October. Most of the reports of submarines sunk, however, were found to be erroneous. Such was the case with the U-boat which the *Lorientaise* reported it had sunk in the Bay of Biscay on January 19, 1940, and which a diver even claimed he had actually seen lying on the bottom. German archives, examined after the war, proved however that no U-boat was lost in that vicinity. Similarly the *U-41*, attacked with gunfire and depth charges by the *Siroco* in the Bay of Biscay on November 20, 1939, and reported sunk, was able to return to port and report the attack. These same German archives, however, confirmed the victory of the *Simoun*, which rammed and sank the *U-54* on February 23, 1940—a sinking which had not been officially recognized by the French Admiralty at the time.

As for other attacks carried out in conjunction with British forces, the degree of success attributable to either will never be known. Such was the case of the *U-55*, attacked simultaneously on January 30, 1940, by the French destroyer *Valmy* and two British destroyers and a British plane.

The really important thing was that the U-boat had been sunk!

In addition to convoy escort and antisubmarine warfare—routine tasks in any naval war—numerous other missions devolved upon the French Naval Forces.

First there was the protection of the heavy troop movements at the beginning of the war: seven convoys transporting two divisions from Africa to the Rhine front; eight troop convoys from Marseilles and Algiers to Beirut, to form the Army of the Levant; and two convoys of British troops from Gibraltar to Malta, which were escorted by the French. In addition a steady stream of native African troops—45,000 men in nine months— began to flow from Dakar and Casablanca to France.

Other important convoys were those carrying the British Expeditionary Force to French soil—four modern divisions in 1939, and thirteen by the end of May, 1940. At first these landed at Brest and in the ports of the Loire, in order to be beyond range of German air raids. The escort was British, though French destroyers and fighter planes often participated in the protection of convoys carrying troops. Local patrols and the sweeping of harbors and harbor entrances for mines was the particular responsibility of the French.

The great minefield barrier which the Allied navies had laid across the Pas-de-Calais at the beginning of the war, had only two narrow passageways through it, each of which was guarded by microphones and other detection gear. One of these passageways was close to the English coast, and opened toward the Downs roadstead; the other was at the foot of Cape Gris-Nez, and opened toward Dunkirk. As its share in the barrier, the French Navy laid 1,000 mines, but within the next few weeks the swift Channel currents tore over 200 of them up and deposited them on the nearby beaches. But just as many British-laid mines washed up on these same beaches. With typical courtesy the French mine disposal officer disarmed these mines, disassembled them, greased them, and returned them to their British owners.

As soon as the Pas-de-Calais mine barrier was in place, the terminal ports for British military convoys were moved closer to the front. Saint-Malo replaced Brest, but the principal port of disembarkation was Cherbourg, where before April, 1940, over 300,000 men were landed without incident. On mail steamers from Boulogne, Calais, and Dunkirk a stream of sick or wounded men, of non-combatants from various organizations, and of men on leave crossed the Channel for England, sometimes as many as 2,000 or 3,000 within a day.

It was not only in the Channel that the French Navy cooperated in ensuring the safety of British troop convoys; in December, 1939, London requested the loan of the *Dunkerque* to escort a Halifax-to-England convoy of seven passenger liners carrying Canadian troops to join the British Expeditionary Corps in Europe.

Other crossings requiring special care were the convoys carrying gold. Not only was the United States of America not in the war at that time, but it was so fearful of being dragged in that a special neutrality law—the "cash and carry" law—governed all dealings with the belligerents. Under the law these latter were required to pay for all purchases in cash and then to transport the goods themselves, as American ships were forbidden to enter the war zone. The Allies had to transport the purchased goods either in their own ships or in neutral ships chartered by them. When the Allies ran out of U.S. dollars, the only currency the Americans would accept was gold.

In November, 1939, the battleship *Lorraine,* escorted by two cruisers, carried the first shipment of gold to the United States; on its return it escorted a convoy of merchant ships loaded with airplanes. When in December the *Dunkerque* went to Halifax to escort the Canadian troop convoy mentioned above, it deposited there, as at a teller's window in a bank, 100 tons of gold. The aircraft carrier *Béarn,* going to pick up airplanes in the United States, took over 250 tons of gold, and the passenger liner *Pasteur* an additional 400 tons. The cruiser *Emile Bertin* started for America with 300 tons, but the armistice intervened and she was diverted to Fort-de-France, in the island of Martinique, instead.

In addition to safeguarding the transfer of all this gold without a penny's loss, the French Navy also rescued, via Beirut, 78 tons of gold belonging to the Republic of Poland—gold which later figured in important diplomatic exchanges at the time of the evacuation of the reserves of the Bank of France when the country was invaded by the Germans.

Nor was the Navy's part confined to the mere convoying of ships; it also mounted offensive operations against surface raiders which threatened them.

The operations of the German surface raiders are now well known, but in 1939 the Chiefs of Staff in London and Maintenon could not deduce the German plans from the maze of information, both true and false, which poured in from all over the world.

On September 30, for instance, news was received of the sinking of the English freighter *Clement,* sunk in the South Atlantic by a German pocket-battleship. The French battleship *Strasbourg* promptly sailed from Brest for Dakar on October 7, to join the British aircraft carrier *Hermes* in forming a "killer group." The *Strasbourg* would be relieved later by two heavy cruisers from the French Mediterranean Squadron. These "killer groups" made periodic sweeps of the tropic seas, and eventually the raider, identified by then as the *Admiral Graf Spee,* was brought to action off the Río de la Plata on December 13, 1939, by a British force under Commodore Henry Harwood. Damaged, and driven into the neutral harbor of Montevideo, the *Graf Spee* scuttled herself. Perhaps her refusal to come out for a final fight was due in part to a rumor, carefully "leaked" by the French, that several large ships were cruising off the Río de la Plata.

A second German raider, the *Deutschland,* was reported loose in the North Atlantic on October 21. The *Dunkerque* and a division of cruisers promptly put to sea to safeguard to its destination an unescorted British convoy from the West Indies.

A month later a British auxiliary cruiser was sunk north of Scotland by the German battleships *Scharnhorst* and *Gneisenau.* Believing mistakenly that the blow had been struck by the *Deutschland,* which in reality had already returned to Germany undetected, the British sent out a search group built around the *Dunkerque* and the British battle cruiser *Hood,* which swept the northern seas unsuccessfully from November 25 to December 2.

In the Indian Ocean the French heavy cruiser *Suffren* was escorting Australian convoys, while in the Atlantic joint patrols searched for the *Altmark,* the *Graf Spee's* supply ship. But the *Altmark* escaped all its hunters until two months later when it was intercepted in Norwegian waters, bare hours from the safety of its home port.

Also watched by the French Navy were certain areas suspected of running supplies to enemy ships at sea. One such area was the Iberian Peninsula. Spain was proclaimedly neutral, but her government was indebted to the Germans for help rendered during the Civil War. Also many German merchant ships, caught at sea by the war, had taken refuge in Spanish ports, especially Vigo. The British and French Admiralties suspected that some of these ships were secretly taking supplies out to enemy submarines or even enemy cruisers at sea. Therefore the French Navy had its light craft, during the entire war, patrolling the approaches to the Cantabrian coast and the principal ports from Bilbao to Vigo. French airplanes and even French submarines participated in these patrols at the beginning. Nevertheless, out of the score or more of German merchant ships that were reported to have slipped out of Spain's northeast ports between September, 1939, and May, 1940, only two were intercepted. Of these one was captured, and the other was scuttled by its crew.

As for German submarines slipping in and obtaining supplies from German merchant ships anchored in Spanish harbors, even today little is really known.[3]

In addition to all the areas mentioned thus far, the French Navy was also responsible for patrolling the regions of the Azores and of the Canary, Madeira, and Cape Verde Islands, where some German freighters and tankers had taken refuge. On several occasions our own submarines or auxiliary cruisers would investigate these suspected areas, and on September 23, 1939, the French submarine *Poncelet* captured the German freighter *Chemnitz,* which had slipped out of Las Palmas and was attempting to get back to Germany. In October a joint Franco-British "killer group" intercepted the German freighter *Halle,* which scuttled itself, and captured the German *Santa Fe.* In the middle of the following month the German freighter *Trifels* was captured by the French auxiliary cruiser *Koutoubia,* while trying to get away with 21,000 cases of gasoline. On February 14, 1940, a prize crew from the small sloop *Elan* sailed into Brest with the German *Rostock,* captured off the Spanish coast three days earlier.

But the most extraordinary episode was that of the German freighter *Corrientes,* which on the night of May 9 suddenly blew up with a mysterious explosion while trying to get under way in the Las Palmas roadstead. Now it can be revealed that the explosion was caused by two audacious officers from the French freighter, *Rhin,* cruising off the port, who swam in and placed limpet mines against the underwater hull of the German ship.

But convoy escorting, blockade duty, and vain "killer" patrols were not enough to fill a need for activity which the Italian status of nonbelligerency left unsatisfied in the Mediterranean. At the suggestion of the French Navy, the Royal Navy accepted the offer of a few French submarines to assist

---

[3] The French naval attaché at Madrid sent in reports giving in detail the identifying numbers of German submarines supposed to have been supplied from merchant ships anchored in Spanish ports. German records examined after the war proved, however, that none of these particular submarines had been within hundreds of miles of Spain at the times cited. On the other hand a German submarine commander made an official report, as evidenced by the German archives, that he had had to forego seeking the shelter of the Spanish coast in order to recharge his batteries, because the sector was too closely patrolled by the French for safety.

in keeping the watch in the North Sea against a possible sortie by the German forces.

The French submarine tender *Jules Verne,* with a division of 600-ton submarines, arrived at Harwich on March 23, 1940. A month later another division of 600-ton submarines as well as a division of 1,500-ton boats reported at Harwich, bringing the total to 12 submarines thus placed at the disposal of the British Command. The force was further increased by the submarine minelayer *Rubis,* since the services of such a vessel had also been requested by the British.

But the hazardous operations of this flotilla in German waters more properly belongs to the account of the Norwegian expedition and therefore will be told in that chapter, along with the equally fascinating story of the super-destroyers of our *Fantasque*-class in the grim battles of the North Sea.

CHAPTER 5

In Search of a Strategy

In modern democracies, the national leaders who direct a war are the statesmen—the political men in power. But they are not capable of conducting war alone; they need the assistance of technicians whose business this is; that is to say, the strategists. Thus at the highest echelons of national defense, the general staffs of the Army, the Navy, and the Air Force have a double function: on one hand, they conduct the actual military operations in accordance with the decisions of the government; on the other, they assist by information and suggestions in the making of those decisions.

In 1939 Admiral Darlan and his immediate colleagues in the French Admiralty were not unaware of their responsibilities. If, up to the time of the formal declaration of hostilities—a purely political action—their role had been limited to completing the Navy's preparations, now the moment had come for them to show how the war could be won.

Truthfully speaking, France entered the war without any definite, actual plan. She had promised to come to Poland's assistance, and she was committed to that action. But within days, within hours, almost, Poland was crushed, occupied, and partitioned without the French Army being able to do one thing to prevent it. What must France do now?

For a long time after the First World War the French were assured that there would be no more wars, and that in any event the fortified Maginot line, facing Germany, guaranteed them security from any invasion. These assurances engendered a defensive psychology which spread throughout the country and pervaded the governing circles and, in 1939, influenced even the military staffs. The sea was forgotten, and the nation's entire attention was given to the land. When the complicated movement of millions of men on innumerable trains was completed without disruption from German air bombardments, every one breathed more easily. The entire French Army was now drawn up at attention back of the Maginot line and the Belgian frontier, which extended beyond it. But that only brought up the question once more: What should be done now?

Whether stated or not, one postulate was universally admitted both in France and in England: the Maginot line was impregnable, and the German

Army would shatter itself in attacking it. But by the same token the French Army would shatter itself if it attempted to pierce Hitler's equivalent, the Siegfried line—though the degree of completion of this latter fortification was perhaps overestimated. So it was a standoff, a checkmate for both sides. This opinion was so universal that at the first meeting of the Inter-allied Supreme Council, held at Abbeville on September 12, 1939, the British Premier, Sir Neville Chamberlain, asked the French as a favor not to risk smashing their army against the Siegfried line for, at best, an uncertain gain. When the French Premier later asked the Chamber of Deputies, assembled as a secret committee on April 19, 1940, whether the French forces should throw themselves against it headlong, the unanimous shout was, "No! No!"

At the worst it was believed that even if the German Army attacked and made some penetration, the frontlines could be consolidated again just as they had been in 1918. The front, everyone believed, was frozen in place, and no decision could be expected for the time being in that quarter.

There was of course the possibility of a flanking movement by one side or the other through Belgium. But Belgium was neutral, and intended to remain so. As to a thrust through Belgium, France gave that country complete assurance that the French Army would enter its territory only if Germany violated it first—and then only if Belgium requested it. To prepare for any such eventuality, General Gamelin wished to draw up defense plans with the Belgian General Staff, but the Belgians, fearful of compromising their neutrality, refused to consider any detailed mutual planning.

The French High Command therefore made the unilateral decision, in case of a Belgian request for assistance against a German invasion, to shift the left wing of the French Army quickly up to the line of the Dyle River. The resulting front from Sedan to Antwerp would be a little shorter than from Sedan to Dunkirk, and the movement should further bring onto the line some 20 Belgian divisions. In order to hold the Scheldt estuaries, it was even planned to extend the line to cover Breda, in Holland. The Navy was concerned in this plan since it would be the Navy's responsibility to transport by sea the Army troops assigned to occupy the islands at the mouth of the Scheldt.

While waiting for any such German movement against Belgium, that part of the French Army which was stationed on the Belgian and Luxembourg frontiers occupied itself in constructing earthworks. The other part, in direct contact with the German Army from Sierk[1] to the Swiss frontier, reconnoitered between the lines and staged minor patrols and raids. The op-

---

[1] A small village in the Department of the Moselle, close to the French, German, and Luxembourg frontiers.

posing forces scarcely fired a shot at each other. In fact the French quietly removed their petroleum stocks from Strasbourg without any opposition from the Germans, though the oil barges passed within 200 meters of the German guns, while, on the other side of the Rhine, infantrymen of the Wehrmacht exposed themselves to work on their casemates without a single bullet being fired to drive them to cover.

It was not this sort of "phony war" that would ever give France a victory.

As a matter of fact, the French Government counted heavily on an economic blockade of Germany to bring Hitler to terms. They envisioned an economic strangulation that would choke Germany without any necessity for seriously waging war on land. To conduct this operation a Ministry of Blockade was set up in the Quai d'Orsay—the French Foreign Office—which, in liaison with London, compiled a list of German commercial representatives in neutral countries. Any merchandise assigned to these representatives was to be seized. All shipping bound for the neutral ports of the North Sea or of Scandinavia was required to pass through clearing stations at the Downs or at Dunkirk where each ship was individually boarded and examined. It was the same in the Mediterranean, with inspection posts at Oran, Gibraltar, and Marseilles. Attempts were also made to negotiate non-reexportation agreements with the neutral countries, and also to restrict not only their imports but their shipping as well to the bare amounts actually needed for national use, with the Allies chartering or purchasing everything in excess. The results from this attempt to control shipping were quite disappointing, however, especially since Italian ships and companies had to be handled with kid gloves. Even in the course of ordinary trade the Scandinavian and Balkan countries, as well as Belgium, Holland, Italy, and Russia, would inevitably contribute toward the provisioning of Germany.

Furthermore, in anticipation of a blockade, Germany had set up a great stockpile of goods. This was increased by the output of synthetic gasoline and artificial rubber processing plants—both unknown to French industry at that time. In addition Hitler had instituted rationing—something which the French Admiralty, concerned over German U-boat successes, also wished to do. But the French Government refused to do this on the pretext that it "would demoralize the people."

In retaliation against Germany's magnetic mine warfare, Great Britain and France had placed an embargo, in November, 1939, not only on German imports but on German exports as well. This was an innovation in economic warfare, its main purpose being to prevent the enemy from acquiring foreign currencies with which to purchase foreign goods. Actual application of this embargo was postponed until March 1940, when it proved ill-advised, indeed, since its first victims were Italian colliers going to Rotterdam to load German coal for Italian industries.

The French Admiralty was of the opinion from the first that a naval blockade of Germany would not be sufficient to bring about a decision, and that in any event the results would be slow. Quite a percentage of Frenchmen were sure that dissension between Hitler and the German generals would bring the war to an end before any real amount of blood was shed, and hence were taking life too easily. The Admiralty felt that the country needed to be shaken out of this passive attitude, even if only for moral and psychological reasons.

Seeking some field for positive action—always with the postulate that the land front would remain frozen in place, of course—the General Staffs decided that there were three weak spots in the enemy's make-up which could be attacked—petroleum, iron ore, and Germany's interior transportation system.

Germany was obtaining natural petroleum—exactly how much, was not known—from the Caucasian oil fields. These oil fields were controlled by Russia which, since its invasion of innocent Finland on November 30, 1939, had been branded as an aggressor by the League of Nations, and placed in the same category with Germany. Russia had already become firmly tied with Germany since her treaty with Hitler, and no one could be sure that she would not change to an outright enemy any day.

Accordingly staff studies began on the problems of air attacks on the Caucasian oil fields as well as naval intervention in the Black Sea itself. Plans for a Balkan operation, outlined long before, were gotten out of the files. Diplomatic activities there, as well as in Turkey, were stepped up. As a measure of precaution, troops were assembled in the Levant—English troops in Egypt and French in Syria. The French Admiralty suggested that Italian expansion be encouraged toward the Levant and the Black Sea oil fields, but the Quai d'Orsay did not agree. In fact the project did not even get beyond the first planning stage.

Germany's interior transportation system, however, became the object of two mysterious undertakings which went well beyond the planning stage. One of these was a pet project of Mr. Churchill, who had the British Navy construct a number of small river mines—"as large as footballs." These he proposed to sow, by planes or otherwise, in the rivers and canals of Germany. But the French Government, fearing German reaction on the land front, delayed the operation indefinitely.

The second project was aimed at blocking the Danube, through which raw materials and goods—especially petroleum—from Roumania and the Black Sea reached the heart of Germany. For years this river had, in principle, been internationalized, and England, France, Germany, Yugoslavia, Hungary, and other countries had large commercial fleets on its waters. The French companies alone owned 73 ships on the Danube, of which 19 were oil tankers and 10 were tugboats. Using their ships alone, the Germans could import 400,000 tons of petroleum products per year via the Danube, and by chartering neutral shipping they could increase this to over 1,000,000 tons.

To cut off these supplies, the British and French secret services began preparations for blocking the Danube, where it flows through the gorges of the Iron Gates, by sinking cement-laden barges in it. If the barges met opposition, they were to fight their way through with arms which would be hidden on board. The cement was purchased, and French and English personnel were assembled who, disguised as civilians, were to attempt the operation.

But Admiral Darlan was lukewarm to the whole project. Why begin something, said he, if we are not in a position to see it through. Then an English barge, loaded with weapons, was captured by the Roumanian Customs Service, and the whole project blew up. The most the French could do was to try to get their Danube shipping out and to Istanbul—and some 50 per cent was, as a matter of fact, thus saved by June 1940.

There remained the third weak spot in Germany's warmaking potential —the problem of iron ore for her industries.

It was well known that Germany imported 50 per cent of her iron ore from Sweden—an import that was vital. If in some way or other those imports could be halted, the war could be appreciably shortened.

The Finnish situation offered one way of approaching the problem. Ever since she had been wantonly attacked by Russia, Finland had been amazing the world with her valorous defense. France, like almost every other country, was warmly sympathetic. A Finnish military mission came to Paris, seeking assistance. Emboldened by the strong stand of the League of Nations, the French Government ordered the General Staffs to provide the Finns with the greatest possible assistance, without worrying unduly about Russian reaction, since Russia was practically in the enemy's camp anyway.

Naturally an expedition to Finland could not be put into operation without Norway and Sweden becoming involved. Obviously—though it is perhaps a bit cynical to say it—the Allies could not hope to hold the entire Russian Army at bay and thus save Finland. But they did hope, by this operation, to get their hands on the Swedish iron ore and prevent its going to Germany—which end would serve the Allies' interests admirably. Furthermore, this project would offer an opportunity to use the great naval superiority of the Allies over Germany—an advantage which could not otherwise be exploited. Other than the navies, it was planned to use only a small land force for this diversion—a force so small that its withdrawal would not materially weaken the principal land front.

Such was the reasoning which led the Allies to initiate the only strategic operation undertaken by them before the French front collapsed. And that undertaking was worthwhile only as long as the hypothesis on which it was based held good: namely, that the frontline facing toward Germany could not be pierced.

CHAPTER 6

The Diversionary Operation in Norway

It was in December, 1939, that the League of Nations had denounced the Union of Soviet Socialist Republics as aggressors for their attack on Finland, and had invited all League members to assist the invaded country.

Accordingly, from December, 1939, to March, 1940, the French loaded aboard Finnish ships at Le Havre or Bizerte the following munitions for shipment to Finland via Norway: seven 305-mm. guns originally taken from the Russian General Wrangel's fleet;[1] some 60 reconnaissance planes; 430 guns (mostly of 75-mm.), with 7,000,000 rounds of ammunition; 5,000 automatic rifles, with 20,000,000 rounds; and 200,000 hand grenades. The contribution of this war material was kept from the French people, but public clamor for aid to Finland caused the Allied Governments to plan an operation.

On February 5, 1940, there was a meeting, in Paris, of the Supreme Franco-British Council, consisting of the Naval Chiefs and the Ministers of Defense of the two governments, and their military advisers. As a result of previous studies, the Staffs were agreed that troops could be sent to Finland's assistance only by routing them through the port of Petsamo, already in the hands of the Russians, or else by sending them across the Scandinavian Peninsula. The Council's decisions, as arrived at in Paris, may be briefly outlined as follows:

Preparations should be made to send a Franco-British Expeditionary Force to Finland—under the guise of "volunteers," if necessary, as certain countries had done during the Spanish Civil War.

The Petsamo region was unsuitable for the project, as operations there might bring on an open clash with Russia.

A landing should be made at Narvik, with the occupation of the Swedish ore region of Gällivare as the first objective; secondary landings should be made at Stavanger, Bergen, and Trondheim.

When all was ready, the Finns should be requested to ask the Allies officially for help, and the Norwegians and Swedes were to be requested

---

[1] In 1920 the Black Sea Squadron of General Pierre de Wrangel's anti-Bolshevik White Russians had taken refuge at Bizerte, where the ships had been interned. The 305-mm. guns had been taken from the old battleships of this fleet.

to receive the Expeditionary Force with open arms. If, through fear of German reaction, these countries demurred, they were to be assured that the Allies were ready to defend them. In any event the landings in Norway were to be "peaceful" operations, with the Norwegians offering no real opposition, even if they could not openly agree.

Since the operation was to take place in a military zone, it was to be conducted under British command.

With these premises, the General Staffs promptly went to work, with the British proceeding perhaps a little more slowly and cautiously than the French—a deliberation arising probably from their greater responsibility and their greater appreciation of the difficulties involved. The French were for staging the operation as quickly as possible, for a few vague rumors hinted that Hitler also might be interested in Norway.[2] They proposed to use the *Altmark*[3] incident as an excuse to intervene immediately; also, in order to save time, the French convoys, which would be ready first, were to sail first. But the British, who had prepared the sailing schedule in as much detail as a railroad timetable, would not consent to any deviation.

As its contribution the French Admiralty secretly assembled in the Brest roadstead and the Channel ports those ships that were to take part in the operation. These ships were placed under command of Rear Admiral Edmond Derrien, but would come under British control once they cleared the French coast. The man-of-war contingent consisted of one cruiser, nine super-destroyers, three fleet-destroyers, and five auxiliary cruisers, plus several tankers. The transport section was made up of eight passenger liners and seven cargo ships. The French Expeditionary Corps totalled 12,500 troops.

Everything was ready by the 2nd of March. But upon being sounded out, Norway and Sweden both refused to permit passage of the troops through their territory for fear of being dragged into the war. And Finland, already at the end of her rope, did not want an intervention that would only prolong the hopeless conflict. In fact, on March 12, despite her knowledge that the Allies were on the verge of sailing, she made peace with Russia.

Finland could no longer be used as an excuse to intervene. The British

---

[2] For entirely different strategic reasons the Germans were also preparing to occupy the Norwegian coast. (See Vice Admiral Friedrich Ruge's history, *Der Seekrieg— The German Navy's Story, 1939-1945*).

[3] The *Altmark*, a German naval supply ship for the *Graf Spee* in the South Atlantic, had been sent back to Germany with some 300 prisoners taken from the prizes sunk by the raider. The British learned of this, found the *Altmark* hidden in a Norwegian fjord, and boarded her to rescue the prisoners despite the fact that she was in the territorial waters of Norway. As grounds, they claimed that the *Altmark* was violating the limited rights granted a belligerent in the territorial waters of a neutral, and that Norway was unable to protect her neutrality.

Admiralty dispersed their expeditionary forces and cancelled all their preparations. The French Navy received orders to do likewise, but Admiral Darlan wanted to retain all the forces he had assembled. He was convinced that the thing was not over yet; the essential thing, to his way of thinking, was to prevent Swedish ore from going to Germany. But the French Government decided otherwise.

The failure to do anything for Finland caused a furor in the Parliament. Premier Edouard Deladier, the head of the Government, resigned, and was replaced by Paul Reynaud, who was reputed to be of tougher fiber. At any rate Mr. Reynaud, after appointing Deladier as Minister of National Defense, rushed off to London to confer on the common strategy.

The meeting of the Interallied Supreme Council took place at No. 10 Downing Street on March 28. It was presided over solemnly by Sir Neville Chamberlain. On one side of him sat Lord Halifax, meditative, and sometimes with his eyes closed. On the other side sat Mr. Churchill, who also closed his eyes at intervals that afternoon—but not always to meditate. Mr. Reynaud sat facing Sir Neville, with the principal military and naval leaders scattered around. The generals and admirals had already conferred the day before, so the Council discussions developed into an almost parliamentary style dialogue between the two chiefs of government.

Other fields having been briefly surveyed—the blockade, the Caucasus, the Danube, etc.—it was decided to take up the Scandinavian affair again by less oblique approaches. The Norwegians and Swedes would be bluntly told that the Allies could no longer stand by idly while Swedish ore destined for the German war industry passed through Norwegian costal channels unmolested—to prevent this the Allies would lay two or three minefields in those channels to stop the iniquitous traffic. At Britain's request it was also decided to mine the Rhine River with Mr. Churchill's pet river mines. And after the luncheon recess, Messrs. Chamberlain and Reynaud quietly announced that during the meal they had agreed on the text of an official statement to be given to the press at the end of the meeting: namely, that the two governments engaged themselves not to conclude a separate armistice or peace with the enemy. To the military people present, such unity of purpose went without saying. In fact no one present attached any more importance to the statement than they would have done to any simple communique intended to bolster the public morale.[4] No Frenchman there could ever have imagined that ten weeks later, under the crucifixion of defeat, this pronouncement would result in attacks on their government as though the declaration had been part of a solemn treaty.

---

[4] In 1914 a similar engagement had been entered into, but only after most careful study and full discussion by the Council of Ministers. (See G. Chastenet, *La République Triomphante*—"The Republic Triumphant.")

Strange to say, not one person around that table raised the question of a possible German reaction to the laying of minefields in Norwegian waters. Admiral Darlan noted this default, however, and winked at Captain Auphan, who sat behind him. But the admiral was afraid that if he spoke, the entire Norwegian question would be reopened, and the project perhaps cancelled.

Once the meeting was over, however, Admiral Darlan conferred with the other military chiefs on the necessity for all haste in staging the Norwegian undertaking. Everyone agreed that a minefield which could not be kept patrolled would be of little use; they must be prepared to occupy the Swedish ore fields themselves before the Germans seized them. The French Admiral of the Fleet wired orders from London to Maintenon, directing that all the forces he had originally promised the British for this project be reassembled immediately.

The British Admiralty was equally prompt, but the British War Office contented itself with hauling out and pouring over boxes full of plans for a "peaceful" landing that had been prepared a month earlier. No consideration was given to the risk that the operation might develop—as indeed it did—in an entirely unexpected manner.

The 2nd of April had been set as the date for launching the operation. But on March 30 the French Government demurred again in the matter of aerial mining of the Rhine River for fear of unleashing the whole holocaust of aerial warfare. Thereupon the British promptly suspended the entire Norwegian operation. Urgent consultations in Paris resulted in a new date—April 8—being set. On that date the Allied ambassadors were to inform the Norwegian authorities that the minefields were being laid,[5] that the British were laying them, and that the first convoy of British troops was already about to sail.

But now the quibbling and the delays of the Allies were to prove fatal. For by a coincidence that no novelist would have dared touch, on that very day the German operation against Norway was launched. Carried out resolutely, with powerful forces, its purpose was to seize all of Norway in order to open up to the German Navy a path to the North Atlantic which the Allies could not block. At the very moment when the French and British diplomats were delivering their messages at Oslo and the Norwegian Parliament was deliberating on the matter, the German Fleet was at sea, heading for various Norwegian ports as far north as Narvik. At

---

[5] Three minefields were planned: one at the entrance to the Vest Fjord, off Bodö; another at Statlandet (not laid because of bad weather); and a third, purely fictitious, at Bud. The *Notices to Mariners,* published immediately, announced these three minefields, as well as a fourth in the Swedish waters of the Baltic, where a few mines were to be dropped by plane.

The destroyer Bourrasque, *crowded with troops evacuated from Dunkirk, sinking off Nieuport on May 30, 1940.*

A VERY OLD COASTAL BATTERY, manned by the Navy, in the sector of Dunkirk, during the winter of 1939-1940.

0900 the British destroyer *Glowworm,* which had been delayed on her way to the Vest Fjord by a man washed overboard, was caught alone by the German cruiser *Hipper* and sunk by gunfire. The following day the British battle cruiser *Renown,* of Admiral of the Fleet Sir Charles Forbes' Home Fleet which was at sea covering the Allied operation, had a fleeting engagement with the enemy battle cruisers *Scharnhorst* and *Gneisenau* which also were at sea covering the German operation.

Notwithstanding these engagements, which should have showed that the Scandinavian sector was just beginning to boil, Mr. Reynaud announced triumphantly, "The iron route is definitely cut!" And from the speaker's rostrum of the House of Commons Mr. Churchill shouted, "That cursed corridor is now closed forever!"

It would require a complete book devoted to the Norwegian campaign alone to cover all the details of that ill-fated operation.[6] The strategic considerations leading up to it have already been described; the campaign itself lasted exactly two months—from April 8 to June 8, 1940—and extended over almost 1,500 kilometers of coastline. The principal events of that campaign are chronologically tabulated below:

The swift occupation by the Germans, within only a few days, of all the principal ports and airfields of Norway, including Narvik, where ten destroyers of the Kriegsmarine put ashore 2,000 crack mountain troops; and the equally swift destruction of these destroyers in the fjord of Narvik by an audacious counterattack by British destroyers in two raids, the second of which was supported by the battleship *Warspite* of the Home Fleet.

Allied irresolution in the matter of a counterattack to eject the Germans, with especial uncertainty as to choice of locations for the landings.

Preparation—then cancellation—of an expedition, exclusively naval, destined to recapture Trondheim.

Franco-British landings at Andalsnes and Namsos intended to recapture Trondheim by a pincers maneuver from inland. Then the evacuation of these same two bridgeheads when it was found impossible to hold them under the continuous attacks of the German Air Force.

Franco-British landings in the fjords in the vicinity of Narvik, resulting in the recapture of that port and the dispersal into the interior of the German garrison.

The eventual evacuation of Narvik, after destruction of all its port installation, followed by the Allied evacuation of all of Norway, whose king left with the evacuating forces to set up a government-in-exile in England.

The French part in this campaign consisted in sending to Norway, via

---

[6] For more complete details, see Jacques Mordal, *La Campagne de Norvège*—("*The Norwegian Campaign*").

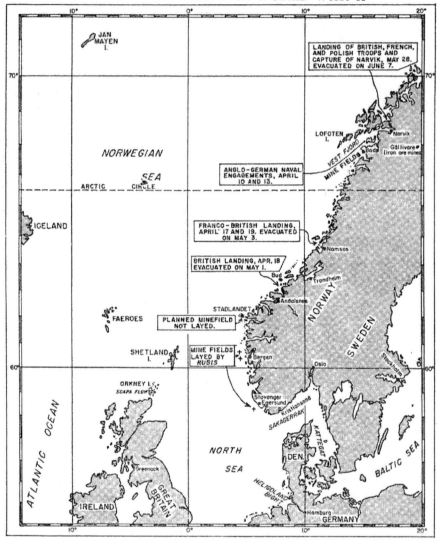

THE NORWEGIAN CAMPAIGN

the British Isles, a total of approximately 25,000 men, 1,200 draft animals, 1,700 vehicles, 170 guns, and 12,000 tons of supplies. That at least was what was routed through the port of Brest for Greenock, the improvised base in Scotland, between April 15 and May 8. But there was time only to send some 15,000 men on to Norway before the expedition was cancelled and the country evacuated. To escort and transport these troops and their supplies, there was assembled 6 fine auxiliary cruisers, 13 passenger liners, and 23 cargo ships, each of which was equipped with antiaircraft guns

(25-mm. and 40-mm.) before leaving Brest. The requisitioning of that many ships strained the national shipping program which was necessary to support the whole wartime economy of France. Since the original plan called for sending over a third French division of approximately 12,000 men, the English promised to provide the necessary transport. When they were unable to do so, the French had to choose between providing the additional shipping for Norway and suspending a good part of the vitally important traffic between North Africa and the French homeland. The plan for sending the additional division was therefore abandoned.

In the man-of-war category the French Navy at one time or another had the following ships engaged in the Norwegian campaign: one cruiser (which was replaced by another when the first was damaged by an enemy bomb), six super-destroyers (two of which were sunk), five destroyers, six auxiliary cruisers, three fleet-tankers, two base repair and supply ships, two patrol vessels, and a hospital ship. At the same time, in the North Sea but operating under orders of the British Admiralty, there were thirteen French submarines and their tender, which, along with the super-destroyers, took effective part in the war against the German lines of communications.

The opening of the Norwegian campaign required the movement of all the Allied dispositions to the north. The English plunged into the Skagerrak, where they carved out some fine successes for themselves at the expense of the German invasion transports. The zones assigned to French ships—notably the approaches to the Heligoland Bight—proved less rewarding, though no less dangerous. French submarines in those waters were detected on a number of occasions, and were hunted and depth charged by the German patrols. In general, they came out of it well. The *Calypso,* caught in an antisubmarine net, managed to free herself; in a cruise of 10 days at sea she had to run submerged for a total of 187 hours. Human errors compounded the risks, while real opportunities for a shot at the enemy were rare. Only the *Orphée* succeeded in getting in two shots at a surfaced German U-boat, which, however, avoided them by putting her helm hard over

Special attention must be made of the bold patrols carried out by French 1,500-ton submarines—such, for instance, as that of the *Casabianca,* which penetrated far into enemy-held Norwegian fjords. It was the same with the activities of the minelaying *Rubis.* On three separate occasions—May 8, May 27, and June 9—she skillfully planted her mines in the channels used by the Germans along the Norwegian coast. The first field was laid to the south of Egersund, the second off Bleivik, and the third in Hjelte Fjord, one of the entrances to Bergen. Inasmuch as the *Rubis* was at sea on this operation on June 4, when the others were recalled to France by Italy's imminent entry into the war, she did not return with the squadron. It was because of the strong urging of the British that she stayed on to lay a fourth minefield—this one off Trondheim, on June 26, only eight days before the sad affair at Mers-el-Kebir—and that the *Rubis* became one of the first units of the Free French Naval Forces.

To upset the German antisubmarine dispositions, which were causing both the French and British trouble off the Skagerrak, the British Admiralty planned to stage a destroyer raid in these waters. But the Commander in Chief of the British Home Fleet opposed the raid as being too risky in light of the enemy's air capabilities. It was finally decided to send in a division of French super-destroyers, whose high speed would permit them to go in and still get clear of the most dangerous areas before daylight.

Leaving Rosyth, the super-destroyers *Indomptable, Malin,* and *Triomphant,* of 3,200 tons each, and all capable of making 40 knots, crossed the North Sea during the day and swept the Skagerrak as far east as the longitude of Hamburg, which point they reached at 0100 the next morning without having sighted a thing. Reversing course and increasing speed to 34 knots, they had a brief engagement around 0300 with some German motor torpedo boats and two patrol trawlers. One of the latter was hit, but succeeded in escaping behind a smokescreen. One or two of the motor torpedo boats were also thought to have been hit and set on fire, but post-war information proved this erroneous. During the remainder of the morning, and despite the presence of British fighter planes, the super-destroyers were bombed by German planes, frequently at close range, but succeeded in returning safely to base. The only casualty was a propeller shaft on one of the ships which was thrown slightly out of line by a near miss.

The French Admiralty proposed that the super-destroyers be sent back immediately for another raid, but the British High Command preferred to employ them in Norway. They accordingly remained in the north until the threat of war in the Mediterranean obliged their recall.

Meanwhile, in accordance with the original plan of the campaign, a British brigade had made an initial landing at Namsos on April 17. Two days later Rear Admiral Jean Cadart's three auxiliary cruisers—*El Djezair, El Mansour,* and *El Kantara*—approached the small harbor under strong escort. They carried three rifle battalions with their light equipment—in all, 3,000 men and 500 tons of supplies. During the course of the afternoon they were subjected to repeated enemy air attacks, during one of which the cruiser *Emile Bertin,* acting as protective screen, was hit and forced to retire. Because of the constant bombing, Admiral Cadart's cruisers could remain in the harbor only during the three or four hours of darkness, but they succeeded in unloading all their troops and all the supplies onto the docks. Neither troops nor material were to remain there very long, however.

On April 22 the auxiliary cruiser *Ville d'Alger* arrived with reinforcements—1,100 men. A snowstorm and the damaged docks prevented her going alongside, and unloading had to be carried out by small boats. In order to clear the harbor before daylight the *Ville d'Alger* had to leave with 350 men, all the transport mules, and most of the antiaircraft guns still on board. However, on April 27 three daring French cargo ships succeeded in landing more food supplies, gasoline, 25-mm. guns, ammunition, etc. Unfortunately all this material was bombed and set on fire by German planes almost as soon as it was landed, thus depriving the troops ashore of material with which they might have been able to hold on.

Before these last ships could leave the harbor, even, the word was given that Namsos was to be evacuated. Taking on board 1,000 men, the ships got under way once again and managed to return home comparatively unharmed, despite a vigorous harassing pursuit by the German bombers.

The task of evacuating the remainder of the landing force was entrusted to a British cruiser and Admiral Cadart's three auxiliary cruisers, the *El Djezair, El Mansour,* and *El Kantara.* Since the *Ville d'Alger* had been disabled in her last trip to Norway, these three ships, plus the British cruiser *York,* left from Scapa Flow and reentered the Namsos rattrap at 2300 on the 2nd of May. The city as well as the docks was still smoking from the previous bombing, and leaping flames occasionally reddened the night.

Reembarkation of personnel was begun immediately; there was no thought of trying to bring off any of the equipment. All that could be done with this was either to blow it up or to dump it into the sea.

As day broke, the troops already embarked grew nervous and impatient to get under way. But gray-bearded Admiral Cadart coolly made an inspection round of the whole dock area to make sure that all the British rear guard troops were off. Finally the ships pulled out, loaded with 1,850 French troops, 2,354 British, and a few Norwegians—plus 38 German prisoners.

The return trip was a nightmare. The German air attacks were continuous. A German dive bomber succeeded in hitting the super-destroyer *Bison* (Captain Jean Bouan, the 11th Destroyer Division Commander). The *Bison's* magazines exploded. From the *Montcalm,* flying Admiral Derrien's flag, one of the *Bison's* 138-mm. guns, with its crew, could be seen flying high in the air. The survivors were picked up by a British destroyer, which itself was sunk only two hours later. Later on, what remained of the *Bison's* survivors barely missed being wrecked still a third time—an experience which the participants would never forget.

The other Norwegian landings were the primary concern of the British, since their main objective was Narvik, the northern terminal of the iron ore traffic to Germany. This port was still held by 2,000 German soldiers, reinforced by some 1,800 sailors from the crews of the destroyers sunk there by the British on the 10th and 13th of April, plus 600 or more soldiers brought in by plane—a total of some 4,400 men.

As an opening move, a powerful British surface and naval air force clamped a tight blockade on Ofot Fjord, leading Narvik. Three English battalions had already been landed outside the port, but though they had the assistance of some Norwegian troops, they had made no headway. The terrain inland was broken, rugged, desolate, and still covered with snow. To assist in the Narvik operation the British Command called in two French forces: one consisting of three battalions of "Blue Devils" (Alpine mountain troops), and the other of two battalions of the Foreign Legion and four of Polish depatriated troops—a total of 11,800 men, with 2,000 tons of light equipment. The heavy equipment was following in many cargo ships.

Notwithstanding frequent enemy air attacks, the landings were carried out under far better conditions than those at Namsos—the only ship casualty was one French super-destroyer slightly damaged. The difficulties were mainly material in origin, rather than human: wharves too short, with no unloading facilities; a shortage of charts and pilots; and the irritating loss of anchors and anchor chains in very deep water. The Alpine troops were landed on the last two days of April, the Foreign Legion and the Poles on the 9th and 10th of May.

On May 27, a grand combined attack of the British Naval Forces, commanded by Admiral of the Fleet Lord Cork and Orrery, and the French troops, commanded by General Marie Béthouart, drove the Germans out of Narvik with heavy loss. To the Norwegians was given the honor of being the first to enter the recaptured city. Only the two senior commanders knew, however, that for the past 24 hours they had carried in their pockets the order to blow up the port installations and to evacuate Norway.

As has been said earlier, the Norwegian operation was undertaken chiefly as a diversion—a flank movement permitting the utilization of naval forces not employed elsewhere—and the whole concept had been based on the supposed impregnability of the Maginot line. But 15 days before, the Germans had broken through this front and the sweep of their armored divisions threatened to encircle the whole left wing of the Allied armies. At the very hour when General Béthouart was making his entry into Narvik, almost 500,000 French and British soldiers stood compressed into the Dunkirk pocket.

Béthouart's few thousand men would have made no difference at Dunkirk, even if they could have been transported there. However, their continued operation in Norway served no useful purpose, either. Furthermore, a declaration of war by Italy was imminent, and France had need of every man, gun, ship, and plane for the defense of the homeland.

The Allied troops at the Narvik bridgehead—24,000 men in all—were evacuated from northern Norway on June 8. Part of these French troops, in addition to those in Scotland who had not yet been transshipped to Norway, were still in Britain during the tragic days of the armistice.

Offhand, the whole Norwegian expedition would seem to have been a defeat for France and Britain. The objective of cutting Germany's iron ore route was not realized. Instead, it was the Germans who, by capturing Norway, would for a long time deprive England of her share of the Swedish exports. And the tragedy of it all was that the results might have been reversed if the expedition had not been delayed for five fatal days by the bickering over Mr. Churchill's pet scheme of sowing the Rhine with river mines.

Yet, there were a few bright entries on the opposite side of the ledger, too. The damages and losses suffered by the German Navy were far greater comparatively than those suffered by the Royal Navy—a fact which was to be enormously important to Britain in the future. And these German Navy losses[7] at this particular time did not encourage it, in case there had been such a thought, to operate in the lower North Sea on the right flank of the German armies during those critical last days of the Battle of France.

One of the most revealing aspects of the Norwegian campaign was the complete degree of collaboration achieved between the British and French Navies. It was during this campaign that the British Admiralty, fully occupied in northern waters, proposed that the French Navy assume responsibility for the Mediterranean.[8] Never in history had there been more cordial relations than those established in the battle area of the sea off Norway. Not merely was this collaboration in the technical field, but in the far more important field of human relations—the spirit of *comraderie* between the French officers and their brethren of the Royal Navy. Whether they sailed with the Home Fleet or on escort duty off the fjords of Norway, French and British ships, side by side, learned to sustain and to parry the fierce attacks of Germany's formidable Air Force.

---

[7] Germany's naval casualties were 3 cruisers, 10 destroyers, 4 submarines, 1 gunnery training ship, and 10 small ships lost; and the battle cruisers *Scharnhorst* and *Gneisenau* damaged. British ship casualties were 1 aircraft carrier, 1 cruiser, 7 destroyers, 3 submarines, 1 sloop, 1 antiaircraft escort ship, and 14 trawlers lost, plus 1 Polish destroyer. French casualties were 2 super-destroyers (the *Bison,* lost under the circumstances already stated, and the *Maillé-Brézé,* destroyed at Greenock on April 30 by the explosion of one of its torpedoes). Despite Germany's Air Force and submarines, not one single British or French troop transport was sunk.

[8] The proposal was presented by the British on April 16, and the French Admiralty immediately gave its agreement. But at a meeting of the Interallied Supreme Command on April 23, it was decided to maintain the *status quo.*

CHAPTER 7

France Invaded

The night of May 9, 1940, the telegraph, the teleprinters, and the telephones crackled and chattered explosively. From the headquarters of Admiral, North, at Dunkirk—from the naval attaché's office at The Hague—from the various intelligence agencies, from the Foreign Office at Paris, and, above all, from Army General Headquarters at Montry, came messages bringing to Maintenon a flood of fragments of information, the very volume of which indicated that something unusual was happening on the land front. The great difficulty, while waiting, was to determine exactly what was taking place.

At sea, the naval forces, in addition to the Norwegian operation which was at its peak, were busy with their usual patrol and escort missions. They were not directly concerned with developments on land—at least not yet. Still, in the event the war moved into Belgium, the Navy was committed to transport, as speedily as possible, a small contingent of troops to Flushing (Vlissingen) as well as to the Dutch islands at the mouth of the Scheldt, in order to flank the left wing of any new front that reached the North Sea. To insure maximum secrecy this operation had been given the code name, "Expedition of the Isles."

Three times before—in November, 1939, in January, 1940, and in April, 1940—similar alerts had occurred. Each time a German attack through Belgium and Holland had been believed imminent, just as in 1914. Each time troops had been hurriedly massed at the frontier; the Navy had readied ships to transport the expeditionary corps to Flushing. Each time the alert had turned out to be a false alarm. Eventually the staffs, at all levels, became rather blasé about them.

This time, however, the thing seemed more serious—particularly to the Navy, which had noted several portentous occurrences. For instance, since April 30 the enemy had been increasingly active in laying magnetic mines off Dunkirk, Calais, and Boulogne. On May 5 the French naval attaché at The Hague brought certain information to Dunkirk which influenced Admiral Abrial in making camouflaged preparations to lift troops to Flushing—not, as he wrote, without causing a certain amount of derision in the

54

general staff of the Seventh Army. Yet it was this very Army which constituted the left wing of the French land forces and which was to advance
beyond Antwerp in case of a German attack through the Low Countries.

The Royal Navy, too, was suspicious of some new activity on the part of
the enemy. On May 6 the British Admiralty set up a barrier of eight submarines—three of them French—off the Dutch coast where a German landing
might be expected.[1] And on May 7 the Dutch Army had been placed on the
alert.

But on May 9 the German Government publicly disclaimed any such
evil intentions as were being attributed to it. With this disclaimer, tension
at The Hague relaxed.

However, the denial was a trick. Beginning that very midnight German
forces were in motion; before daybreak, Belgium, Holland, and Luxembourg had all been invaded. Belgium appealed for French assistance. At
5 A.M. Admiral, North, reported: "Region Dunkirk-Calais is at this moment
the target of a heavy air attack. Incessant bombings. Magnetic mines."

A great many French airfields, spared up until then, were attacked at the
same time. At 0635 Supreme General Headquarters ordered the execution
of Plan "D," which provided for the entry of the Allied armies into Belgium
as far as the Dyle River, and into Holland as far as Eindhoven.

The die was cast. The Battle of France had begun.

For the time being, the Navy only had to carry out its routine escort
and patrol duties and transport the expeditionary forces to Flushing, not
far away. Despite magnetic minefields and repeated enemy bombing of the
port of Flushing, 3,150 men, with an artillery group and all necessary
supplies, were landed there without loss on the 11th and 12th of May from
four small passenger ships and two freighters. Air cover for the operation
was provided by naval air units, which here first encountered the Luftwaffe
—and successfully, for while the faster Messerschmitts brought down two
French fighters, they in turn had five or six bombers shot down.

The naval units assigned to support the troops and safeguard their
lines of communication were under the command of Rear Admiral Charles
Platon, who installed himself at Flushing. These units consisted of two

---

[1] This barrier was to produce no results, as the German surface forces did not take
any part in this phase of the offensive. On the contrary, with ships so close together,
the danger of mistaken identities was considerable. To avoid regrettable errors, the
commanding officer of each submarine received orders not to attack any other submarine! Thus it was that the German *U-9*, prowling in the area *and knowing that it
was the only German submarine there,* was able to surprise and torpedo the French
submarine *Doris* (Lt. Comdr. Jean Favreul) shortly after midnight on May 9. This
was the first French submarine destroyed by enemy action.

divisions of small destroyers, five submarine chasers, and some twenty minesweepers and smaller craft. The constant enemy air attacks made life very difficult for these ships at the mouth of the Scheldt, where two sweepers were lost on May 15.

To defend the Belgian coast against enemy attack from the sea, two mobile coastal batteries of the Navy, each made up of four 155-mm. guns, were positioned on the south bank of the Scheldt. At the urgent request of Army General Headquarters, also, a mobile naval 90-mm. antiaircraft battery from Dunkirk was placed to defend the tunnel under the Scheldt at Antwerp, which was of vital importance to the French troops, who by now were in Breda. Also, two divisions of magnetic minesweepers were sent to Ostend and Zeebrugge to assist in insuring supplies to the Army. Antwerp itself was the responsibility of the British Navy.

The Flushing expeditionary force had one serious weakness, however: the troops assigned to the outpost of Walcheren Island were lightly armed, green troops originally intended for coast defense duty. Although the Walcheren Island force was doubled on May 13 by an additional detachment detailed to the advanced post of Zuid Beveland, these were mainly Reservists, with little training and with a commanding officer who shortly had to be relieved. His successor was capable and valorous, but had no time to bring the troops to the high state of morale necessary in such an exposed position.

The French High Command had expected to find prepared positions in Belgium against which the German offense would exhaust itself, but the assault was so fierce that the newly arrived troops on the Dyle and on the Gembloux plateau did not have time to catch their breadth.

Dutch resistance began to crumble on May 14, and the French Seventh Army had to pull its advance elements back south of Antwerp. On the 16th the French High Command had to order a general withdrawl from Belgium, because, three days earlier, German tanks had broken through the Meuse River front between Dinant and Sedan. The order, unfortunately, came too late; most of these troops were to find themselves hemmed in shortly in the Dunkirk pocket.

Walcheren and the Zuid Beveland outpost were left uncovered by the precipitous withdrawal. On May 14, a French naval reconnaissance party penetrating the Hollandsch Diep found German tanks already crossing over the bridge at Moerdijk. The German advance captured Bergen op Zoom on the same day and arrived at the Zuid Beveland isthmus by 3 P.M. Despite constant attacks by the Luftwaffe, the French submarine chasers *No. 6, No. 9,* and *No. 41,* and the torpedo boat *L'Incomprise* fired on the Germans until their magazines were empty. On the 16th and 17th the fleet-destroyers

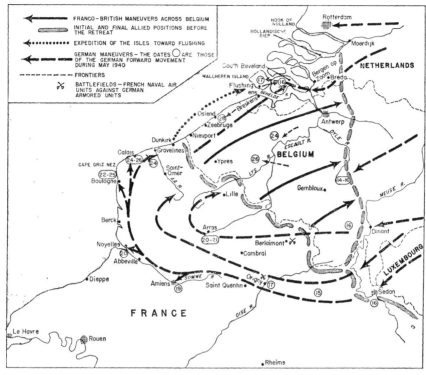

FRANCE INVADED

Fougueux and *Frondeur* joined in the action, assisted by the destroyers *Cyclone* and *Siroco,* two naval air attack squadrons, and two 155-mm. batteries firing from the vicinity of Breskens.

Unfortunately, the regiment holding Zuid Beveland gave way that afternoon, and only 300 men succeeded in reaching Walcheren. The next day Walcheren too was taken, despite the bravery of its commanding officer, General Marcel Deslaurens, who fell at the head of his men, rifle in hand, like any private. Admiral Platon, with five sub-chasers, succeeded in rescuing 1,800 men, the only ones rescued of the 6,000 men stationed there. The harbor installations had already been so badly bombed that the torpedo boats were unable to go alongside the docks. While trying to do so, Commander Charles de la Fournière, of the *Bouclier,* had both cheeks pierced by an automatic rifle bullet when his mouth was open to give the order to the men on the docks to take his lines. The men were German soldiers, advance troops in the assault! Equally strange, Commander de la Fournière did not lose a single tooth!

The Expedition of the Isles was over. During it—a week of almost continuous air attacks—the French, however, lost only three small sweepers sunk, and two sweepers and one torpedo boat damaged. The British escort ships, fighting valorously to fend off the enemy bombers, suffered losses also.

The period following the failure in Flanders was to be spent by the Navy mostly in evacuating everything that was mobile in the path of the enemy's advance, and destroying everything else. This painful task was to occupy them for the next month—a period during which they had to witness the fall of the North Sea ports, the Channel ports, and then the Atlantic ports before the overland sweep of the enemy.

Ahead of that tide rolled an equal wave of refugees. Everything that floated in Dutch and Belgian waters, everything that moved on the roads, was attempting to flee before the invasion. Despite all the traffic congestion, however, the three naval batteries that had been positioned at the mouth of the Scheldt succeeded in reaching Dunkirk without loss of a gun or a man.

The destruction of Antwerp and the bottling up of the various ports was the responsibility of the British, who had made preparations for such an emergency a long time before. The French had the assignment of destroying the installations at Ostend and Zeebrugge.

The King of the Belgians, concerned over what might be the results to his countrymen, objected to the destruction. Consequently the enormous petroleum stock at Antwerp fell into the hands of the Germans before more than 10 per cent could be sabotaged.

Also, through improper liaison, the French battalion[2] defending Zeebrugge had not been informed of the British plans to block the navigation channels, and they opened fire on the blockships, impeding the work for some time. However, Admiral of the Fleet Sir Roger Keyes, hero of the famous Zeebrugge raid of World War I, made it a special point to congratulate these French soldiers for their faithfulness in carrying out their orders.

Differently from Zeebrugge, which was thoroughly sabotaged and blocked, Ostend was evacuated intact on May 28, only two hours before the arrival of the Germans. However, over 25,000 Belgian and 28,000 British soldiers were successfully evacuated from its harbor, which had been kept open by French minesweepers despite the numerous bombs and magnetic mines dropped by the enemy throughout the whole period of the offensive.

---

[2] This battalion, oddly enough, belonged to one of the two divisions the elements of which had made such a poor showing at Walcheren and Zuid Beveland. Later it was to distinguish itself by its last-ditch stand in defense of the beaches of Dunkirk—proving that all the division lacked was training under fire before the decisive battle.

The German invasion of Holland and Belgium was in reality only a deceptive maneuver to conceal the direction of their real thrust, which was to be at Sedan, pivot point of the Allied left wing just beyond the Maginot line. Convinced that the Franco-British left wing, containing the Allies' best divisions, would swing around into Holland and Belgium at the first sign of a threat there, the German High Command had determined to deliver their principal attack on the Meuse River front, between Sedan and Dinant. The attack was to be made through the wooded mountains of the Ardennes, supposedly impassible to tanks—yet the Germans had assigned to this attack seven of their ten armored divisions, containing 1,800 tanks, and two air fleets.

The breakthrough exceeded even their fondest hopes. After a short pause to regroup, the Panzers drove swiftly ahead toward the Channel coast, thus cutting off and trapping the Allied troops which had advanced into Flanders. These troops, already fighting off attacks from the north, had no time to disengage, change front, and attempt to cut their way through the enemy now to their southward.

What would have happened if the Allies had not been duped into advancing into Belgium—or whether better technical preparation or less rigid strategy on the part of the French Army might have checkmated the German maneuver—is open to debate. What is certain is that the maneuver succeeded—although perhaps its success lay less in the boldness of its conception than in the daring and precision with which the envelopment was executed.

The German tanks first crossed the Meuse on May 13. Two days later they had broken completely through the front. On May 17, having taken scarcely any losses, they drove down the Oise River, beyond Saint-Quentin.

On May 19, only two days later, two new Panzer divisions were hurled through the gap between Saint-Quentin and Sedan. These were tanks which had originally been used in the deceptive opening attack in Belgium. When they encountered stiff resistance there—proof that the Allies had advanced into Belgium in force—they were shifted around to the Sedan front.

In this area there were now nine armored divisions—a concentration of practically the entire German tank strength—and all traveling at full speed over the excellent French roads to the sea. On May 20 the first detachments arrived at the mouth of the Somme River. Such speed left the French general staffs hopelessly behind. The French tank divisions, although as well equipped and as well manned as the enemy, were poorly placed; they found it impossible to intercept the fast moving Panzers.

Strong, well-handled airpower might have done something toward stemming that German tide. But the only attack squadrons existing in

France at that time were the Navy's Air force, operating under the orders of Admiral, North.

At the urgent request of the Army High Command these magnificent squadrons, especially trained to fight at sea, were thrown against the German tanks in the Oise valley on the 19th and 20th of May, at the cost of half their strength. The sacrifice of this elite group was the result partly of lack of fighter protection, which could not be given, and the highly effective German antiaircraft fire. Both here and at the Meuse the German flak had proved astoundingly accurate.

Appalled at the crushing breakthrough, Prime Minister Reynaud made an impassioned appeal to the French public to emulate the military glories of their fathers in World War I. Although with few illusions as to the outcome, but with unselfish devotion, Marshal Philippe Pétain—despite his eighty-four years—accepted the post of Vice President of the Council of Ministers. Similarly, General Maxime Weygand, former Chief of Staff to Marshal Fredinand Foch, and himself seventy-three years old, consented to replace General Gamelin at the head of the French Army.

General Weygand's first act as Commander in Chief was to see what was happening to the Armies of the North, already isolated from the rest of the country. On May 21, following an eventful trip to Ypres, he held a conference with King Leopold III, commanding the Belgian Army, General Gaston Billotte, commanding the French First Army Group, and Admiral Abrial—Admiral, North. Unfortunately he was not able to have a talk with General Lord Gort, commanding the British Expeditionary Force, to discuss the preparation of a counteroffensive toward the south, which was mandatory in order to close the gap opened by the German tanks.

Weygand's plan for a counteroffensive along the entire front had already begun that day, below Arras, where two English divisions, along with elements of the French cavalry corps, had been hurled against the enemy Panzers. The attack started off well, yet the day ended with no decisive results. The next day the English were no longer available. The French attacked again, this time alone, and made some progress toward Cambrai, but were eventually brought to a halt by heavy enemy air attacks. The attempt to break out of the German encirclement was doomed to failure.

The causes for this failure were many. Outstanding were the death of General Billotte, killed in an automobile accident; the caving in of the Belgian front; the withdrawl of the British toward the sea; the compromising situation of the French divisions, making it impossible for them to pull quickly out of Belgium; the disorganized state of communications and resulting confusion; and the excessive delay in concentrating the divisions which were to attack from the south.

Half a million French and British soldiers were to remain cut off from their supplies and their normal lines of communication—with the two Navies the only hope of supplying them or of evacuating them from the beaches.

Such was the situation around Dunkirk, headquarters of Admiral, North. But there were two other large ports threatened by the German advance: Boulogne, a fishing port and the most important such on the European continent, with over 30,000 inhabitants, and Calais, an ancient city of 50,000 souls, terminus of the rapid cross-Channel traffic to Dover. These two ports had been handling practically all the British Expeditionary Force's lighter traffic with the home country—both light material and individual passengers going on leave or to hospitalization in England or on errands of military importance.

With the exception of French and British workers attached to the various auxiliary services there, these two cities had no garrisons, even.

Yet there did exist an element of defense. In France it is the Navy which is charged with defense of the coast against attack from the sea. On that basis Boulogne and Calais were surrounded by a certain number of rather antiquated coast defense batteries, all primarily mounted to fire toward the open sea. Never, before this war, did the Navy ever expect to engage in a critical battle in that region; the officers and men who manned these batteries—or the Navigation Police Service—were mostly reservists who had not been on active duty for years. There were practically no anti-aircraft defenses. The beaches themselves were patrolled only by a few territorial troops.

Boulogne and Calais had been subjected to initial heavy air attack on May 10. This was soon to become a daily occurrence. Numerous magnetic mines menaced the ship channels, despite constant sweeping by the Navy. Victims of either bombs or mines, many ships which had escaped safely from Holland and Belgium ended their cruising forever in the Boulogne roadstead.

Moreover these ports were the Meccas of the innumerable Belgian or French men, women, and children fleeing before the German approach. Many civil servants thought they were carrying out their duties by trying to carry their archives to safety. The prefect of the Pas-de-Calais Department was preparing to evacuate all able-bodied men. Mingled with these refugees were even some disorganized persons in French or Belgian uniforms. All surged toward the ports seeking to embark. The most pessimistic rumors were rife. The imaginative populace saw German parachutists and spies everywhere.

Everyone was confused by the speed of the Panzers. The lessons of the Polish campaign had not been well learned. It was practically the first time in history that a great battle had been fought on land at the speed of an automobile. In fact, when questioned by the Navy, the Army High Command did not imagine it possible that the Germans could be in force in the port areas of the north, and put all such reports down as cases of "audacious infiltrations by isolated units."

The French Admiralty, nevertheless, was distinctly uneasy over the situation. The revictualling of the encircled armies depended entirely on the ports. Holding on to them was a vital necessity. No sooner had he returned from Ypres, than General Weygand asked Admiral Darlan to do the impossible—defend the ports against enemy land attack by checking them with Navy personnel.

To Admiral Abrial—Admiral, North—was given the responsibility of carrying out that hopeless mission. As early as May 17 the French Admiralty had informed him that "the axis of advance of the enemy armored divisions is westward." The Panzers were even then at Saint-Quentin, and on the direct road to the outskirts of Boulogne. And on the 20th the Admiralty ordered: "Direct your efforts in the defense of the ports against all enemy armored or motorized vehicles and against parachutists or planes landing on the beaches."

It was understood, of course, that in case of an attack in force, and if no Army troops were covering the port, the Navy had only to destroy everything it could, and then evacuate.

Before all these various directions reached their proper destinations, however, a tragic incident had occurred at Boulogne.

On May 17 the British had begun the evacuation of noncombatants. This evacuation gave rise to various comments, not altogether inspiring. During the night of the 20th a French general, separated from his troops and demoralized, arrived at Boulogne and informed the captain in command of the naval unit that the Germans were almost on his heels. The Navy captain telephoned immediately to inform Admiral, North, and to ask instructions. Unluckily he did not succeed in getting a message through to Dunkirk. Convinced thereupon that the Germans indeed were at the gates, and laboring under the general delusion, the naval commander gave the order to evacuate. A few hours later an emphatic counterorder came from Admiral, North. Unfortunately a great deal of destruction had already been done, and many of the sailors had already sailed on the better ships that were available. The remaining ships had been scuttled.

For that temporary lapse, the naval captain was tried by general court-martial at Cherbourg within three days, and was sentenced to twenty years at hard labor. Admiral Darlan wanted to make an example: a Navy man must not lose his head. It is regrettable, perhaps, that this procedure was not followed in dealing with other leaders—civil or military—who gave way under less dramatic circumstances.

On the afternoon of May 22, Captain Audouin de Lestrange arrived from Cherbourg on a fast motor boat to take charge of the defenses of Boulogne. By then the situation had been somewhat remedied, due to the efforts of Commander Henri Nomy,[3] commanding the naval air force at Berck, who had hurried to Boulogne late the preceding day. Later a few troops returned to man the installations. For the French, General Pierre Lanquetot brought in about two battalions and some artillery, drawn from a French division retreating from Belgium. To these were added a British brigade sent from Dover, as London was anxious to keep communications open with Boulogne as long as possible.

The German attack began that very evening and continued throughout the night. Although the guns of some of the coastal batteries could not be brought to bear on the inland roads, they entered the fight and continued firing until overrun by the enemy infantry.

The morning of the 23rd, the defenders suddenly received powerful support from French naval forces under Captain Yves Urvoy de Porzamparc, commanding the 2nd Destroyer Flotilla and flying his flag in the *Cyclone*. Backed up by naval aviation, two super-destroyers and eight destroyers, plus additional small craft, fired on the advancing German columns until they had exhausted their ammunition, after which they had to return to Cherbourg to replenish. The naval gunfire had momentarily checked the German tanks, and General Heinz Guderian, commanding the armored corps, had to call on the Luftwaffe for assistance. The latter had responded in force. The destroyer *Orage,* commanded by Lieutenant Commander Vanblanc, took a direct hit and had to be abandoned, its flaming wreck illuminating the battlefield for a long time.

But the garrison ashore had been bolstered long enough to permit a squadron of British destroyers from Dover to evacuate 4,368 British troops from almost under the enemy guns. This was a magnificent accomplishment by the Royal Navy, although it had no effect on the battle for Boulogne itself.

For by now the battlefront had reached the heart of the city. Captain de Lestrange was captured at his command post after a bitter hand-to-hand fight during which a French petty officer shot down a German soldier attempting to hoist the swastika flag over the building.

Fierce fighting still continued at centers of resistance through the night of the 23rd. At daybreak a small sweeper succeeded in landing a few supplies for the defenders despite heavy machinegun fire from nearby enemy

[3] Now an admiral and Chief of Naval Operations.

posts. With dawn the Luftwaffe reappeared. The super-destroyer *Chacal,* under Commander Jean Estienne, took two direct bomb hits and sank just off the jetties with heavy loss of life. Other ships were more or less seriously damaged.

General Lanquetot, holding out in the citadel, received his last telephone message from Admiral Abrial, at Cherbourg, on the morning of May 25. The message said, "Warmest congratulation of the High Command on your heroic resistance!"

But the fight was coming to an end. One by one the last defenses fell. General Lanquetot accepted the German terms, and the citadel's defenders surrendered with the honors of war.

Similar battles were taking place at the same time at Cape Gris-Nez and Calais.

At Gris-Nez itself there were no coastal batteries. Construction of a battery to control the channel between the minefields and the shore had been started several months before, but never completed. The four 100-mm. guns which constituted its armament had been installed a few days previously but not yet supplied with ammunition. The several hundred Navy men stationed there had nothing but a couple of 37-mm. guns, 4 machine-guns, and 20 rifles. Yet their commanding officer, Lieut. Commander Ducuing, refused the German demands to surrender. After resisting all attacks for 24 hours he met his death at 0900 on May 25, under the flag which he himself had hoisted during the height of the fight.

Calais had no stronger French garrison than Boulogne, but the British Army was doubly interested in holding on to the port as a vital link in the British communications with England. On May 19 British infantry, coming from the front, installed themselves in the city, along with strong artillery and searchlight detachments. During the next few days a fresh infantry brigade and a regiment of tanks arrived from England. These forces made a series of attacks in an effort to cut through the enemy to the south and relieve Boulogne, as well as to rush 350,000 rations through to Dunkirk for the use of the British Expeditionary Force pocketed there.

Not one of these attempts succeeded. Upon their failure, the British set fire to their truck trains, destroyed their tanks, and prepared to evacuate. Dumfounded, the naval commander at Calais informed Admiral, North, of the British intentions.

Admiral Abrial had just been personally directed by General Weygand to defend the northern ports at all costs. For without entry ports for supplies, the surrounded troops could not be maintained.

The British War Office, upon receiving the French protest, changed its orders. The English troops in Calais remained. It was in the ensuing siege that Brigadier C. N. Nicholson, in command of the polyglot collection of

English troops and French soldiers and sailors, was to win honor and fame.

With all its forces fully occupied elsewhere, the French Navy was unable to send any combatant ships to Calais. The British Admiralty sent one cruiser and five or six British and Polish destroyers, of which two were seriously damaged in bombing raids by the Luftwaffe.

Training their guns inland over the roofs of the city, the French coastal batteries fired on all targets that appeared in the field of fire. When the shifting zone of battle rendered the guns of Bastion No. 2 (three 194-mm. guns) useless, the gun crews received orders to destroy their guns and attempt to cut their way to freedom through the German lines already encircling the city. But in the effort another tragic mistake occurred. The lieutenant who had commanded the bastion stumbled into an English position, gave the wrong answers to the questions—which he did not understand —and was shot on the spot as a spy.

Bastion No. 11 was defended until May 25 by a handful of French sailors and soldiers, aided by some 30 Moroccan infantrymen and a detachment of British soldiers. Before overwhelming the position the Germans had to call in all their artillery and air forces in that sector.

Finally, on the evening of May 26, after a heroic resistance that lent added luster to the proud history of the ancient city, General Nicholson was forced to surrender to overwhelming forces.

When one hugs the French coast from Gris-Nez toward Calais and Dunkirk, the cliffs dominating the sea fall away to make room for a flat and sandy moor, intersected, 20 kilometers from Dunkirk, by the river Aa. The Aa is a canalized stream, not over 20 meters wide a little bit up from Gravelines. Under no circumstances could it be considered a serious military obstacle. Yet, other than the Aa, there was nothing else in the plain that could stop even an automobile driving toward the waterfront at Dunkirk.

It was at the Aa, therefore, that Admiral Abrial made an attempt to throw up a barrier to check what he was still advised were no more than mere "infiltrations" by isolated German tanks.

As a matter of fact, on May 22—just when the first assaults were taking place at Boulogne and Calais—a third German armored division was arriving in sight of the Aa. The only Allied forces there, at Gravelines, were some units of the Services of Supply, which, finding their further retreat blocked, had stopped there, all mixed in with a horde of refugees.

During the day, however, Admiral Abrial brought up some detachments of reconnaissance groups retreating from Belgium, the two mobile batteries he had pulled back from the mouth of the Scheldt, and an infantry battalion. Other elements were to follow—among them isolated groups of sailors from the ships that had been sunk in the harbors. In all, there were around 4,000 or 5,000 men, to which were to be added a very weary British battalion, which took position before Gravelines—and then retired as soon as the French arrived.

There were also two motorized 75-mm. guns and three English tanks which arrived from Calais. How they got there in the night, they did not know—but when daylight came, they found themselves practically surrounded by German tanks! From seaward, the coastal batteries of Fort West (164-mm. guns) and of Fort Philippe (95-mm. guns) provided supporting fire on the improvised front, and the 194-mm. guns of the Mardyck fortifications also chimed in. These latter guns were entirely manned by the crew of the French destroyer *Adroit,* which had just been sunk off Dunkirk.

Fortunately the German tank division headed for Gravelines was delayed by a confusion of orders and then counterorders from the German High Command. But, farther upstream, one SS division and two other Panzer divisions took position on the left bank of the Aa all the way up to Saint-Omer, 28 kilometers above Gravelines. This was a far stronger force than would be required to break through the improvised French positions.

The critical battle began on May 24, and for a time all went well at Gravelines. The morale of the French Army, Navy, and Air Force, as well as of the British units participating, was, as Admiral Abrial reported that evening, exceptionally high. The three British tanks did wonders. The Navy's 155-mm. guns fired through open sights on the German tanks, stopping them dead in their tracks, though not without suffering considerable loss in return. An intercepted German message testified to the stern resistance encountered on the lower Aa.

But, farther upstream, the river was crossed at several points. Nothing—nothing except an order from Adolph Hitler—could now prevent these enemy columns from emerging the following day on the very docks of Dunkirk and thus completely encircling a half million French and British fighting men in this Flanders trap.

Nothing except an order from Hitler. And, amazingly, that order came!

The reasons for it are still being debated.

One contention is that the German High Command had already begun planning for the operations to come. It considered—too soon, no doubt—that this first phase of the Battle of France was virtually over—and won. The tanks needed a breathing spell; they should be regrouped before driving ahead in the second phase—the march on Paris and the annihilation of the remaining French Armies.

Another view is that Reichsmarschall Hermann Göring had persuaded Hitler that he could eliminate the Dunkirk pocket with his Luftwaffe alone —the psychological value of which would have been tremendous.

At all events the German generals, acting under strict orders, but mad with rage, halted on May 24 on the left bank of the Aa. There they remained immobilized for three days—a delay that was to prove the salvation of the trapped men of Dunkirk.

Even so, there is no doubt that had it not been for the unexpected resistance at Gravelines, and, to a lesser degree, the heroic combats of Boulogne and Calais, the order to halt would have found the German tanks at Dunkirk instead of still back at the Aa. It can even be supposed, without too great a stretch of imagination, that General Guderian would have been better advised to proceed with his Panzers directly toward Gravelines instead of delaying for the capture of Boulogne and Calais. Those two by-passed cities could have no effect on the main German drive, and thus Guderian would have been at Dunkirk itself before he received the order to halt.

The French Navy's role in all this had been extraordinary in that it is not part of the naval profession to fight on land. Nevertheless it had done its utmost to hold back the land forces of the enemy. It had made possible the delays which immediately preceded Hitler's amazing order to his tanks to halt—delays without which the British Expeditionary Force would most likely never have seen England again.

CHAPTER 8

The Miracle at Dunkirk

Few cities in the Republic of France have had as stormy a history as Dunkirk. In early days it had been the lair of corsairs, whose hunting grounds had been the rolling seas, and France, England, and Spain had each in turn sought to capture or destroy it, depending upon the circumstances of the moment. During the French Revolution, the War of 1870, and the First World War, Dunkirk had been a focus of conflict. The heroic conduct of its inhabitants had twice gained for it the accolade of the French Assembly that "Dunkirk deserves well of the Republic."

This time the city was to undergo an even more severe trial.

Immediately after the failures in Belgium and Holland, the port and roadstead were filled with warships and merchantmen returned from that northern essay. The night of May 17 was filled with air raid warnings, followed by the explosions of bombs, machineguns, and magnetic mines. The return antiaircraft fire of the ships was incapable of stopping the enemy planes. Two piers were set on fire, another was blown apart. The inner harbor locks were temporarily disabled. The 11th Torpedo Boat Division, which was cruising offshore, had two of its three 600-ton torpedo boats seriously damaged.

The local naval commander no longer had any air protection at his disposal. The squadrons of the aircraft carrier *Béarn*, which had already lost part of their strength on the Oise River, had to evacuate the Dunkirk airstrips and fall back to Cherbourg, whence they were very quickly ordered to the Mediterranean. An Air Force fighter group, assigned to the Navy, was called to other duty, and left without notice. The British had sent their units back to Britain one after the other as the German advance reached their respective bases in France.

Nevertheless an attempt was made to evacuate everything not essential to the safety of the Army. In succession there were lost immediately off the jetties almost a dozen ships: the freighter *Pavon,* loaded with bales of wool, and with 1,500 Dutch soldiers on board—sunk on May 20; the destroyer *Adroit,* the fleet-tanker *Niger,* submarine chaser *No. 9,* and six minesweepers—sunk on May 21. On the 22nd it was the turn of the *Jaguar,* a super-destroyer, which, after having survived almost continuous air attacks, was struck during the night almost off the entrance to the port by a torpedo from a German motor torpedo boat.[1] The officers and crews of sunken warships were immediately sent to coastal batteries in the neighborhood to bring their complements up to strength.

Confusion and chaos reigned in the city and the suburbs. The roads were filled with refugees of all nationalities. The area was without water and light. The shops were practically empty of both customers and goods. Many of the inhabitants, fleeing the bombardment, joined the refugees who were milling about in the suburbs without anywhere finding an avenue of escape.

There was no naval base at Dunkirk. Like all other cities on the front, Dunkirk lay within the zone of the Armies. Nevertheless the port was of such importance that the Navy obtained, from the Army High Command, the post of governor for an energetic naval officer. This officer was Rear Admiral Platon, just returned from Walcheren, who in the trials to come gained the respect of everyone. He was everywhere, looking after all needs; he was unperturbed even under the most intense bombardment, often stopping to adjust his monocle as an example of coolness to others. To bolster the civilian morale, he started a newspaper, the *Jean Bart*. A few of the leading citizens who had not fled the city—the Assistant Prefect and the Archpriest of the church of Saint-Eloi, among them—aided him devotedly and untiringly. Had it not been for Platon's success in restoring order in the martyred city, the ultimate evacuation of the Allied troops might have been far less successful.

The appointment of an energetic governor was not the only thing done to strengthen Dunkirk. On May 21, after his conference at Ypres, General Weygand paid a short visit to Dunkirk in company with the Commander in Chief of the Naval Forces of the North—Admiral Jean Abrial. The two men knew each other well, and they were well matched—Weygand, the old soldier and Generalissimo, and Abrial, a former Commander of the Mediterranean Squadron and an officer who had held many staff positions. Weygand, greatly concerned for the safety of the Armies, yet still confident that a counteroffensive would be successful, had no need to impress Abrial with the vital importance of the northern ports. In entrusting their defense to the Admiral, the Generalissimo said, in conclusion, "I know to whom I am talking."

Abrial called attention to the unpreparedness of the Navy for such a task, as well as the inadequate means at his disposal.

"Means?" retorted Weygand. "I will give you all I can. But what is

---

[1] It is known today that this success on the part of the German motor torpedo boats based on the Dutch coast was due in part to their deciphering the message which the *Jaguar* sent to Dunkirk giving the time of her arrival.

needed above all is a stout heart. I am counting on you to save everything that can be saved—and, above all, our honor!"

On May 23 the appointment became official. Hitherto, the Admiral, North, had only had the responsibility of protecting commercial shipping in his zone and defending the coast against attacks from the sea. Henceforth he had the duty of building an impregnable bulwark around Dunkirk against enemy attack by land as well as by sea in order that, first of all, the Allied armies could continue to live—and then, if all else failed, to insure their safety in embarking.

To assist him in carrying out his orders, Admiral Abrial was given an able Army officer, Lieutenant General Marie B. A. Fagalde, as aide, and the remnants of two Army divisions which had escaped from the trap of Flanders by retreating along the coast.

Ever since May 20 no supplies had been able to reach the surrounded troops except by sea. The Army High Command had asked the French Admiralty to arrange for the transport to Dunkirk of approximately 3,000 tons of munitions and provisions daily. Since the Seine estuary was filled with enemy magnetic mines, the cargo ships requisitioned by the Navy were loaded at Cherbourg instead of at Le Havre, and then were sent across the Channel to the Downs. From there they were to slip into Dunkirk.

This plan was put into effect on May 22, and the first convoy of seven ships reached Dunkirk three days later. In the Channel they had come under the fire of several German coastal batteries situated to the east of Calais, and had returned the fire vigorously. Now, in the port, they were subjected to continuous air raids. The electric wires to the piers had already been knocked out by enemy bombs, and consequently no mechanical unloading facilities were available. Discharging the cargoes by hand was a slow and tedious job, all of the time under enemy bombardment. Some munitions trains were blown up almost as soon as they were formed. A good part of the remaining cargoes was set afire as soon as it reached the shore. Four freighters were sunk.

Manifestly it was impossible to continue under these conditions. Accordingly the French Admiralty sent the supply ships thereafter to Dover, where the cargoes were to be transshipped on a multitude of small fishing boats for the final run to Dunkirk. To provide the numerous fishing boats necessary for the operation, groups of French sailors, under junior officers, were sent to all the French Channel and even Atlantic coast ports, with orders to requisition everything that floated—including the Belgian trawlers which had fled from their home country at the coming of the German invasion.

If the crews of the requisitioned ships volunteered, they were reinforced by two or three naval ratings armed with automatic rifles, or sometimes only with carbines or revolvers. If they did not volunteer, they were replaced promptly by naval personnel. In this way more than 200 small vessels displacing between 10 and 150 tons were sent on their way, but it would take them several days to reach Dover, and meanwhile the situation had changed radically. As for the cargo ships similarly requisitioned, 25 out of the 30 got as far as the Downs; of these 25, only 13 arrived at Dunkirk— and only 8 returned from there, the other 5 having been sunk.

At Dunkirk, however, the landing of supplies had become a matter of purely secondary interest. The land front facing the Germans had become disorganized; no counteroffensive could succeed in consolidating it. The few munitions and rations which the ships succeeded in landing, often at cost of heavy casualties, found no takers to deliver them to the troops. The latter surged constantly toward the sea in ever thickening masses. The problem of evacuation would soon take precedence over that of supplies. During the last days of the battle the only supplies landed from the incoming vessels were some loaves of bread thrown quickly over onto the docks; the supplies loaded aboard at Dover remained in the holds, while the decks were jammed with troops seizing every means of escape from the closing trap.

At the beginning of the Dunkirk tragedy, the French Admiralty, motivated by a deep attachment to the soil of France, urged that the port be reinforced rather than evacuated. It declared, on May 19, that without air support any attempt to reembark the troops would be "doomed to disaster."

The British viewed the matter in a more realistic light. They did not have the same feeling toward the Dunkirk soil that the French did. What came first with the Commander in Chief of the British Expeditionary Force was to insure the safety of the only army the United Kingdom had. With less illusions than the French, he was little inclined toward the launching of a counteroffensive without the means to sustain it. In fact it is now known that on the same day, May 19, General Lord Gort advised his Government that it would be prudent to contemplate the evacuation of the whole British Expeditionary Force to England.

The British Admiralty, like their French allies at Maintenon, replied that such an operation would be both hazardous and impractical—a unity of viewpoint that was flattering, since the two organizations had not conferred on the subject. But from then on, urgent natural interests dictated diverging courses of action. The French planned to give their best efforts to revictualling Dunkirk; the British moved quickly toward the evacuation of their Army without even informing their ally of their decision. Although a meeting of the Franco-British War Council was held on May 22 at Vincennes, headquarters of General Weygand, Mr. Churchill did not breathe a word of the British intentions during the conference.

It was not until May 25 that the French Government and French High Command received real intelligence of the matter. On that day a liaison officer, Major Joseph Fauvelle, came to Paris from the Armies of the North. He did not hesitate to deliver his message in plain language, and the Prime Minister, deeply impressed, that evening for the first time used the word "armistice." For Fauvelle had described the military situation as tragic, and had added that from information he had personally gathered, the British Expeditionary Force was preparing to disengage and to reembark for England.

Up to that moment the French had had no thought except to continue fighting to hold Dunkirk—"to save, above all, the honor of the flag," as was repeated in one of General Weygand's telegrams that day. But although Admiral Abrial had momentarily checked the Germans on the Aa River, he did not conceal from the Admiralty his opinion that the situation was extremely critical. The Admiralty, reading his telegrams, received the impression that at any moment everything could break wide open—particularly if, as Fauvelle had just indicated, the British were thinking more of evacuating than of holding. It was necessary to prepare for the worst.

It was under these conditions that Captain Auphan, Deputy Chief of Staff of the French Admiralty, was sent to Dover on May 27 to make an on-the-spot estimate of the situation. He arranged for a meeting there with Vice Admiral Odend'hal, Chief of the French Naval Mission to the British Admiralty at London, and with Rear Admiral Marcel Leclerc, Chief of Staff to Admiral Abrial. Naturally he was to confer also with the British naval authorities.

While awaiting the arrival of Leclerc, who had left Dunkirk in a fast motor boat, Odend'hal and Auphan exchanged information at the Allied Officers Mess. Both were considerably astonished at the large number of British naval officers in battle dress who were present.

Living at London and mingling in British naval circles, Admiral Odend'hal knew many of these officers, at least by sight. All these officers, he learned, had been assigned by their various branches to the task of manning the hundreds of small craft which had been requisitioned at Dover and other English ports several days before. In khaki, and carrying gas masks over their shoulders, they were at work on the plans for evacuation, which had already been in preparation since the day before.

It was thus—that is to say, by chance—that the French High Command learned of a decision already made of vital importance to the battle then raging, and, in fact, to the future of the whole alliance. When Weygand and Darlan learned of it, through Auphan's report, they had some rather sharp words to say about the British—not because of the decision itself, which time was to prove was highly correct, but because it had been made unilaterally, and because the evacuation thus made would disorganize the entire defense. When, two or three weeks later, the question of a separate

Franco-German armistice arose, it was the opinion of the majority of French leaders that after such a breach of trust and disregard for the spirit of teamwork, France was not required to make a greater sacrifice for the common cause than England had.

At Dover Captain Auphan met Admiral Sir Bertram Ramsay and Admiral Sir James Somerville, who briefed him on "Operation Dynamo"—the evacuation of Dunkirk—which was already in progress under their direction. Auphan agreed with them upon a plan whereby the French could join the operation without delay. This plan was approved by the French Admiralty the day after Auphan's return.

Now the requisitioning of the small vessels in the Channel and Brittany ports proved an enormous advantage. Orders were sent out to the requisitioning officers to expedite the program to the maximum. Even so, the British, who had had much more time than the French to set up their program, began complaining that the French vessels were not arriving quickly enough.

On May 28 Rear Admiral Marcel Landriau was designated to command all the small French naval vessels assigned to the operation, which would be called the Pas-de-Calais Flotilla. This short-lived naval force consisted of two super-destroyers, seven fleet-destroyers, six 600-ton torpedo boats, four sloops, some twenty patrol vessels, submarine chasers, or fast motor boats, and a host of miscellaneous small craft—approximately 200. Landriau hoisted his flag on the antiaircraft sloop *Savorgnan de Brazza,* and proceeded to Dover. At Admiral Abrial's direction he joined Admiral Ramsay's force in establishing a shuttling bridge of ships between the English coast and Dunkirk. Although the Royal Air Force provided some protection, mostly the shuttle ships operated without air cover.

As his part of the operation, General Weygand sent one of the generals of his staff to the Armies of the North to order them to counterattack once more. But in view of the inability to stage such an attack, and in light of the collapse of the Belgian front and the withdrawal of the British, all General Weygand could do was to order a general withdrawal of the French also. At 0720 on May 29, he telegraphed[2] General Georges Blanchard, General Billotte's successor, "Fight your way through to the coast!"

However, only a few divisions succeeded in getting through; the remainder sacrificed themselves before Lille in order to cover the retreat of the others.

Despite the speed with which they acted, the French naval operation was always one week behind that of the British. This, added to the fact that the

---

[2] Ever since the fall of Abbeville, when the last remaining land wire was cut, all messages between Supreme General Headquarters and the First Group of Armies were handled by the Navy.

Royal Navy had greater means at its disposal, explains why the French Navy rescued fewer people than its ally. But if Abrial and the Dunkirk defenders had not checked the German attacks for several days, neither the British nor the French would have brought as many men out of the trap as they did.

When the Dunkirk evacuation is mentioned, one thinks almost entirely of the British operation. The two authors of this book, one of whom was at French Admiralty headquarters and the other at Dunkirk itself, were in an excellent position to observe the "magnificent work" and the personal bravery of the British crews,[3] who, with their French comrades, rescued from that infernal trap some 338,000 men, of whom 120,000 were French. The British operation is known to the world. What will be attempted here is the account of the French part in that operation.

To evacuate anything at all, it was first of all necessary to hold on to Dunkirk. It would serve no useful purpose to send evacuation ships there if they found the Germans already occupying the wharves and the beaches when they arrived.

The entrenched camp established around Dunkirk by Admiral, North, extended in the main from La Panne and Bray-Dunes to Mardyck, via Bergues. As they fell back, all French forces came under the orders of Admiral, North, as soon as they entered this defense perimeter. Many, however, were not fit for combat. Only the freshest troops were sent to man the lines.

As far as the French generals were concerned, no command difficulties confronted Admiral Abrial, as all had received definite instructions from General Weygand. On the British side, however, the situation was more delicate. A single command did not exist, which resulted in frequent consultations at Government level. On May 31 the Supreme Allied War Council decided, in principle, in favor of Abrial, but then it was too late. Too late also was another decision on that date—demanded by Mr. Churchill as a matter of honor for the British Army—that the British be assigned the rear guard. The British, acting independently, had already taken their dispositions, which often superimposed themselves on Admiral Abrial's.

When orders are contradictory, incidents are bound to occur. For instance, the British demolition parties wished to destroy immediately certain installations which the French wanted to hold to the very end.

In general, the British undertook to defend the Eastern Sector, while the French took over the Western. In reality, however, by the 1st of June the British rear guard had already been reduced to 4,000 men, and General

---

[3] Extract from Admiral Abrial's official report.

Sir Harold Alexander, to whom Lord Gort had given this command, made it known that he had orders to withdraw this last contingent on the following night. However, as a result of a decision of the Supreme Allied Council, he actually held on for another 24 hours. Nevertheless, during the last 48 hours—the most critical period of the entire evacuation—the French found themselves alone in manning the defenses of the entrenched camp.

At sea, collaboration was infinitely easier. Even after departure of the last man of the British Expeditionary Force, the Royal Navy, exhausted as it was, continued its efforts for another two days—all for the exclusive benefit of the soldiers of France. That, France will never forget.

Meantime the state of the defense perimeter was precarious in the extreme. The Navy could provide some precious artillery support for that front—four coastal batteries with 164- and 194-mm. guns (not counting the less important batteries), and the two mobile batteries of 155-mm. guns which had fought at the Scheldt and on the Aa. Whenever the enemy came within range, these batteries never stopped firing, notwithstanding intense enemy air attacks and counterbattery fire. When not a single shell remained, the crews destroyed their guns, but continued to resist with small arms alone. Particulary notable was the Third Mobile Battery, under Lieutenant Henri Jabet. After destroying their guns, the crew of this battery, only a few thousand yards from the embarkation points, fought the Germans for every inch of ground during the night of June 3 to cover the escape of their comrades. Jabet was killed in this action.

In the matter of seaborne artillery, the French Admiralty could provide a great deal more support to Dunkirk and the evacuation. Two veteran battleships, the *Courbet* and the *Paris*, each with ten 305-mm. guns, were overhauled in 96 hours at Brest, equipped with antiaircraft guns, and sent to Cherbourg on May 28—there to await the Admiral's orders as "expendable." It was Admiral Abrial's intention to use these ships at pointblank range to support a counterattack planned to extend the perimeter of the Dunkirk entrenched camp to the westward, toward Calais. If successful, this enlargement would have greatly facilitated the troop evacuations. Lacking sufficient ground troops, however, the operation was cancelled.

On account of shallow water and enemy mines, the evacuation and escort ships—even those of shallow draft—could not enter and leave Dunkirk by the shortest route. Only two routes existed—or rather two channels which were regularly cleared by French sweepers.

Route Z, the shortest, and the one used by commercial shipping before the war, followed the coastline to the west before heading for the open sea and Dover. However, it passed close under the guns of German batteries now installed between Calais and Gravelines, and was seldom usable except at night. It was to clean out these batteries that the French and British

Admiralties had planned the counteroffensive to the west previously mentioned.

Route Y followed the coast toward the east and passed around the northern edge of the French minefields, but it was exposed to the fire of the more distant batteries which the Germans had installed at Nieuport. By day, if the ships shied away from the German shore batteries, they took the risk of running afoul of the minefields. At night they ran the still greater risk of being attacked by German motor torpedo boats at the Hook of

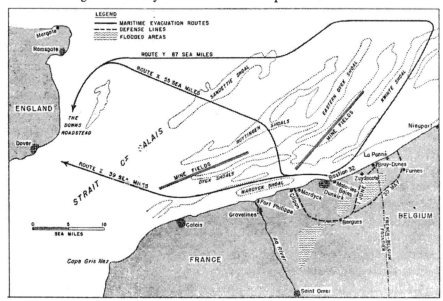

EVACUATION ROUTES FROM DUNKIRK

Holland. As a matter of fact, several French and British destroyers and many transports were thus torpedoed. Admiral Abrial offered Admiral Ramsay the assistance of his super-destroyers and of the special sloop, the *Amiens,* to fight the German MTBs but the operation never materialized and Route Y eventually had to be abandoned.

A third route was then established—Route X, the best but the most difficult from a navigational point of view because of the shallow waters and the minefields it skirted. It was practical to use it only in clear weather and at certain hours of the tide. Furthermore it could be reached by fire from the German battery installed at Clipon, nine kilometers west of Dunkirk, which the R.A.F. had been unable to knock out.

In brief, from May 26 on, German artillery within range of the port and beaches of Dunkirk kept the points of embarkation under continuous fire, day and night. This was the cause of heavy losses among the evacuating vessels and many casualties among the troops waiting to embark.

Such was the setting in which was accomplished the miracle of Dunkirk—an accomplishment which neither the French Navy nor the Royal Navy—not to mention the Germans—believed in any way possible.

The first to be evacuated were the wounded. This was natural, as the longer they were denied the necessary medical care and hospitalization, the worse their condition became. At Dunkirk the French Navy medical units were bombed out of one first aid station after another and finally had to establish themselves some ten kilometers to the east of the city, close by an Army field hospital set up in the sanatorium of Zuydecote. Here conditions were really tragic. Some 600 to 800 wounded were always waiting for treatment by the first aid surgical teams, which were already working 24 hours a day, without a break. Many of the wounded died without ever having seen a doctor. Others were killed by bombs. In the midst of an operation, one surgeon had to take his anesthetized patient in his arms and quickly dump him under the operating table in order to protect him from German 77-mm. shellbursts which were riddling the operating room.

Ever since May 20, Admiral Abrial had been making a determined effort to evacuate the wounded at every opportunity. The mail steamer *Rouen* took 420 patients to Cherbourg on May 26. The following day two minesweepers disembarked 175 more in England.

An attempt to bring in French hospital ships was without success. One evening a large convoy of ambulances, waiting at the waterfront for the expected arrival of a hospital ship, came under heavy enemy fire directed at the quays. They were forced to leave and return to the hospital at Zuydecote; only a few ambulances and a few men survived the round trip. The British were having enough trouble with their own hospital ships, so finally the French Admiralty had to resign itself to giving evacuation priority to combat-fit soldiers.

Next on the priority list were certain categories of specialists whose return the Army asked for prior to the issue of the general evacuation order. For their sake Admiral, North, assembled a convoy on May 28 in which 2,500 men were embarked. Scarcely had it cleared the harbor when the cargo ship *Douaisien,* with 1,000 men on board, hit a magnetic mine. The majority of its passengers were rescued by small trawlers en route to Dunkirk.

On the following day, May 29, general evacuation began. The English generously offered space for 5,000 men on their ships. The French Admiralty sent three destroyers of the *Cyclone* class and five sloops from Dover to Dunkirk. The destroyers arrived in midafternoon, under a violent German bombardment. The *Cyclone* got away without damage, and returned to Dover that evening with 733 passengers, of whom 158 were survivors of a sunken English sloop picked up on the return trip. The *Siroco,* also undamaged, brought away 509 men. But the *Mistral,* her superstructure shattered by a bomb bursting on the quay alongside and with her commanding officer mortally wounded, had to back out at full speed without being able to take on board any troops whatsoever.

As a matter of fact, there were no longer any evacuees on the quay, everyone having taken shelter wherever he could find it. The port was now completely untenable. When the *Mistral* cleared the harbor, there was no longer a single ship left afloat there. The English had not been spared, either, and, as Admiral Ramsay wrote in his report, "The day closed with a formidable list of ships lost or damaged."

The sloops arrived after nightfall and waited until dawn to enter the harbor. For once the air raids were lacking and they encountered only enemy artillery fire. They took safely away a full load of passengers, despite the interference of a German battery which saluted them off Nieuport. In all, embarkation figures for the 29th amounted to 5,178.[4]

May 30, however, was a disastrous day. It brought the end for three ships: the *Bourrasque,* sunk off Nieuport; the *Siroco,* hit by two torpedoes from a German *Schnell-Boot*[5] and then finished off by two bombs; and the *Cyclone,* disabled through having her bow blown off by a torpedo. This glorious ship of Captain de Porzamparc had participated in every engagement from the very first. She had fought at Flushing, at Boulogne, at Ijmuiden. She seemed invulnerable. But this time she got it. She did manage to reach Dover under her own power, and later crossed to Brest. There she had to be scuttled while in drydock, on June 18, the very day the Germans arrived.

Notwithstanding all these losses, 6,363 French soldiers were embarked on the 30th and safely landed, thanks to a decision to risk five supply ships which had been anchored in the Downs. These ships were able to evacuate a total of 3,000 men, with very few losses and only minor damage. In addition, two small torpedo boats of 600 tons each brought back survivors. The *Branlebas* evacuated 520 men, including a great number from the *Bourrasque;* the *Bouclier* saved 767 men—a prodigious number to those familiar with that type of ship.

The following day saw the entry into Dunkirk of four more of these small torpedo boats, and five more of the 600-ton *Elan*-class. All handled extremely well, and were skillful at evading bombs. They yielded remark-

---

[4] Counted from 0800 on May 29 to 0800 on May 30. In principle, evacuees embarked on a ship that was sunk are not counted; instead, they are credited to the rescuing ship.

[5] Fast, small German craft, similar to the U.S. PT-boat.

THE BATTLESHIP DUNKERQUE *after the second attack by torpedo planes from the* ARK ROYAL. *Abreast No. 2 turret can be seen the hole caused by the explosion of depth charges carried by the* TERRE NEUVE, *sunk alongside the battleship.*

MERS-EL-KEBIR, JULY 3, 1940. *The battleship* STRASBOURG *underway within seconds after the first British salvo. The super-destroyer in foreground is getting underway.*

TORPEDO PLANES *from the* ARK ROYAL *attacking the* DUNKERQUE *at dawn on July 6, 1940.*

MERS-EL-KEBIR HARBOR *during the battle on July 3, 1940. In the foreground is seen the super-destroyer* MAGADOR *after being struck in the stern and set on fire by a large shell.*

able returns.[6] Unfortunately the French Admiralty recalled these ships to escort transports which, in compliance with the Army's urgent demand, were returning the Dunkirk evacuees from England to France.

Finally, acknowledgment should be made of the services of the three mail steamers, *Côte d'Argent, Newhaven,* and *Rouen,* which between them transported almost 12,000 men during the evacuation.

At last, on May 31, there arrived the horde of small fishing craft which had been requisitioned. Admiral Landriau had established control stations in the Dover roadstead and was sending to Dunkirk everything that arrived. Needless to say, the trips were made under the least orthodox methods of navigation. There were insufficient charts—compasses were lacking— courses were mainly set by following the ship ahead. It was easy enough proceeding to Dunkirk, for the lofty columns of flame and smoke were visible from miles away. But the return trip was less easy, and many boats missed the mouth of the Thames altogether.

Also, there were engine failures. Thus, the motor of the little *Jacqueline* positively refused to function after arrival at Dover. Never mind—its crew of three sailors from the destroyer *Triomphant* set off boldly for Dunkirk *under sail,* and returned the same way, bringing off 33 men.

In all, 48 ships brought back 9,967 men on May 31. On the 1st of June, 38 craft brought off 7,483. Forty-three ships had actually started out, but five were sunk off Dunkirk, including the *Foudroyant,* last survivor of Porzamparc's flotilla,[7] and three sweepers sunk by the Luftwaffe. On the 2nd of June, 43 ships evacuated 6,177 men, and on the 3rd in a last go, with both Navies vying with each other, 63 ships brought off 10,248.

It was scarcely hoped to continue the evacuation as late as the night of June 3. The enemy was already nearing the inner defenses of Dunkirk. Admiral Abrial was burning his codes. But from Dover the English and French were preparing one final *coup* in force. When Admiral Abrial left his headquarters in Bastion 32, to view the last embarkations from on board a MTB, a tremendous activity was taking place in the harbor of Dunkirk. For the moment the sky was clear of enemy aircraft, but the furor of the land battle was increasing minute by minute. In an uproar of

---

[6] The record for these ships belongs to the *Impétueuse* (Lieutenant Commander François Bachy), which disembarked 649 men at Dover on May 31. In time of peace no commanding officer would dream of embarking half that number on a ship of that class.

[7] Captain Urvoy de Porzamparc, well known and very popular in the Navy, commanded the 2nd Flotilla, based on Brest, which consisted of 12 destroyers of the *Cyclone* class (1,500 tons). Of the 9 placed under the orders of Admiral, North, 5 were sunk and 4 damaged. Only the *Ouragan,* undergoing repairs at Brest, and the *Boulonnais* and *Brestois,* sent to Norway and then to the Mediterranean, were absent from this battle.

sirens the torpedo boats maneuvered at full speed—went alongside, took on their loads without making fast, and backed full away in brief minutes—crossed each other and sheered off in a whirlpool. The final miracle of Dunkirk is that there were not more collisions that night. Only one serious collision occurred, and even then, thanks to the fog, the ships succeeded in getting away to sea. The last loss of Operation Dynamo was the French minesweeper *Emile Deschamps,* which on the morning of June 4 blew up on a magnetic mine within sight of the North Foreland. Of the 500 men aboard, only 100 or so were rescued.[8]

Plans had been made to save everybody, but the dispositions taken to embark the defenders of Dunkirk were defeated by the sudden appearance of thousands of men, coming from no one knows where. Out of caves, out of shell and bomb holes, came disarmed men, forming small human streams converging toward the jetty and joining together to form a huge, impressive human river almost congealed on the spot. With all approaches to the jetty blocked, the real last ditch defenders looked on in silence from a distance and saw the last embarkation leave the quay and the last ships clear the

---

[8] Note by Jacques Mordal: Among them I was fortunate to find myself with Lieutenant Jacquelin de la Porte de Vaux, one of my shipmates in the *Jaguar,* sunk 15 days before. The *Emile Deschamps* went down in a few seconds, taking with her a great many of our sailors, as well as a number of the survivors of the *Jaguar.* But, as in all tragedies, this event had its lighter side. After I had surfaced and recovered my breath, I heard myself being hailed by de la Porte de Vaux with, "Hello, Hello! Let's sing!" And he began singing "The Song of Departure (*"Le Chant du Départ"*), one of our most famous military marches.

I was picked up by the British sloop *Albury;* I do not remember the ship which picked up de la Porte de Vaux. But it so happened that the same ambulance carried us both to the first aid station at Margate. En route I was strongly reproached by him for not having sung while in the water, "as all sailors with their hearts in the right place must do in such circumstances."

I had been in no more of a mood to sing patriotic songs than my clothing could be said to give me a martial appearance. In fact, I was covered by a single blanket, which I felt sliding off me while I was being carried by a big devil of an Englishman toward a group of nurses who were attending the wounded. An indignant "Shocking!" coming from the lips of a blushing young nurse finally conveyed to me the fact that the said blanket and I had parted company.

It so happened that I was repatriated to France shortly afterward, while de la Porte de Vaux was still in a hospital in England at the time of the armistice between France and Germany. I continued to serve in what became known as the "Vichy Navy," while he joined the Free French Naval Forces. The reverse could just as well have happened; and astute is he who will tell me what my feelings would have been if I had been in my comrade's place. Meeting unexpectedly one evening in Paris after the liberation, we fell into each other's arms, calling each other "You dirty Vichyite!" and "You dirty De Gaulliste!" Then we ran together to the nearest bar to swap reminiscences. We almost left our whole month's pay there!

harbor. The night paled and the early dawn rose over an empty sea from which no further help could be expected.

And thus the bravest remained in the hands of the enemy. In all, there were from 35,000 to 40,000 prisoners, but 215,000 British troops and 123,000 French had been snatched from the hands of the enemy. Of the total, the French Navy had evacuated 44,352 men landed in England, 3,936 sent directly to Le Havre or Cherbourg, and the passengers of a few transports who were not counted. The total was in the neighborhood of 50,000.

The French Army Command was naturally in a great hurry to recover the use of the troops of the Armies of the North evacuated to England, as well as those waiting in Scotland or returned from Norway. The French Admiralty therefore set in motion, even during the evacuation, a continuous shuttle of transports, mostly French, between the English ports and Cherbourg and Brest. By June 9 one hundred thousand men had been repatriated without a single loss. At any other time the escorting of so many transports across the Channel with means primarily French would have been considered quite a feat; in view of what was taking place at Dunkirk, it received scarcely any attention at all.

In addition to the evacuation, one last duty had been left to the defenders of Dunkirk—to make the port useless to the enemy thereafter. Despite repeated orders from Admiral, North, the British had begun to bottle up the port with blockships on the night of June 2; the following night the work was completed, this time in agreement with the French. The hulks of four sunken ships, each over 100 meters in length, blocked the inner harbor for a long time—in fact the Germans were still complaining about them in 1941.

In addition the French Navy completed the Pas-de-Calais minefields. Between the 6th and 12th of June the *Pollux* and three other French minelayers from Cherbourg finished blocking the channel along the French coast there in an operation that was full of danger.

On the 4th of June the following Navy communique was published to an anxious France:

> During the night of June 3, the last Army and Navy units which, under the orders of Admiral Abrial, had been defending Dunkirk to permit the withdrawal and embarkation of the allied Armies of the North, were, in their turn, evacuated in good order after having rendered the port unusable. The British and French Navies, by their close collaboration, successfully concluded an operation unique in history which permitted them to rescue over 300,000 men of the Allied Armies. . . .

This was followed by the names of the ships lost. At that time only part of the French losses were given out. Moreover, on June 4 the actual losses were not even known to the Navy. The casualties, as finally tabulated, amounted to 2 super-destroyers, 5 fleet-destroyers, 30 auxiliary mine-sweepers (armed trawlers), 5 tugs, 3 oil tankers, 12 cargo ships, 1 passenger liner, and several other small vessels of which no trace has ever been found. Numerically these losses amounted to approximately one-fifth of the 300 ships of all sizes which the French Navy had committed to this operation.

Thus ends the story of the miracle at Dunkirk. It was successful beyond all expectations. Even if the results had only been half so great, the incalculable importance of the defensive measures taken by the Commander in Chief of the Naval Forces, North, should always be remembered. There were countless others who contributed their share to that triumph, but it would be impossible to do justice to them all. Pilots of the Royal Air Force —ships' gunners—firemen— infantrymen on the Mardyck Canal—masters of fishing boats or captains of destroyers—all of these, and others, share with Admiral Abrial and Admiral Ramsay in the glory of the feat which robbed Germany of a great part of her victory in the West. And who knows if it did not later influence Germany's decision to forego the invasion of England?

CHAPTER 9

Fall of the French Atlantic Ports

Day after day the inspiring message had gone out over the radio to a breathless France: "The entrenched camp of Dunkirk still holds fast." Now it was over. Dunkirk had fallen.

But thanks to the Navies, all had not been lost. And remembering 1914, when a new line of defense had been created, even after days and weeks of suspense, the French wanted to believe that a new front could again be established—this time on the Somme.

But the French Navy could think only of its immediate job—keeping open the seaways, the only means by which France could continue to live. The northern ports had fallen, but the Atlantic and Channel ports still remained.

And the Navy's prestige had never stood so high. Admiral Abrial's name was on every lip. The survivors of Dunkirk, returning from England, were loud in their gratitude.

One of the immediate results was that on June 8, 1940, a Government decree placed all the Channel and Atlantic ports under the authority of the Commander in Chief of the Naval Forces in the same manner as the cities on the land front came under the authority of the Army.

The majority of those ports were in desperate situation. Their harbors choked by refugee ships, their roadsteads blocked by enemy magnetic mines, they were in danger of quick strangulation. The French Admiralty immediately sent to each port a qualified senior officer, with the title of "Delegate of the Admiralty," to coordinate and direct the action of all services, civil or military, concerned with the operation of the port. It was hoped that these *Missi dominici*[1] would clear the waterways and speed up traffic. But they arrived only in time to preside over the evacuation of the operable ships, the scuttling of those not able to get under way, the burning of petroleum stocks, etc.

For after the collapse of the Meuse front, nothing could stop the German tide from sweeping over the country and engulfing the ports, one by one, from the rear.

For fifteen days General Weygand had been working diligently to set

---

[1] Messengers of the Lord.

83

up a new front on the Somme, but it never existed except as a few isolated fortifications. And on June 5, within 24 hours after the fall of Dunkirk, the enemy attacked again along the entire line from the Argonne to the sea.

Against them the small observation posts on the coast, with batteries hastily strengthened with guns borrowed from the Navy, fought to the last. At the request of the Army, the *Léopard, Epervier,* and *Savorgnan de*

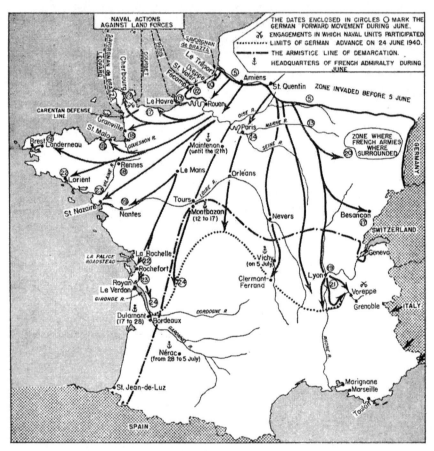

FALL OF THE CHANNEL AND ATLANTIC PORTS

Brazza laid down a barrage on the roads from inland. The old battleship *Paris* took firing station off Le Havre, but a direct bomb hit forced her to Brest for repairs.

As at Dunkirk, the danger came from inland. A German armored corps crossed the Somme between Amiens and Abbeville on June 5, and reached the Seine three nights later. On June 9 the German tanks were at Rouen.

Here, Captain de Porzamparc had been assigned as Delegate of the Admiralty. Leaving his disabled destroyer *Cyclone* at Brest, he arrived at Rouen only in time to witness the destruction of the bridges just ahead of the advancing Germans, to rescue personally some sailors stranded on the opposite shore, and to evacuate anything that could be evacuated. He arrived at Admiralty headquarters, only 85 miles from Rouen, that same day, with the news of the enemy's approach. Within two days the French Admiralty was forced to withdraw from Maintenon and to move southward, beyond the Loire.

The Germans' lightning advance cut off all the Allied divisions which were still in upper Normandy. They no longer had any bridges—only ferries, with which to cross the Seine downstream from Rouen.

An attempt was made to rescue them by sea from Le Havre just as had been done at Dunkirk. All the small trawlers of the Pas-de-Calais Flotilla were sent for. Twenty freighters got under way from Brest and Cherbourg. The ferries were manned with armed sailors. The huge oil stocks at Port Jérôme were set on fire, to blacken the skies for days with smoke.

At Le Havre itself, Admiral Platon, who had assumed the command, did his utmost to insure the escape of the exhausted infantrymen. Motor busses were requisitioned to bring them out. But they were still 100 kilometers away, and the Germans moved too fast. On June 10, General Erwin Rommel reached the coast in the vicinity of Fécamp, where a small group of soldiers and of sailors from a minesweeper under repairs held him up for 24 hours.

Out of the five encircled Allied divisions, only a few French units and two motorized British brigades succeeded in reaching Le Havre. The remainder dug in at Saint-Valery-en-Caux, 53 miles up the coast from Le Havre, to await rescue that could only come by sea.

But miracles take place only once. Despite fierce resistance by the French and Scottish troops, the Germans drove forward until their artillery could sweep both the port and the beaches of Saint-Valery with shellfire, ending the Allied hopes. General Rommel announced the capture of 46,000 men.

A few thousand troops were saved by the Navy, however, from the beaches of Veules les Roses, seven kilometers to the east, on the night of June 11. Here the beached patrol vessel *Cérons,* under pointblank fire from German 88-mm. guns, succeeded in knocking out two of them before herself being blown up by the explosion of her own depth charges. The French armed freighter *Granville,* arriving next day and unaware that Saint-Valery had fallen, was knocked out by German artillery which let it approach to within 700 meters before opening fire.

But the resistance at Saint-Valery at least permitted the evacuation of

Le Havre, with no interference except by the Luftwaffe. The Navy was able to tow away a few sub-chasers under construction at Fécamp and in the shipyards of the lower Seine, and also the submarine *Créole,* which had been launched at Le Havre on June 8. But the Luftwaffe's bombs sank half a dozen transports, including the *Niobé.* This ship, although loaded with ammunition which had been intended for Dunkirk, was evacuating refugees from Le Havre. The ammunition was set off by the bombs, causing the death of 800 soldiers, sailors, workmen, women, and children. Only 11 out of all those aboard were saved.

On June 13, Le Havre and the whole north shore of the Seine estuary were in German hands. On the south bank a few guns sent over from Cherbourg were still manned by survivors from Dunkirk, but upstream from Rouen the river had already been crossed in half a dozen places. The front was nothing more now than a thin line of troops, outnumbered three to one, and with no reserves behind them. Several million refugees were crowding all roads to the south. In order to prevent useless destruction, General Weygand had ordered a general withdrawal and had proclaimed Paris an open city.

Italy now had declared war on France.

Generalissimo Weygand informed the Government that he saw no other solution to the situation than to ask an armistice from the Germans. Churchill heard the news, with tears in his eyes, at Tours on June 13, and admitted the probability involved, yet he interposed no conditions.

Even in the hour of decision the Government ordered the organization of a bridgehead in Brittany which France possibly could hold through the assistance of England and with supplies brought in by sea. General Charles de Gaulle, who since June 9 had been Assistant Secretary of the Army, went to Rennes to study the organization of this "Breton Redoubt," whose front was to follow the courses of the Couesnon and Vilaine rivers. The defense forces were to consist of a few regiments assembled from within the area, plus a Canadian division which was even then disembarking at Brest, and General Béthouart's troops just back from Norway. But the project was entirely visionary for several reasons: lack of planes, lack of antiaircraft guns to defend the ports, and, above all, lack of time. To organize a worthwhile defense would take a month—some of De Gaulle's generals and engineers said three months. And the Germans would be there in less than a week.

Admiral Darlan, in Admiralty headquarters now at Montbazon, near Tours, knew the bitter truth. Every evening since the beginning of the German offensive, liaison officers from the Supreme General Headquarters of the Army had brought the latest information on the situation.

This Admiral Darlan had promptly passed along to his subordinates, so that while many authorities in France and overseas were poorly informed, the Navy's principal commanders usually were fully and accurately informed. This sense of sharing in the problem would be a tremendous psychological factor in maintaining the Navy's cohesion in times to come.

"In case we should be surprised by the rapidity of events" the Commander in Chief of the Naval Forces, acting on his own initiative on June 14, drafted a set of directives to take effect "in the case of an unfortunate armistice." These directives, which called for the Fleet to sail for Great Britain or for French colonial ports, were coded in advance in order that they could be sent out immediately upon receipt of orders from the Government.

Those orders from the Government never came. But the frame of mind of the Admiralty can be clearly deduced from the two important messages it sent to the western naval bases on June 15. The first suspended further drydocking of any ships; it ordered a speedup in repairs to the Fleet, and the loading of spare parts and ammunition reserves on requisitioned cargo ships; and it directed all men-of-war to be ready to get under way at a moment's notice. The second message concerned the two powerful battleships still under construction: the *Richelieu,* which was undergoing trials at Brest, and the *Jean Bart,* which was still on the building ways at Saint-Nazaire. In case of being threatened by the German advance, these two ships were to be sent to England in accordance with arrangements which had been concluded by Admiral Odend'hal with the British Admiralty. The outline for these arrangements had been taken to Admiral Odend'hal at Dover by Captain Auphan just three weeks earlier.

The next day, June 16, the French Admiralty received definite information that two German armored divisions had just gotten under way in a drive toward the Cotentin Peninsula and Brittany. In that direction lay both Cherbourg and Brest.

Cherbourg, the headquarters of a naval district, was where Admiral Abrial had set up his command post after the evacuation of Dunkirk. It, like most other such ports, had sent the majority of its small guns to Paris or to the banks of the Seine for antitank defense. The result was that it had little left now in the way of mobile artillery. As for defenders, there were a few second-rate battalions. Other than these there were only noncombatant specialists—mechanics, yeomen, stewards, air technicians, and the like—men more used to handling a typewriter or a kit of tools than a machinegun or a rifle.

On the evening of June 17 the German tanks arrived at the Carentan lines. These are natural defense lines which, as far back as the Hundred Years' War, have been relied upon to defend the approaches to the Cotentin Peninsula. Here Vice Admiral Jules Le Bigot, Commandant of the District and a veteran of the famous Marine Brigade of 1914, had attempted to establish defense lines. But on account of the many other tasks assigned to Cherbourg, he was never able to do so.

On June 17 the radio announced that a new Government, now headed by Marshal Philippe Pétain, had asked the Germans for an armistice. But Admiral Darlan directed that the fight must continue with fierce energy as long as the negotiations were not concluded. Consequently the sailors opened fire on Rommel's advance guard and held them the whole night. The next morning the drive on Cherbourg continued, but under fierce harassing fire from men-of-war which Admiral Abrial had positioned on each side of the Cotentin Peninsula.[2] A few defensive positions in the outskirts of the city also held up the enemy advance so that it was not until the afternoon of the 19th that Cherbourg finally was taken.

The forty hours thus gained, however, had insured the evacuation of the last British troops there as well as all the French ships in the harbor. A submarine, not quite ready for launching, was dynamited on the ways. All of the coastal batteries were blown up, as were the forts on the main breakwater, which did not surrender until the 20th. Nothing of any use whatsoever was left for the Germans.

Determined to share the fate of his men, Admiral Abrial refused all opportunities of escape and let himself be taken prisoner, along with Admiral Le Bigot and the Cherbourg garrison.

Brest, situated at the very tip of Finistère—"the end of the earth"—could not believe that it was threatened. Despite numerous attacks in its long history it had never been overrun since Brittany had become a part of France in the Middle Ages. Powerful forts defended the roadstead and its approaches. Unfortunately none of these forts faced inland. Worse still, a telegram from the French Admiralty, warning against parachutists landing on the beaches, had resulted in wide dispersion of all the light guns which had not already been sent off to defend Paris.

Brest was the headquarters of a naval district and the command post of Admiral de Laborde, Commander in Chief of the Naval Forces of the West. The Admiral, a vigorous, quick-tempered officer, was very popular in the Navy, especially among those not in a position to encounter his formidable wrath. Up to now the duties of Admiral, West, had been concerned purely with nautical affairs—escort and convoy duty, antisubmarine warfare in the Atlantic, and launching the expeditions to Norway and Finland.

---

[2] The firing ships on the east coast were the old battleship *Courbet,* escorted by two 600-ton torpedo boats and one antiaircraft sloop; on the west coast, the *Léopard, Savorgnan de Brazza,* and two torpedo boats. The effectiveness of their fire was attested by French prisoners whom Rommel had placed at the head of his column.

At the beginning of June, Brest had become crowded with French troops escaping from Dunkirk or returning from Norway, as well as British troops en route to the east—100,000 men in all, in four weeks. It was the duty of Admiral, West, to protect this heavy traffic and to keep open the sea-lanes which fed France from the Atlantic. The last thing he had time to think about was what was going on inland.

The Commandant of the Naval District and Governor of Brest counted on the Breton Redoubt to stop the enemy, at least for several days. He was confirmed in this impression by the passage through Brest, on June 15, of General de Gaulle, who was on his way to London on a mission. General de Gaulle gave out no information regarding his trip, and the authorities at Brest naturally imagined that he was going to work with the British on an interallied organization for that famous redoubt.[3]

The first note of alarm that reached Admiral de Laborde was a message from the French Admiralty on June 16. The message directed Admiral, West, to load onto Admiral Cadart's auxiliary cruisers, then in port, all of the gold of the Bank of France, as well as the reserves of the Banks of Belgium and Poland. These gold reserves, which had been collected at Brest and Lorient, were to be sent to safety in French West Africa.[4]

In addition to this worry, Admiral, West, had the problem of the British troops who were falling back to Atlantic ports, abandoning their weapons and supplies, and making ready to take English transports back home.

Admiral, West, wondered whether the requested armistice would be effected before the worst occurred.

He had not long to worry. At 1100 on June 18 the telephone rang in the office of Vice Admiral Marcel Traub, the Naval District Commandant. The call was from General René Altmayer, at Rennes, who wished to speak with Admiral de Laborde. The General reported that he was already a prisoner, but the Germans had carelessly forgotten to cut his telephone wire. The important part of the message, however, was that a German

---

[3] General de Gaulle's actual mission was to obtain ships from the British to evacuate as many French troops as possible to Africa.

[4] It is perhaps thanks to the French Admiralty that the gold of the Bank of France remained on French territory. In early June, 1940, Paul Reynaud, President of the French Council, had negotiated with the American Ambassador at Paris for the evacuation of 200 tons of French gold to the United States. American warships were to take this gold aboard at Saint-Jean-de-Luz. Concerned over the risks of such a transfer in an open roadstead, the French Admiralty loaded this gold on the French auxiliary cruiser *Ville d'Oran* at Pauillac on May 29, and transported it to Casablanca, where on June 10 it was transferred to the U. S. cruiser *Vincennes.*

This was the only transfer of gold to a foreign country for the sake of security, all the rest of the gold reserves being entrusted to French overseas possessions. It was thus that approximately 1,000 tons of gold were transported to Dakar, in French West Africa, without the loss of a penny.

motorized division was passing through the city unopposed—and that there were no French troops between Rennes and Brest.

A glance at the map showed that the Germans could be in Brest before 9 o'clock that evening. It was useless to expect any real defense at the close-in lines which General Jean Charbonneau had been trying to develop over the wishes of the civil authorities. There were just ten hours left. Ten hours in which to clear from the port 83 men-of-war and 48 French merchantmen, plus 10 English and 18 Dutch, Belgian, and Norwegian. Ten hours in which to get 159 ships to sea, either under their own power or under tow—or else to scuttle them. Ten hours in which to wreck the workshops, blow up the gates of the locks, set fire to the petroleum stocks—destroy everything that could be of use to the enemy if left behind.

Such a task usually requires detailed preparation. In this case the measures to be taken were totally unexpected by those who were to carry them out—a complete surprise. Several years later, when Admiral de Laborde was being tried for scuttling the Fleet at Toulon, and was asked why he had failed to answer the call to arms of General de Gaulle from London on that June 18, his answer was quite understandable, "That day, I had other things to do besides listening to the British Broadcasting Corporation."

Seventy-four out of the 83 warships in port were able to get away to sea. The *Paris,* being repaired after damages suffered at Le Havre, was rushed out of drydock. The precious *Richelieu* was one of the first to leave; it departed at 1600, with all of the midshipmen of the French Naval Academy on board. The large submarine *Surcouf,* undergoing machinery overhaul, got under way with one diving rudder jammed hard over and with only her electric motors for power. Some ships departed at the end of a tow line.

Only nine ships had to be destroyed to save them from falling into German hands. Among these were four submarines and the redoubtable *Cyclone,* which had escaped from Dunkirk with her bow blown off, only to be destroyed now by her crew at the Brest navy yard. The sloop *Vauquois* struck a German magnetic mine off the town of Le Conquet as she reached the seaward end of the Brest channel, and was blown up.

Of the merchantmen in port, all escaped except one, which had to be scuttled. Of the others only one was sunk by enemy action on the way out. Before sailing, three of the transports took aboard, at the last moment, 6,000 men of General Béthouart's brigade who had just returned from Narvik a few days earlier.

After a heroic but utterly ridiculous defense of a small, untenable defensive position at Landerneau, the city of Brest capitulated in the evening of June 19. When German Vice Admiral von Arnaud de la Périère, the commander of *U-35* in World War I, arrived to take over the command, he found nothing afloat but an old six-stack cruiser which had been used by the Air Training Command, and a few old wooden lighters belonging to the apprentice seamen's school which it had not been thought worthwhile to scuttle.

Winston Churchill was considerably in error when, in his memoirs, he wrote that at the time of the German invasion, "Not one French warship moved in order to place itself out of reach of the German troops." [5]

Following Cherbourg and Brest, all of the other French Atlantic ports were engulfed in that same German tide. And in every case, despite the Government's request for an armistice, and despite a hasty proclamation declaring all cities of more than 20,000 to be "open cities," the French naval authorities had orders to defend the military ports—something which they resolutely tried to do, regardless of how limited were their means of defense.

For instance, at the repair and construction center of Lorient, there were 15 warships and 35 sweepers or patrol craft. All put to sea on June 18, except three which had to be scuttled. Admiral Hervé de Penfentenyo de Kervéréguin, the naval commandant of the port, remained behind to hold the Germans off for three more days of heroic but hopeless resistance—an act which won the respect of even the Germans themselves.

At Saint-Nazaire, the measures taken by Admiral André Rioult permitted the British transports to evacuate 40,000 British soldiers and 2,500 men of the Polish division. Despite heavy enemy bombing, the multitude of merchant ships crowded into the harbor and roadstead were gotten safely away—including three precious cargo ships which had just arrived from America with full loads of airplanes.

The most spectacular escape, however, was that of the battleship *Jean Bart,* commanded by Captain Pierre Ronarc'h. That escape is now legendary. The uncompleted ship, with workmen's scaffolds still covering the decks, was afloat in an open basin separated from the ship channel by an earthern dike. This dike had to be dredged out before the ship could reach open water.

In normal years there would have been ample time to complete the dredging before the ship's scheduled departure in October. But without waiting for orders the commanding officer had begun dredging on May 25, when the military situation had begun to turn worse. From then on it was a race against time.

But even with the dike dredged away, it would be necessary to get the ship out on the high tides between June 18 and 22, or else to wait weeks for the next ones. And there could be no waiting. The high tide of the night of June 18 was selected for the departure. But within that short time

---

[5] French edition, Book II, Volume I, page 228.

it would be possible to dredge only to a depth of 8.1 meters, which meant that the ship would have to go out almost completely stripped—no water, no provisions, no fuel oil, and only one of her 380-mm. turrets in place. Also, there would be no time to dredge the channel any wider than 50 meters; the *Jean Bart* herself was 35 meters wide. By extraordinary exertions the dredging was completed by 2 o'clock on the morning of the 19th.

One boiler in the fireroom had been ready since June 11, but only two of the four propellers were in place. The turbine drives for these two propellers had been hurriedly installed, but the engines had not yet been turned over under their own power. Not a gun aboard was in condition to fire, so a few antiaircraft machineguns, a few 37-mm. guns, and two 90-mm. twin mounts were hurriedly swung aboard and bolted down.

Already, it was learned, the Germans were at Rennes; they would reach Saint-Nazaire the next day. If the *Jean Bart* did not leave that very night, there would be nothing left to do but blow her up.

At 0330, the time of high tide, the operation began. There was no power on the main engines, or on the rudder, or the windlass, or the after winches. Everything had to be done by hand—with capstan bars aboard and pushing tugs outboard. The ship managed to get clear of the basin without too much difficulty, but in the darkness she missed a buoy in the too narrow channel and ran aground. It took six tugs to pull her off again. Then at 0440, just as the *Jean Bart* was clearing the entrance to the Loire, the Luftwaffe appeared. The ship sustained but one hit, and that caused only minor damage. Then after the German air attack was over, the French fighter planes, which had been scheduled to give air cover, belatedly arrived—and were warmly greeted by the *Jean Bart's* gunners. Luckily only one Morane fighter was hit, and no lives were lost.

Then, little by little everything straightened out. Luck was with the ship. The main engines began to turn over; there was steam for the auxiliaries, and electric power for the steering; the oil tankers were on time at the refueling rendezvous; and two German submarines, which had been lying in wait, never made contact.

The *Jean Bart* was saved. Even though she had no steering compass, she could follow the destroyer *Hardi,* on which Admiral de Laborde had hoisted his flag. At 1700 on June 22, the *Jean Bart* steamed into Casablanca harbor, in French Morocco, having made the whole trip at an average speed of 21 knots.

Meanwhile, back in France, as the enemy advanced south along the coast, the French shipping fled constantly before them, until no ports were left. The large fishing trawlers had pushed straight on toward the Mediterranean. At Rochefort and La Pallice and in the Charente River 36 ships out of 40 escaped. At the Rochefort Air Base Rear Admiral Jean

Lartigue, Chief of Naval Aviation, was killed while directing the shift of naval air groups to Hourtin and Marignane.[6]

At Bordeaux the Admiralty Delegate, Rear Admiral Gaston Barnouin, had held that post only since June 13. Convoys of 10 to 15 ships were still arriving from the Atlantic. From June 23 on, the port at the mouth of the Gironde was under attack from three directions—bombing from the air, magnetic mines in the sea, and German artillery fire from Royan, on the north shore of the estuary. The port itself, from the docks to the suburbs, was a human ant hill of civilian refugees and military evacuees, most of the latter being supply service troops.

The Navy had been asked to provide passage for 30,000 young recruits to North Africa, but at the last moment the Army was unable to muster the recruits. The Navy was next asked to evacuate important stockpiles as well as several thousand specialists, principally from the Air Force.

On June 13 the French Admiralty had given orders for 8 large passenger liners, with suitable escort, to be made ready at the mouth of the Gironde, but by June 20, only 4 were available—the *Mexique* having been lost to magnetic mines at Verdon and the *Champlain* at La Pallice.

The morale among merchant marine sailors was very low. No one wanted to be "the last man killed in the war." Some crews deserted their ships in order to be with their families ashore if the Germans came. Two passenger liners loaded with military personnel refused to get under way. The crew of a third one, taken firmly in hand by the Admiralty Delegate, carried off all the personnel of the Hourtin Air Base under direct fire from the Germans. The fourth ship—the *Massilia*—was assigned to carry those members of Parliament who wished to leave for North Africa; it required the captain's best arguments to persuade the crew to evacuate men whom many among them regarded as fugitives from their duty in France. One freighter loaded with valuable war material got under way with naval officers replacing the usual ship's officers, but it was too late to cross the bar and the ship had to be scuttled to prevent the Germans capturing her. In all, some 30 transports, sweepers, or patrol vessels left the Gironde, the majority of them heading for Casablanca.[7] The last shipment of gold was sent to North Africa on the cruiser *Primauguet* and on a few of the patrol vessels.

---

[6] Airfields near Bordeaux and Marseilles, respectively.

[7] A few ships, however, headed for England under pressure of the British destroyers cruising off the Gironde. Among them was the freighter *Fort Médine*, which was of particular interest since it carried the archives of the Gnôme and Rhône aircraft engine factory. The British liaison officer at Bordeaux had received orders to do his utmost to persuade the freighter captain to sail for England, and, if necessary, to bribe him. (A British Admiralty dispatch, 1937 of 22 June, specified 100 pounds sterling.)

As a cheerful change from these depressing incidents of defeat there was the exploit of the destroyer *Lansquenet.* Like the *Jean Bart,* she was uncompleted when the order came to evacuate. She was first floated on June 17, without ever having turned her engines over. She received her turrets that afternoon, was towed to the supply and oil docks, got under way under her own power on June 23, and cleared the mouth of the Gironde under fire of the arriving German guns.

Why, it is often asked, did all of these ships head for French Africa, and not, as had been planned several days before, for England?

The answer is that the situation had radically changed since the military collapse of France.

On May 28, when the evacuation of Dunkirk had scarcely begun, in strictest confidence Admiral Darlan had given a personal, handwritten memorandum to his chief of staff, Rear Admiral Le Luc. The memorandum began with these words: "In case military events lead to an armistice, the conditions of which would be set by the Germans, *and if these conditions include the surrender of the Fleet, I have no intention of carrying out that order."* Then followed a list of detailed instructions which were to govern in that case.

Certainly no sailor could have been found in France who would have turned over the Fleet intact to the Germans. But, fearing a moment of weakness on the part of the Government, Darlan was taking no chances. In fact, only the day before, the French Admiralty had inquired into the possibility of completing the *Jean Bart* and the *Richelieu* in an English navy yard.

But if no surrender were required, or if the dishonor of a capitulation were not imposed on the Navy, the latter had no reason not to remain faithful and obedient to the legal government of France, as required by every commissioned officer's oath.

On June 14, Darlan, believing that the Government intended to continue the war from overseas, had plans prepared so that the Fleet could proceed to some English or French colonial port and continue to fight from there. But not one single person in the Reynaud Government—where César Campinchi was Minister of the Navy and General de Gaulle the Assistant Secretary of the Army—gave orders to execute those plans.

On the contrary, the group in power, faced with the tragic reality of defeat, resigned and was succeeded in an orderly manner by another Government, which then asked for an armistice.

An armistice is not a peace treaty concluding a war; it is merely a truce, a cessation of hostilities. And one could not ask for a cessation of hostilities on land yet still continue the fighting at sea. The new Government, of which Darlan was a member, had taken the firm position that no armistice would be concluded if it involved surrendering the Fleet to the Germans. All that remained for Darlan to do was to regroup the ships in the ports remaining to France, and to continue the fight as directed until he received orders to the contrary. The interests of the Fleet could not be considered ahead of the interests of France.[8]

It was a bitter pill for the Navy. Driven out of the Atlantic bases without having any real opportunity to fight, it had only the satisfaction of not having left the enemy anything usable. Yet its morale was high. The eagerness with which it availed itself of the last days of the war to defy the enemy fleet in the Mediterranean bears witness to that fact.

---

[8] On the evening of June 18, Admiral Darlan had telegraphed this message to his principal subordinates: "The President of the Council reminds all combatants that no armistice has yet been concluded, and their duty remains to resist to the utmost. In case of necessity, all ships and planes will withdraw to North Africa. Combatant ships and planes unable to reach there, and running the risk of falling into enemy hands after a fight, must either destroy or scuttle themselves."

CHAPTER 10

Fifteen Days of War in the Mediterranean

It was a strange aberration that led Benito Mussolini to the balcony of the Palazzo di Venezia on June 10, 1940, to announce to the world the entry of Italy into the war. Strange, because he had made apparently sincere attempts to prevent the outbreak of war during that month of August, 1939. Upon the outbreak of hostilities he had immediately declared his country a nonbelligerent. Like the democracies, he had sided with Finland against the invading Russians. All along he had permitted Italian industry to fill French orders for war materials. In short, while remaining technically faithful to the Axis pact, he had given proof of intelligent moderation. Now he had suddenly given France the "stab in the back." In actuality it was not France, but his own country, to which he was giving the *coup de grâce*.

There is no doubt that the Allies' decision at London to blockade Germany by placing an embargo on her exports, even though these were carried in neutral ships, was a serious blunder. The Italians were exasperated by the stopping and boarding of their colliers bringing German coal to Italy, and still more exasperated when the embargo forced them to import this needed coal by rail over the Brenner Pass. Also there was undoubtedly a deep aversion between the Fascist leaders and many statesmen of the democracies. Nevertheless none of these reasons was sufficient to bring Italy into the war—which in the case of France could be considered almost fratricidal—and Italian opinion, including the military, was all against it.

The only explanation for Mussolini's declaration of war is, perhaps, the slogan that circulated in Rome: "To participate in the peace, one must participate in the war." Germany's quick success in Norway had disturbed Mussolini. Now, with France apparently breaking up, he thought he had better get in a few quick shots if he wanted to sit down as a conqueror at the peace conference afterward—a conference where he could demand Nice, Corsica, Tunis, etc., as Italy's legitimate compensation for participating in the victory.

The Allied Navies had been preparing against just such an action by Mussolini ever since the beginning of April. At that time responsibility for the Mediterranean was divided by agreement between the two Allies: the

French Navy was to have responsibility for the western half, the Royal Navy for the eastern half. Although the British, strained by the demands of the Norwegian campaign, had given thought to asking the French Navy to take over the responsibility for the entire Mediterranean, it had been decided to adhere to the original agreement, with some slight modifications.

For instance, it was decided that as a precaution against Italy's entry into the war, the French Raiding Force should be transferred immediately from Brest to the western Mediterranean, and that in addition another French squadron should be sent temporarily to the eastern Mediterranean where at the time the English had only some light forces.

In accordance with this plan, Admiral Gensoul's squadron, consisting of the *Dunkerque, Strasbourg,* and several light groups, sailed for Mers-el-Kebir, French Algeria, arriving there on April 27. An improvised squadron called Force X, consisting of the old battleships *Lorraine, Bretagne,* and *Provence,* plus several heavy cruisers and some light craft, all commanded by Vice Admiral René Godfroy, were sent to Alexandria. They joined Admiral Sir Andrew Cunningham's two old British battleships which had just arrived there. Three weeks later, when Admiral Cunningham's squadron was reinforced from England, the *Bretagne* and the *Provence* returned to the western Mediterranean; the *Lorraine* remained, to form part of a British division.

Thus, in order to cope with the Italian Fleet, the Allies had made strategic dispositions as follows: at Toulon, the Third French Squadron, of 4 heavy cruisers and a dozen destroyers; at Mers-el-Kebir and Algiers, Admiral Gensoul's fast battleships *Dunkerque* and *Strasbourg,* and two older and slower battleships under Rear Admiral Jacques Bouxin, plus two cruiser divisions and many destroyers; at Bizerte, six divisions of French submarines; at Malta, a number of British submarines; and finally, at Alexandria, a British squadron and Force X, under the over-all command of Admiral Cunningham.

In basing the large ships of the Allied navies at the ends of the Mediterranean, far from Italian airfields, the Allied leaders were perhaps according the Italian Air Force the same respect they gave the Luftwaffe—something which experience later proved was overrating it.

Admiral, South (Admiral Esteva), who had cordial personal relationships with Admiral Cunningham, set up his headquarters at Bizerte. In anticipation of hostilities with Italy, British maritime traffic between the eastern and the western Mediterranean had been suspended and the ships routed around Africa. But in the western waters, traffic between France and North Africa continued as usual, under protective cover of the air forces of the 3rd and 4th Naval Districts and of the escort and patrol divisions in that area.

On May 15 the strategic plan had been formed that, if Italy entered the war, the Allies should attack that very night, should bombard her bases and industrial centers, and should shoot up her coasts to try to provoke the Italian Navy into coming out to fight. For aerial bombing, some Royal Air Force squadrons had been based in Provence, where they were in striking distance of the Po valley factories. The French 3rd Cruiser Squadron was to bombard the petroleum tank farms and other military installations in the Gulf of Genoa. The code name for this operation was "Vado."

Other operations were to follow without delay: the Toulon forces were to strike in the Tyrrhenian Sea; the forces at Bizerte and Algiers were to raid southern Italy and Sicily; and the Alexandria forces were to strike in the Dodecanese and along the coasts of Cyrenaica.

Hostilities began at midnight on June 10. At 0850 on the morning of June 11 the French Admiralty sent out the order to execute Vado that evening. The English were informed that the French would rely on the assistance of their aviation units as previously planned. Admiral Emile Duplat, of the 3rd Cruiser Squadron, received orders to go ahead even if the French Air Force could not provide him with air cover. When the order was confirmed at 1735 that afternoon, the cruiser force was assembled in the Salins d'Hyères roadstead, with turbines warmed up, waiting for night to fall so they could get under way and strike the target at daybreak.

Then, 22 minutes later, came the unexpected counterorder: "Cancel Vado. Cancel preceding dispatches. This is a Government order."

Admiral Duplat sent a respectful but firm protest, but all in vain. Once more he was told that it was not the Admiralty but the Government which had given the counterorder.

Gloom settled over the ships. The crews had to be informed. The squadron made a crestfallen return to Toulon, since the Salins roadstead was poorly defended against air attacks.

What was going on?

The truth gradually came out. At Briare that day, during a Ministers' conference one of them had remarked that, considering the position of France at the time, it seemed to him foolish to provoke the Italian Air Force unnecessarily by taking the offensive. This opinion had prevailed, and Admiral Darlan had had to abide by it. General Joseph Vuillemin, Chief of Staff of the French Air Force, received orders to stop the R.A.F. squadrons which were just getting ready to take off.

The decision thus made created considerable excitement. Churchill mentions it with decided acidity.

It is known that on June 10 the Italian Air Force was under very restrictive instructions: reconnaissance flights alone could be made, and these could not fly over the French coasts. It was really a most unusual war!

But the next day Mussolini lifted these restrictions. On June 12, some 21 Italian Savoia-79 bombers attacked Bizerte, damaging a few planes and setting fire to some gasoline drums on the Sidi Ahmed airfield.

Darlan thereupon managed to obtain a reversal[1] of the counterorder. Vado would be carried out. Not that night, because there was not time enough, but on the night of June 13.

As if to sweep away all French scruples, the Italians bombed Toulon that night, but so timidly that the French commander requested the anti-aircraft batteries to save their ammunition.

The exact results of the shelling by the ships of Admiral Duplat at daybreak on June 14 have never been assessed. What counted were the exultant reports brought back by those who had participated in the action.

The squadron had approached the Italian coast in two groups,[2] and despite enemy fire had carried out the bombardment exactly as planned. The Italian resistance had been feeble. Enemy aviation did not show up at all. Four or five motor torpedo boats attacked, but without success, and lost one ship for their temerity. Only one French ship was hit—the destroyer *Albatros,* which was struck in the fireroom by a 152-mm. shell, resulting in 10 men burned to death. She continued her firing, however, and returned with the rest of the squadron at 25 knots.

That same night the R.A.F. attacked the industrial centers of northern Italy, and the airplane *Jules Verne,*[3] of Naval Air, gained laurels by bombing the gasoline storage tanks of Porto Maghere, at Venice.

---

[1] "Bizerte having been bombarded, the Government authorizes reprisals. The 3rd Squadron will carry out Vado the night of June 13. . . . Give British air squadrons freedom of action to attack." Admiralty message, 2250, June 12.

[2] The first group consisted of *Algérie* and *Foch;* the second, of *Dupleix* and *Colbert.* Each group was escorted by two divisions of destroyers.

[3] The *Jules Verne* was a 4-engine commercial-type Farman plane with a 6,000-kilometer range of action. It had been requisitioned by the Navy to carry out scouting missions over the Atlantic. Though it had a negligible armament, it could carry over 4 tons of bombs. Manned by a crack crew under command of Lieutenant Commander Henri Daillière, the *Jules Verne,* during May and June of 1940, carried out a series of very risky operations over the enemy's lines at Aachen, Flushing, and Rostock. It even ranged as far as Rome, where it flew several times to drop propaganda leaflets.

Its most famous operation was the bombing of Berlin—the first such action of the war—which it accomplished on June 8, despite violent antiaircraft fire. When the bombing officer had nothing left to drop on his objective, he took off his hobnailed boots and held them threateningly over the heads of the Berliners. The same petty officer, on a trip over Rome, became very worried because a bundle of leaflets he had dropped had failed to open. His comrades assured him that without a doubt he had made a direct bull's-eye on the Vatican!

The following day Admiral Cunningham carried out a raid in the Dodecanese with two battleships, an aircraft carrier, and light forces. From Beirut, in Lebanon, Admiral Godfroy led the cruisers of Force X to the vicinity of the straits of Casso. The Bizerte submarines set up a barrier line in the central Mediterranean. Admiral Gensoul had sortied from Mersel-Kebir on the false report[4] that a German squadron was preparing to drive past the Straits of Gibraltar into the Mediterranean.

Surprisingly, almost no enemy submarines were sighted during all these operations. One launched an unsuccessful torpedo attack against a cruiser of the Raiding Force; another sank a Swedish freighter and a British cargo ship; a third, damaged, had to intern itself at Spanish Ceuta. Not a single enemy surface ship had shown itself.

Despite the entry of Italy into the war, French morale was high, and neither they nor their English allies had any idea of giving up control of the Mediterranean.

Merchant shipping in the western Mediterranean, which had been suspended on June 10, was resumed on the 12th. The ships followed the French and North African coastal routes as far as Port Vendres and Oran, respectively; there they were formed into convoys and routed, under escort, well to the westward of the Balearic Islands, as far as possible from enemy bases. One of these escorts, the French sloop *Curieuse,* rammed and sank the Italian submarine *Provana* 30 miles south of Cape Palos, on June 16.

Meanwhile, back in France, General René Olry's Army of the Alps, reduced to three divisions, was holding its own against Italian attacks on the frontier. But on June 18, the Germans, rushing down the valley of the Saône, entered Lyons; on the 21st they occupied Clermont-Ferrand. To prevent his flank being turned, General Olry had to pivot hurriedly along the line of the Isère River. Instinctively reacting in the same way it had done when Paris was threatened, the Toulon navy yard rushed twenty 47-mm. and 65-mm. guns to that front, where their sailor crews distinguished themselves against German tanks at Voreppe, near Grenoble.

Here was the enemy in the valley of the Rhône. The usual throng of fugitives was swarming on all roads leading south. On June 21 a German bombing attack on Marseilles sank the passenger liner *Chella* and killed or wounded hundreds of civilians.

The port of Marseilles was one of the principal evacuation ports of southern France. Through here were routed not only many civilians, but also large detachments of troops and enormous quantities of raw materials

---

[4] The origin of this false bit of intelligence lay in two suspected shadows—German supply ships, in fact—which had been detected in the Iceland-Faeroes channel several days earlier by the Northern Patrol, at the time of the sortie of the *Scharnhorst* and *Gneisenau,* during the evacuation of Narvik.

—copper, brass, zinc, tin, molybdenum, petroleum etc. These invaluable strategic materials were hustled out of France ahead of the invaders, and were hidden in North Africa on the chance that there would come a day when France would reenter the fight.

During the days preceding the armistice, the majority of merchant vessels in French harbors got under way as soon as loaded and proceeded without waiting for convoy protection. But contrary to what was happening on the Atlantic side, shipping in the Mediterranean did not sustain a single loss from enemy mine, plane, or submarine.

People have asked why at this time the Navy did not evacuate a large part of the French Army, in order to continue the war from Africa.

As a matter of fact, all military groups which arrived at the docks of the French Mediterranean ports were evacuated. Even the Polish troops, for whom the Navy had no transports available when they first arrived, were safely carried away by the English[5]—especially since they wanted to go to England, and not North Africa.

One of the most interesting of such operations was the evacuation to Algeria of the entire movable stock of the French Air Force—trucks, cranes, tank cars, repair shops, spare parts, bombs, etc. This important material arrived at Port Vendres in sufficient time because the Air Force General Staff issued the necessary orders far enough in advance. At the same time all operational planes were being flown to North Africa.

The only way more troops could have been evacuated would have been for half of them to dig in and hold the Germans off while the other half hurried to the seaports and embarked. Such an operation would have been possible only if the plans had been made three or four weeks earlier, when there was still something of a front on the Somme and on the Aisne. But it was impossible for a single force to hold a front on the north and simultaneously retreat toward the south.

Also, it would have been necessary to assemble the required number of transports well in advance. At Dunkirk all that had been required was to evacuate, across a narrow strait, troops who had abandoned all of their equipment. But in the Mediterranean, if the evacuated troops were to carry on the war, it would have been necessary to load aboard with them the material they would need overseas—arms, ammunition, food, vehicles, petroleum—everything.

And to transport a single division overseas, with its necessary supplies

---

[5] After the evacuation of Dunkirk and the ports of the north, the Royal Navy extended its evacuation operations—"Operation Aerial"—to retrieve all British troops and supply services still in France. It succeeded in evacuating approximately 180,000 men—including Polish troops—through Atlantic ports as far south as Saint-Jean-de-Luz, and slightly more than 10,000 through French Mediterranean ports.

and equipment, it was estimated that 20 suitable ships would be required. By violating all rules, it could have been done with half that number—but this would mean carrying men and nothing else, for while men can be squeezed, equipment is incompressible.

Briefly, it would have required 100 ships if it had been desired to embark, for example, 100,000 to 120,000 troops. And because of the demands for vessels in the Norway operation and in the evacuation of the Atlantic ports, the bulk of French Mediterranean shipping had been rushed to the Atlantic side of France. The same was true of English shipping, as the Mediterranean in principle was closed to it and everything was being routed around the Cape of Good Hope. Lastly, up until June 15, there was still talk of establishing a Breton Redoubt, which would have required additional shipping.

It is true that around June 12 the French Government did ask the Navy to plan for the evacuation of several hundred thousand men, without being able to give the dates or even the embarkation ports, Atlantic or Mediterranean. In order to obtain the necessary tonnage, the President of the Council, Paul Reynaud, had decided to ask the British for assistance, and had sent General de Gaulle, Assistant Secretary of the Army, to London on that mission, as has been previously mentioned.

General de Gaulle's trip was useless insofar as that mission was concerned. For the British had no time or ships to spare. Furthermore, there were no troops to embark. There were French ships in the Mediterranean sufficient to evacuate—as they did—all those who presented themselves at the evacuation ports during those days just before and after the armistice. These evacuations averaged several thousand troops each day, plus some civilians.

Since it was well known that armistice talks were in progress, there was not a person in the Navy who was not aching to fire a few last rounds or drop a few last bombs on the enemy before the end of the war—a day which they anticipated with great bitterness.

They just missed such an opportunity in the western Mediterranean on June 23. Some important French convoys were at sea that day between Marseilles and Oran. The 4th Cruiser Division, under Rear Admiral Jean Bourragué, with escorting destroyers, was convoying them. Coming out of their lethargy, the Italians had sent out a light task force, the Sansonetti squadron, the day before. After having steamed as far west as Minorca, these Italian ships were returning to their Sardinian bases when they were sighted by a French plane. The 3rd Cruiser Division, under Rear Admiral André Marquis, immediately got under way from Algiers to intercept them, but contact was lost and the enemy was not brought to battle.

In the eastern Mediterranean, the *Lorraine* sortied on June 20 with the British division to which she was attached. She bombarded Bardia, in Italian Cyrenaica, on June 21.

The French armistice delegation was meeting with the Italian delegates in Rome at that very time. When the news of the Bardia bombardment, as well as of the bombing of Trapani and Leghorn by French naval air squadrons, was given to the French delegates, a furtive smile lit up their faces. The Italians had the good taste to consider it all just a routine matter.

On the evening of June 22 the entire Franco-British squadron at Alexandria was scheduled to put to sea to bombard Augusta and to raid toward Messina, and to wipe out all Italian communications with Libya. The French cruisers were about to cast off from the buoys when suddenly the British battleships reversed course and Admiral Cunningham sent a signal cancelling the operation. The French were to learn later that the order to do so came from London direct.

The armistice with Germany had just been signed, and Churchill was taking no chances. In Churchill's eyes it was imperative that French Force X be immobilized in the Alexandria roadstead, under control of the British, the moment the armistice became effective. It was the same pattern as was to be followed in the case of all French ships taking refuge in Great Britain; in fact the British admirals at Portsmouth and Plymouth were receiving orders to that effect at that very moment.

The French Navy had fired its last shots. But it was only now that its real trials and tribulations were to begin.

CHAPTER 11

The Armistice Between France and the Axis

The German Army had launched its offensive against the Somme front on the 5th of June. By the 12th it was evident to the French military leaders that the situation was hopeless. The Seine between Paris and the sea had been crossed in numerous places. In Champagne, after a hard three-day battle, the German Panzers and infantry had broken through the front on the Aisne. The tanks of Generals Guderian and Ludwig von Kleist prepared to drive ahead, some toward the Swiss frontier, thus turning the Maginot line, and the others down the Rhône valley, threatening the rear of the Army of the Alps. On June 12, a meeting of the French Supreme Council was held at General Headquarters at Briare. There Generals Weygand and Alphonse Georges made the tragic announcement: "The capacity of the French Army to resist is coming to an end, and within a short time an honorable armistice will be the only solution possible."[1]

No one disputed the gravity of the situation. But a certain number of French Ministers saw another way out. Instead of an armistice—a political action negotiated by the Government—they desired a capitulation by the Army—a nonpolitical action performed by the Commander in Chief, as was done in Holland, which would leave the Government free to continue the war from overseas at Britain's side. In one case, it was the political leaders who would bear the brunt of the defeat; in the other, the military leaders would take the onus of the failure. In the first case, the Government, having put an end to a sacrifice henceforth hopeless, would remain on French soil to protect its citizens as well as possible; in the second, it would abandon to their fate all military personnel and men subject to draft, either free or prisoners, as well as the entire civilian population, in order to link themselves with the destiny of England. On one side was the more humane solution, but grievously humiliating in its stark realism; on the other was a more grandiose gesture, but a huge gamble, since the United States had refused to enter the war, and England might one day willingly accept a favorable compromise. With Russia practically aligned with Germany, no one could foresee how the occupation of France might end.

---

[1] Maxime Weygand, *Recalled to Service.* Page 206.

104

Moreover, a rapid exchange of dispatches with General Charles Noguès, French Commander in Chief in North Africa, revealed that a successful resistance overseas was by no means certain. No appreciable part of the French Army had been able to escape overseas; there was no modern equipment in Africa; Britain could do nothing to assist the French forces there, for she had lost practically all her own equipment at Dunkirk and elsewhere. Despite the Allied Navies, the cordial relations existing between Germany and Spain would probably gain the Wehrmacht and Luftwaffe a foothold in Africa, if only in Spanish Morocco. And then the French African ports, like those on the French Atlantic coast, would have every chance of being taken by an attack from the land side.

After the defeat at Baylen in 1808, in the First Empire, the French Government had passed a law punishing with death any general surrendering in the field. That law had never been repealed. Without even taking the trouble to call attention to that law, General Weygand absolutely refused to consider a military capitulation which he, in complete agreement with his subordinates, considered dishonoring. No other general in his place would have done differently. As General Weygand pointed out, opening and suspending hostilities are political acts; it was up to the Government to assume its proper responsibilities.

To assemble Parliament while France was being overrun by the German Panzers was manifestly impossible. The Ministers—for the most part senators or deputies—together with the President of the Republic and the Presidents of the Assemblies, represented the only credible official opinion. Despite their being scattered in the environs of Tours, they met almost every day. But they were hopelessly at variance and no amount of discussion could bring about an agreement. Marshal Pétain and General Weygand, whose only concern was for the soldiers who were daily dying and the civilians who were suffering while these endless discussions went on, grew impatient.

Not a single Minister wished to break with England, therefore before committing themselves on the armistice question they wished to know what the British reaction would be to an eventual suspension of hostilities on the part of France. At Tours, on June 13—only a few days before—Churchill had shown himself quite understanding of France's tragic position. But Premier Reynaud—perhaps not without an ulterior motive—had not informed his colleagues of Mr. Churchill's fraternal understanding.

Fundamentally the President of the French Council was too intelligent a man not to be aware that an armistice was inevitable. However, Mr. Reynaud considered himself bound by the "joint declaration" which he himself had read to the Interallied Supreme Council in London on March 28, and by which he had engaged himself not to conclude a separate peace.

That had been the political policy for which he stood, and he could remain in power only so long as he adhered to that policy.

And, strange as it may seem in a country such as France, where public opinion never gets very excited over matters pertaining to the sea, it was the French Navy that was at the bottom of the dispute.

One of the strongest arguments of those who were opposed to an armistice was that the Germans would not fail to demand the surrender of the Fleet, just as the Allies had done in 1918.[2] But to turn the ships over to the Germans, to be used against France's allies, would be dishonorable.

There was no disagreement on that point. Those in favor of an armistice wanted it only under "honorable conditions." If the Germans put forward the slightest claim on the French Fleet, these people were in favor of carrying on the war, anywhere, any time. Therefore before any armistice was considered, it was necessary to know the conditions the Germans would present, and also whether the English would take exception to any such proceedings.

Resigning himself to the inevitable, Mr. Reynaud finally asked London, on the night of June 15, whether the British Government would release France from the engagement contracted on March 28.

The answer was made through the British embassy, the next day, in the form of a telegram authorizing a French request for an armistice from the Germans—"provided, *but only provided,* that the French Fleet sailed immediately for British harbors pending the armistice negotiations." A little later a second telegram notified the French Prime Minister that the British Government expected to be consulted on whatever conditions were offered by the enemy.

Mr. Reynaud had not had the second message in his hands twenty minutes before he saw Sir Ronald Campbell, the British Ambassador, coming back. Sir Ronald's mission was to take back both telegrams, which were officially considered null and void.

What was going on? Was the British Government withdrawing its agreement in principle, or was it cancelling the restrictions it had stipulated as requirements for its agreement?

In his memoirs, published after the war, Mr. Churchill has explained what was taking place just then in England. For one thing, he had suddenly realized how diplomatically rude—in fact, how cold and inhuman—the phrasing of the two messages was. In the second place he had just worked

---

[2] The armistice of November 11, 1918, provided, in Article 23, for the German Fleet to be interned in a neutral or Allied base. Of course, no neutral base was considered suitable, and Admiral Ludwig von Reuter was required to take the High Seas Fleet to Scapa Flow—where he scuttled it on June 21, 1919.

out with General de Gaulle a plan for a Franco-British Union,[3] which was immediately telephoned to Mr. Reynaud and confirmed by Mr. Churchill personally.

"Thus," writes Mr. Churchill in his memoirs, "the British War Cabinet had not altered its position in any respect. We felt, however, that it would be better to give the proposed Franco-British Union its full chance under the most favorable conditions. If the French Council of Ministers were encouraged by it to continue the war . . . the removal of the Fleet from the German threat would follow automatically. If our offer did not find favor, our rights and claims would revive in full force."

That was the explanation given by Mr. Churchill ten years after the event. But at the actual time, the French did not see matters in the same light at all. The French Government had been at Bordeaux since the day before. Mr. Reynaud had not showed either of the telegrams to the Ministers when they arrived, and he did not even mention them now, since he no longer had them in his possession—the telegrams having been withdrawn both figuratively and literally. On June 16, when matters came to a head, none of the Ministers had any knowledge even of the existence of the telegrams, much less of their contents. Consequently the offer of a Franco-British Union did not appear as an alternative to the British stipulation that the French Fleet be sent for safety outside of French waters before Britain agreed to France separately requesting an armistice from Germany.

Nay more, this offer of a Franco-British Union, which might have received serious consideration under other circumstances, appeared in those tragic days to be only a political trick designed to stop any French movements toward an armistice and to force the French Government to leave France and set up a government-in-exile elsewhere. Consequently the entire French Council, without even going into the details of the proposed union, rejected the British offer unanimously.

From then on, the die was cast. The last moment appeal to President Franklin D. Roosevelt—a gesture simply for the sake of "getting on record"[4] —having brought no practical results, Reynaud himself recommended to the President of the Republic, on the evening of June 16, that he form a Government presided over by Marshal Pétain[5] in order to ask Hitler's terms for an

---

[3] Under the proposal, the two countries would have joint defense, foreign, financial, and economic policies; joint citizenship, joint War Cabinet with over-all control of all forces of both countries; resources of both countries would be mutually used for repair of all war damages in either country.

[4] *The Memoirs of Cordell Hull.*

[5] In France, the term Chief of State refers to the President of the French Republic; the term Chief of Government refers to the Premier. When Marshal Pétain relieved

armistice. Perhaps Reynaud vaguely hoped that those terms would be so harsh there would be nothing left except to continue the war—under *his* leadership, of course.

The new Government, with Pétain at its head, was established during the night of June 16. It immediately asked the Spanish Ambassador to act as intermediary between France and the German Government.

Everyone in the new Ministry, of whom 11 had been members of the previous one, agreed that in no case was the French Fleet to be surrendered. Moreover, Marshal Pétain, as a first step, appointed Admiral Darlan, Commander in Chief of the Naval Forces, as his new Minister of the Navy. To the British, as well as to the French sailors who knew Darlan well, this choice constituted a full guarantee. In fact, only a few weeks before, at Briare, on June 11, Winston Churchill had taken the future Minister aside and had said in heartfelt tones, "Darlan, I hope that you will never surrender the Fleet!" And to that Darlan had replied, "There can be no question of that. It would be contrary to our naval traditions and to our honor."

Darlan assumed office as Navy Minister on June 17. His first message to his subordinates was to make clear that, "All naval operations must be carried out with the fiercest energy," and to assure them that, "No matter how the situation develops, the Navy can be certain that in no case will it be delivered intact." Then, on June 18, he sent out the general message, previously quoted, ordering, in case of German threat to the Atlantic ports, a withdrawal to Africa of everything that floated and the scuttling of all ships not in condition to get under way.

While Darlan took on the heavy duties of Navy Minister in addition to those of Commander in Chief of the Naval Forces and also Minister of the Merchant Marine, the British Ambassador went to the Secretary-General of the Foreign Office and handed to him the two telegrams which he had given to, and then withdrawn from, Mr. Reynaud the day before. The Secretary-General was completely astounded and began an investigation. Up to that moment no one had even heard of these telegrams except Mr. Reynaud. Paul Baudouin, who had succeeded Reynaud as Minister of Foreign Affairs, questioned the British Ambassador on the exact implications of these messages. The latter requested a few minutes to consult his instructions. On his return he stated that in his opinion the telegrams constituted the elements of an exchange of views which had ended with the

---

Paul Reynaud as Premier on June 16, 1940, he became Chief of Government. However, when, on July 10, 1940, the United Assembly of the French Parliament at Vichy gave "all powers of the Government of the Republic, under the signature and authority of Marshal Pétain, etc.," that Government, made up of the President of the Republic and the French Parliament, in effect abdicated; Marshal Pétain became Chief of State, and the Premiers under him (Laval, Flandin, and Darlan) became Chiefs of Government.

famous offer of a Franco-British Union. He added that he did not consider that his gesture in returning the telegrams for the French Foreign Office files reopened the subject. Hence, as far as the French were concerned, departure of the Fleet before opening armistice negotiations was not required. These texts, returned to the files, had only historical interest now.

Baudouin took advantage of these interviews to repeat to the Ambassador the assurance that the Government unanimously rejected any thought of surrendering the Fleet to the Germans, and that the British Government could rest assured on that subject.

That same day, June 18, President Roosevelt stepped in with a personal message to Admiral Darlan asking him to take the necessary steps immediately to insure that the French Fleet would not fall into the hands of the Germans. It was almost identical with the request that President Roosevelt had made on the British Premier a few weeks earlier with regard to the British Fleet. Mr. Churchill states in his memoirs that he had answered President Roosevelt, "The British Fleet constitutes the only bargaining point for any British Government abandoned by the United States and obliged to sue for peace."[6] Admiral Darlan, who took a seaman's view of such matters, had the Foreign Office reply to Mr. Roosevelt that any surrender of the French Fleet was completely out of the question.

Despite all assurances, the British Admiralty was deeply concerned over the fate of the French Fleet. If the French destroyers, submarines, and, especially, the large French battleships were incorporated into the German Fleet, there would be a turning of the tables in seapower which could be disastrous to England.

The British First Sea Lord, Sir Dudley Pound, made known these fears to the Chief of the French naval mission in London, Vice Admiral Odend'hal. The latter suggested that Sir Dudley make them known to Darlan in person. Darlan and Sir Dudley had fought the war together; they had met often and had a high regard for each other. Between sailors, they would speak frankly.

The meeting took place at Bordeaux, the afternoon of June 18.[7] Admiral

---

[6] This was not a flash of wit. On June 28 Churchill replied to a new American demand to send the British Fleet to America, that this Fleet "would constitute the tangible means by which a peace-minded Government could obtain better conditions from the enemy."

[7] Several authors, including Admiral Auphan, had fixed from memory the 19th as the date of that historic meeting because Mr. Alexander and Lord Lloyd had spent that day at Bordeaux and had had many conversations with French politicians. But Admiral Pound was there only for a brief time on the 18th; the Biscarosse Air Base logged in his arrival at 1300 on the 18th and his departure at 0100 on the 19th. The meeting therefore took place on that same day, and at almost the same hour, that General de Gaulle was delivering his first speech over the BBC at London.

Pound arrived with A. V. Alexander, British First Lord of the Admiralty. To balance the meeting Admiral Darlan took with him Rear Admiral Auphan, who had recently been promoted to that rank. Admiral Auphan had often gone to London with his chief and the English knew him well.

Both sides were sad and solemn. It might be that the English hoped to inherit some French men-of-war, but they did not voice any requests in that respect and imposed no conditions. Firmly resolved to continue the war, they emphasized what a tragedy it would be to them if the Germans got the French Fleet, and they asked what the French intentions were.

Darlan pointed out the tragic state of France, already half overrun, the obligation to put an end to an unequal struggle, and the impossibility of continuing the war with the French naval forces at the same time that they were requesting a suspension of hostilities ashore. Perhaps, later on, they could again take up arms at the side of the British; in the meantime they would keep their ships up for that purpose. In any case, if those ships could not remain French, they would be destroyed.

With a warmth unusual in him, Darlan gave Admiral Pound his word of honor that in no case would the French Fleet be turned over to the Germans —a pledge in which Auphan joined. If the Germans insisted on this as a condition of the armistice, then there would be no armistice. Marshal Pétain and all the Ministers were agreed on that point. And he, Darlan, had already issued—and would reissue—orders that all ships in danger of being taken by the enemy, even under the excuse of an armistice, should be immediately scuttled and destroyed.

Admiral Pound returned immediately to London, where he gave Admiral Odend'hal the impression of not being too happy over his trip, but the other British officers who had accompanied him were full of confidence.

Mr. Alexander remained at Bordeaux. Accompanied by another British Minister, Lord Lloyd, he visited Marshal Pétain and the Minister of Foreign Affairs. These gave their British visitors the same solemn assurances regarding the Fleet that Admiral Darlan had given.

Lord Lloyd saw Darlan once more before flying home on June 20. Admiral Darlan manifested the same determination he had shown in the meeting two days before. This brought an emphatic reply from the English Minister: "Then we are still Allies!"

However, in a matter so vital to them, the British had difficulty in trusting others than themselves—be they an Admiral of the Fleet or a Marshal of France.

In the forest of Compiègne, at the crossroads of Rethondes, there was preserved the identical railway carriage in which Foch and Weygand in 1918 had laid down the armistice terms to the defeated Germans of World

THE BATTLESHIP RICHE-
LIEU, *a light cruiser
(probably the Mont-
calm) and a colonial
sloop in the harbor of
Dakar prior to the An-
glo-Free French attack
on September 23, 1940.*

AFTER THE ATTACK ON
DAKAR. *General Barrau,
Admiral Landriau, and
Captain Marzin, confer
on board* RICHELIEU.

THE FREIGHTER TACOMA, *set afire during the battle of Dakar is towed out.*

A MAIN BATTERY NEAR-MISS *on a super-destroyer during the battle of Dakar.*

War I. With typical irony the Germans had set this as the meeting place for the negotiations of June, 1940, at which the French would fill the seats of the defeated.

The trip of the French delegation across the German lines was hard for them, both physically and spiritually. The delegation was headed by General Charles Huntziger. Others were Léon Noël, of the Foreign Office; Vice Admiral Le Luc, chief of staff of the French Admiralty; General Henri Parisot, formerly military attaché at Rome; and General Jean Bergeret of the Air Force. Tired but impassive, the French were lined up facing a row of German uniforms, in the middle of which was Hitler in person. The latter lingered for the reading of a labored preamble by General Wilhelm Keitel, then withdrew.

The delegates on both sides sat down for the reading of the convention. One by one, each article was translated by the interpreter. After the conditions concerning the territory already conquered and held by the Germans, the disarmament of the military forces, the surrender of arms, etc., they came to the essential clauses concerning the Navy:

> The Fleet must be assembled and disarmed in ports to be specified. . . .
> The German Government solemnly declares that it has no intention of utilizing the French men-of-war for its own use. . . . The German Government solemnly and formally declares that it has no intention of claiming any part of the French Fleet at the conclusion of peace. . . .

"I saw," Admiral Le Luc was to recount later, "all the members of our delegation turn toward me with a gleam of admiration and envy in their eyes."

Yet it was these selfsame conditions which were to lead to the tragic Franco-British misunderstanding later.

From the moment that turning over the French Fleet had been so solemnly ruled out, the conditions of the armistice, so harsh otherwise, did not appear dishonoring. Notwithstanding these terms being presented in the form of an ultimatum, the French delegates, who were in continuous telephone connection with their Government, sought for 24 hours to have certain conditions modified. It was thus that the airplanes of the French Air Force, initially scheduled to be delivered to the Germans, were simply disarmed and immobilized.

The armistice with Germany was signed at 1800 on June 22, but the German Government withheld applying its terms until the French had also concluded an armistice with Italy.

The French delegates therefore left for Rome. They feared that Italy would demand Tunisia or else some part of the French home territory not occupied by the Germans. Before leaving Compiègne, General Huntziger had bluntly told General Keitel that if the Italians wanted more than they had taken by arms—which is to say, practically nothing—the French would refuse to sign.

Whether because of this or for some other reason, the Italian conditions did not go beyond the German ones. After discussions and the modification of certain points, the Italian armistice was signed on the evening of June 24. The two treaties were to become effective six hours later. Hostilities ceased at 0035 on June 25, 1940.

During these crucial days, Admiral Darlan, while energetically continuing regular naval operations, sent out repeated instructions reaffirming previous directives that in no case should any French naval ships be allowed to fall into the hands of foreigners.

The French Admiralty was at that time located in a castle, the Chateau de Dulamont, near Bordeaux, at the junction of telegraphic cables and close to the radio station of Bouscat. Communications with the French Naval Mission in London, which had always been sent through British channels, were slow and precarious; it had been practically impossible to obtain telephone connections with London since June 14. This difficulty also contributed its share to the later Franco-British misunderstanding. In fact, in order to maintain radio communications with their own embassy in France, the English were obliged to station, first, a destroyer, then a cruiser in the Bordeaux region.

However, the French Admiralty's communications with the Mediterranean ports and the naval forces overseas continued to function satisfactorily. In addition to officer messengers traveling by plane, a deluge of coded messages transmitted over land wire and by radio made known the views of the High Command to all echelons of the naval forces.

Here are a few extracts:

On June 20, after having established the succession of command of the Navy in case he should be made a prisoner, Darlan directed:

> Fight fiercely so long as a legal French Government, independent of the enemy, has not given orders to the contrary. . . . No matter what orders are received, never abandon to the enemy a ship-of-war intact.

On June 22, while the armistice conditions were being discussed at Rethondes:

> Negotiations not having been completed, further instructions will be sent later. I wish to make it clear once more, while coded message transmission is still open to me, that a resolute party must be organized and maintained secretly on board each ship in case of an armistice. That party will have as its mission the destruction of the armament and the scuttling of the ship if the enemy, taking an unfair advantage of the armistice and contrary to his promises, attempts to utilize for his own use one or several men-of-war. These considerations apply to all foreigners.

On June 24:

In this message I refer to the clauses of the armistice now being telegraphed in plain language by other channels. I am taking advantage of the last coded messages I may have opportunity to send in order to make known to you my views on this matter.

First—The demobilized ships-of-war must remain French, with French flag, French crews, and based in a French port, either metropolitan or colonial.

Second—Secret precautions for automatic sabotage must be taken in order that any enemy or foreigner seizing a ship by force cannot make use of it.

Third—If the commission charged with interpreting the armistice text decides contrary to the first directive above, without further orders the ships-of-war will be either taken to the United States or scuttled if there is no other way of keeping them out of reach of the enemy. In no case must they be left intact in the hands of the enemy.

Fourth—Ships thus taking refuge abroad must not be employed in operations against Germany or Italy without orders of the Commander in Chief. . . . 1245, 24 June 1940.

A few hours later, the ships of the Fleet immobilized themselves in their respective bases. The national flags were flown at half-mast as a sign of mourning. All radio posts and stations of the Navy ceased operating, as required by the terms of the armistice. However, negotiations on that score had been immediately opened with the Germans, and the Navy's radio posts and stations awaited permission to resume radio traffic.

Thus ended another chapter in French naval history.

CHAPTER 12

The Misunderstanding Over Article 8

It is certain that the signing of an armistice between France and the Axis constituted a severe blow to the British. They did not realize the possibilities which French-controlled bases in the western Mediterranean and North Africa, out of reach of the Germans, held for the landings of 1942—the first step in the liberation of Europe.

At the moment, the resentment of the British was understandable. Yet, fundamentally, following the trend begun at the time of the evacuation of Dunkirk, France and England had begun to diverge in their viewpoints. This was largely because England has always been protected against continental invasions by the intervening Channel, while France has always been menaced by such attacks.

As was to be expected, the Franco-German armistice convention provided for the occupation of a large part of European France. Mainly this included the territory which the Wehrmacht had overrun up to the time hostilities ended. However, to insure control of the coast between the Gironde River and the Spanish frontier, the enemy agreed, in exchange for the requisite territory, to evacuate a number of cities which he had taken in the Massif Central and in the Rhône valley—notably, Lyons and Saint-Étienne. Three-fifths of France was thus occupied by the enemy; the country was cut in two by a line of demarcation.

Geographically speaking, the military clauses of the armistice convention considerably increased the naval potential of the enemy, because they meant that henceforth, in their fight against England, the Kriegsmarine and the Luftwaffe would enjoy the use of French bases all the way from the Belgian frontier to the Spanish border.

The clauses concerning the French Fleet appeared in Articles 8 and 9 of the Franco-German armistice convention. They are quoted exactly herewith:

> Article 8.—The French war fleet, with the exception of that part permitted to the French Government for the protection of French interests in its colonial empire, is to be assembled in ports to be specified and disarmed under German or Italian control. The choice of these ports will be deter-

114

mined by the peacetime stations of the ships. The German Government solemnly declares to the French Government that it does not intend to use for its own purposes in the war the French Fleet which is in ports under German control, with the exception of those units needed for coastal patrol and for minesweeping. Furthermore, it solemnly and expressly declares that it has no intention of raising any claim to the French war fleet at the time of the conclusion of peace. With the exception of that part of the French war fleet, still to be determined, which is to represent French interests in the colonial empire, all war vessels which are outside French territorial waters are to be recalled to France.

Article 9.—The French High Command is to provide the German High Command with detailed information about all mines laid by France, as well as all harbor and coastal barriers and installations of defense and protection. The clearing of minefields is to be carried out by French forces to the extent required by the German High Command.

In the Franco-Italian convention signed at Rome on June 24, the naval clauses, strictly speaking, were the subject matter of Article 12. Like the German Article 8, this article in the Italian convention stipulated that the home ports of the ships in times of peace were to be the ports where the ships were to be disarmed.

Articles 8 and 9 in the Franco-German armistice convention created a great deal of excitement in England. If carried out to the letter, they involved the return of the French Navy's best squadron to Brest, a port now occupied by the Germans. In particular the British were seriously disturbed by the word "control," which appeared twice in Article 8. In the English language, "control" means "the power of directing and restraining" —a much stronger meaning than it has in French, where "control" merely means "administrative verification, inspection, censorship."

The French Government did not even wait for British reaction before requesting a modification of Article 8. While the French were still negotiating in the railroad car, they submitted a counterproposal to the Germans as soon as they knew the armistice terms: "control" would apply only to the unloading of ammunition and supplies, and the men-of-war were to be disarmed at Toulon or in the French ports of Africa.

For reasons of prestige the Germans would not accept any modifications in their draft. But they did not reject in principle the proposal of having the ships generally stationed in the Free Zone or in the empire ports overseas. It was merely a question, General Keitel said, of the armistice commissions working out a practical application of agreed-upon principles.

These armistice commissions were to be permanent bodies whose responsibility it would be to resolve all the problems arising from application of the texts of the convention.

The question of the French Fleet was the first matter taken up by Admiral Fritz Michelier at Wiesbaden, seat of the Franco-German armistice commission, and by Admiral Duplat at Turin, seat of the Franco-Italian armistice commission.

Thus, as early as June 30, both Axis powers had accepted the principle that the French Fleet should be immobilized in the Free Zone or in empire ports overseas. This, it would seem, should have assured the English that the principal French combatant ships would remain out of reach of the German and Italian forces.

If the British and French had been able to communicate their viewpoints promptly and freely to each other, things might have turned out differently. However, communications between Bordeaux and London became progressively more uncertain, and the misunderstanding between the two countries worsened in proportion.

In addition to the French Fleet, the question of the French merchant marine also was a cause of contention. When Denmark had been occupied by the Germans some weeks earlier, simultaneously with the Norwegian campaign, the French and British had arbitrarily taken over all available Danish shipping between them. Now that France had been invaded and was on the point of succumbing, the British were attempting to do the same thing with French ships and were directing them into British ports. This they were readily able to do, inasmuch as practically all of the overseas convoys came under British escort at the approaches to Europe.

The French, however, were equally determined to retain these French merchant ships "under the orders of the naval command." However, during the days preceding the armistice, and despite French radio orders to the contrary, many French merchant ships and fishing boats were herded into British ports.

Of immediate and particular urgency was the matter of Force X, at Alexandria, and of men-of-war which had fled from the French Atlantic ports and had taken refuge in England.[1] In the eyes of most of the commanding officers of these ships, entering British harbors was merely a first stop; as soon as they had made necessary repairs and had taken aboard necessary supplies, they would proceed, in accordance with the general order already issued by Darlan, toward their designated African bases. On June 21, while the armistice negotiations were still under way at Rethondes, the French

---

[1] Ships-of-war and naval auxiliaries taking refuge in British ports—mainly Portsmouth and Plymouth—were as follows: The two old battleships *Paris* and *Courbet,* 2 super-destroyers, 8 destroyers, 7 submarines, 13 sloops, 16 submarine chasers, 3 minelayers, 1 target ship, 7 motor torpedo boats, 98 patrol craft or minesweepers, 42 tugs and harbor craft, and 20 requisitioned trawlers.

Admiralty had sent out confirming orders, directing all ships with sufficient steaming radius to get under way for a Mediterranean or African port.

The British Admiralty at first agreed to their departure, and then abruptly changed its mind. Under its instructions the naval authorities at the various ports conjured up a variety of pretexts to prevent the French ships getting under way. In fact, the plans for "Operation Catapult"—the seizure of French ships—were already being prepared.

Every defeat brings its own disgrace. While the French Admiralty was struggling with its especial difficulties, the French Government was faced with no less painful problems of another sort, both inside and outside European France. At Bordeaux, on June 21st, the Government first learned of repeated attempts on the part of the British consuls at Rabat, Algiers, and Tunis to incite the French governors or residents to break with the home government in Europe. Three days later Lord Gort and Duff Cooper, the British Minister of Information, made a trip to French Morocco, with the intention of establishing a dissident French government there. This government, of course, would be built around those members of the French Parliament who had been evacuated on the *Massilia*.

Back in London, Mr. Churchill had not waited for the outcome of the French armistice negotiations. On June 22 he broadcast a short speech over the radio in which he warned that, if the armistice were signed, "All the resources of the empire and of the French Navy would pass rapidly into the hands of the enemy." A few hours later General de Gaulle himself spoke over BBC along the same lines. In this speech he called the French Government "a makeshift government." For this he was later to be tried *in absentia* by a military tribunal on the charge of "refusing to obey orders while in the presence of the enemy, and inciting the military to disobedience."

Relations were not improved by the return, at this time, of Pierre Laval to a post in the French Government. Mr. Laval was reputed to be an Anglophobe, and up to this time had been excluded from the Government as a sop to English public opinion.

On the night of June 22 there was a new break in relations. Around midnight the British Ambassador rang the bell at the private residence of the French Minister of Foreign Affairs. The Minister himself, in pajamas, opened the door. The Ambassador informed him that in advance of instructions from his Government, he was returning to England. That same evening Captain the Honorable A. Pleydell-Bouverie, R.N., Chief of the British Naval Mission, called at the ministerial residence of Admiral Darlan, but the admiral was prevented from seeing him by urgent official business. The remainder of the British naval officers attached to the Naval Mission, however, departed abruptly, without any notification, and the French

Admiralty, whose offices were only a few kilometers from Bordeaux, only learned of their departure some time afterward.

Aside from any personal feelings involved, the departure of the British Naval Mission took away the last direct means of liaison between the French Admiralty and the British Admiralty. After that, the French Admiralty at Bordeaux would be able to communicate with London only by telegram through the roundabout and uncertain Spanish communication system. Article 14 of the Franco-German armistice convention required the sealing of French naval radio stations from the moment the armistice took effect. In consequence French Admiralty messages were to take an average of 35 to 40 hours to reach their addresses through other means of communication. Sometimes the lapse was as much as three days! Thenceforth communication between the French Admiralty and Admiral Odend'hal, its sole liaison with the British in London, took on many of the one-sided aspects of a dialogue between two deaf persons.

To add to these blunders, Mr. Alexander and Admiral of the Fleet Sir Dudley Pound sent two messages to Admiral Darlan, via the British destroyer *Beagle* at Bordeaux[2] on June 23. In his message the Minister of the British Navy offered his French colleagues the choice between "continuing the struggle at our side or sending the French Fleet to our ports." In the other message Admiral Sir Dudley Pound, as First Sea Lord, objected to the requirements of Article 8 of the armistice convention, and pointed out the danger of having the four modern French battleships utilized by the Germans. He further emphasized the point that the condition laid down by Great Britain for a Franco-German armistice was that, "The Fleet be sent beforehand to English ports[3] in order to be certain that it would not fall into the hands of the enemy."

Admiral Darlan was greatly perplexed by these two messages. Offhand, he asked himself if these rather confusing messages were not related to the

---

[2] HMS *Beagle* had been sent to Bordeaux to demolish—without the knowledge or consent of the French—the harbor and petroleum installations in the Gironde River.

[3] The best proof that the British Admiralty did not consider the withdrawal of the French Fleet to English ports as being an absolute essential is the telegram sent to the British admirals at Portsmouth and Plymouth on the afternoon of June 22, ordering them "to grant all facilities to French ships for their departure to North Africa." At that time Sir Ronald Campbell had already sent home the terms of the armistice, and from the fact that the Germans had made no demands for the French Fleet, it must have been known in England that France would sign the armistice. It was during the course of the night that the Admiralty decided to send the two messages to Darlan, which were received by the *Beagle* at 0045 on June 23, and to countermand the instructions previously sent to Portsmouth and Plymouth furthering the departure of the French ships. (Telegram of 0133.)

attempts at this time in Morocco and in the French empire to induce the French leaders to desert. Moreover, practically speaking, what could the chief of the French Navy do on receipt of these messages? He had been informed, only after the event, of the two diplomatic notes which Sir Ronald Campbell had given, then withdrawn, then returned once more to the French Government. Moreover, the British Ambassador had declared that in his opinion these messages had now only documentary value. Above all, five days earlier, Darlan had had a meeting with the two authors of these new messages, and they had not laid down any conditions and had spoken to him in an entirely different vein. He had already pledged that in no case would the French ships be utilized by the Germans, and had issued the necessary orders to insure this. As for the armistice, it had been signed the evening before, and there was nothing the Navy could do about it. Short of leaving immediately on the British destroyer to join De Gaulle, Darlan really could not see what was expected of him.

The radio message which the captain of the *Beagle* sent back to his superiors was brief:

No satisfactory answer obtainable. Am leaving Bordeaux now.

Those days were the darkest the French Navy had yet known. In all the ports and roadsteads the feverish bustle of war's operations was followed by a painful silence.

Mail service had stopped. Urban centers began to feel the pinch of shortages. The seamen became anxious about the fate of their families, many of whom were now in the German-occupied zone. Some Reservists, now that the war was over, fell into slovenly habits and thought only of going home. The crews of ships detained in British ports suffered from their poorly defined status, and were demoralized by false rumors. Those in overseas parts of the empire had no knowledge of what had really happened in France. Instinctively, in order to guard against despair, the Navy, at all echelons, clung to discipline. Without that, it felt, no recovery was possible.

At the French Admiralty, they were being squeezed—as they were to be for two and a half years—between the stiffening attitude of the British and the unreasonable demands of the Germans.

It was on June 24 that Admiral Darlan had broadcast his last message, directing all ships, in danger of being seized by the Germans, to sail for America or else scuttle themselves.

English historians have since said that if these directives had been known in London at that time, things might have turned out differently. As a matter of fact the chiefs of the British did know; they had heard all this directly from Darlan's own lips. Also, from the notes of the First Sea Lord, which corresponded exactly with those of Admiral Darlan, it is certain that on June 25 Vice Admiral Odend'hal handed over to his British colleagues a note to the following effect:

> I have just received a message from Admiral Darlan stating that the armistice clauses were accepted only on the condition that the French Fleet would remain French, under the French flag, with reduced French crews, and would definitely remain French thereafter. Admiral Darlan considers that these arrangements are not prejudicial to British interests. But he is sadly disappointed to learn that the British Admiralty opposes the departure of French men-of-war presently in their harbors, and he urgently requests a modification of this prohibition.

Of course the value of German promises could be questioned in London, as well as the ability of the French Navy to protect themselves against German violations. The one thing the British could not doubt, however, was the sincerity of the French Navy's intentions and its determination to live up to them.

As has been said, the French brought up the question of the demobilization of the Fleet at the first meeting of the armistice commissions, on June 29. At Turin, Admiral Duplat obtained from the Italians their assent to the French warships being demobilized at Toulon and in the North African ports—this being contingent upon the Germans agreeing likewise. The French Admiralty immediately telegraphed Admiral Odend'hal as follows:

> Italian Government authorizes the stationing of the Fleet, with half crews, at Toulon and in North Africa. I have firm hopes that it will be likewise with the German Government, whose reply we are now awaiting. Under these conditions all British pretexts for detaining our forces are without foundation, and I beg of you to insist on our men-of-war and merchantmen being released. 1430 June 30.

Unfortunately this message was garbled in transmission, and all words after "I have firm hopes" were lost. Even so it should have provided valuable information to the British Admiralty, to whom[4] it was promptly delivered.

Of course it would have been even better if Admiral Odend'hal could at the same time have given the British the assurance that the consent of the Germans had also been obtained on that point. This consent was, in effect, obtained the same day, because the German armistice commission agreed to accept the recommendations of Italy on all questions concerning the Mediterranean. Unfortunately there was not sufficient time for that

---

[4] The message was received at the British Admiralty by Admiral Sir Tom Phillips, RN, Deputy Chief of Staff.

information to reach Admiral Odend'hal before the irreparable took place.

But while affairs in the Mediterranean were progressing favorably, the problem of the French ships in English harbors was becoming more acute. This time the troublemakers were the Germans, who were insisting that the French obtain the release of all French ships detained in England.

From a strictly logical standpoint, the Germans were justified in their demand. They were perfectly willing to renounce taking over French ships, but only on condition their antagonist, England, did likewise. Fearing that the French Navy might be doubledealing in this connection, the Germans demanded that they be shown all French orders which had been and were being sent to England on that point. Finally, on July 3, they sent an ultimatum: All French ships must return to France, or the entire armistice would be reconsidered.

The Navy remained in the center of the squeeze. But the drama that day was to be played at Mers-el-Kebir.

CHAPTER 13

The Drama of Mers-el-Kebir

Even with the French Navy and its bases neutralized, the Royal Navy was large enough to hold its own against the united German and Italian Fleets. The only risk was that some of the powerful modern ships of the French Navy might be seized by the Axis powers. And even if there were only one chance in a thousand of this happening, it was a risk the British Government refused to take.

Perhaps, too, Churchill needed a spectacular stroke to brace British morale, which had been sadly shaken by the knockout blow to France. The United States Secretary of State, Cordell Hull, gave one of the keys to the British decision when, after having discussed it later with the British Prime Minister, he wrote in his memoirs: "Since many people throughout the world believed that Britain was about to surrender, he wanted by this action to show that she still meant to fight."[1]

The idea of taking precautions to insure that the French Fleet would never be used against England went back perhaps to the day when the word "armistice" was first enunciated by Paul Reynaud, in the presence of General Sir Edward Spears, as a logical consequence of the evacuation of Dunkirk, which was taking place at that time. The first concrete trace of any such precautions was seen on June 17, when Admiral of the Fleet Sir Dudley Pound reported to the Prime Minister that, in accordance with his instructions, he was assembling a Force H at Gibraltar to "observe" the movements of the French Fleet. Force H was to be built around the battle cruiser *Hood* and the aircraft carrier *Ark Royal,* and was to be commanded by Vice Admiral Sir James Somerville. In Admiral Pound's thinking, this naval force would also serve to relieve, on the strategic level, the French squadron at Mers-el-Kebir, which up to that time had been the only one operating in the Gibraltar area. At any rate this is what he told Admiral Darlan at Bordeaux on June 18, when they were discussing, solely from the professional point of view, the effect of the coming neutralization of the French forces.

Measures were also being taken to retain the French ships which were at that time in the ports of the United Kingdom and in British bases over-

[1] *The Memoirs of Cordell Hull.* Vol. I, page 799.

seas. In England, the commanders in chief at Portsmouth and Plymouth received their orders on June 27. In Africa and other overseas ports, attempts were made to incite the French forces to dissidence. Admiral, South, at Bizerte, Admiral, Africa, at Casablanca, and the Naval Commander at Morocco, all were solicited by the British admirals to disobey their Government. Admiral Sir Dudley North left on a destroyer for Oran on June 24 in order to approach Admiral Gensoul, commanding the French Atlantic squadron at anchor in the port of Mers-el-Kebir. Everywhere the representatives of the British Navy developed the same subject. Everywhere they were answered that the French sailors would follow the orders of their Government, but these orders provided that in no case was the French Fleet to be allowed to fall into the hands of the enemy. The British liaison officers attached to the French naval forces returned to London convinced of the sincerity of the French Navy and also of its firm resolution. They said as much. But evidently they were unable to take back the formal guarantee that this firm resolution would be effective.

It is known with certainty today that the British Navy did not accept the orders of their Government with a light heart. The memoirs of Admiral of the Fleet Sir Andrew Cunningham need no comments on that point, and the views of Admiral North and Admiral Somerville were plainly stated in the House of Lords in 1954 in terms which merit reprinting here:

> Admiral North had visited the French admiral at Oran and had received an assurance that French ships would not be surrendered to Germany or Italy, and he was not alone in being appalled at the decision to attack these French ships at Oran. Admiral Somerville was ordered to carry out the attack, and he and all the officers concerned were horror struck by the decision. Admiral Somerville intended to protest, but before he could do so, he was informed that the decision was the irrevocable decision of the War Cabinet.[2]

There was only one discordant note, that of Admiral Sir William James, who unreservedly described in his memoirs the Indian wiles employed to seize the French ships at Portsmouth before they could fire a shot.

It was not that there would be any difficulty in taking the crews by surprise; they were all blindly trustful, feeling safe in the protection of a friendly port or roadstead. The difficulty was in keeping the preparations secret.

Yet, all things considered, it must be conceded that if affairs of this sort are to be accomplished, it is perhaps better to stoop to unethical procedures than to risk regrettable bloodshed.

Nevertheless the two French admirals in command of the collection of

---

[2] Lord Winster in the House of Lords; reported by *The Times,* Tuesday, July 27, 1954.

variegated ships at Portsmouth and Plymouth had issued instructions in case of such an action by the British. To their credit, the French admirals did not believe it would ever occur; the worst they expected was some sort of internment of their ships for the duration of the war. This idea had finally been accepted by even the most distrustful commanding officer. Thus the commanding officer of the *Surcouf,* who had not shed his uniform since leaving Brest, considered on July 2 that he could go to sleep between real sheets in perfect tranquility!

The first measure taken by the English was to remove from the ships the numerous passengers, or refugees who had been brought from Brest or Cherbourg. Seven or eight thousand men in all were thus concentrated in a camp at Aintree, on the outskirts of Liverpool, to await their departure for Casablanca in English ships on July 1.

The men-of-war, which were mostly anchored in the Spithead and Cowesands roads, were invited on some pretext or other to shift their anchorages to the harbors of Portsmouth and Plymouth. Wardroom calls of British officers to the French ships—social visits, presumably—were increased in number. Liaison officers were designated—in reality they were nothing but future boarding officers.

The stage had been set. On July 2 the British admirals received orders to execute the plan the following morning at dawn. Everywhere, in the English ports, the action followed an almost identical pattern.

On the stroke of the bell, at predawn of the 3rd of July, a British officer presented himself at the gangway of every French ship. Aboard, all was quiet and peaceful. No extra watches had been posted, and the sentry on watch was alone.

"An urgent message for the commanding officer," the visitor announced. "It must be delivered into his own hands."

"Very well," the sentry replied, without suspicion, and left to awaken his captain.

This was exactly what the British had planned for. Groups of armed English soldiers were waiting nearby, hiding behind a building, or a hangar, or a pile of coal or under the canopy of a boat. With one leap they were on board and in command of every hatch and passage. Meanwhile the officer, gun in hand, had followed close on the sentry's heels, and his silhouette was framed in the doorway before the commanding officer, abruptly awakened, knew what had happened. Ten armed men crowded around him while he was handed a memorandum from Admiral James or Admiral Sir M. Dunbar-Nasmith stating that he must hand over his ship. It was a grotesque and humiliating experience which the French officers would have difficulty in ever forgetting. Elsewhere in the ship the surprise was equally complete—the crew locked in their compartments, still in their night clothes, isolated from the other compartments, with sentries blocking every exit.

Naturally, all of this did not take place without protests and without incidents.

At Portsmouth nothing happened other than the simple act of seizure by armed force; no blood was shed. But at Plymouth the officers of the *Mistral* found opportunity to open the sea valves and flood a number of compartments. Complete scuttling of the ship was checked only after the commanding officer was unequivocally threatened with having his men, who were locked in their compartments, go down with the ship. On board the *Surcouf* the French fought back with revolvers, and four men were killed—three of them English. Among these were Commander D. V. Sprague, commanding the British submarine *Thames,* moored close by, and Lieutenant Commander Griffiths who, since the arrival of the French ships, had been designated liaison officer for submarines.

Each of these officers had been cordially received on board the *Surcouf* during the preceding days. Now they had returned, gun in hand, at the head of a boarding party and had demanded the immediate evacuation of the ship by her crew. Seeing his comrades threatened, the French gunnery officer drew his pistol and killed both of them. A few steps away the *Surcouf's* medical officer fired a whole clip at an English sergeant who was rushing at him with a bayonet. In falling, the sergeant ran his bayonet through a young officer of the *Surcouf,* whom he carried to his death with him.

As the French crews were forced from their ships they were herded on the docks or in neighboring buildings. Later they were allowed to return on board, in small closely guarded groups, to collect their personal belongings.

Unfortunately, in the haste in which the operation had been mounted and carried out, the British authorities had not always been able to institute the necessary precautions to safeguard personal property. Inevitably, more than one French sailor was disappointed in not recovering his watch, his camera, his binoculars, and, in some cases, even his medals and decorations. The resulting bitterness manifestly did not tend to ease the already strained relations.

Presently guards with fixed bayonets marched the crews to the railroad station, locked them in the coaches, and transported them to the camps in the vicinity of Liverpool just as though they had been prisoners of war. In this manner some 10,000 men spent several months in tents under conditions that were uncomfortable physically and even more painful mentally. They were separated from their officers, a great number of whom were interned on the Isle of Man. They were deprived of correspondence with their families, and they were subjected to incessant propaganda to join the Free French Legion which was being organized under General de Gaulle.

The mud in the camps, the lack of comforts, the mediocre food—all could have been forgiven. But they bitterly resented the moral pressures to which they were subjected. The enthusiasm, the will to fight, and the patriotism of the sailors would certainly have led many of them to continue the war at the side of the English if that option had not been presented to them as a disavowal of their Government. After all, one member of that Government was Admiral Darlan, their own Commander in Chief, whereas those who attempted to enlist them appeared to them somewhat as accomplices of their jailers.

When all these sailors were repatriated during the course of the months to come,[3] the mere account of the manner in which they had been treated contributed more than the aggression at Mers-el-Kebir, perhaps, to strengthen the Navy in its loyalty to the Government of Marshal Pétain.

The French ships thus taken over in English waters represented, in tonnage, barely a tenth part of the French Fleet, and much less than that in military value. The essential part was in African ports, principally at Mers-el-Kebir. Here the French were in their own territory, hence it would be impossible to board them surreptitiously under cover of darkness. Nothing less than an operation of battle proportions could take these ships from the control of the French.

For such an operation the British wanted an unquestionable superiority in strength. Admiral Somerville, who commanded the operation, had under

---

[3] The French admirals held in England demanded, as a matter of principle, that the crews be returned to their ships, but on July 22 the British authorities began to load the sailors at Camp Aintree on French merchant ships to repatriate them to the Free Zone of France. Two days later the passenger ship *Meknès* left Southampton at 1600 with all lights burning and with 1,100 passengers on board. At 2200 she was hailed by a German motor torpedo boat which first fired a few machinegun bursts into her and then sank her with a torpedo. Almost 400 French sailors lost their lives in this disaster.

Nobody in France had been advised of this trip, and consequently the German armistice commission had not been informed. There is of course no excuse for the motor torpedo boat attacking this ship, with all its lights burning, without first taking the trouble to identify it. Nevertheless the greatest part of the responsibility must rest with the English for sending out an unarmed "neutralized" ship without informing the other belligerent in advance.

After this tragedy, which deepened French bitterness, further repatriations were suspended except for those that could be transported on the hospital ships *Sphinx* and *Canada*. Later they were resumed, but only after laborious negotiations with the United States, Britain, and the German armistice commission. With safe conduct guaranteed by all belligerents, the repatriations extended through December, and landed in France 21,000 naval personnel, 2,000 merchant seamen, over 7,500 troops, and 200 civilians, including those repatriated in July.

him a formidable task force: the battle cruiser *Hood,* the battleships *Resolution* and *Valiant,* two cruisers, eleven destroyers, and the aircraft carrier *Ark Royal.* In addition, since the French ships would be anchored unsuspectingly in the harbor, he could choose his own time to surprise them, and also could place his own ships behind the cover of a promontory so that they could fire over it without themselves being in sight of their opponents. To keep himself advised at all times of the disposition of the French Fleet, he stationed a submarine off Oran and Algiers for several days preceding the attack, and also had a plane fly from Gibraltar to keep an eye on them as well.

The setting of this tragedy was the Bay of Mers-el-Kebir, which opens onto the sea a few miles west of Oran, at the foot of the Djebel Murdjadjo. Here the French Navy, before the war, had begun the construction of a deep water port capable of sheltering all its squadrons. The breakwater, resting on a bottom a hundred feet deep, consisted of stone blocks quarried from the Murdjadjo. Though incomplete at the time of the attack, it still extended almost a mile from the shore.

Here, on July 3, 1940, were assembled Admiral Gensoul's squadron, consisting of the battleships *Dunkerque, Strasbourg, Provence,* and *Bretagne,* the superdestroyers *Volta, Mogador, Tigre, Lynx, Kersaint,* and *Terrible,* and the seaplane tender *Commandant Teste.* Of the battleships only the *Dunkerque* and *Strasbourg* were modern.

The large ships were moored with their sterns toward the breakwater and their bows toward shore, a normal moor in times of peace but particularly unsuited for bringing the powerful main batteries of the *Dunkerque* and *Strasbourg* into action quickly, as the main turrets of these ships were located entirely forward.

At Oran, a few miles to the east, were anchored or moored a conglomeration of destroyers, patrol vessels, minesweepers, sloops, ships under construction, etc., which had withdrawn from Toulon. At Algiers there were six 7,800-ton cruisers.

Confident in the results obtained by its negotiations with the German armistice commission, the French Admiralty had issued orders to begin demobilizing the ships at Mers-el-Kebir. No one thought of sending them back to Brest, for in Africa they were out of reach of the Germans, unless the Wehrmacht were to invade Spain and chase the English out of Gibraltar. That was something that could not occur overnight. In the meantime the French ships remained under the constant surveillance of Force H and could not leave without the English becoming aware of it. In fact they were in greater safety at Mers-el-Kebir than Admiral Godfroy's ships at Alexandria when in July, 1942, Rommel's Afrika Korps approached to within less than 50 miles of them!

Nothing, then, seemed to justify the precipitous haste of the British Government, and, even now, all of the principal actors of that drama remain convinced that an amicable accord could have been reached, thus preventing the unnecessary loss of many lives.

On June 24, as previously noted, Admiral Sir Dudley North paid a personal call on Admiral Gensoul at Mers-el-Kebir, while at the same time Captain C. S. Holland, commanding officer of the aircraft carrier *Ark Royal,* called on the commander of the French naval forces at Casablanca. Not a word in the conversation of these two officers gave the slightest inkling of what was to come.

The first intimation the French at Mers-el-Kebir had of anything unusual came via the British destroyer *Foxhound,* which entered the harbor at 0700,[4] Greenwich time, on July 3. On board was Captain Holland, who informed the French flagship that he had an important message for the admiral.

Captain Holland had formerly been British naval attaché at Paris, and had many close friends in the French Navy. Under normal circumstances Admiral Gensoul would have received him most cordially. However the lookouts had just reported the presence, offshore, of an imposing array of British battleships, cruisers, and destroyers. Not having received the customary courtesy of advance notification of their visit, Admiral Gensoul suddenly wondered whether the message Captain Holland was bringing was not some sort of ultimatum.[5] If so, he had no intention of engaging in any discussions under such threat. He therefore refused to receive Captain Holland, but sent his flag lieutenant, Lieutenant Bernard Dufay, to represent him.

Dufay was a close personal friend of Holland, and spoke English perfectly. His fortunate choice as representative prevented an immediate break, and the negotiations continued, with many ups and downs, almost all day.

The proposition which Captain Holland presented gave the French five options: (1) they could join the British and continue the war at their side; (2) they could take their ships to a British port; (3) they could get under way for the West Indies or a port in the United States; (4) they could scuttle themselves; or (5) they could fight.

There could be no thought of accepting either of the first two alternatives. Compliance with the British wishes in either case would have been a direct violation of the armistice. That armistice had been signed by the French

---

[4] Greenwich time, which is the only time used in this narrative unless otherwise indicated.

[5] Admiral Somerville had foreseen this, but if he had acted otherwise the French squadron would have had time to prepare to get under way if the negotiations failed, which would have radically altered the combat conditions.

Government, and it was not within the province of the Navy to contravene an obligation formally recognized by its Government. Scuttling was equally out of question. As to fighting with a presumed friend and ally, Admiral Gensoul would in no case assume the responsibility of firing the first shot.

Admiral Gensoul gave so little consideration to the third option offered by the British—that of taking the Fleet to the West Indies or the United States—that he did not even mention it in his message reporting the ultimatum to the French Admiralty. Later on, politicians were to hold that against him on the grounds that the French Admiralty itself had contemplated such a withdrawal as a checkmate to any attempt to seize the ships. But at that time the only threat came from the Germans, not the English. In any case, internment in America was contrary to the terms of the armistice, which specified that all French naval ships should be demobilized in French ports. No modification of the armistice terms in that respect could be made without consent of the German armistice commission. The likelihood of the Germans agreeing may be inferred from their ultimatum that same morning from Wiesbaden: "Either return all ships from England, or the whole armistice will have to be reconsidered."

At 0900 Lieutenant Dufay transmitted to Captain Holland the reply of Admiral Gensoul:

(1) The assurances given to Admiral Sir Dudley North still held good. In no case would the French ships be allowed to fall intact into the hands of the Germans or of the Italians. They would not be given up, as Dufay reiterated emphatically, in English, "Any time, anywhere, any way, and without further orders from the French Admiralty."

(2) In view of the substance and form of the unmistakable ultimatum presented to Admiral Gensoul, the French ships would defend themselves by force.

At 1000, Admiral Gensoul's Chief of Staff went personally to confirm Admiral Gensoul's reply, and to invite Admiral Somerville's attention to the fact that, "The first shot fired against us will have the practical effect of lining up the entire French Fleet against Great Britain—a result which will be diametrically opposite to that which the British Government seeks."

At 1050 the *Foxhound* signaled that, in accordance with his orders, Admiral Somerville would not permit the French squadron to leave port unless the terms of the ultimatum were accepted. This declaration was emphasized by English seaplanes which at 1230 dropped several magnetic mines into the channel leading into Mers-el-Kebir.

The English ultimatum was to expire at 1400. The *Foxhound* emphasized this by signaling, at 1310, "If you accept the proposals, hoist a square flag at the main mast; otherwise we will open fire at 1400."

All hope of a peaceful settlement seemed lost. However, Admiral

Gensoul tried hard to prolong the negotiations. At 1315 he signaled that he was waiting for a reply from his Government. Then at 1330 he signaled that he was prepared to receive Admiral Somerville's representative for an honorable discussion.

Obviously Admiral Somerville was waiting only for that, as the British ships were ordered not to open fire. At 1500 Captain Holland stepped on board the *Dunkerque* to confer with Admiral Gensoul.

It was during this interview that the French admiral showed Captain Holland a copy of the French Admiralty's message of June 24, of which Holland knew nothing. The Englishman seemed staggered by what he read. Then Admiral Gensoul put forward the same idea for a "gentlemen's agreement" that Admiral Godfroy was proposing at Alexandria at that very hour—an agreement that he would personally guarantee.

Admiral Gensoul gained the impression that the ultimatum presented by the British was not arbitrary or final. But to end the dispute without a catastrophe, more time was needed for discussion. Unfortunately things were taking place elsewhere which militated against that.

For the French Admiralty was in the process of moving from Bordeaux to Vichy, with a stopover at Nérac, when news of the British ultimatum reached them. Two of the three sections of the Admiralty had already left Nérac. Admiral Darlan was temporarily with the Government at Clermont-Ferrand, and could not be readily reached by telephone. Admiral Le Luc was still at Nérac with a radio truck and a few men. His first action was to alert all French naval forces in the Mediterranean, especially the 3rd Squadron, consisting of four heavy cruisers and three divisions of super-destroyers at Toulon, and the six cruisers at Algiers: "Get under way, ready for action, and report to the admiral in the *Dunkerque* at Oran." And, as if the British were not expecting such a move, he sent a plain language message to Gensoul ordering him to so inform them.

At London, they were becoming impatient. In his memoirs, Churchill tells how he paced the council chamber like a caged lion during that famous day. "Settle the affair quickly, or you will have reinforcements to deal with," radioed the British Admiralty to Somerville.

The day was indeed getting on. At 1615, when Holland and Gensoul were still trying to arrive at an amicable arrangement, a message from Somerville interrupted the discussion: "If none of the propositions is accepted before 1730 B.S.T. (British Summer Time)—I repeat, 1730 B.S.T. —it will be necessary to sink your ships!"

All hope was now gone. The battle would take place, and under tragic conditions, as Admiral Gensoul had forbidden his ships to get under way during the negotiations lest this immediately bring on the fight.

However, the hours since the *Foxhound's* first appearance had not been

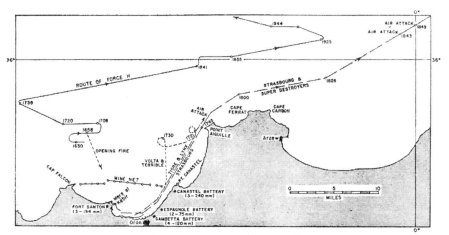

THE ENGAGEMENT AT MERS-EL-KEBIR

wasted. All ships now had steam up and crews at their battle stations. The coastal batteries, whose disarmament had begun, were now again in readiness to fire. On the airfields, 42 fighters were ready to take off. The ships at Oran were ready to get under way. Minesweepers had been busy sweeping part of the channel clear of any possible English mines. Four submarines at Oran were ready to get under way at the first shot in order to establish a barrier line between Cape L'Aiguille and Cape Falcon.

At 1635 Captain Holland left the *Dunkerque*. At 1656 the British squadron opened fire. It had been 125 years since the French and the British had last fired on each other—at Waterloo!

At that moment Somerville was in a position north-northwest of and approximately 14,000 meters from Mers-el-Kebir lighthouse, with battleships in column on course 70 degrees, at speed of 20 knots. The first salvo landed north of and close to the breakwater. The order was immediately given to the French ships to open fire. The *Provence* fired the first answering shots within one minute and 30 seconds after the British began the action. She had to aim her 340-mm. guns directly between the *Dunkerque's* masts.

Admiral Gensoul had no intention of fighting while at anchor, but in the crowded anchorage all of the ships could not get under way at the same time. The battleships were ordered to form column with the *Strasbourg* leading, and then the *Dunkerque, Provence,* and *Bretagne.* The superdestroyers were to sortie separately.[6]

The *Strasbourg,* under command of Captain Louis Collinet, got under way within seconds. The berth she had just left was immediately struck by

---

[6] See map, page 132, showing the anchorage berths.

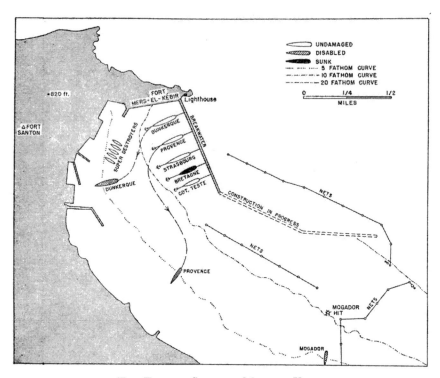

THE FRENCH SHIPS AT MERS-EL-KEBIR

a salvo of British shells, and one shell fragment cut the flag halyards. At 1710 the *Strasbourg* was steaming through the Mers-el-Kebir channel at 15 knots and firing at a British destroyer which promptly retired behind a smokescreen.

The other battleships were not so fortunate. The *Dunkerque* was struck the moment she slipped her moorings. A 380-mm. shell hit, followed by a 3-shell salvo of the same size, caused serious damage and left her half paralized. With electric power gone she could no longer fire her guns. She headed toward the far end of the bay, where she anchored at 1713. Within that brief time, however, she had managed to fire some 40 shots at the *Hood*.

The *Bretagne* was also hit before being able to get under way. She began to sink by the stern, with an immense cloud of smoke rising above her. At 1707 she was on fire from stem to stern, and two minutes later she suddenly capsized and sank, taking 977 men[7] down with her.

_____

[7] This loss may be compared to that of the USS *Arizona,* which was bombed and which capsized during the Japanese raid on Pearl Harbor. Out of a total of 100 officers and 1,411 men on board, the *Arizona* had 47 officers and 1,056 men killed or

The *Provence* was hit at 1703, while waiting for the *Dunkerque* to pass up the channel ahead of her. A serious leak and fire breaking out aft induced her captain to beach her at the edge of the five-fathom line. The *Commandant Teste,* fifth combat ship to get under way, miraculously escaped being hit, and immediately went to the rescue of the survivors of the *Bretagne.*

The super-destroyers had all succeeded in getting under way. They would probably have gotten out of the harbor unscathed if the *Mogador* had not been forced to stop in the channel to avoid a tug. Seconds later a 380-mm. shell struck her aft, setting off the 16 depth charges in their racks. With her stern blown off to the after engineroom bulkhead, the *Mogador* anchored in three and one-half fathoms of water, where small craft rushed from Oran assisted in putting out the fires aboard her.

The fire of the British had been very heavy, very accurate, and of short duration. At 1712 Somerville ceased firing and took cover under a smokescreen.

At that time Gensoul had left with him only the disabled *Dunkerque, Provence,* and *Mogador* and the *Commandant Teste,* which had neither fired, nor been fired upon. The field of battle was moving out to sea, where the British were attempting unsuccessfully to intercept the *Strasbourg* and the super-destroyers, who had now been reinforced by destroyers from Oran. The pursuit did not last long; the British battleships gave up the chase at 1925 and headed for Gibraltar. The *Ark Royal's* planes attacked the *Strasbourg* on three occasions, but did not make a hit, as the torpedo boat *Poursuivante* from Oran alerted the *Strasbourg* in time for her to put her rudder over and evade.

The submarines from Oran were depth bombed by British destroyers and planes, and did not succeed in getting within torpedo range of the British capital ships. The fighter planes, with no bomb sights and only 75-kilogram bombs aboard, were almost equally unsuccessful. Some Air Force pilots boldly machinegunned the English ships, and several shot down English planes. But there were other Air Force pilots who could not seem to bring themselves to attack their comrades of the day before.

The coastal batteries undoubtedly contributed a great deal to the escape of the *Strasbourg* and the super-destroyers by keeping the British largely to the western end of the bay.

At 2010 the next day, the *Strasbourg* entered Toulon undamaged, along with the *Volta,* the *Tigre,* and the *Terrible.* They were received with tremendous cheering from all the ships in the roadstead, where they were to

---

missing—a casualty percentage of almost three-fourths of the entire ship's complement. (See Samuel E. Morison, *History of U.S. Naval Operations in World War II,* Vol. III, page 109.)

be joined shortly by the six cruisers from Algiers. The destroyers and sloops from Oran withdrew to Algiers. It was in this withdrawal that the colonial sloop *Rigault de Genouilly* was torpedoed and sunk in sight of the harbor by a British submarine[8] at 1415 on July 4.

From a purely military standpoint, Force H had accomplished only a part of its objectives: one old battleship sunk, another disabled, and the *Dunkerque* damaged to an extent which at that time could have been easily repaired. On the other hand the encounter almost resulted in what had been predicted by Gensoul and feared by the British themselves: a complete about-face by the entire French Navy, which up to then had been 100 per cent pro-British. Darlan, feeling it a personal insult that his word had been doubted, was blazingly indignant over this new "Copenhagen."[9] His first reaction was to send out orders, at 2000 on July 3, to attack all English ships met. The next day he obtained from the German armistice commission a cancellation of all requirements that French ships be disarmed. But on July 5 he substituted for the order of the 3rd a new and wiser order, warning that, "All British ships approaching to within less than 20 sea miles of the French coast are open to attack." This warning was widely broadcast immediately.

During the night of July 4 a few naval planes were sent to attack Force H, which had returned to Gibraltar, but no hits were scored.

On July 6 the British returned to Mers-el-Kebir. Perhaps they were tipped off by a press communique of Admiral, South, who unwisely announced, "The damages to the *Dunkerque* are minor and will be quickly repaired." At dawn three waves of torpedo planes from the *Ark Royal* appeared simultaneously over the Mers-el-Kebir roadstead. The antiaircraft defenses only partially broke up their attack. A torpedo hit one of the small

---

[8] The British had posted the submarines *Pandora* and *Proteus* to the north of Algiers and Oran, respectively. These did not take part in the Mers-el-Kebir battle, but at 2150 on July 3, they received orders to attack all French men-of-war on sight. The next afternoon the *Proteus* sighted the *Commandant Teste* but could not get into firing position. The *Pandora* had better luck with the *Rigault de Genouilly*.

During the night of July 5, Admiral Sir Tom Phillips, Deputy Chief of the Naval Staff, had Admiral Odend'hal awakened in London especially to tender him his regrets at this torpedoing. It was due, he said, solely to an error on the part of the Royal Navy, while the attack at Mers-el-Kebir had been strictly a decision of the British Government, and the Royal Navy could do nothing except obey.

Obedience of the military to the civil authority is, as a matter of fact, the rule in all navies. That rule was respected in France as in England.

The order to attack had been given the submarines by Admiral Sir Dudley North, flag officer commanding in the North Atlantic, at 2316 on July 5.

[9] In 1807, the British, although at peace with Denmark, had suddenly demanded the temporary internment of the Danish ships of the line in one of His Majesty's ports, and upon refusal, had attacked them at anchor in the harbor of Copenhagen.

craft which were grouped around the battleship to assist in repairing her. The torpedo exploded the depth charges on the small craft, which in turn blew a large hole in the side of the *Dunkerque,* killing 150 men. New graves had to be dug in the cemetery where the first victims had just been buried, bringing the total of the dead, including those lost in the *Bretagne,* to 1,297.

Another French counterattack on Gibraltar was considered. But to carry it out, the assistance of the Air Force was required. Apart from the fact that the Air Force had been disorganized by the defeat, and was partially disarmed, the aviators in Africa showed themselves lukewarm. They lingered over the preparations for days. Wisely the French Government cancelled an operation which would no longer carry the weight of a prompt reprisal. On July 12 the French Admiralty sent a message to all of its naval attachés abroad: "Our position remains defensive. The surprise is over and we count on defending ourselves by returning blow for blow—but by ourselves and without enlisting the assistance of our former enemies. We shall know how to maintain our dignity during misfortune."

Meanwhile, both at Alexandria and at Dakar, French and British relations had come to near crisis.

At Alexandria, Admiral Cunningham had received orders to seize the ships of Admiral Godfroy's Force X on the same pattern as Admiral Somerville at Mers-el-Kebir. But here the situation was even more delicate. The French ships had been operating as an integral division of Admiral Cunningham's force; in fact they had been scheduled to take part in a combined operation on June 22, which the British had cancelled at the last moment. Then, during the night of the 24th, Admiral Godfroy received orders from the French Admiralty to leave Alexandria at the earliest possible moment.

But Admiral Cunningham had likewise received very definite orders from his Admiralty. In view of these he respectfully asked Admiral Godfroy to remain in port.

Godfroy did not insist on leaving. He still hoped that an armistice would not be signed—at least with Italy—and he did not wish to provoke a bloody engagement which could benefit no one except the enemy. Cunningham engaged himself to attempt nothing against the French squadron; in return Godfroy promised not to leave during any absence of Cunningham from the port.

No French sailor will ever forget the chivalry and the intelligence which Admiral Cunningham displayed in arriving with Admiral Godfroy at a solution to the crisis of July 3. A brutal application of the orders of the British Government would undoubtedly have resulted in a tragedy, as at Mers-el-Kebir. Without detracting in any way from Admiral Cunningham's generous conduct, it must be admitted, however, that his situation was better than Somerville's. Somerville had to accomplish his job as quickly as possible, under penalty of having additional French forces appear on the scene, which might have radically changed the situation to his disadvantage. Cunningham, on the other hand, had the French ships cut off in Alexandria harbor, an English base, and he could take all the time that was necessary.

Cunningham was fundamentally hostile to the "senseless" operation which he knew was taking place at Mers-el-Kebir at that moment. He would not admit the possibility that he also would have to employ force against his French comrades.

The day of July 3 passed without any tragic incident. Both admirals had agreed to maintain the *status quo* until the next day. However, when the news of the attack at Mers-el-Kebir was received on the flagship *Duquesne,* Godfroy hardened immediately. The radio added its complications. London was broadcasting, "Destroy the French Fleet at anchor immediately!" From the French Admiralty were coming orders such as, "Get under way fighting, whatever the cost! At least exact an eye for an eye, a tooth for a tooth!"

However, the night went by, with the English perhaps under greater tension than the French. On the morning of the 4th, the ships of Force X saw all the guns of the British ships, tompions out, trained on them. When this was called to Cunningham's attention, he immediately ordered the guns trained fore and aft.

That was already one point gained. The tension was further lessened by the coolness and quick wit of the French commanding officers. One of them replied to the menace of the English guns by sending his men topside to wash down the decks.[10] On the *Duguay-Trouin* they rigged stages over the side and began wire-brushing and painting the rusted areas. The *Lorraine* sounded swimming call and sent swimmers over the side!

The unexpected appearance of an Italian plane created an even more effective diversion, because the *Tourville,* believing the *Duquesne* threatened, opened up on the Italian with her 75-mm. guns.

After many discussions, the crisis was settled at the end of the day. The English would make no attempt to seize French ships by force. The French, on their side, would unload their fuel oil, and would store all the breech-

---

[10] The officer responsible for this action was Captain André Marloy, commanding officer of the *Tourville.* In his memoirs, Admiral Godfroy wrote: "These dispositions kept busy an important part of the crew for whom an occupation was necessary. No better work could be found than that laid down by the standard routine—washing down decks, shining brightwork, etc. This cool carrying on of ship's routine astonished the British, who talked about it a long time afterward. Admiral Cunningham's sailors, tensely waiting behind their armor, could see their French comrades continuing their usual shipboard life as if nothing unusual were occurring, and as if they did not even see the guns of the British Fleet trained on them."

blocks of their guns and the firing pins of their torpedoes at the French consulate.

A written agreement was signed on that basis by both Commanders in Chief on July 7. Its main provisions were:

(1) The French ships would be maintained in their present condition of matériel. They would not be scuttled.

(2) No attempt would be made by the British to seize them by force.

(3) The personnel on board would be reduced, with the excess being returned to France; the complement of each ship would be established by mutual agreement.

(4) The personnel remaining on board would not engage in any hostile act against the British, and would not attempt to leave port.

Articles 5 to 10 covered regulations concerning the food, clothing, and medical care, etc., of the French sailors, who could not possibly be subsisted without British assistance. Then came Article 11.

(11) In the event that French men-of-war were seized and utilized by either the Germans or the Italians, this agreement would be reopened for further discussion.

This "gentlemen's agreement" was scrupulously observed, until 1943, by Admiral Godfroy as well as by Admiral Cunningham and his successor, Admiral Henry Harwood. "It would be insane to fight each other," radioed the British admiral on July 4.

Admiral Darlan, who was still seething with anger, accepted the compromise without any great confidence. As for Churchill, he desecrated the spirit in which the agreement had been achieved by reporting to the House of Commons the next day, "Measures have been taken to insure that the French ships, commanded by a very gallant admiral, shall either be sunk or accept our demands."

The British aggression was to extend as far as Dakar, where the incompleted *Richelieu* had taken refuge after escaping the Germans at Brest on June 23.

No one in this French West African colony had any real knowledge of the true political situation in France. In all good faith, a number of French military and civilian officials, who did not have a clear picture of the collapse of France, talked of continuing the war. They were confused by the British men-of-war which stayed on at Dakar after the armistice. To get away from that environment, the *Richelieu* put to sea on June 25, planning to go to Casablanca. But the British sent forces to intercept her, and when the cruiser *Dorsetshire* began shadowing her, Admiral, South, ordered her back to Dakar.

There, on July 8, she was attacked at dawn by planes from the aircraft carrier *Hermes.* This ship was well acquainted with the harbor and its approaches, as she had often been there while operating under the orders of Admiral Duplat.

The *Richelieu* had never fired her main battery, and her antiaircraft battery was not yet in working order. The ship received a torpedo hit aft which was to prevent her getting under way for some time. With this torpedo, Franco-British relations in Africa began to split wide apart.

The French politicians surrounding Marshal Pétain, being realists, had been forced to submit to the Germans to end a fight for which they could see no possible success. But not a single one had ever desired, or till then had desired, to break with England. No one—or almost no one—thought that it would be possible to entertain any relations with the Germans other than those required under the armistice conditions. In fact, it was generally believed that the armistice would apply only for a limited period, and that then all Europe, including England, would in some measure or other arrive at a common understanding.

But these illusions were completely wrecked by the tragedy of Mers-el-Kebir. Till then France had felt some shame at abandoning their fighting comrades and concluding a separate armistice with the enemy. But from the moment those comrades turned their guns against France, the French no longer entertained any scruples. They had been freed from any such. The English had thought only of themselves; now France had only to imitate them and think of France first.

The break could, of course, only profit the Germans. In fact, with a certain audacity, they had immediately cancelled the naval disarmament provisions of the armistice. How Hitler must have gloated!

But the French Government knew how to temper its actions and to avoid the trap. A reversal of alliances would have nothing but fatal consequences for France.

Churchill, knowing privately that he had the support of President Roosevelt,[11] understood this when he declared, on the day following Mers-el-Kebir, that he considered the matter closed, and when on July 12 he issued orders that French men-of-war were not to be interfered with unless they

[11] We know today from reading *The Challenge to Isolation,* by Langer and Gleason, page 573, that the British Prime Minister secretly had obtained the approval of President Roosevelt before ordering the operation at Mers-el-Kebir. Neither Cordell Hull nor Sumner Welles in the U. S. Department of State had been notified. There exists among the Roosevelt papers a note in the handwriting of the British Ambassador at Washington, Lord Lothian, dated July 4, 1940, which states, "You will see that Winston Churchill has undertaken the actions against the French Fleet which we discussed and which you approved." (Roosevelt Papers, Secretary's File, Box 71.)

headed for a port in the German-occupied zone.[12]

Once Darlan's anger had passed, the French also understood that it was not to their interest to add a definite quarrel with the British to the woes they already had from the German occupation. As Laval himself said, "A defeat is more than sufficient."

Officially, diplomatic relations, already suspended by the British, were broken. Unofficially, contacts with Britain were still maintained by a French consul general and a commercial mission, presided over by a diplomat, remaining in London.

As far as the French Navy was concerned, the day of July 3 had two consequences of major importance.

The first was to isolate the Navy further from the military and the remainder of the country. The Germans were by now counting their prisoners—one and a half million—sorting their booty, and infiltrating themselves into the administration of the Occupied Zone. The suffering mass of Frenchmen began to be aware of the rigors of occupation. They were thinking a great deal more about what was happening at home than about those battles in faraway African ports of which the average citizen understood nothing. The sailors, was the popular thought, were wrong; it was not England, but Germany, that was the enemy. "I cannot believe," one of Admiral Gensoul's acquaintances was to say later, "that the English were the first to fire."

The second consequence of that day was the return to Toulon of the bulk of the French naval forces. If it had not been for the aggression of the British, the principal French squadrons would have remained in North Africa, out of reach of the Germans. Under the original applications of the armistice, there would have been only one naval force based in European France, and that would have been merely "a police division," made up of light craft. But with the ports of Casablanca, Mers-el-Kebir, Algiers, etc., all directly on the coast, at the mercy of another British attack, the remaining capital ships of the French Navy—including the *Dunkerque* when she was temporarily repaired—took cover under the protection of the powerful coastal batteries of Toulon. They thus came nearer to the German forces in the Occupied Zone.

The French Navy, driven out of its Atlantic bases by the Germans, and then out of its African bases by the English, had nowhere to go but Toulon. And there, by their very nearness, they offered a constant temptation to the Germans—a temptation to which the Germans finally succumbed on November 27, 1942, when they attempted to get their hands on it.

---

[12] This agreement did not take in merchant ships. All French merchantmen immobilized in the Suez Canal were seized on July 18. It was neither the first nor the last violation of the international treaty signed at Constantinople in 1888.

PART II

CHAPTER 14

Naval Politics Under the Armistice

In order to understand the sentiment that motivated the French Navy from 1940 until late 1943, it is necessary to know the peculiar conditions under which it functioned after the armistice.

It was not the first occasion in modern times that France had been occupied by foreign troops. In 1815 and again in 1870 victorious invaders had been stationed in the country for long periods. France herself had occupied part of Germany after 1918.

But these occupations were different. They came into effect as the result of treaties ending wars, and affected the people themselves very little. Mainly they were established to guarantee the execution of the terms of the treaty, such as the payment of a war indemnity or the reparation of damages.

But in 1940 there was no treaty of peace, and there could be none as long as the war lasted. The Franco-German armistice was purely military in nature, with no provisions for the continued economy of the country, or the establishment of frontiers, or the return of prisoners. All these matters were left for settlement in the final peace treaty. Legally a state of war continued and diplomatic relations had not been reestablished,[1] even though the guns had ceased firing. If Germany suspected the French of circumventing the armistice conventions, she could at any time reopen hostilities—and this

---

[1] There was an ambassador of the German Government, Otto Abetz, at Paris; he was the only ambassador who had not followed the French Government to Vichy. But there was no French embassy at Berlin—only a transient envoy who looked after the welfare of French prisoners. Anything in the nature of diplomatic business was transacted by the military with the armistice commission.

was a threat she often made during the next four years. But if France had a complaint against Germany, there was nothing she could do about it, because she had been disarmed and all her strategic points were occupied.

Vae victis—woe to the vanquished—was as true in 1940 as when the Gallic chieftain Brennus captured Rome.

The armistice had been intended to last only a few months; instead it was to last almost four years. During that time it was necessary to provide the 40,000,000 Frenchmen in the homeland with a living, not counting the 60,000,000 inhabitants of the colonies overseas who depended more or less upon France. The purely military clauses of the armistice had no concern with such civil problems. Administrative matters, the public safety, employment for the unemployed, the equitable distribution of food—all these questions had to be taken up with the occupying power. Hence constant negotiations were required with the armistice commission and between other corresponding French and German organizations—negotiations even at the Government level, and once, at Montoire, between the Heads of State themselves. It was in connection with the Montoire conference that a press communique mentioned for the first time the word "collaboration," for which Marshal Pétain was later reproached. As a matter of fact, the term was used in connection with a meeting totally devoid of the usual connotations of the word.

The British, and the few French who had joined up with them, sternly disapproved of these contacts with the "enemy." This was easy to condemn over the radio. But with the majority of Frenchmen under the heel of the invaders, such contacts were necessary for France to continue to live.

It was not necessary for Germany to reopen hostilities in order to bring pressure on the French. There was the daily cost of the German occupation —300,000,000 to 400,000,000 francs—as well as the numerous taxes the Germans placed on French trade and produce. Then there was the demarcation line between Occupied France and the Free Zone. Similar lines of demarcation between North Korea and South Korea, and between East Germany and West Germany, have shown the advantages that can be gained from such divisions. To cross the line of demarcation in France, a German permit was necessary. A great many French government officials, engineers, industrial leaders, etc., had urgent business which frequently required crossing this line. Ordinarily crossing permits were fairly easy to obtain. But if at any time the Germans wanted to apply pressure, all they had to do was to delay or halt the traffic across the line.[2]

For example, in December, 1940, when public opinion compelled the

---

[2] The Russian squeeze on Berlin, which forced the democracies to institute the Berlin airlift, is an excellent example of this sort of economic pressure.

dismissal of Laval from the Government, not one Minister or French official was allowed to cross the line for several weeks. No correspondence, official or private, went through. Since the service units of the various government agencies and the heads of many companies were scattered throughout both zones, the nation's administration completely broke down. It was only after patient and repeated argument that the French succeeded in getting the armistice commission to relax its stranglehold.

There was also the question of the location of the national government. Paris has always been the hub of all government administration, all large business enterprises, all main highways, and all railroads. Marshal Pétain had hoped that after the armistice the Germans would permit the Government to return to the capital—the only place, he believed, from which it was possible to effectively govern the country. His request for a demilitarized enclave, free of German troops, was refused—and refused time and time again. Of necessity the Government remained at Vichy, the only city in the south of France with sufficient hotels and other accommodations to provide lodgings and office space for all the government personnel. That provisional capital was to last for four years. Yet Marshal Pétain, as an old soldier, always kept his trunks piled up in his room, ready to move at any time.

Vichy was the temporary capital of a country cut in two—or even in three or four parts, if you count the prohibited zones of Alsace and the sections north of the Somme which Hitler intended to annex or to separate from France. In fact the northern zone was much more in the hands of the German occupation authorities than it was under the French Government. Nowhere did the French flag fly; the only uniforms seen on the street were those of the Wehrmacht. Directly or indirectly the Germans controlled the press, the radio, the police, the railroads, and the censors. The prefects and the mayors were responsible to them for public safety, and the task of these prefects and mayors in defending the interests of the people was more than difficult—it was heroic.

In addition to the Franco-German armistice commission at Wiesbaden, there were numerous other organizations in Paris with whom the French authorities had to deal—the German military command, the embassy, the economic departments. Unfortunately, when arrangements were completed with one of these organizations, some other organization was likely to come forward with still other demands.

Life in the southern or Free Zone was entirely different. Instead of a populace gloomy and sullen, overrun by foreign uniforms, people here were animated and exultant in being able to return to traditional standards. From sheer need to demonstrate outwardly their love of country, the

MARSHAL PÉTAIN AND ADMIRAL DARLAN.

ADMIRAL
DE LABORDE

THE ARMISTICE
COMMISSION AT
WIESBADEN. *Admiral Michelier,
Chief of the
French naval delegation, conferring with Kapitän
zur See Wever,
representing the
German Navy,
September 1940.*

schools and youth groups everywhere adopted the ceremony of hoisting the colors in the morning and lowering them at night, thus imitating what is done by all the navies of the world. This piece of France was small, but it was home. And it had the sea at its back, and, beyond that, the whole colonial empire.

That the legitimacy of the Vichy Government could ever be questioned occurred to no one in France or in any of the other leading powers of the world. All the foreign embassies had followed it to Vichy, and in turn it had diplomatic representatives in each of the neutral countries. On July 10, 1940, by an overwhelming majority—87 per cent of all those present— the united assembly of senators and deputies had given to it "all powers of the Government of the Republic, under the signature and authority of Marshal Pétain, for the purpose of promulgating, by one or several acts, the new constitution of the French State." What had happened on that July 10 was the abdication of the Government which was considered, rightly or wrongly, to have been responsible for the defeat.

Later, there were to be many long-winded discussions concerning that vote. But at the moment the 40,000,000 Frenchmen of the homeland, in the Free Zone as well as in the Occupied Zone, were not giving much thought to Parliament. They had too many worries. And the soldiers and the sailors, whether they had returned from German captivity or English detention, thought only of licking their wounds.

After the armistice of 1871, the triumphant Prussian Government had required that a national election be held in France; that election had resulted in an enormous majority in favor of the ratification of the armistice and of peace. There is no reason to believe that a similar election held in 1940 would not have produced the same result. But there was no way to hold such an election, with the country occupied and so many soldiers still prisoners. It was equally impossible to legislate by the customary parliamentary debates. Marshal Pétain, who was already 85 years old, could only rely on himself and his Ministers and on a National Council of approximately 200 persons working behind closed doors.

The civilian ministries—Finance, Industrial Production, Education, etc. —had reassembled the bulk of their personnel at Paris, retaining only a skeleton organization at Vichy.

On the contrary, the national defense ministries were located almost entirely at Vichy or in the vicinity. The French Admiralty had established itself in a modest hotel, the Helder, which it arranged like a ship and manned entirely by sailors. At Toulon it had been possible to set up a powerful communication network, practically the only one that could operate reliably with French overseas possessions. In times of crisis, it was the Navy which insured the transmission of government messages—a fact which led ill-disposed persons to believe that the Navy was directing politics.

Permission thus to resume radio traffic between French authorities had, as a matter of fact, been granted by the armistice commission only after the Navy turned over to the Germans and the Italians the keys to all its codes and ciphers. It was only natural that the conquerors should want to be in a position at any moment to decipher all the French radio messages. People who later criticized certain messages forgot that the enemy too could read them like an open book. Naturally the French Navy kept for themselves a secure system for the transmission of messages over French landwires. Moreover, when it was imperative that a message be kept secret, it was not even put down in writing, but was delivered orally by an officer messenger.

The terms of the armistice allowed the French Navy only one "division of police," of several thousand men. All ships other than those needed for this purpose were to be disarmed, with crews reduced to practically caretaker status and all other personnel sent back to civilian life. The affair at Mers-el-Kebir changed all this, and on July 4 the requirement for the Fleet to be disarmed was cancelled. Consequently, following the British aggression, all combat vessels at Toulon and in the African ports were allowed to have crews large enough to man and fight their ships.

On July 15, while the Vichy Government was still considering the matter of an air reprisal against Gibraltar, the German armistice commission presented a letter from Hitler requesting authorization for the German forces to occupy all the ports and bases of French North Africa. It had been less than three weeks since the armistice had been signed, and not fifteen days since British shells had fallen on the French Fleet at Mers-el-Kebir, and already the Germans, reopening the whole matter, wanted also to go into Africa. If this permission had been granted and the planes of the Luftwaffe had landed at Port Lyautey and Dakar in July, 1940, the war's whole future aspect might have been radically changed.

Naturally, however, the reply of the French Government was a decided "No!" Marshal Pétain even went so far as to order Admiral Darlan to be prepared to resume the fight in Africa if the Germans violated the armistice terms.[3] Instantly the German attitude stiffened. They required a stricter interpretation and execution of the armistice clauses—an attitude which ended only when France was liberated.

War, it has been said, is but a continuation of politics by other means. The state in which France found itself after the war was neither war nor peace, yet it very definitely provided "another means" of pursuing politics and of achieving one's aim. But, in the case of France, what were these politics? And what part did the Navy play in them?

---

[3] Paul Baudouin—*Neuf Mois Au Gouvernment* ("Nine Months With The Government"), Paris, 1948. Pages 277, 278.

France had requested the armistice just as a drowning man grabs at a straw. With the United States not in the war and with Russia practically an ally of Germany, the French expected that shortly after the armistice the conflict would end in a compromise between Britain and Germany. Any such compromise would largely be governed by German considerations. Hence grew the policy of certain French political leaders—of whom Pierre Laval was the most representative—of conceding advantages to Germany in order to gain favors in return. Up until 1944 Laval was convinced that through secret weapons which he knew the Germans were developing, Germany would win the war; in fact he never changed his mind.

However, when in late 1940 the Germans had not been able to land in England and the British were as determined as ever to fight to the end, French opinion at the Government level began generally to change. England, with its seapower, could—as the French Navy consistently argued—hold on for a long time. At the same time she was not strong enough to overcome Germany on the land, so the latter could hold on there for a long time also. For France the problem became one of outlasting the conflict. From this stemmed a home policy of building up the nation's economy, and a foreign policy of safeguarding the national heritage, caught as France was between the British hammer and the German anvil. It was a policy of neutrality and of waiting, with due respect for the terms of the armistice. But it was also a policy of alert watching. Watching international events in order to take advantage of any opportunities that presented themselves.

In this program the Navy had an essential task to perform. Differently from the other governmental departments, which were absorbed with the grievances of the Occupied Zone, the Navy was oriented entirely toward the sea and the empire.[4] As the only effective weapon remaining to France, it not only maintained the ties between France and the overseas possessions, but also constituted the best safeguard against undertakings in French ter-

---

[4] An odd situation arose at the military ports of the Occupied Zone after their capture. While the admirals and the majority of the line officers were taken away to military prisons, the officers of the other corps were permitted to stay at their posts, where they did their utmost to protect the civilian personnel and the families of absent sailors. At Cherbourg the chief medical officer of the naval hospital assumed the functions of Senior French Naval Officer Present. At Brest, at first, it was a senior naval paymaster. At Lorient, it was an admiral in the Engineer Corps.

At Brest, as an example, a certain number of naval officers had succeeded in getting themselves assigned, with their men, to the shipyard. They constituted a French unit which the officers of the German Navy, arriving in the Army's freight cars, regarded with easy tolerance.

Thus it became possible to reestablish veritable Navy commandants in the occupied ports who, from 1942 on, came under the authority of a Director of Naval Services in the Occupied Zone, with headquarters at Paris. The men who occupied these unenviable posts waged a continuing and amazingly successful war with the armistice authorities in their effort to prevent the deportation of navy workmen, who otherwise would have been forced to do obligatory work in Germany.

ritory which would violate the terms of the armistice, and, inevitably, bring interference from the Axis. To carry out its mission, the Navy continually sought to obtain greater and greater exceptions to the original disarmament clauses. Thus, instead of the three or four thousand sailors originally permitted as a maximum in July, 1940, the Navy had increased its authorized personnel strength to 75,000 men in November, 1942. And this was without counting a considerable number of the noncombatant corps, more or less reduced to civilian status.[5]

The Navy's personnel was not only sizable, it was also highly select. The "fleet in being" which it manned was from half to three-quarters, depending on types, of all the combat units of the Fleet.[6] The remaining ships were in caretaker status, with skeleton crews. Although the Navy, by the terms of the armistice, had had to declare the amount of fuel stocks on hand, the Germans had not seized them, but had merely limited themselves to controlling their use. By careful economies, the Navy was able not only to provide escorts for its convoys, but also to give the combatant ships a minimum of training up to November of 1942.

After Mers-el-Kebir, the combat ships of the French Navy were deployed generally as follows:

(1) At Toulon, the main squadron, commanded by Admiral de Laborde. This consisted of the battleship *Strasbourg*, 3 heavy cruisers, 2 light cruisers, 10 super-destroyers, 3 destroyers, and a number of submarines. Three naval air squadrons were stationed at Berre, near Marseilles.

(2) At Oran or Mers-el-Kebir, 1 super-destroyer, 6 destroyers, and a dozen submarines. Four naval air squadrons were based at Lartigue-Oran.

(3) At Dakar, the battleship *Richelieu*, 3 light cruisers, 3 super-destroyers, and 7 or 8 submarines. Five naval air squadrons were stationed at Ouakam.

(4) At Casablanca, the battleship *Jean Bart* (uncompleted, but capable of firing), 1 cruiser, 9 super-destroyers and destroyers, and 12 submarines. Four naval air squadrons were stationed at Port Lyautey.

In addition, small naval forces, consisting of light craft and submarines, were based at Beirut, Lebanon, at Fort-de-France, Martinique, at Diego Suarez, Madagascar, and at Saigon, Indochina. Also at Fort-de-France was

---

[5] In order not to have them counted as military personnel, the Navy renamed its Engineer Corps and classified them as civilians. The same was done with personnel on board ships in a caretaker status. The officers attached to those ships wore their uniforms, but without insignia of rank, and with black buttons instead of gilded ones.

[6] Attention should be called to the fact an oath of special loyalty to Marshal Pétain, as Chief of State, was required of all officers, government officials, and civil servants, as has always been done in troubled periods in the history of France. This oath was in addition to the normal oath of allegiance, which required obedience to legitimate authority; the oath now taken to Marshal Pétain personally bound the officer on his word of honor. This fact must not be forgotten in studying the events of November, 1942.

the *Béarn,* a former battleship that had been converted into an aircraft carrier.

The principal group in caretaker status was at Toulon. It consisted of 2 heavy cruisers, 14 super-destroyers or destroyers, and a dozen or so submarines. To this group was added, in the spring of 1942, the battleship *Dunkerque,* brought back from Mers-el-Kebir to be repaired.

Finally some 60 sloops, torpedo boats, and patrol boats were scattered along the lines of communication between the ports of the Free Zone and North Africa, Morocco, Dakar, Madagascar, Indochina, and the West Indies. Their duty was to escort French commercial shipping moving between those ports.

The German or Italian "control," the mention of which in the armistice terms had so disturbed the English, was practically nonexistent except on paper or at the shore establishments. The Axis inspectors were never lied to; their questions were answered and they were shown what they asked to see—but no more. They had the good taste to forego visiting any commissioned combatant ship, where the routine on board functioned pretty much as usual.

In the face of a Navy so little disarmed and so little controlled, the armistice commissions were baffled. Would not this fleet some day shift base to Africa and turn against the Axis? Accordingly the Germans and, particularly, the Italians systematically opposed any requests made by the French Admiralty. But when informed that the changes requested were absolutely necessary in order to protect the colonies against British encroachment, there was nothing they could do but consent.

The standing order of the Government, strictly carried out by the Navy, was, "Defend the empire against anyone." The word "defend" had a double meaning. Applied to the English, it meant returning blow for blow on the spot, but without spreading or generalizing the conflict, and particularly never taking the initiative. It also applied to the Germans, but in their case the French would have fired with gusto, had any occasion been provided. The Germans, however, gave no such occasion, as they had numerous other ways of exerting pressure without resorting to arms.

In addition to building up the Fleet's fighting potential, the Navy accomplished certain other little things of an unpublicized nature. By increased shipments of war materials, often without the authorization of the armistice commissions, they gradually built up the strength of the Army of Africa. Cautiously and cunningly—as, for instance, by granting concessions which the Germans could have taken anyway—the Navy sought primarily to maintain a maximum of naval forces. Sooner or later, it was sure, these would once more be useful to the country.

The Navy had also acquired another and heavy responsibility at the time of the armistice—that of administering the merchant marine.

France has always needed maritime imports in order to live. But after the armistice and occupation, the English had set up a blockade of the French coasts. To try to break the blockade by force would merely have been playing the enemy's game, even if the French Navy had had the power to do it. On the other hand, France could not do without the food and raw materials the colonies supplied, and the colonies could not do without the manufactured products of the home country. Hence the Navy had to maintain these vital ties between metropolitan France and the empire.

One other thing occurred which was to add to the prestige of the Navy, and yet at the same time lead to its being accused of too close affiliation with what has been called the "Vichy regime." For the senior admiral of the Navy was to become practically the Chief of Government, with a heavy share in all the formidable political responsibilities that go with that position.

At the beginning of May, 1940, Marshal Pétain, on a visit to Maintenon, had been struck by the orderliness and efficiency of the French Admiralty. A few weeks later, when the Marshal became head of the State, he selected Admiral Darlan as Minister of the Navy.

From June to December of 1940, Darlan was responsible only for the Navy. To Admiral Auphan, whom he had brought with him as Chief of Staff, he entrusted the management of the merchant marine, whose offices had been integrated with or joined to those of the Admiralty. For his own particular responsibilities Darlan took over the safeguarding of the war navy, the defense of the empire, and the work of obtaining the release of 12,000 sailors still held as prisoners of war by the Germans.

But on December 13, 1940, at the end of a session of the Ministers, Marshal Pétain had each member submit to him a letter of resignation. When the meeting reconvened a few moments later, he announced in the grim and glacial tone so typical of him at times, that all resignations were refused except those of Mr. Laval and one other member.

There was complete amazement at this action, to be known later as the "coup of December 13." But the Marshal was merely checking the "Ship of State" in what he, as well as public opinion, considered a headlong rush onto the rocks.

The following day a particularly irksome task fell to the lot of the Admiral of the Fleet. Pierre Laval had connived with the Germans for Marshal Pétain to journey to Paris in order to receive the ashes of the son of Napolean Bonaparte—the "Eaglet"—who had died at Vienna in 1832. This theatrical gesture had appealed to Hitler as promising possible political advantages. However, Marshal Pétain refused to go to German-occupied Paris and be received with honors by German troops. Someone else would have to substitute for the Marshal in order to avoid further aggravation of the Germans, who had already been angered by Laval's dismissal. Darlan was designated. Thus he had his first contact with the high officials of the Reich.

Laval had been replaced as Minister of Foreign Affairs by Pierre Étienne Flandin, a former President of the Council. However, Flandin could not establish effective relations with the Germans, still furious over the ouster of Laval. Relations became so strained that it was feared the Germans would take over the entire country. The Wehrmacht recalled its personnel on leave. The previous autumn General Weygand had been forced to leave his government post and go to Africa; now Flandin in his turn had to leave.

At this critical moment, Marshal Pétain remembered his sailor Cabinet member, Admiral Darlan. On February 12, 1941, he appointed Darlan to be Vice President of the Council—that is to say, Chief of Government—and also Minister of Foreign Affairs. Darlan still retained his post as Minister of the Navy. Within the next few weeks he was also given the additional posts of Minister of the Interior and Minister of Information. That autumn he was also to be made interim Minister of War. Never before in the history of France had so much power been concentrated in the hands of any single person.

One immediate result was that many naval officers suddenly found themselves called upon to take over some rather unexpected functions. The admiral had confidence in them. They were seen at the Ministry of the Interior, as chiefs of various departments, and even at the headquarters of the Paris police. Sardonic critics complained that two-thirds of France was overrun by the Germans, and the remaining third by the Navy.

The majority of the officers so detailed acquitted themselves with honor in carrying out their heavy responsibilities under the occupation. Several made the acquaintance of German jails. Many government departments carry to this day the imprint of their work and methods.

In his new position Darlan promptly found himself faced with some of the difficulties that had defeated his predecessors. At his first personal meeting with Hitler, at Ferrières-sur-Epte, on December 25, he received a broadside of insulting remarks, which, however, according to the German interpreter Paul Schmidt, "seemed to make as little impression on him as green seas sliding off the oilskins of an old sea dog."

But facing the music wasn't enough. France had to live, and the Germans were literally strangling her. Darlan took the reins in his hands. Only by direct contact, he believed, could the stranglehold be loosened. Under these circumstances there developed an unavoidable foreign policy, marked by concessions and speeches quite disagreeable to French ears, which brought him to his second meeting with Hitler—this time at Berchtesgaden—on May 12, 1941.

The Germans were then at the height of their power. The Balkans campaign had ended in triumph. In Greece the English had been thrown back to the sea.

Darlan had come as a petitioner. He was promptly and curtly told that he would receive favors exactly in proportion to the favors he would give.

Darlan had already granted the Luftwaffe authority to land their planes on the airfields of Syria. As this was en route to Iraq, where the Germans were intervening, Darlan considered it in the same light as a belligerent vessel putting into a neutral port for a limited stop—something universally permitted under international law.

But now the Germans wanted something more—a great deal more. What they really were after was French Africa, and, above all, Bizerte, for which both the Italian command and Rommel clamored. In actuality, no one could have stopped them from taking the territory by force if they had wanted to do this.

The discussion was now shifted to Paris, where it was renewed with bitterness by both sides. On May 27 Darlan seemed to be on the point of consenting to a protocol which in effect would have opened Bizerte and the African ports to the Germans. But at the last moment he inserted an escape clause which made the use of the French African ports contingent upon concessions which Darlan was sure the Germans would not make.

Although this was the clause that later was to save everything, the Germans seemed at the time to regard it as a mere formality. But the French leaders in Africa—Weygand, Esteva, Pierre Boisson, etc.—who had been called to Vichy for a conference, violently opposed the protocol. Darlan let himself be abused unmercifully without saying a word in his own defense, so confident was he in the escape clause. Finally the French Government, *including Darlan,* unanimously refused to carry out the terms of the protocol until the Germans themselves granted all the concessions which had been requested. All that the Germans ever got out of the protocol were a few shipments made in the Mediterranean by French vessels for the Axis account.[7]

---

[7] These shipments, supposedly for the benefit of the Axis, have given rise to so many fantastic tales, that they need clarifying. Negotiated on the economic rather than the military level, they involved little more than the following:

(From March, 1941, to November, 1942)—a monthly shipment of 25,000 to 30,000 tons of African phosphates to Germany and Italy. The Axis replaced all fuel and lubricating oils consumed in the shipping, and paid for the phosphates themselves in food products badly needed by the French populace. These purely commercial shipments were the price France had to pay to be allowed to operate the remainder of its shipping in the provisioning of France.

(Between January and March of 1942)—the shipment of nonmilitary merchandise (3,000 tons of food and 78 trucks, in all) from Marseilles to Tunis, where the Axis took over to forward to Rommel's army. These shipments were immediately stopped the first time a ship was torpedoed. As a gauge of how much these small shipments benefited Axis operations in Africa, it must be realized that the Axis armies in Libya required from 150,000 to 200,000 tons every month. The French also exchanged 500 tons of diesel oil in storage in Tunisia for the same amount delivered to Toulon.

Neutral countries, such as Sweden or Switzerland, which were not under the yoke of an armistice, probably contributed much more to the German economy. In addition

Darlan's real objective was to gain time—always to gain time. In effect he had his eyes glued on the calendar. He had learned confidentially from the French military attaché in Roumania that Hitler was going to attack Russia. That information completely swept away any lingering doubts Darlan might have had as to how the war would end. To him it was only a matter of time until the Wehrmacht became bogged down in the Russian morasses. After that France could again breathe.

The German offensive against Russia, launched June 22, 1941, was brought to a halt in October by the severe winter weather. Meanwhile, with the Germans fully engaged in the east, Pétain and Darlan consolidated their position in the west. In a November interview at Saint-Florentin, Göring angrily inquired of the old Marshal, "Is it you or we who are the conquerors?" Darlan kept his *sang-froid*—and also his policy of watchful waiting. He was more than ever convinced that, for France, passive resistance was the best policy, especially when the December 7 attack on Pearl Harbor finally brought the United States into the war.

Passive resistance was not achieved, however, without small services, generally disagreeable, having to be rendered to the Germans; nor without tragedies, either, as the Germans carried out bloody reprisals each time one of their military or civil personnel was the victim of some infuriated Frenchman.

So the year 1941 went by without a single Axis soldier being able to put a foot on French African soil. And now that they were beset with troubles in their Russian venture, there was even less probability that they would ever be able to do so in the future. Thanks to Darlan, the "void" in Africa would not be filled until November, 1942—and then by the Americans and British, not by the Axis.

Sooner or later the Germans would inevitably get rid of Darlan. He succeeded in holding on for some time. In April, 1942, however, the German embassy sent word that it no longer wanted to have any official dealings with him. Under pressure, Marshal Pétain dismissed him from the Government and returned Laval to power. However, as Marshal Pétain did not wish to trust the administration of the armed forces to Laval, Darlan remained as Commander in Chief of the Army, Navy, and Air Force, and responsible as such only to Pétain himself. This bypassing of the new Chief of Government was in truth a rather clever scheme on the part of the old Marshal—and something that could have been done only in those troubled times.

In leaving the government, Darlan had also given up his post as Minister of the Navy. The selection of a successor would be necessary. But Darlan

---

Sweden granted passage to German troops en route to northern Norway and also to Finland, later on. Swedish naval forces also escorted the German cargo ships carrying iron ore in the Baltic.

had anticipated just such an eventuality ever since the arguments over the May, 1941, protocol, and had privately fixed on Admiral Auphan as his successor. To prepare him for that position he had had Auphan designated as Chief of Naval Operations in addition to his regular duties of administering the merchant marine. Thereafter Auphan had been responsible for all military and economic tasks which devolved upon the French Admiralty. He was Darlan's executive officer in all matters—but an executive officer with a relatively free hand, since Darlan had three or four other Ministries in his charge. It was only natural that Auphan, as second in command, should succeed him.

Auphan, however, was not inclined to become a member of any government directed by Mr. Laval. He firmly refused the offered post. Finally, after two or three days in which no other acceptable substitute had been found, Darlan went personally to Auphan and reminded him of the pledge they had together made to the British at Bordeaux in June of 1940—that no ships of the French Navy would ever be allowed to fall into the hands of the Germans, and that if such an eventuality seemed likely, they would be destroyed first. Darlan advised Auphan that it was his patriotic duty to accept the post in order to reassure the British, who were already suspicious of the new government of Laval.

Auphan accordingly accepted, but only after writing personally to Marshal Pétain, asking for assurances that the lives of the sailors "would not be needlessly risked in pursuing a policy too strongly dominated by foreign influences."

By taking such a firm stand the new Minister of the Navy immediately became the leader in the Cabinet of all those who were morally opposed to the policies of the new government headed by Laval.

To those who knew Pierre Laval, there was no question about his personal patriotism, courage, and devotion to the public welfare; his tragedy lay in the fact that he let himself be influenced more by sentiment than reason. Ever since the defeat of the famous Hoare-Laval agreements of 1935, he had strongly disliked the English. All he talked about was depriving them of their fertile territory of Nigeria. Firmly convinced that collaboration with Germany would be to the best interests of France in the Europe of the future, he was determined to pursue this policy to the bitter end.

Admiral Auphan, on the contrary, was opposed to such collaboration with Germany, and equally opposed to measures that would result in any form of civil war among the French people. He was an advocate of adhering strictly to the stated terms of the armistice—and of "watchful waiting" until new developments materialized. His known sentiments at times brought forth from Laval, at Cabinet meetings, such sarcastic remarks as, "Hey, you over there! You don't have to say anything; we already know what you are going to say. You still believe in an English victory!"

To Laval, such an assumption represented the height of ignorance.

For France that year of 1942 became one of increasing difficulty. Up till then the conflict had been confined to Europe only. Thanks to continuous negotiations with the armistice commission, as well as to a few artful tricks, such as the May, 1941, protocol, France had gained breathing room and was beginning to reorganize herself. But now, with the entry of Russia, the United States, and Japan into the arena, the war had taken on added impetus and was extending around the globe. Up until this time, the leaders of the German Reich had felt almost certain of winning. Now they began to fear that victory was escaping them. Faced with a France that was sturdily recovering, they became jealous, demanding, and aggressive.

At the same time France had to face new difficulties on every side: American pressure in the French West Indies; a Free French blockade of Djibouti; English aggression at Madagascar; recurring incidents at sea with the British; and Japan's requisitioning of French merchant ships in Indochina. Pinched for manpower to continue the war, Germany was raiding the personnel of the industries in all the European countries she had occupied.

The greatest reservoir of skilled labor anywhere in the world, probably, is that represented by the mariners of the nations of the world. By adroit negotiations and by a few secondary concessions, the French Navy had secured exemptions not only for its increased naval personnel but for the sailors of its merchant marine as well. It had even done more than that. Its navy yards had had a force of some thirty or thirty-five thousand skilled civilian workmen. The Navy had also managed to retain these except for some small token groups of volunteers headed by their own engineers—and these, too, the Navy generally managed to retrieve on some excuse or other.

As for the personnel of its merchant marine, whether afloat or ashore, the French Admiralty made special arrangements with the armistice commissioners, as well as with the Chief of the French Government, so that not a single officer or man could be drafted by Germany. Once, just prior to the departure from Paris of a trainload of drafted workers for Germany, the representatives of the Navy were seen, papers in hand, discussing the matter with the occupation authorities. The result was that two office employees of a steamship company, who had been drafted through error, were removed from the train.

While the great majority of the sailors, faithful to Marshal Pétain, busied themselves supporting their countrymen, and thus served as a shield to France, there were certain others, absent from the country at the time of the armistice or who had left afterwards to continue the fight, who were serving her as a sword.

CHAPTER 15

The Free French Naval Forces

The Free French Naval Forces (abbreviated F.F.N.F.) were born at Gibraltar on June 28, 1940, from the romantic circumstances of a meeting between an admiral who had escaped from France and one of those adventurous figures who seem to emerge from all wars.

Vice Admiral Emile Muselier, Navy Commanding Officer at Marseilles at the beginning of hostilities, had been placed on the retired list on October 21, 1939, as a result of disagreements with Admiral Darlan, his superior officer. Being a retired officer, with no further responsibilities, he decided to leave France at the time of the armistice and go to England to join with the British in the fight. He had left Marseilles on June 23 on an English collier bound for Gibraltar.

Lying at Gibraltar was the cargo ship *Rhin.* Ostensibly she was just another freighter; actually she was employed at times on very special missions by the French Secret Services.[1] The radio officer on the *Rhin* was a certain Claude Péri, who should have lived in the era of the buccaneers instead of the 20th century. Always armed to the teeth and with his pockets bulging with explosives, he exerted an extraordinary influence over the personnel under him. It was he who provided Admiral Muselier with providential assistance in starting the F.F.N.F.

Péri started by stirring up a lively brawl on the *Rhin,* at the end of which he was alone on board with six other men, the rest of the crew having fled the ship. The *Rhin* then joined with three other French cargo ships in the port, and an auxiliary vessel of the Navy, the *Président Houduce,* in forming the first force of the new movement.

It is worth noting that the *Rhin* never was any part of the F.F.N.F. which later operated under De Gaulle. Péri, who had a fiery disposition, never took kindly to the orders which one of General de Gaulle's officers tried to give him. Instead, he offered his services to the English, and the *Rhin* went through the rest of the war under the name of the HMS *Fidelity.*

---

[1] For example, the *Rhin* had just completed the mission of blowing up the German freighter *Corrientes,* which had taken refuge in the harbor of Las Palmas, Canary Islands. Swimming in from offshore, French underwater teams had placed limpet mines against the freighter's hull. (See *H.M.S. Fidelity,* by Marcel Jullian.)

Back at Gibraltar, Admiral Muselier, as soon as he had organized the first units of the new French Navy, took off for England. As the plane carrying him circled over the harbor in its takeoff, Admiral Muselier looked down and noticed that the ships which had joined him were flying the identical national ensign as the only other French freighter present—which had refused to join. That fact, he said later, suggested the idea for a special, distinctive emblem. He decided that his ships would fly at the flagstaff an ensign with a blue field and a white diamond-shaped center on which was imposed the Cross of Lorraine in red—"in opposition to the German swastika." The Cross of Lorraine was eventually adopted by all those who, under the name of "Free French," were to join with General de Gaulle.

Admiral Muselier arrived in London on June 30, and was received that same day by the First Sea Lord of the British Navy, and, in the evening, by General de Gaulle. The General immediately offered him the command of the naval and air forces in the "Legion" he was in the process of creating.

It is traditional that an Army man, accustomed to working with huge drafts of civilian conscripts, who in peacetime return to their normal civilian occupations after their conscript period, finds it difficult to understand the Navy, with its highly trained, technically educated, longtime career personnel. In addition, General de Gaulle had a deep personal sense of being called to save France in her desperate hour, and was impatient with anyone or anything that seemed to interfere with that mission. It was inevitable that differences would arise between the Navy man and the Army man, even though the admiral found that his actual command was confined to the naval contingent of the Free French Forces.

Anyone would presume that the new F.F.N.F. would have drawn many recruits from among the 20,000 sailors who were then in England after retreating from France. Many had fought heroically at the side of the English or had escaped with their boats for the sole purpose of continuing the war. But the Free French propaganda[2] with its attacks on the legal government of France, only succeeded in recruiting a few hundred men from all those French sailors who had been quartered on shore. Of the crews of French ships in the ports, the F.F.N.F. obtained not a single recruit.

The crews of these ships in English ports amounted to around 12,000 men. Their will to continue the fight might perhaps have triumphed over their sense of discipline if the British had not perpetrated the tragedy of

---

[2] ". . . Since it is proved that the men in power at Vichy are but tools subject to the will of the enemy, I solemnly declare in the name of France that the Empire must not comply with their disastrous orders. . . ." From General de Gaulle's broadcast speech of July 30, 1940.

Mers-el-Kebir and the seizure of the ships at Portsmouth and Plymouth. These actions almost killed the F.F.N.F. in the bud.

There were, of course, other factors as well. Rightly or wrongly, there were wide differences of opinion over the personal characteristics of Admiral Muselier, and especially over his differences with Darlan. Men who were penned behind barbed wire, separated from their officers, and deprived of all news except through British sources, were naturally resentful of such treatment, which was no different essentially from that being experienced by their comrades in German prison camps.[3] It was but a natural defensive reaction on their part to distrust anyone who was apparently allied with their jailers. This reaction expressed itself in the camps by very active counterpropaganda against the British and the associates of General de Gaulle, primarily. Much less resentment was felt against Admiral Muselier, who had a far better understanding of the feelings of the restricted French sailors.

These men of the Navy asked themselves, where was the truth? Where did their duty lie?

Here and there were sincere and generous souls for whom these questions presented no problem at all. They either decided to continue the war to the death against the Germans, or they chose to remain in the path of discipline and obey a government dignified by the names of Pétain and Weygand.

But there were many, many others who did not find the issues so plainly resolved. Some would have remained with the F.F.N.F. if they had not had families in France to look after—families from whom they had had no news. Some few looked forward to being completely free of any of the military services with their traditional bonds of discipline. Still others were without any ties whatsoever, and were attracted by the promise of a new adventure. And there were officers who took the considered stand of refusing to consider any change until they could no longer do anything for the men of their crews who were so dependent upon them.

The sentiments of the officers on both sides cannot better be depicted, perhaps, than by reproducing the following sentences of an appeal sent out by the officers of the F.F.N.F., and the resulting reply to it.

> We appeal to the youth, to those who have faith, to those who believe that our country has not merited its present humiliation; to those who believe in the immortal destiny of the French people; to those who are prepared to act and, if necessary, to die, in order to create a new France, more radiant than ever . . .

---

[3] On July 7, 1941, a seaman of the *Savorgnan de Brazza* was killed by a British sentinel at Aintree for approaching too close to the stockade fence.

. . . . If, in spite of this appeal, you should all abandon us, we shall none the less maintain our faith in a final victory. . . . We shall remain proud of having been those who swore not to return to our native land until after having driven out the enemy; not to return to our harbors except in our victorious ships—those same ships which have never ceased to fly the eternal flag of France.

Such was the appeal sent out by the F.F.N.F. Equally noble was the reply of those among the interned survivors who rejected that appeal.

In order not to permit our ships to fall into the hands of the enemy, our crews accomplished prodigies. We left behind us only wrecks. We carried out that day, without doubt, the greatest sacrifice that can be made in a lifetime. Then we came to the English ports, seeking hospitality and friends —still expecting to supply ourselves and repair our ships, in order to continue the fight.

Then the armistice was signed. We experienced the same inner feelings of rebellion as you did when the news of the defeat was officially acknowledged. But we ascertained that the orders of the Government were being carried out by the Navy and the empire. We have taken the decision to do likewise. . . .

We are neither vanquished nor desperate men. Our faith in a final victory is equal to yours. England continues the war. Her insular position permits her to do so. We fervently hope that she will be victorious. But, we desire that a new France emerge from that victory. The Navy, which has not been defeated, which has remained intact and sound, which was, in short, an elite service, must have a major part in the task of restoring France while waiting to reenter the fight for the final liberation of our country. . . .

Although we have chosen to follow different paths, we fervently hope that we shall meet again some day. May it be within the bosom of a strong, independent, and united France, restored to its social, national, and Christian ideals by the energy of her sons, the virtues of her race, and the tribulations of her ordeal!

Such were the sentiments which sustained all French sailors, even up to the supreme sacrifice; sailors who, notwithstanding the different paths they followed, died for France—as did Bertrand de Saussine on one side and Honoré d'Estienne d'Orves on the other.[4]

Not only did the problem of personnel face the new Free French Navy,

---

[4] Lieutenant Commander de Saussine, commanding a submarine disabled and put out of action by the British off Gabon, French Equatorial Africa, voluntarily went down with his ship.

Lieutenant Commander d'Estienne d'Orves, after having joined the F.F.N.F., was executed as a spy by the Germans despite repeated attempts by the Vichy Government to save him.

but the problem of matériel as well, dependent as it was on the subsidies and the naval bases of the British.

On July 3, 1940, the personnel strength of the F.F.N.F. was about 400 men, of whom about a dozen were officers. Notwithstanding the intervening crises of Mers-el-Kebir and Dakar, by November a total of 3,100 men had been recruited from among those quartered in the camps. That source dried up when the last sailors loyal to the Government had been repatriated to France.[5] From then on, the only additional recruits joining the F.F.N.F. were volunteers escaped from France, recruited from overseas territories going over to the F.F.N.F., or men enlisted from the crews of French ships captured at sea by the English. From 3,100 in November, 1940, the F.F.N.F. grew to 4,700 on January 1, 1942, and to 5,314 by the following January. At the time of the American and British landings in North Africa, some 2,000 or 3,000 more men from the French naval forces in Africa came over to the new movement. The Free French recruiting methods to which the regular French Navy had so strongly objected came to an end when, on August 2, 1943, the F.F.N.F. was merged into the whole national liberation movement.

At the time of the merger, the F.F.N.F. had sustained a loss of 567 killed, dead, or missing—a percentage of 7.45 of the total personnel in the F.F.N.F.[6]

French men-of-war seized by the British while in English ports included two old battleships, two super-destroyers, two 1,500-ton destroyers, six torpedo boats of 600 tons, fifteen sloops, five submarines, twenty-three submarine chasers or motor torpedo boats, and seventy-one patrol vessels or auxiliary minesweepers, plus a host of tugs and smaller craft. In addition there were scooped up in the English harbors 140 merchant ships and fishing craft of all sizes, to which should be added some 60 French ships taken over by the British elsewhere up to November, 1942.

Very evidently the officers and sailors recruited by the F.F.N.F. were nowhere nearly sufficient to man all these vessels.

As a consequence, the old battleships *Paris* and *Courbet* remained tied up in English harbors throughout the war, as part of the antiaircraft system.

---

[5] Practically all the shore establishment personnel of Cherbourg, Brest, and Lorient had been repatriated to Casablanca by English transports before the July 3rd attacks on French ships.

[6] These figures have been taken from a report prepared by Captain Georges Jaquet, chief of staff of the F.F.N.F. from March 13, 1942, to August 7, 1943. Even more of the F.F.N.F. were to fall on the field of honor after the merger. It does not seem logical to give separate statistics for the F.F.N.F. after both sections of the Navy were united against the common enemy. This will explain apparent discrepancies in figures published elsewhere.

The *Paris* was manned by the English and the *Courbet* by the F.F.N.F., for whom it also served as station ship. Admiral Muselier's men also manned the super-destroyers *Triomphant* and *Léopard*. The British attempted to place the 1,500-ton destroyer *Mistral* and the 600-ton torpedo boats into service, manning them with English, Dutch, or Polish crews. But the *Branlebas,* with a British crew, broke in two during a storm in the winter of 1940, and the English gave up the idea of using the others. The *Melpomène,* returned to the F.F.N.F., was employed for two and a half years in escorting coastal convoys. The remaining four 600-ton torpedo boats were utilized as school ships, repair ships, or depot ships, as were the 1,500-ton destroyers and the sloops. Other than the super-destroyers, only the submarines and the fairly new sloops and patrol vessels had enough military value to be worth modernizing and manning.

As for the seized merchant ships, they were quickly incorporated into that multitude of cargo ships for which the English had such a pressing need. The crews of some of these had been kept on board under armed guard; others had been herded into internment camps near London. Many of these sailors refused to join their comrades who were actively continuing the war. Only one-third of these ships could be manned under the French flag; the rest put to sea with mixed crews. But even on such vessels flying the Union Jack, the crews in the majority of cases included a certain number of sailors from the F.F.N.F. or of the French merchant marine.

Of the 140 French ships seized by the English, 60 were lost during the war.

The first ship of the new F.F.N.F. to be lost in combat operations was the small patrol vessel *Poulmic,* which was blown up by a mine off the south coast of England on November 7, 1940.

Among the first French ships to reenter the fight were two submarines. One of these, the *Narval,* was with its division in the harbor of Sousse, Tunisia, at the time of the armistice. Without saying a word to anyone, her commanding officer, Lieutenant François Drogou, took her to sea and proceeded to Malta, from which place he later announced his accession to the Free French forces. His career was to be a short one. The *Narval,* due to return to Malta from her third war patrol on December 16, 1940, was never to return. It was not until October, 1957, that her wrecked hull—the bow split open by a mine—was found by Italian divers near the Kerkenna Islands, off the Tunisian coast.

The case of the *Rubis* was quite different.

This submarine minelayer had been operating with the British forces in the Norwegian campaign, during which it distinguished itself by its boldness and effectiveness. When, at the beginning of June, 1940, France had recalled all her submarines in the North Sea, the British had been so insistent in their request to retain the *Rubis,* that the ship had been left under their orders. At that time the Royal Navy was particularly short on minelayers.

When the armistice talks began, the *Rubis* was at its base in Dundee. At the urgent request of the British Admiralty, Vice Admiral Odend'hal consented to its making a last trip on June 21, to use up the supply of mines which it had just taken aboard. In return Admiral Phillips solemnly promised that the moment the armistice went into effect, the ship would be recalled, as otherwise its crew might run the risk of being treated as pirates if she were captured by the Germans.

That promise was not kept. On June 26, the day after the armistice went into effect, the *Rubis* was permitted to plant mines in the approaches leading to Trondheim. Two days later a German submarine chaser was lost on that minefield.

It was the *Rubis'* fourth victory, and the previous ones had already won the respect of the British Admiralty. All this, however, did not spare her the indignity of being forcibly seized, along with the other French ships, on July 3. Her seizure was particularly easy since all her crew had been granted a well-earned rest ashore.

After a week's deliberation, her commanding officer, Lieutenant Georges Cabanier,[7] overcame his feelings of rancor, and he and his men decided to continue the fight on board the ship which they had handled so well. Under his command, and later under Lieutenant Henri Rousselot, his successor, the *Rubis* was to make an exceptional record. She carried out 22 war patrols along the enemy coasts, always under perilous conditions. Reliable German sources later confirmed that she was responsible for the sinking of 17 enemy ships, 15 of which have been positively identified.

Outside of these two ships, which had joined the Free French fully manned and trained, only the colonial sloop *Savorgnan de Brazza* had been able to recruit an important portion of her former officers and crew. In the case of all others, it was necessary to supply practically all new complements, and their return to active service was relatively slow.

As early as July 14, 1940—"Bastille Day," the national holiday—Admiral Muselier created a battalion of *fusiliers marins*—"marines." The French who continued the fight took pleasure in seeing this successor to the famous marine brigade of 1914, *"Les demoiselles au pompon rouge"*— "the maidens with the red pompons." This new battalion, of about 200 or 300 men, the kernel of a future regiment, first were engaged in the overseas operations undertaken by General de Gaulle, at Dakar, at Gabon, and in Syria. Later they were seen at Bir Hacheim, under the command of Lieutenant Commander Hubert Amyot d'Inville, fighting this time with General Pierre Koenig's brigade in action against the Germans. Still later, after their

---

[7] Today a vice admiral.

merger with the forces of Africa, they took part in the campaign in Italy, in the landing in Provence, and in the final breakthrough in Germany which took them to the Danube.

Although Admiral Muselier disapproved morally of the expedition to Dakar, he provided General de Gaulle, for that undertaking, the colonial sloop *Savorgnan de Brazza,* the minesweeper sloops *Commandant Duboc* and *Commandant Dominé,* and the first of the patrol vessels to join him, the *Président Houduce.*

Later, after taking part in the blockade of Djibouti, the *Savorgnan de Brazza* was employed in escorting Atlantic convoys. Under the command of Commander André Jubelin,[8] it distinguished itself on March 19, 1943, by shooting down at least one German plane. The two minesweeper sloops did escort duty off the coast of Syria in 1942, along with the *Moqueuse* and the patrol vessel *Vikings.* The latter vessel was sunk off Saida, Lebanon, on April 18 by the *U-562.*

Admiral Muselier had planned to form a Mediterranean division of the super-destroyers *Léopard* and *Triomphant,* which were ready for service in late 1940, but organized them instead into a group called the "Free French Naval Forces of the Pacific." Administratively, these forces were under Rear Admiral Georges Thierry d'Argenlieu,[9] at Noumea, but for operations they came under the orders of Admiral Robert L. Ghormley, U.S. Navy, commanding the American forces in the South Pacific. Thierry d'Argenlieu's mission was in part political, as he also exercised the functions of High Commissioner of the Free French in the Pacific.

The *Triomphant* got underway for the Pacific, via Panama, in August, 1941. After performing escort duty between Australia and New Caledonia, she spent most of 1942 undergoing repairs in Sydney. The *Léopard* had to have extensive repairs, and did not get away from Greenock until June 30, 1942. However, she soon repaid the costs by assisting the HMS *Spey* and HMS *Pelican* in sinking the *U-136.* Unfortunately she was in a collision with the British corvette *Lowestoft* the next night, and spent two and a half months in the repair yards at Simonstown, South Africa. She left on No-

---

[8] Jubelin escaped from Saigon on April 11, 1940, on board a plane whose regular tanks could not hold the fuel necessary to reach Singapore. But Jubelin succeeded in reaching that city by pouring gasoline from spare cans into the fuel tanks while the plane was still in flight. Today he is a vice admiral.

[9] George Thierry d'Argenlieu, today an admiral, left the Navy after the first World War in order to enter the order of Carmelites. In June, 1940, he was a lieutenant commander in the Naval Reserve. Made a prisoner at Cherbourg, he escaped and reached Jersey. From there he crossed to England where he was among the first to join the Free French. The seizure of the ships on July 3 so disturbed him that he temporarily left the F.F.N.F. However, he changed his mind and played an important role in the operations against Dakar and Gabon before going out to the Pacific.

vember 12, under Commander Jules Evenou[10]—alias "Richard"—to carry out a raid on Reunion Island. The British had completed the conquest of Madagascar from its regular French garrison, and Reunion was the next French territory on the program. The *Léopard* arrived off Reunion on November 27 and secured its accession to the Free French on the 30th by the persuasive effect of 200 shells fired into the battery at Point Galets, where the defenders put up considerable resistance. Altogether the operation resulted in four deaths.

But the *Léopard* did not have enough steaming radius to be effective in the vast Pacific, so she was diverted to the Indian Ocean and then to the eastern Mediterranean where she was lost by grounding on May 27, 1943, while escorting a convoy along the coast of Cyrenaica.

Outside of the *Narval* and the *Rubis,* only three French submarines could be put back in service: the *Minerve,* the *Junon,* and the *Surcouf.*[11] This latter vessel was, at that time, the largest submarine in the world, and carried a battery of 8-inch guns in addition to her regular torpedo armament. To recommission this outsize ship, with no spare parts available and beyond reach of all navy yards, constituted a notable feat of skill on the part of her crew and her commanding officer, Lieutenant Commander Paul Ortoli.[12]

All these efforts went practically for naught. After carrying out several missions in the Atlantic, she participated in the expedition to Saint Pierre and Miquelon Islands in December, 1941, but never found a fit target for her powerful guns. On February 18, 1942, while en route for Panama and the Pacific—for reasons which appear to have been primarily political—she was rammed at night in the Caribbean by an American freighter and sank with all hands.[13]

Admiral Muselier decided to form a submarine division with the *Junon* (Commander Jean Querville, commanding the 1st Submarine Division) and the *Minerve* (Lieutenant Pierre Sonneville). They would be based at Dundee and operate under the command of the British commander of submarines. Both ships had been towed to England, with repairs not yet completed and with no spare parts on board. Readying them for service was a long and difficult task.

On January 31, 1941, the *Minerve,* the first one ready, began a long

---

[10] Today a rear admiral.

[11] The *Orion* and *Ondine* were in too poor material condition to warrant repairs. The *Créole,* only 68 per cent complete when towed to England, was completed after the war.

[12] Today a vice admiral, and Inspector General of the Navy.

[13] It was at that time commanded by Commander Georges Blaison, who had formerly been Ortoli's executive officer.

series of patrols in the North Sea and off the coasts of Norway. In May, 1941, she was in the Skagerrak at the time of the sortie of the *Bismarck,* which probably passed not too far from her torpedo tubes. She was in the vicinity of Trondheim, in March, 1942, when the *Tirpitz* left there to intercept Convoy PQ-12 headed for Murmansk. The following July the *Minerve* was one of a barrier of submarines stationed between Bear Island and the North Cape, at the time when the unfortunate Convoy PQ-17 was suffering its tragic fate.

The *Junon,* somewhat deferred to permit a more rapid recommissioning of the *Minerve,* was not ready until December, 1941. Before reporting to the base at Dundee, she was sent to the Gulf of Gascony with British submarines to bar the passage to an eventual sortie of the *Scharnhorst* and *Gneisenau* from Brest. She obtained a few successes against German shipping off the Norwegian coast.

Finally the *Junon* and *Minerve* participated in the search for the *Tirpitz* during the passage of Convoy PQ-12. The *Junon* also landed secret agents and commandos in Norway. On one of these trips she landed the British commandos who blew up the German heavy water production plant near Glomfjord on September 15, 1942.

A few French submarine chasers, perhaps a dozen, were commissioned at Cowes and thereafter operated in the English Channel. Several participated in the commando raid on Bruneval[14] and the affair at Dieppe in August of 1942.

A flotilla of motor torpedo boats, designated the 23rd Flotilla and commanded by Lieutenant Commander Ernest Auvynet—alias "Meurville"—and later by Lieutenant Pierre Iehlé, operated for a long time off the coasts of the Occupied Zone of France.

The brightest stars in the crown of the F.F.N.F. in its fight against the Axis forces were without doubt the operations of the nine corvettes acquired from the Royal Navy in 1941. Three of these corvettes operated in the South Atlantic.[15] The other six plied the North Atlantic, that disagreeable, tedious, dangerous stretch of water between the British Isles and the shores of Newfoundland and Canada. It was here that the *Alysse,* under Lieutenant Jacques Pépin Lehalleur, was torpedoed and sunk on February 8, 1942, by the *U-664.* Lost also to U-boats in the same waters was the *Mimosa,* under command of Lieutenant Roger Birot, which went down with her entire crew except three lonely survivors.

[14] Translator's Note: This was a technical intelligence raid to gather information on new German radar equipment installed in a station at the top of a 400-foot cliff, some 20 kilometers from Le Havre.
[15] They were named after the first three officers of the F.F.N.F. killed in action—the *Commandant Detroyat,* the *Commandant Drogou,* and the *Commandant d'Estienne d'Orves.*

Against these losses, however, the ships flying the Cross of Lorraine could point to at least three German submarines sunk by them.

The first, the *U-609,* part of a wolfpack which had been attacking a convoy for several days, was sunk on February 7, 1943, by the *Lobelia,* under Lieutenant Pierre de Morsier. The two others—the *U-444* and the *U-432*—were both sunk on March 11, 1943, within twelve hours of each other by the Free French corvette *Aconit,* commanded by Lieutenant Jean Levasseur.

The *Aconit,* in company with the *Renoncule,* was shepherding the stragglers of Convoy HX-228, bound for Europe from Halifax. On March 10, 1943, the convoy was struck at night by a German wolfpack. The escort commander, in the HMS *Harvester,* signaled in the middle of the night that he had disabled his ship by ramming a German submarine, and he ordered the *Aconit* to stand by him. Very shortly after, the *Aconit* saw and rammed a submarine—the *U-444,* the very same that had been slightly damaged by the *Harvester's* ramming. Four German sailors picked up out of the water were proof of the *Aconit's* effective maneuvers.

But the U-boat pack still dogged the convoy, and at 11 o'clock the next morning the *Harvester* was torpedoed and sunk. Rushing to her assistance, the *Aconit* glimpsed the guilty U-boat well on her way to escape. The *Aconit* attacked with both gunfire and depth charges, and finally ended the battle twenty-three minutes later by ramming her opponent, the *U-432,* and cutting her in two. Thus the *Harvester* was avenged within less than an hour after she had been sunk.

Twenty of the U-boat's crew were picked up. They were, they said, eating their lunch when the *Aconit* attacked.

"I hope," said Lieutenant Levasseur in reporting the encounter, "that they enjoyed my dessert of depth charges!"

As some indication of the nature of the activities of these small ships, statistics compiled from the *Aconit's* log may be of some interest.

She went into service under the Free French on June 19, 1941. During the next two years she was at sea for a total of 405 days and steamed 84,000 miles; she escorted 34 North Atlantic convoys and participated in many rescues and a dozen engagements of the type already described.

Another of the Free French corvettes was the *Roselys,* commanded by Lieutenant Commander André Bergeret, which left the North Atlantic lanes only to take part in the more dangerous convoys to Murmansk. In July of 1942 she distinguished herself by boldly steaming into a minefield in order to pick up 177 survivors from an American transport.

No sailor can read the account of these stubborn fights in the open Atlantic without having the greatest respect for all the participants on both sides. He might even have difficulty in determining who was the most deserving of his respect—the almost superhuman courage of the submariners, the sacrificial fortitude of the merchant mariners, or the aggressive intelligence and tenacity of those who manned the escort ships.

Officially, however, whatever might be the secret feelings of the sailors remaining in France toward their comrades who were continuing the war, the Government at Vichy could not do otherwise than disavow the F.F.N.F.

For one thing, one of the armistice clauses obliged the Government to forbid all of its citizens entering the service of a foreign power in order to take up arms against the Axis. In addition, the first operations of the Free French Navy surface vessels, instead of being directed against the Germans, had been operations against their fellow Frenchmen at Dakar and Gabon, and as such partaking of the characteristics of a civil war. And when, in October and November of 1940, General de Gaulle announced at Brazzaville that he was creating a new government-in-exile to replace "a French Government that no longer existed,"[16] there was nothing the Vichy Government could do except to meet the challenge if it were to retain any semblance of authority as a government responsible not only to its citizens but also to the Axis powers for the honest observance of the armistice terms which it had legally accepted. In fact the severe, and, at times, almost unendurable measures which the Germans took against anyone in France suspected of "dissidence" stemmed largely from such actions as this, just as some of General de Gaulle's actions later perhaps stemmed from personal reaction to the court-martial sentence imposed upon him *in absentia.*

At any rate, there was nothing to do but to try General de Gaulle *in absentia,* as well as the officers and men who had joined him. It was remarkable, though, how long the courts delayed in completing these trials, and how many cases were discreetly suppressed. However, the courts were forced to condemn the members of the F.F.N.F. as a matter of principle.

Any anxiety the sailors of the F.F.N.F. might have had for their families back in France was quickly dispelled. These families were of course immediately dropped from the list of naval personnel receiving the legally established allotment of the husband's or father's pay and allowances. But they were just as promptly taken up on another list, entitled "Assistance D" —D for "dissidents." Here they received exactly the same allotments as

---

[16] ". . . . Giving way to inexcusable panic, the fortuitous leaders submitted to the laws of the enemy. . . . Millions of French subjects have decided to continue the fight for liberation . . . now that there no longer exists a French Government. The organization sitting at Vichy and which pretends to that title is unconstitutional and submissive to the invader. . . ." From General de Gaulle's speech broadcast from Brazzaville on October 27, 1940.

was prescribed by regulations for the families of men in the regular Navy. Even those in the Occupied Zone received this money. Thus, the wife of a F.F.N.F. petty officer living in her small Breton village found herself in the same financial situation as her neighbor whose husband was serving on a cruiser at Toulon. A similar system was instituted for the families of the merchant marine seamen.

Later, during the dark hours of 1944, a few extremists at Vichy insisted that these payments be stopped, but the new measures applied solely to the families of a few leaders—and only in theory, at that. For instance, the family of the chief of staff of the Navy at Algiers, now associated with the Allies, continued to receive the regular monthly allotment from secret funds.

One extremely delicate problem was the encounters that were bound to happen between ships of the regular French Navy and those of the Free French meeting by accident on the high seas. After a few early tragic episodes such as happened at Dakar and Libreville, to be described later, the French Admiralty had adopted a hardened attitude and had issued strict combat instructions for such eventualities. Copies of these instructions had fallen into the hands of the British, who promptly passed them on to the F.F.N.F.

But shortly afterward, Captain Paul Maerten, former Commandant of the French Navy at Madagascar, who had been interned in South Africa after the conquest of that island, happened to meet there Lieutenant Pépin Lehalleur, commanding the F.F.N.F. sloop *Commandant Duboc*. The meeting gave them the opportunity to discuss the difficult situation that would inevitably occur when ships of the two forces happened to meet. Both officers decided that the only reasonable solution was for the ships to *ignore each other!* Pépin Lehalleur sent his superiors the draft of a message which he proposed should be sent by all F.F.N.F. ships, by visual means, to all vessels of the regular French Navy whom they happened to meet at sea. The message simply recommended that no mention of the meeting be entered in either ship's log, and that the ships should continue on their way as if they had never met. The proposal was approved by Admiral Philippe Auboyneau, who issued instructions to that effect to all F.F.N.F. commanding officers in a circular dated November 3, 1942.[17] Events which shortly occurred were to make these instructions no longer applicable, but the sentiments that inspired it should always be remembered.

But it was not alone with the Navy of the Government at Vichy that the F.F.N.F. had problems. In England the relations between the staff of the F.F.N.F. and the staff of General de Gaulle were not too amicable. From being strained, they eventually developed into a bitter crisis. On January 2,

---

[17] *Circular—Personal and Secret*. No. 214, F.F.N.F./3, dated November 3, 1942.

1941, Admiral Muselier was suddenly arrested at his residence by two inspectors from Scotland Yard accompanied by an intelligence officer of the Royal Navy.

He was at first imprisoned in a common jail, but then was shifted to the supervision of the British Admiralty under more decent conditions. Ten days later he was released with a letter of apology signed personally by Anthony Eden on the part of the British Government.

Neither the memoirs of the admiral nor those of General de Gaulle shed complete light on this extraordinary occurrence. However, it is known that a set of charges, largely false, had been filed against Admiral Muselier. But by whom were they filed? And why?

One of the charges alleged collusion with Vichy. Another one would have given the impression that the defeat sustained at Dakar had resulted from indiscreet remarks of the admiral, whose disapproval of the whole undertaking was no secret. Whatever the reasons or source, the repercussions shook the staff of the F.F.N.F. right down to its lowest echelons. Incidents like Admiral Muselier's arrest did nothing to ease the strain between the staff of the admiral and the over-all staff of the Free French Forces.[18]

Admiral Muselier returned to his duty with the Free French Committee and as head of the F.F.N.F., just as though nothing had happened. However, the breach between him and General de Gaulle widened until a definite break occurred over the expedition against Saint Pierre and Miquelon that winter.

These two islands, with their 3,500 inhabitants, were the microscopic remains of what had once been French Canada. They had no strategic value, they constituted no threat to the Allies—in fact they had only four policemen as a garrison. After the armistice they had been included along with the French West Indies in the special agreements made between the United States and the French Government, and they came under the administration of Admiral Robert, at Martinique, the High Commissioner of the French Antilles.

These agreements respected the *status quo* of the islands in their loyalty to Marshal Pétain, but specified that they should have no contacts with the Axis.

As their consideration under these agreements, the United States, which had an embassy at Vichy, received facilities useful for propaganda and other action, especially in North Africa. The Americans were especially anxious that this arrangement not be disturbed, and made that fact known to the Free French Committee.

---

[18] Admiral Muselier, in his book, *De Gaulle Contre le Gaullisine,* states that the entire incident had been created by the chief of General de Gaulle's security service.

The Free French, however, felt that annexation of the islands would publicize the Free French movement and would demonstrate that it was not merely a creation of the British, but was a spontaneous movement which operated in complete independence and which was just beginning to develop.

Accordingly Admiral Muselier embarked on the *Lobelia* at Greenock on November 24, 1941, ostensibly on an inspection trip of the corvettes which had just been placed in service on the North Atlantic run. On reaching the coast of Iceland, he inspected two or three corvettes that were there, and then transferred to the *Mimosa* and headed for St. John's, in Newfoundland, where he joined up with the *Alysse* and the *Aconit*.

This abnormal concentration of Free French Naval Forces did not go unnoticed. Commodore Leonard W. Murray, of the Canadian Navy, remarked dryly to Muselier that he was not sure it was prudent on his part to allow such a strong F.F.N.F. group to cruise in the vicinity of Saint Pierre.

Admiral Muselier did not turn a hair. The recent entrance of the United States into the war decided him to rush matters. Reinforced by the *Surcouf* and her 8-inch guns, he descended in force, on December 24, on the islands and their four-man garrison.

The affair was over and the governor arrested within twenty minutes. The plebiscite which was held afterward resulted in the islands' decision to join the Free French. But the phrasing of the question was such that the choice given the islanders was not that between the Vichy Government and the Free French Committee proclaimed by General de Gaulle, but rather that of "joining the Free French" or "collaborating with the Axis powers"—an option in which the result was a foregone conclusion.

This adventure in power politics, however, had unexpected repercussions in the American hemisphere—a veritable "tempest in a teapot." The U.S. State Department was furious at this action which imperiled its whole agreement with Vichy. The United States was on the point of demanding the restitution of the Islands, but the attack on Pearl Harbor had just occurred and they would have their hands full in the Pacific for a long time to come.

Admiral Muselier did not return to England until February 28, 1942. Then the long smouldering feud between him and General de Gaulle exploded at the first meeting of the Free French Committee, where he had gone to report on his mission. That very evening he submitted his resignation as a member of the Committee and as Commissioner—that is to say, "Minister"—of the Navy. He retained his position, however, as Commander in Chief of the F.F.N.F.

Commander Auboyneau,[19] who commanded the *Triomphant* in the Pacific

---

[19] Liaison officer to Admiral A. B. Cunningham during the war, Commander Auboyneau had remained on Admiral Godfroy's staff at Alexandria, until he left to join the Free French on August 20, 1940. He is a vice admiral today.

with the temporary rank of captain, was immediately promoted to rear admiral by De Gaulle and appointed Commissioner of the Navy. On March 11 Admiral Muselier received a sentence of thirty days under arrest in a fortress. On his release he was relieved of his command and placed on the retired list, for the second time in his career. However, the world was to see him again on active duty in 1943 in Algiers!

This account of the activities of the F.F.N.F. up to their merger with the naval forces of Africa after the Allied landings in November of 1942 would not be complete without some mention of the heroic adventure of Lieutenant Commander d'Estienne d'Orves.

A descendant of a well-known family of Provence, Honoré d'Estienne d'Orves was, in 1940, on the staff of Admiral Godfroy, commanding Force X at Alexandria. He was a magnificent officer—well thought of by his seniors, liked by his comrades, and idolized by his men. After a bitter inner struggle he had joined the Free French movement on July 11, 1940. A long trip around Africa brought him to London in October.

There he was promptly assigned the duty of Director of Intelligence of the F.F.N.F. However, d'Estienne d'Orves would not acknowledge any right to order other people on dangerous missions to the Occupied Zone of France without first having gone there himself. Notwithstanding the expressed opposition of Admiral Muselier, he had himself assigned to one of these missions.

It was the last occupation in the world for such a straightforward, courageous individual. He did not know how to dissimulate, he knew only how to fight in the open. The inevitable occurred. Scarcely had he landed in France before he was arrested by the Gestapo at Nantes. Taken to Paris, he was tried before a German military court and sentenced to death.

When his sentence became known at Vichy, it caused consternation. Admiral Darlan immediately gave orders to his representatives in Paris to attempt the impossible with the German authorities, and, incredibly, a delay in executing the sentence was obtained.

Everybody believed that d'Estienne d'Orves had been saved, when, on August 21, a German midshipman was assassinated in one of the Paris underground railway stations. In reprisal the Germans shot all the hostages they had in hand. d'Estienne d'Orves and his comrades were executed at Mont Valérien[20] on August 27, 1941.

The letters which he wrote in prison, and which were later published, bear witness to the fact that, regardless of the diverging paths they followed, the officers of the Navy had retained their traditional resolution of spirit, and, in their thinking, they were not so far apart.

---

[20] A hill fortress dominating Paris.

CHAPTER 16

Feeding France Under the Armistice

With the signing of the armistice the offensive role of the French Navy disappeared—except for those of its members who still continued the war as part of the F.F.N.F. But the other missions of the Navy still continued. In short, these were the provisioning of the country, the maintenance of the ties of sovereignty with the empire overseas, and the preparation of the overseas forces for the day when France would once more enter the conflict.

The first of these missions required a sturdy merchant marine. By orders of the Pétain Government the French merchant marine had been placed under the Navy. But when the Navy began to look for the ships with which to carry out its mission, it found but a small percentage left.

At the beginning of the war, France possessed 3,000,000 tons of merchant ships, and had under charter 1,900,000 tons of neutral ships—Greek, Swedish, Dutch, Norwegian, and Danish. But shortly after the armistice she found that she had sustained a tremendous decrease:

271,000 tons lost through enemy action;

450,000 tons sequestered in English ports by the British for their own use in continuing the war;

196,000 tons interned in U.S. ports, including the liner *Normandie,* 3 oil tankers, and 16 cargo ships, and 25,000 tons similarly detained in Argentine ports;

257,000 tons either captured or requisitioned by the Germans in the Occupied Zone.

Furthermore, of the chartered ships, almost all had proceeded immediately to British ports. On July 4, despite the armistice and what had happened at Portsmouth, Plymouth, and Mers-el-Kebir, the French Admiralty engaged itself to transfer all charters to Great Britain, and to sell the British, at cost, the cargoes[1] of all chartered ships in transit, and also to send to England all neutral ships still on hand. Of this latter, only half were able to get under way before the Germans took over control of the departure

---

[1] The total value of these cargoes represented a considerable sum, which probably constituted the first financial backing in Great Britain for the benefit of the Free French.

170

ports. The French ultimately retained the other half—approximately 150,000 tons—as compensation for the French ships seized by the British and also to keep them out of German hands.

Summarizing, France had available, in July, 1940, only 1,650,000 tons of shipping as against the almost 5,000,000 tons she had had the use of previously. And almost two-thirds of the ships now available were oil burning. As France was very low on fuel oil, she had to convert most of these oil burners to coal.

Since Article 11 of the armistice had required the suspension of all French maritime traffic, the first thing the Navy had to do was to negotiate for its resumption—with the Italians for the Mediterranean and with the Germans for the Atlantic. Permission was finally obtained, but only provided certain conditions were met.

The first condition was that the French must submit a detailed schedule of all ship movements several weeks in advance, and that all French convoys should pass certain points at specified times, correct within an hour. This latter condition was, perhaps, necessary in order to prevent mistakes, but it placed a tremendous burden on the French, since ships might have to sail half loaded in order to reach the control point at the specified time.

The second condition was that the French Admiralty had to pledge itself to scuttle any ship threatened with seizure by the British. The Germans, naturally enough, did not want the British thus to be able to replace the ships which the U-boats were striving so desperately to sink.

But there are many ways of doing things. After one or two scuttlings, only sabotage was carried out—and that was almost completely limited to a symbolic gesture, such as putting part of the machinery out of action.

The Germans were furious and threatened personal reprisals against the individual ship captains, but they could not be reached because, with their ships, they were already in British hands. Moreover Admiral Auphan, in charge of the French merchant marine, stepped in and declared that he himself was the person responsible; he had issued written orders that a ship was not to be scuttled if so doing would endanger human life.

As a result, in 28 months, out of 104 French ships stopped and examined at sea by the Royal Navy, only two steamers and two small sailing vessels scuttled themselves; 43 were released or were retaken[2] by the French naval

---

[2] Some of these recaptures took place under very picturesque conditions. The crew of the small trawler *Joseph Elise,* taken by the British, got their English captors drunk, locked them in the hold, and then returned with their prisoners in triumph to Casablanca.

The *Ville du Havre* lost her propeller and was adrift in the mid-Atlantic when intercepted by a British cruiser. A tug boat from Dakar meanwhile had been sent out

forces, and the remaining 57 were taken into British ports for use thereafter by the English.

With each of the 57 captures the Germans threatened to stop French traffic completely; they also demanded that French tonnage be turned over to them equal to what the British had taken. By a few concessions here and there, mostly of small account, the French Navy managed to keep traffic going until the next outburst.

The Axis armistice commissions exercised little or no control over the passengers carried or the merchandise transported by the French merchant marine. It has been said that the occupation authorities systematically took for their own use a considerable portion of all French imports. Actually, the only item of which the French were required to turn over a certain percentage of the amount imported was peanuts from Senegal, and this requirement was effective only for the first year or so. Germany did lay a heavy tribute on French economy, but this was irrespective of any imports by sea.

What the Germans were really anxious to do was to establish consulates in all the French colonial ports, especially Dakar. The French successfully opposed these demands until the Americans began increasing their own consular representation in French Africa. Thereupon the Germans demanded that these new consuls be sent home or they themselves be given equal rights.

The Americans, who were in North Africa supposedly to give humanitarian aid to Algeria, did not want to go home—for reasons which became manifest the following November. So the French Government had to concede the Axis powers the right to station armistice commissions at Algiers and Casablanca. They never succeeded in getting one at Dakar or in other more distant colonies.

Such were the conditions under which the Navy gradually reestablished maritime traffic between France and Algeria, Tunisia, Morocco, Dakar, the Gulf of Guinea, the Antilles, Madagascar, and Indochina. French Equatorial Africa and the French possessions in Oceania had already passed under Free French control.

In the beginning, all ships sailed from ports in the Free Zone—Marseilles, Caronte, Port Saint Louis du Rhône, Sètes, and Port Vendres[3]—and a top

---

to assist the *Ville du Havre*. The British cruiser ordered the tug to tow the disabled ship to Freetown, in British Sierra Leone (W. Africa). The tug boat captain defiantly refused. Not being able to tow the *Ville du Havre* himself, and tired of trying to argue in another language with an obstinate French sailor, the English captain gave up and went away.

[3] French maritime traffic with the Occupied Zone had not completely ceased. For reasons of morale as well as to prevent actual suffering when the Germans closed the

flight organization was necessary to keep an even flow of heavily laden ships moving in accordance with a tight schedule. This became the task of the "delegates of the Admiralty."

Traffic with Algeria generally sailed without escort, and this quickly reached the 65 to 80 crossings per week averaged before the war. But every ship was now much more heavily laden.[4] Despite all efforts to keep ships out of combat zones, France had ten ships sunk and three damaged in two years in the Mediterranean—four casualties from Italian mines, two from German bombs or torpedoes, and seven from English bombs or torpedoes.

Ships that were routed through the Strait of Gibraltar were generally convoyed. The escort was usually only a token one; the sloop or patrol vessel so assigned was there mainly to answer signals coming from the shore or from British warships, and to intervene as far as it could in case of incidents. In no case was the escort vessel to take the initiative in opening fire.

On one occasion, in January, 1941, a four-ship convoy was attacked, without apparent reason, by five small British destroyers. But there were two empty oil tankers in the convoy, and perhaps the Royal Navy had need of tankers. One passenger ship in the convoy apparently did not stop soon enough, so she was halted by a burst of machinegun fire which killed or wounded several passengers. The escort vessel did not reply. The entire convoy was seized.

A little later, in March, another convoy, escorted by a destroyer, was attacked but ran in under the shelter of a coastal battery at Nemours. The guns of the battery kept the English well away, but several officers and men of the French gun crews were killed or wounded.

---

demarcation line, the economic authorities in the Occupied Zone begged the Admiralty to keep sending in a few shiploads of urgently needed foodstuffs: bananas from the Antilles, wine from North Africa, peanuts from Senegal. In compliance, 120,000 tons of merchandise were delivered through the ports of Bordeaux, La Pallice, and Nantes.

All the inbound ships arrived safely. On their return trip to Africa, however, three ships were captured by the British and a fourth sunk.

In addition, the French Admiralty found dealings with the German-held ports both disagreeable and open to misunderstandings. Hence traffic with the Occupied Zone was terminated at the end of 1941.

In return for the 1941 shipments, however, the Germans returned to the French 28 coal burning cargo ships which they had detained since the armistice. These formed a most welcome addition to the French merchant marine in the Mediterranean. It was surprising that the Germans agreed to release these ships when they so badly needed them themselves.

[4] During the period from the armistice until the Allied landings in Africa in November, 1942, the French merchant marine unloaded in the Mediterranean ports of European France a total of 4,400,000 tons of merchandise—or more than 220 pounds per inhabitant.

Such incidents, however, were rare. It was much easier for the British to pick up their prizes in the distant sealanes where no French vessels could interfere.

Between September of 1940 and November 8, 1942, exactly 540 French convoys, comprising a total of 1,750 merchant ships, passed through the Strait of Gibraltar in one direction or the other. These convoys brought to European France some 3,000,000 tons of badly needed provisions.

Official records show that without the peanuts from Dakar, the individual ration of fats to the people of France would have been reduced by half, and that the lack of oil cake for the cattle would have reduced the production of milk by twenty-five per cent. Without the phosphates from Africa, French crops would have fallen off at least thirty per cent. Without the early wheat from Tunisia there would have been a deficit in bread. Without the fruits and vegetables from Africa, continental France—especially the southern zone—would have suffered a great deal more from famine. Up until 1943, almost half of what the average Frenchman ate, he owed directly or indirectly to the Navy.

All this, however, was not attained without constant disagreements with England.

The British, by an Order in Council, dated July 31, 1940, had declared a blockade of the entire coast of France. In the eyes of the British, all that entered France, even in the Free Zone, indirectly served the enemy. The Free French radio broadcasts from London were spreading the word that 80 per cent of maritime imports were going to the Reich. The British Ambasador at Madrid mentioned a figure of 50 per cent. If there had been suitable liaison with London it would have been possible to show how false or exaggerated this information was, but diplomatic relations remained broken and Mr. Churchill continued to support the Free French wholeheartedly.

The French Admiralty tried by every means possible to enlighten the English on the real nature of this commercial maritime traffic. When, in September, 1940, it organized the first convoy through the Strait of Gibraltar, the French naval attaché at Madrid gave exact information in advance to the British naval attaché there. A little later, conversations took place at the ambassadorial level. Unfortunately Sir Samuel Hoare, for the British, wanted from François Pietri, the French Ambassador to Spain, a formal guarantee that no merchandise imported into the Free Zone would be forwarded to the Occupied Zone and that the Germans would get none of it. The French Ambassador could not give him any such precise guarantees. Above all, the English desired that the conversations be continued at London without the knowledge of the Germans. This was impossible, and the negotiations came to an end.

ADMIRAL AUPHAN, the Chief of Naval Operations, inspecting a naval detachment during a visit to Marseilles and Toulon.

THE ENTRANCE CHANNEL *to the navy yard at Brest.*

Even at Vichy, Admiral Auphan tried to reestablish contact with the British Admiralty via the Canadian Minister, Pierre Dupuy. At his instigation Lord Halifax, British Foreign Minister, was contacted by Jacques Chevalier, a French Minister who knew him well. Several letters were exchanged. Marshal Pétain himself sent an unofficial emissary, Louis Rougier, to the British Government. From these exchanges there resulted a tacit agreement in which England, without ceasing to seize French ships at sea or to encourage the rival government of De Gaulle, permitted the traffic between France and Africa to continue.

Communications with Indochina were as necessary from a political point of view as for rotating the troops stationed there. It was also necessary to transport coal from Tonkin to Madagascar to fuel the ships there, and rice from Cochin China to Dakar to feed the native population of Senegal, but the British would not grant free passage to and from the Orient even for the purpose of repatriating invalids or the families of service men. In particular, ships carrying rubber especially aroused their resentment. After having had several such ships confiscated, the French Admiralty decided to gamble everything, and sent the cargo ship *François Louis Dreyfus,* with 6,600 tons of raw rubber, home via Cape Horn.

The *François Louis Dreyfus* started out ostensibly for Japan, but once past Formosa it changed course across the Pacific, rounded Cape Horn and the Falkland Islands, and arrived safely in Casablanca two months later.

But voyages of this sort were not always so successful. Out of 52 ships on the regular Saigon-Diego Suarez-Dakar route, 19 were taken. These captures were not always accidental. One convoy of five ships, escorted by the sloop *D'Iberville,* ran into a screen of six patrol ships supported by four British cruisers on November 3, 1941, far south of the Cape of Good Hope. Perhaps the presence of the British men-of-war at that precise moment might have been due to the coincidence of 900 tons of graphite on one of the French vessels. Only a few days earlier, the French had ceded 5,000 tons of Madagascar graphite to the American freighter *West Hardaway* in the hope that this might purchase a safe conduct for the convoy, which was also carrying 30,000 tons of rice.

Unfortunately the results were not as anticipated. Thenceforth commercial traffic beyond Dakar was suspended, and the only communication with Madagascar was by naval sloops or submarines.

The traffic between European France, Casablanca, and Dakar functioned at the rate of several convoys per month. In two years only four ships were seized, and in each case they were sailing without convoy. Incoming vessels brought in as many imports in the nature of peanuts, oil, cocoa, coffee, lumber, and bananas, as outgoing ships carried out manufactured goods, coal, troops, arms, and ammunition. By special agreement with Portugal a branch line joined Casablanca to Lisbon, by which roundabout way certain needed products were supplied to Morocco.

The commercial traffic with the Antilles was also important, not so much because of the 100,000 tons of sugar and 9,000 tons of rum imported from there, as because of the part it played in diplomatic negotiations with the United States.

That nation, though still neutral, was concerned over the possibility, no matter how faint, that Martinique and the other French possessions in the West Indies might come under German control as a result of the defeat of France. Vice Admiral John W. Greenslade, U.S.N., came to the islands and brought Admiral Robert, High Commissioner and Commander in Chief of the French Antilles, some rather formidable demands. As a good Norman, Robert made friends with Greenslade, and, aided by parallel negotiations between Vichy and Washington, concluded an agreement with him: the Antilles would remain faithful to the Vichy Government, but everything of military value there—100 planes, 150 tons of gold, a few warships, and some 20 merchant ships—should remain there, with no attempt to return them to France. In addition, an American observer was to be stationed permanently in the islands. In return the islands could purchase in America anything necessary for their maintenance.

The German armistice commission was never told anything more about this arrangement than was absolutely necessary to obtain their consent for the resumption of transatlantic traffic.

These communications with her colonial possession were absolutely necessary to France, both from the political and ideological point of view. Nevertheless, the British, who were not parties to the agreement, continually intercepted French ships in the open seas off the African coast or in the vicinity of Martinique. In eleven months, six out of 20 large vessels in this traffic were seized. One of these ships, the freighter *Fort de France,* was recaptured west of the Canaries by a French naval force and taken into Casablanca, along with the British armed guard that had been placed on board.[5]

---

[5] The recapture was planned in greatest secrecy by Admiral Jean d'Harcourt, Commandant of the French Navy in Morocco, and was brilliantly executed by the light cruiser *Primauguet* and the destroyers from Casablanca. The *Fort de France* was intercepted en route to Gibraltar, within 24 hours after she had been seized by the British. The English armed guard found on board was transferred to the super-destroyer *Albatros.*

An amusing incident took place on the way in. The *Albatros* had the greatest difficulty in convincing their British prisoners that there was not a single German on board. In order to convince them, they were taken on a complete tour of the ship, with authority to open any door or panel behind which a representative of the Kriegsmarine might possibly be hidden!

To make these crossings, the French ships had to take on fuel at the United States island of Saint Thomas. In May, 1941, the Americans suddenly stopped deliveries. French ships were again allowed to refuel at Saint Thomas in September, but only on condition that all food products from the Antilles should remain in North Africa, where the American consular representatives could make sure they were not being reexported to Europe.

Such checking naturally required enlarged consulates—in evident accord with the wish of the Washington Government to increase its influence in Morocco and Algeria. In March, 1941, Admiral Darlan, as Minister of Foreign Affairs, and Admiral William D. Leahy, the American Ambassador, approved an agreement which had been drawn up at Algiers between General Weygand and Robert Murphy, Consul General of the United States. The object of this agreement was to arrange for the importation into French North Africa—thus placed "outside the blockade"—of certain vitally needed products, such as petroleum and fuel oil, but only on condition that these not be reexported to France.

The difficulty in carrying out the agreement lay in the matter of transport. The Germans, furious at increasing American influence in Africa, would not authorize this traffic unless it were carried out solely in the French ships then interned in the United States—which would have the effect of returning these ships to French control. For exactly the opposite reasons, the Americans and British insisted that it be carried on only in ships from the ports of European France.

The impasse was resolved by a unique system of transatlantic exchange. Two freighters and one tanker, all in ballast, left the shores of European France exactly at the same time that two freighters and one tanker, fully laden, left the American shores. In this manner each adversary held a hostage from the other of equal value.

To add to the difficulties, considerable advance notice and other diplomatic red tape were required. As a result French Africa received, over the period of a year, just 40,000 tons of liquid fuel, 18,000 tons of coal, 20,000 tons of sugar, and some cotton goods, nails, binder twine, insecticide powder, etc.—only about what was necessary to justify the maintenance of the network of American consulates.

In all this complication of political, diplomatic, and operational activities, the French Admiralty thought only of keeping France alive and of defending its maritime interests. But the commerce destroying tactics of the belligerents were steadily and surely diminishing the world's shipping tonnage. Whether belligerent or neutral, every nation needed ships. It was becoming more and more difficult to keep ships in an unemployed status, like the idle vessels in French ports.

Germany was keeping constant pressure on France in this regard. Their operations in the Black Sea and in Libya were limited by the amount of supplies they received by water. It is a matter of wonder even today that the Germans, masters of France, did not force the French to charter to them the numerous fine ships laid up in French ports because of lack of fuel. Perhaps the Germans had no extra fuel oil themselves. Be that as it may, France did not turn over to them one single merchant ship before the decisive turning point of November, 1942, when the Allied landings in North Africa threw all previous arrangements into the discard.

The Germans did cast far more covetous glances at the 150,000 tons of Greek, Norwegian, and Danish ships which the French were operating under charter. This is all the more understandable in that the Germans had conquered and completely occupied those countries. In August, 1942, the French Government was forced to agree, under pressure, to return these vessels to their "legitimate owners"—when, of course, the Germans planned to charter them immediately afterward themselves. The French Admiralty thereupon sent word that under these conditions it would have to reduce the corresponding amount of French shipping being used to transport phosphates for German account.

The Germans were indignant beyond words. "If Admiral Auphan were at Paris," threatened the chief of the German economic delegation at Wiesbaden, "the matter would not end on that note!" However, only a few of the chartered vessels had been returned to their foreign owners when the events of November transpired.

In the United States, matters took a similar turn after Pearl Harbor. Even before then the Americans had wanted the charter all the French vessels laid up in their ports as well as in the Antilles, especially the eight tankers. However, the Germans, forewarned, had exacted a pledge that the French Government would have the tankers scuttled before allowing them to be taken over by the Americans.

Upon entry of the United States into the war on December 8, 1941, naturally she immediately requisitioned and took over all French vessels in American ports. Workmen began converting the giant *Normandie* into a troop transport; however, she took fire from a workman's blowtorch and burned for hours before capsizing, a total wreck, in New York harbor.

On the opposite side of the world, Japan acted in a similar manner toward the 27 ships, totalling 161,000 tons, which the French were operating in Indochinese waters for local needs. Both at Vichy and at Saigon the Japanese representatives asked that the French charter them every vessel over 4,000 tons, in exchange for which they would give more support to the maintenance of French sovereignty in Indochina.

Although France was not in position to oppose any demands in that quarter, the Vichy Government kept Washington fully informed of all the proceedings in order to avoid any misunderstandings.

Washington's reply was that chartering by mutual agreement would be considered a hostile gesture of a nature that might result in serious consequences to all French maritime traffic.

After holding off the Japanese as long as they could—until June, 1942, in fact—the French were forced to permit the Japanese to unilaterally requisition the ships, which they were going to take anyway.[6] Perhaps it was due to France's endeavors to resist the Japanese demands that the Strait of Gibraltar was open to French traffic until the very end.

But the best of ships wear out, even with the best of facilities for upkeep. The French not only had few such facilities, but they were working their ships overtime. Also, because of shortage of fuel oil, most of the vessels they were using were coal burners, hence the most antiquated ships in the French merchant fleet. A few new ships had been converted to coal. This would not have been so bad if they could always have obtained good coal, but this, again, was rarely the case.

In January, 1942, a severe storm struck the western Mediterranean. The passenger ship *Lamoricière,* en route from Algiers to Marseilles, struggled with insufficient power against the storm for hours. Her firerooms became flooded one after the other, her pumps gradually lost suction, and she finally went down to the northeast of Minorca. Despite all the assistance sent from Toulon and Algiers, it was possible to save only 94 of the 350 souls on board the *Lamoricière*.

The freighter *Jumièges* was lost without further trace after the S O S she sent out during the height of the same storm. The cargo ship *PLM 16* was only fifty miles away when she heard the S O S, but could not cover even that short distance. Owing to poor coal, the steam pressure in her boilers had fallen to less than 11 pounds, and her speed to 3 knots. In fact she had to ask for the assistance of a tug in order to make port herself, as she could not maintain steerageway.

Everywhere throughout the world the French merchant marine was the center of conflict between two violent, warring worlds. Its mariners found

---

[6] Translator's Note: In April, 1942, a few days after Admiral Auphan assumed the additional office of Minister of the Navy, I made an official courtesy call on him. During the course of my call, the Admiral briefly discussed the Japanese demands on French shipping in Indochina.

I asked the Admiral what he would do if he were the commander of an Allied submarine operating off the coast of Indochina and encountered these French ships operating either under the Japanese flag, with Japanese crews, or under the French flag and with French crews but under charter to Japan.

Admiral Auphan's reply was vigorous and unhesitating: "I would torpedo them!"

themselves shot at, torpedoed, sequestered, imprisoned, as the varying tides of fortune shifted. Yet, through it all, the merchant marine and the equally dedicated fishing fleet fought to keep essential food flowing into starving France. Only through them was France able to survive. And only through the armistice were they, in turn, able to operate.

And at the other end of the ship lanes, in the overseas parts of the empire, the trials were no less severe.

CHAPTER 17

Defending the Empire

The armistice had left intact the French territories overseas. With their sixty million inhabitants, these territories constituted the second largest colonial empire in the world.

After a momentary hesitation on the part of those who had not witnessed the defeat, the chiefs and the inhabitants of the empire remained faithful to the Government in France. It is significant that these immense territories scattered throughout the world and living within themselves, with only intermittent communications with the home country, should have no thought of withdrawing from it for any advantage to themselves. Any such idea was only to come later—and from without.

This overseas empire, along with the French Fleet, was one of the few trump cards remaining to European France after its reverses. It was going to be necessary, however, to maintain it against those who might have profited from its dissolution.

There was Germany, which, goaded by Italy, regretted not having demanded part of North Africa under the armistice, and which could not forget what an ideal submarine base Dakar would make.

There was England, to whom the ports of French North and West Africa would have been invaluable as way ports on the long route from England to South Africa, especially with the Mediterranean and Suez subject to blockade.

There was Japan, for whom the ports of French Indochina would have been equally valuable in its already projected expansion into the Netherlands East Indies and southeastern Asia.

There was Siam, egged on by Japan, which had long burned to press its claims to Cambodia. There was Spain, which had not forgotten its claims on Morocco and Oran. There was even the United States, concerned over the possibility of Germany advancing into the French West Indies.

And lastly there was the Chief of the Free French Committee, who naturally wished to shift the Free French headquarters from the foreign soil of England to some territory which was unquestionably French.

Faced with all these threats to its territorial integrity, the French Government could not take any position other than maintaining its territory and defending its neutrality against all comers. That defense would be first of all against the Germans, who waited only for an excuse under the armistice terms to move into French overseas territory the moment France gave indication that she herself could no longer defend it. Secondly, it would be against the Allies, who, no matter how well intentioned they might be, were supporting a separationist movement designed to alienate from the home country the African territories at a time when neither England nor the United States was in a position to defend them against a German landing there.

It was General de Gaulle who made one of the opening movements in the overseas campaign.

His proclamation of June 18, 1940, brought results in only a few scattered island territories. In the far Pacific, cut off from communication with France and surrounded by British possessions, the New Hebrides acceded to the Free French Movement on July 21, and was followed, on September 2nd, by Tahiti, also isolated from the trade which she vitally needed in order to subsist. Several days later M. Sautot, administrator of the New Hebrides, arrived at New Caledonia on board the British cruiser *Adelaide*. The only French naval ship present was the station ship *Dumont d'Urville*, a 2,000-ton sloop whose armament of three 138-mm. guns offered no chance of resistance against the powerful *Adelaide*. Upon the appeal of M. Sautot—who was later to be expelled from the Free French Movement— New Caledonia announced her accession to the Free French on September 22.

The *Dumont d'Urville* did not fall into the hands of the Free French, however. Her commanding officer, Commander Pierre Toussaint de Quièvrecourt, was a stout loyalist, so Admiral Muselier had sent a message to his executive officer, ordering him to take over the command. Commander de Quièvrecourt had replied in plain language in a single word which has the same ribald connotation in all languages. Then, unwilling to fire on fellow Frenchmen, Commander de Quièvrecourt took his sloop to Saigon, where it was to do notable work against the Siamese Navy the following year.

General de Gaulle's troubles in French Oceania were not yet over. In August, 1941, he appointed Captain Thierry d'Angenlieu as High Commissioner, with temporary rank of Rear Admiral—and promptly aroused the ire of Admiral Muselier, Commander in Chief of the F.F.N.F., who had not been consulted at all.

Then in the following May, after Admiral d'Argenlieu had arrested former Governor Sautot, the inhabitants of New Caledonia rioted and arrested both the admiral and his assistant, Commander Cabanier, former commanding officer of the submarine *Rubis*. They were extricated from this awkward situation only by the intervention of General Alexander M. Patch, U.S.A., who had landed with American troops at Noumea two months earlier to forestall possible Japanese acquisition of the territories. Both Noumea on New Caledonia and Espiritu Santo in the New Hebrides were to become notable as U.S. naval bases later in the great Pacific war.

Neither New Caledonia nor the New Hebrides nor even Tahiti would serve as a satisfactory capital for General de Gaulle's new Free French government, however. They were too distant, too isolated, too unimportant politically. Something nearer, something more important internationally, was needed. Dakar, the naval base and capital of French West Africa, seemed the best immediate possibility.

Dakar exactly fitted in with Winston Churchill's own strategic requirements also. With Britain's Mediterranean lifeline blocked since May, the alternate route around Africa had to be kept open. But along that whole long stretch of water, Britain had only one base—Freetown, in the British west coast territory of Sierra Leone. Dakar, with its excellent defenses and the only drydock between Gilbraltar and Cape Town, was infinitely superior.[1] In addition, Mr. Churchill, like the Free French, had his eye on the gold of the Bank of France which had been spirited away to Dakar ahead of the German advance.

The planning immediately began.

But even before the plans had begun to mature into preparations, Mr. Churchill had given his approval to support the Free French in an effort to extend their control to French Equatorial Africa, consisting of the Congo, Ubangi-Shari, Chad, Gabon, and the Cameroons. These territories formed an aggregate that was four times larger than France; they were isolated from the mother country, and all their political actions depended entirely upon a few senior officials. Chad had the additional value, in British eyes, of possessing an airfield at Fort Lamy, an indispensable stopover for planes being ferried to the Middle East by way of the Gold Coast and British Nigeria.

On August 13, 1940, two of General de Gaulle's representatives, Captain Philippe de Hautecloque (the future "General Leclerc") and René Pleven, suddenly appeared before the Governor of British Nigeria at Lagos, and through him made contact with Felix Eboué, French Governor of Chad.[2] Leclerc then proceeded to Duala with two dozen Free French adherents and on August 27 took over control of this important seaport and the whole of

---

[1] The British sea lanes through the eastern Mediterranean had been closed by Axis operations since May, and all British reinforcements for the Middle East had to make the long voyage around the Cape of Good Hope. On this route Dakar had the only drydock between Gibraltar and Cape Town.

[2] Eboué had some 70 millions of francs' worth of cotton to export. The planters were awaiting advances from the Treasury in order to pay the natives for harvesting the

the Cameroons in the hinterland. The following day Brazzaville was taken over by General René de Larminat, and Pointe Noire three days later. All of the French Congo thus came under the Free French flag. Ubangi-Shari also made no resistance, and General de Gaulle was able to announce over the radio that the four immense territories of the Congo, Chad, Ubangi-Shari, and the Cameroons had rallied to the Free French standard without a drop of blood being shed.

In Gabon, however, the sentiment of the French at Libreville and the unexpected arrival of the loyal submarine *Sidi-Ferruch* kept the colony loyal to the regular French Government.

However, General de Gaulle was able to announce over the radio that the four immense territories of the Congo, Chad, Ubangi-Shari, and the Cameroons had rallied to the Free French standards without a drop of blood being shed.

As a result of the news from Equatorial Africa, the authorities at Dakar had immediately dispatched the submarine *Poncelet* and the freighter *Cap de Palmes,* with a detachment of native Senegalese infantrymen aboard, to Libreville, the seaport and administrative center of Gabon. At the same time the Government at Vichy had decided to send a stout naval force of three cruisers and three super-destroyers to Dakar in order to restore order in the Gulf of Guinea. This task force—Force Y—left Toulon under command of Rear Admiral Bourragué on September 9.

Meantime, ever since August 6, another force had been in preparation to sail for almost the same destination. The landing force part of this expedition consisted of approximately 2,400 men of the Free French troops, of whom most were members of a Foreign Legion detachment that had recently participated in the capture of Narvik. Accompanying these as a support forces were some 4,000 English troops, but these were only to land in case of necessity. The six transports left Liverpool on August 31. The French were embarked on two Dutch passenger liners, the *Pennland* and the *Westernland,* the latter carrying General de Gaulle and his staff. Four cargo ships and a tanker had sailed five days earlier, escorted by the F.F.N.F. sloop *Savorgnan de Brazza* and the armed trawler *Président Houduce.*

In command of the whole expedition was Admiral Sir John Cunningham, commander of the British First Cruiser Squadron, but for politic reasons

---

crops. The Governor did not see how he could hold the territory if conditions reached the stage where the natives could no longer carry on their affairs. Unemployment and it aftereffects quickly led to dangerous unrest. Therefore, immediately after the armistice, Governor Eboué sent his principal assistant to Nigeria to discuss with the British officials agreements vital to the economic life of the Chad.

he was to issue orders to the F.F.N.F. only with the concurrence of General de Gaulle.

At the start, Admiral Cunningham's force consisted of only two heavy cruisers from the Home Fleet, but off Gibraltar he was to be joined by two battleships and the aircraft carrier *Ark Royal* of Force H, with their destroyer screen. At Freetown, the final concentration point, two additional cruisers from the South Atlantic Naval Forces were to join. Finally, in addition to the F.F.N.F. ships already listed, the 600-ton minesweeping sloops *Commandant Duboc* and *Commandant Dominé,* took part. The entire force was designated as Force M—the "M" being the first letter of the code name of the operation. That code name was quite appropriate— "Operation Menace."

The events of the next couple of days were to cause heated discussions in a number of countries, but especially in England.

For one thing, it was thought in England that the French Government had got wind of the Anglo-Free French expedition and had hastily dispatched Admiral Bourragué's force to forestall them. This was completely erroneous. The French Government had dispatched Force Y to counter the separationist movement instigated in French Equatorial Africa by Leclerc and Pleven. They had never anticipated that the French empire overseas would be attacked by a major expedition staged in part by their recent ally, Britain.

On the other hand, the British did have advance information of the movement of Bourragué's fleet. Two days before its arrival off Gibraltar, a Free French sympathizer had reported the fleet's movement to the British consul general at Tangier. In addition, the French naval attaché at Madrid, acting on direct orders from the French Admiralty, had given to the British naval attaché their notice of the force's imminent passage through the Strait of Gibraltar—though not far enough in advance to permit any interference with its passage.

However, Admiral Sir Dudley North, commanding the British North Atlantic Squadron and hence in control of the British forces at Gibraltar, had received no orders from the British Admiralty to depart from his previous instructions relative to French naval vessels. These orders, issued on July 12, stated, "No opposition is to be made to the movements of French naval vessels unless they head toward a port occupied by the enemy."

Consequently Admiral Sir Dudley North made no movement to stop Admiral Bourragué's peaceful passage through the Straits,[3] and Force Y arrived that evening at Casablanca.

But, back in Gibraltar, by that time things were in a turmoil. The British

---

[3] For this dereliction Admiral Sir Dudley North was relieved of his command and placed on the retired list a few weeks later. Since then he has vainly demanded the

destroyer *Hotspur,* which had sighted Admiral Bourragué's westward-bound force at daybreak, had notified both Gibraltar and London. At Gibraltar, Admiral Somerville had ordered the battle cruiser *Renown* to get up steam, mostly as a matter of precaution. But it was not until 1400 on September 11 that London ordered the British forces at Gibraltar to intercept the French.

The *Renown* and her escorting destroyers got underway at 1600, but by then Force Y was already under the protection of the French guns at Casablanca.

The only result of the *Renown's* vain chase was that she had been sighted and reported by a lookout at Cape Spartel. Alerted by this report to the fact that something unusual was brewing. Admiral d'Harcourt at Casablanca instructed Admiral Bourragué to get under way again the moment he had completed taking on fuel and stores. As a result, Force Y was again at sea by 0400 on the morning of the 12th, and en route to Dakar.

Meanwhile the Free French expeditionary force, supported by Admiral Cunningham's ships, had been proceeding southward also. But inasmuch as the bulk of Force M had left from the Clyde, it was still some distance from Freetown, the final staging point, when Admiral Cunningham gave General de Gaulle the surprising news that 48 hours earlier a French squadron had passed Gibraltar, headed for the Atlantic.

It was Admiral Bourragué's squadron.

Admiral Cunningham did try to deploy his ships in a last moment attempt to intercept Force Y. But when, a few days later, he received news that the French ships had already arrived at Dakar, there was nothing to do but return to Freetown and proceed with the expedition as originally planned.

There was still ample opportunity for bloodshed, however. Force Y had been sent to Governor General Boisson, High Commissioner for French West and Equatorial Africa, to reestablish order and French sovereignty in the dissident colonies. He immediately issued orders to Admiral Bourragué to proceed to Libreville in order to insure the security af Gabon and, at the same time, to study the possibility of recapturing Pointe Noire, the seaport of the Congo.

The urgency of the matter was stated plainly in a message just received from Rear Admiral Platon, Colonial Secretary in the Vichy Government. What the French Government was afraid of was German intervention. On September 11 they had received a note from Major General Karl Heinrich von Stülpnagel, President of the German Armistice Commission, which

---

right to justify himself before a court of inquiry. In 1954, five British Admirals of the Fleet publicly intervened in his favor. His case has been publicly debated in the House of Commons and the House of Lords. The British Admiralty has remained adamant in refusing him a hearing.

stated: "In the event the French Government does not succeed in reestablishing order in the threatened territories, the German and Italian Governments will take such action as they deem necessary."

Completely ignorant of Admiral Cunningham's force ahead, Admiral Bourragué set out with his three cruisers on September 18 without even waiting for his super-destroyers, as these lacked sufficient steaming radius anyway. Since there were no fuel stocks at Libreville, the tanker *Tarn* had been sent ahead under escort of the light cruiser *Primauguet.*

On the morning of September 19 Admiral Bourragué found himself being trailed by the British cruisers *Cumberland* and *Australia,* but determined to push on as if nothing had happened. During the course of the afternoon, however, he received a radio message from Captain Pierre Goybet commanding the *Primauguet,* a thousand miles ahead, informing him that the British cruisers *Cornwall* and *Delhi* were now blocking his way. Goybet was prepared to fight, but Bourragué was of the opinion that a pitched battle with the English must be avoided at all costs—a decision on which he was later to be congratulated by both Mr. Boisson and Admiral Muselier.

All that remained for Admiral Bourragué to do was to return to Dakar. What could he have done at Libreville without fuel on arrival? Increasing speed, he left the *Cumberland* and *Australia* behind. However, the *Gloire* developed engine trouble, and the British cruisers caught up with her and forced her to proceed to Casablanca instead of Dakar. The *Tarn* and *Primauguet* were also turned toward the same port.

Admiral Darlan, however, was very angry. No sooner had Bourragué arrived at Dakar with his remaining cruisers, the *Georges Leygues* and the *Montcalm,* than he was relieved of his command[4] (September 22) by Vice Admiral Emile Lacroix, flown by plane from the 3rd Squadron at Toulon.

Nothing of the combined Anglo-Free French expedition was as yet known at Dakar. However, a Spanish newspaper had announced the departure from England of General de Gaulle for an unknown destination—perhaps Morocco. After conferring with Rear Admiral Landriau, French naval commandant at Dakar, Lacroix informed the French Admiralty that the British attitude might indicate either a blockade of or an attack on Dakar. He added that the latter still appeared problematical, and that, after all, every effort must be made to reach an agreement with the British by doing everything to avoid open conflict between France and England.[5]

By this time the Anglo-Free French expedition was under way, having left Freetown on September 21. Two days later, at daybreak, Admiral

---

[4] Admiral Darlan soon recognized the soundness of Bourragué's decision and promoted him to Vice Admiral, with duties at Government headquarters.

[5] Telegram 1840 of 22 September 1940.

Cunningham's ships appeared off Dakar, preceded by planes dropping leaflets which announced the arrival of General de Gaulle and his troops, come to "defend and provision Dakar."

The answer to the leaflets was a prompt burst of antiaircraft fire directed at the visitors. And so began the Battle of Dakar, at 0610, in a dense early morning fog.

Initially General de Gaulle had believed that he would be welcomed at Dakar without having to fire a shot. He had since abandoned that hope—along with his original determination not to fire on his fellow countrymen.[6] Hence he had worked out with the British a sort of triple-barreled tactical plan: (1) Undercover agents would be slipped into the city several days in advance in order to instigate a separationist movement; (2) a delegation would be landed openly under the leadership of Commander Thierry d'Argenlieu to try to persuade the authorities of Dakar to accede to the Free French movement; and (3) a surprise attack should be launched against the airfield at Ouakam by half a dozen determined aviators who would be landed there in two innocent looking pleasure planes of the "Luciole" type, which would take off from the *Ark Royal.* Possession of the airfield would remove the greatest threat to the attackers—the air force of the defenders.

The three-way tactical plan, however, did not work out as it had been hoped. The "Luciole" planes landed unsuspected at Ouakam airfield on the outskirts of Dakar, and their Free French occupants quickly made a prisoner of the airfield commandant, who had come innocently to meet them. However, their intentions were soon discovered and they were overpowered and made prisoners in turn.

Commander d'Argenlieu's delegation had fared no better. Landing in two motor boats from the *Savorgnan de Brazza,* they asked to be taken at once to the authorities. Admiral Landriau had been alerted, however, by the leaflets and he sent word that he would not see them. Then, after second thought, he ordered them arrested. However, d'Argenlieu, quickly sizing up the situation, reembarked and got under way for the *Savorgnan de Brazza,* pursued by a wheezing old tug and a burst of machinegun fire which only succeeded in wounding d'Argenlieu and a Free French army officer.

The "fifth column," which had secretly infiltrated into the city several days before under the direction of Lieutenant Claude H. de Boislambert,

---

[6] "Besides, I specified, over the objections of the British, that in no case would the volunteers bear arms against France. That did not mean that they might never fight Frenchmen. It was necessary, alas, to expect the opposite, the Vichy Government being what it was and not France at all." From *Memoirs* of General de Gaulle.

had no luck, either. No one would listen to them.

As a climax to these more or less peaceful attempts to sway Dakar to the Free French movement, two small sloops had been sent into the harbor to land detachments of marines who were charged with inciting the crew of the *Richelieu* to shift to the Free French side.[7] The battleship, however, threw a couple of shots their way and they discreetly retired.[8]

General de Gaulle no longer had any delusions about the sympathies of Dakar. One after the other, he broadcast three messages to the defenders.

The first one, put on the air at 0700, announced the arrival of General de Gaulle and his forces, accompanied by "a powerful English squadron and numerous British troops," which, however, "would not intervene if all went well."

The second message, broadcast at 0807, was more threatening:

If such opposition continues, the enormous Allied forces which follow me will enter into action, and the consequences will be serious.

The third message, sent out at 1020, had all the marks of an ultimatum, and was treated as such:

Free French Forces before Dakar.
The authorities of Dakar have refused to negotiate with the officers that I have sent them. The *Richelieu* and the coastal batteries of Gorée have fired on the *Savorgnan de Brazza,* the *Commandant Duboc,* and the *Commandant Dominé.* The French ships and troops which accompany me must enter Dakar. If they are opposed, the important Allied forces which follow me will take over responsibility for the matter.

With that the guns opened up, as the coastal batteries, carrying out their orders,[9] opened fire on the British ships which had just become recognizable through the fog.

The English fired back.

In that opening duel the French submarine *Persée* attempted to torpedo an English cruiser in a surface attack, but was hit and sunk. On the British side the cruiser *Cumberland* was struck by a shell from the coastal batteries and had to withdraw from action.

There was still an alternative way to attack Dakar—to turn its flanks by

---

[7] That, at least, was how their operations orders read.

[8] On his return to Freetown, the captain of one of these sloops, Lieutenant de la Porte de Vaux, sent a telegram to Captain Paul Marzin, commanding the *Richelieu,* to the effect that he did not consider it cricket on the part of the *Richelieu* to open fire on his small ship, particularly since their children attended the same school at Brest!

[9] Since the July attack-seizures, the French Admiralty had issued orders to fire on all British men-of-war approaching inside 20 nautical miles of the French shores.

an amphibious attack in the Bay of Rufisque, in the rear. At 1700, the *Savorgnan de Brazza,* the *Commandant Duboc,* and the *Commandant Dom-iné* made an attempt to land troops there, but were driven off by the fire of two old 95-mm. guns installed in a battery at the foot of the lighthouse, and by machinegun fire from a platoon of Senegalese infantrymen posted on the shore. The amphibious attack was given up after a short exchange of shots.

The worst blow suffered thus far by the defenders was the tragic loss of the super-destroyer *Audacieux.* This ship was struck by a salvo of 8-inch shells from the British cruiser *Australia,* only dimly seen in the fog. With her bridge blown up and fire flaming in the wreckage, the *Audacieux* beached herself in shallow water, where she burned all the next day. Eighty men died in the catastrophe.

At this stage of the affair General de Gaulle, according to his own memoirs, would have been glad to call off the action. But apparently Mr. Churchill then instructed Admiral Cunningham to take over the operation personally. At one o'clock the morning of the 24th, Cunningham sent Governor General Boisson an ultimatum calling upon him to deliver the place over to General de Gaulle by 6 A.M.

The message was not very tactfully phrased, inasmuch as it accused the defenders of preparing to hand over Dakar to the Germans.

The indignation of Mr. Boisson and the generals and admirals around him was extreme. Someone proposed that he answer with an insulting refusal, but Boisson contented himself with a reply that was as dignified as it was curt:

"France has entrusted me with Dakar. I will defend Dakar to the end."

Admiral Cunningham's squadron consisted of two battleships; the aircraft carrier *Ark Royal,* with some 30 planes of the Swordfish and Skua types; plus two heavy cruisers, one light cruiser, and some ten destroyers. This force was exclusive of the damaged *Cumberland.* The defenses of Dakar now consisted of the coastal batteries of nine 240-mm., three 155-mm., and four 138-mm. guns, plus the eight 380-mm. guns of the *Richelieu,* which was moored in the harbor but unable to get under way. There were also two cruisers, two super-destroyers, one destroyer of 1,800 tons, six sloops, two submarines, and some ten naval planes. At Ouakam airfield there was one fighter group, and at Thiès one bomber group. At Dakar and in the vicinity were five regiments of troops.

The morning of September 24 started off badly for the defenders. At 0700 the submarine *Ajax* was disabled by depth charges and her crew taken prisoner. The British battleships then opened up with a bombardment which lasted 34 minutes, but inflicted no appreciable damage to the defenses. The guns of the *Richelieu* and of the cruisers replied briskly. The fog had begun to clear, forcing the British to stay at long range. In addition the antiaircraft guns of the defenders had brought down three English planes, and the fighters had shot down a fourth.

Following a lull, the bombardment began again near noon, and even more furiously. The city was swept by shellfire, and some damage occurred among the mass of freighters anchored in the roads and in the harbor. Yet despite one hundred and sixty 15-inch shells fired at them, the *Richelieu* and the cruisers were practically undamaged. The cruisers evaded injury by constant zigzagging and salvo-chasing inside the torpedo nets at the entrance. Another attack from the *Ark Royal's* torpedo planes resulted only in two more British planes being shot down. The city's civilian population suffered some of the heaviest losses, with 84 killed and 197 wounded.

The British returned to the attack early the next day, with disastrous results to themselves. Lieutenant Commander Pierre Lancelot, commanding the *Béveziers,* the only French submarine remaining after the loss of the *Ajax* and *Persée,* now knew the bombardment positions of the British ships. So, before dawn, he placed himself in a favorable position, and when they approached to resume their bombardment, he put a torpedo in the *Resolution,* blowing a large hole in her, forward.[10] It was months before she could be repaired in a U.S. navy yard and take part in the war again. At 0925 the *Barham* was sprayed by shell fragments of a 380-mm. shell from the *Richelieu.* That was enough. Admiral Cunningham withdrew his ships from the action.

The repercussions of the battle were considerable. In England, General de Gaulle's prestige dropped tremendously, and even Mr. Churchill had to face an angry House of Commons demanding an explanation of the failure. For the men of the French Navy, the successful defense was a great tonic.[11] They were almost grateful to their adversaries of the day for providing them

---

[10] Promoted to Commander as a result of this exploit, Lancelot later commanded the super-destroyer *Terrible,* and eventually served under Sir John Cunningham, Interallied Commander in Chief in the Mediterranean, after the French Navy reentered the war. Awarded a British decoration for his services there, he was asked by Sir John how he had managed to get that hit on the *Resolution.* Lancelot told him. "Good shot!" said the admiral, with fine sportsmanship, and pinned the decoration on Lancelot.

After the war Lancelot was naval attaché at Washington, then commander of the antisubmarine groups of the French Navy. At the time of the Suez crisis in 1956 he commanded the French naval forces in Egypt. He was a Vice Admiral and Director of Naval Personnel when he was unfortunately killed in an airplane accident on October 7, 1957.

[11] Considering the duration and heat of the bombardment, French military losses at Dakar were remarkably small—100 killed and 182 wounded. Of these casualties the Navy suffered the greater part—87 killed and 118 wounded.

with an opportunity to erase the inferiority complex that had beset them since the surprise attack at Mers-el-Kebir. Strange as it may seem, Franco-British relations actually improved after the Dakar battle.

Disappointed in their hopes of winning Dakar to their cause, the Free French set about staging an operation to gain control of Gabon. Here the advantages were more on their side, as, in addition to the British blockade, there were only a few native troops for defense, plus the guns and crews of the French sloop *Bougainville* and the submarine *Poncelet*.

After the opening skirmishes on the Ogooué River, the first Free French Air Force (F.F.A.F.) planes appeared over Libreville and attacked the *Bougainville* at her anchorage in the harbor. Commander Thierry d'Argenlieu commanded the Free French naval forces, and Colonel Leclerc was in command of the over-all operation. The British confined their participation to a tight blockade of the whole Gabon coast.

On November 7 Colonel Leclerc began landing his Free French brigade from the transports *Fort Lamy, Casamance,* and *Nevada* on the shores of the Bay of Mondah, to the north of Libreville. Commander Robert Morin, commanding the *Bougainville,* ordered the *Poncelet* to attack the invaders. But in the afternoon of the next day the *Poncelet* was sighted by the British patrol vessel *Milford,* and, after desperate evasive maneuvers, was forced to the surface in a disabled condition. The submarine's commanding officer, Lieutenant Commander Bertrand de Saussine,[12] saw his men over the side to safety, and then, rather than have his vessel fall into the hands of the enemy, returned to the control room, opened the sea valves, and went down with his ship.

The next day, November 9, witnessed the sad sight of two French vessels, sister ships and flying the same national flag, firing upon each other until one was blasted beneath the waves.

The *Bougainville* was cruising in the river when the *Savorgnan de Brazza* appeared. It was not the Free French ship that fired first; in fact the tragic duel might not have occurred if Free French planes had not begun the action by bombing the *Bougainville.* The latter then opened fire on its adversaries wherever they were seen.

But a good third of her crew were on shore where they had been sent to reinforce the troops resisting the land attack, consequently the *Bougainville's* fire was slow and erratic. After twenty minutes of battle, the *Bougainville* was hopelessly disabled and on fire.

The resistance ashore against the superior Free French forces was as

---

[12] Lieutenant Commander de Saussine was an officer of great promise, and extremely popular throughout the Navy. He was a close friend of d'Estienne d'Orves, in the Free French forces, who was also to give his life under heroic circumstances.

futile. The Free French entered Libreville on the morning of November 10, and were in possession of Port Gentil four days later. The conquest of French Equatorial Africa was now complete.[13]

This territory was the base from which, the next year, General Leclerc began his march that led to the conquest of the Cufra Oases (Italian Libya). It was from Brazzaville that General de Gaulle, on November 16, 1940, broadcast a declaration which, with his broadcast of October 27, completed his political break with Vichy and explained why he had assumed power.[14]

---

[13] Up until 1942 the French Government was under constant pressure by the Germans to allow them to reconquer the dissident colonies—Chad, in particular. Laval discussed the matter with the Germans in Paris in 1940, the day before he was dismissed from his Government office. Only by constantly finding new pretexts—rainy season, poor communications, insufficient means—was the French Government able to dodge the issue until changing events made the Chad no longer of importance.

[14] ". . . . In short, despite the outrages committed at Vichy, the Constitution still remains legally in effect. Under these conditions, therefore, all Frenchmen—and, notably, all free Frenchmen—are released from all obligations toward the pseudo-government of Vichy—a Government derived from a feeble imitation of a National Assembly; a Government which by all its actions proves conclusively that it is under the domination of the enemy. . . ."

CHAPTER 18

Threat and Crisis in the Far East

Meantime, in the Far East, French territory was also under threat, but from different sources.

There Japan had become bogged down in her war with China. Both France and England had been sending supplies to the Chinese, the former by the Yunnan railroad, and the British by the famous Burma Road. Taking advantage of France's reversals in 1940, the Japanese had demanded that these shipments be stopped. The French Governor General of Indochina, General Georges Catroux, conferred with Admiral Decoux, commanding the French Naval Forces in the Far East, as well as with Admiral Sir Percy Noble, commanding the British Naval Forces there.

At that time the French Naval Forces in the Far East consisted of the cruiser *Lamotte-Picquet,* of 8,000 tons and eight 155-mm. guns, the sloop *Amiral Charner,* of 2,000 tons and three 138-mm. guns, as well as two ancient sloops of 600 tons, the *Marne* and the *Tahure,* and a scattering of survey vessels, auxiliary minesweepers, and river gunboats. The British were no stronger. Against these was ranged the entire Japanese Fleet. All the Allied leaders in the Far East were aware that they were not in a position to oppose the Japanese, especially with the United States not prepared to give any support, either morally or politically.

Admiral Decoux, no defeatist, nevertheless perceived that the only way for France to hold on to Indochina was to stay on good terms with Japan. The British naval officers were of the same opinion: "The enemy is in Indochina, now is not the time for France to leave!" General Catroux was of the same opinion and bowed to the Japanese demands.

Nevertheless, the French Government, then at Bordeaux, was displeased with Catroux for assuming the power to make such decisions, as well as for giving in so quickly. They accordingly replaced him with Admiral Decoux.

The concessions extorted from General Catroux did not satisfy the Japanese. On August 1, 1940, they presented new demands, this time for five airfields in northern Tonkin, and the right to quarter 30,000 men there.

Again France turned to America for any support she might give. But the Acting U.S. Secretary of State, Sumner Welles, could only reply, "The De-

194

partment of State understands the difficult position of the French Government . . . and does not believe it has the right to reproach France for granting military facilities to the Japanese."

Admiral Decoux therefore entered into an agreement with the Japanese, but conceded them only three airfields and the right to station 6,000 men there. The Japanese practically ignored these limits, and on September 22 made a surprise attack on the garrison at Langson, and four days later bombarded Haiphong. Only hasty negotiations by Vichy directly with Tokyo prevented the beginning of a general conflict.

But concessions made to Japan did not prevent actual conflict with Siam. This country took advantage of France's difficulties, in Europe and with the Japanese, to put forth her demand for part of Cambodia, on the right bank of the Mekong River.

The Siamese forces were not negligible. Their Air Force consisted of 120 training planes and 150 combat planes—more than three times the total French air forces in Indochina. The Siamese Navy included two coast defense battleships with 203-mm. guns, two gunboats with 152-mm. guns, and some ten torpedo boats, sloops, and minesweepers—unquestionably a force superior in material strength to the five old French men-of-war stationed in Indochina.

War with Siam was never actually declared, but incident piled up on incident until by the beginning of 1941 hostilities were general all along the frontier. Finally Rear Admiral Jules Terraux, commanding the French Navy in Indochina, determined to come to the aid of the hard pressed Army by striking a decisive blow at the Siamese Navy. Disregarding their numerical superiority, he directed Captain Régis Bérenger, commanding the *Lamotte-Picquet,* to take that ship and the 2,000-ton sloops *Amiral Charner* and *Dumont d'Urville,* along with the 600-ton sloops *Marne* and *Tahure,* and seek out the enemy.

Aerial reconnaissance had located the Siamese Fleet off the Koh Chang Archipelago, and Captain Bérenger surprised them there before dawn on January 17, 1941. The great danger was not the enemy's firepower, but the numerous unknown shoals in the area where the slightest grounding would have been disastrous.

The French plane, an old Loire 130, which had located the enemy had alerted the Siamese gunners, who promptly opened fire on the French ships through the curtain of the morning mists.

This was a mistake, because up until then the French gun pointers had not been able to see the Siamese ships. As it was, they opened fire at 0614 and within half an hour had sent the small torpedo boats *Songkla, Chonburi,* and *Trat* to the bottom.

The *Lamotte-Picquet* chose as its main adversary the coast defense battleship *Thomburi,* whose 203-mm. guns should have far outranged the French cruiser's 155-mm. guns. There then took place a lethal game of hide and seek in the maze of small islands into and out of which the enemy constantly popped. Eventually the *Lamotte-Picquet* drove her foe into the shallow water where she could not be reached, but where she capsized later when her consorts attempted to tow her away.

On the way back to Saigon, Bérenger's squadron was attacked twice by enemy planes but received no hits. The only damage received at all during the whole combat, in fact, was that caused by the shock of the fire of the ships' own guns.

A particularly pleasant ending to the campaign was added when the news was received that not only the *Thomburi,* but her sister ship, the *Aytuthya,* had been put out of action, probably by one of the torpedoes fired early in the engagement by the *Lamotte-Picquet* at an ill-defined target dimly seen through the mists.

The Japanese were disconcerted by this resounding defeat suffered by their Siamese friends, and they hastened to act as "mediators" in drawing up a peace to end the hostilities.

But the Japanese had no idea of making any peaceful gestures themselves.

On July 12 Ambassador Sotomatsu Kato asked the French Government at Vichy for the use of eight Indochina airfields, the port of Saigon, and the excellent roadstead of Camranh Bay. Officially the excuse was made that Japan needed the airfields and seaports to help in "the common defense" of Indochina. In actuality the Japanese General Staff was preparing its bases of operations against Malaya and the Netherlands East Indies.

No more help could be expected from the English or the Americans this year than the previous year. After toying with the idea of a caustic refusal, Admiral Darlan bowed to the inevitable. But Indochina was not occupied, and except for the conceded bases, the entire territory remained under French administration.

Without doubt the use of the bases by the Japanese forces was one of the reasons for their swift success in Malaya. It was the Japanese planes taking off from airfields in the vicinity of Saigon that sank the *Repulse* and the *Prince of Wales.* But what could France have done in Indochina with an army of 30,000 men and five old men-of-war against the whole war machine of Japan, allied as it was with the country which even then was occupying two-thirds of France?

The United States, however, reacted violently, particularly against Japan. In a statement on July 24, 1941, Acting Secretary of State Sumner Welles showed great understanding of the French Government's situation in Indochina. He said: "The present unfortunate situation in which the French Government at Vichy and the French Government of Indochina find them-

selves is, of course, well known. It is only too clear that they are in no position to resist the pressure exercised upon them."

The pressure in Indochina was no greater than was being applied at that
same time in the Middle East. There, on June 8, 1941, British forces led by
General Sir Maitland Wilson and the Free French First Division, commanded by General Paul Legentilhomme, attacked Syria and Lebanon,
states under French mandate.

The reason given for the attacks was that Darlan had granted German
planes the right to land there on their way to Iraq, under the circumstances
previously stated. However, on June 8, when the attack was made, there
was not a single Axis plane in either Syria or Lebanon. Not one member of
the Axis military forces resided there. And the Iraq question had already
been completely settled to the advantage of the English. The operation had
been in the planning stage for some time, however, judging from the memoirs
of Winston Churchill and General de Gaulle, and all that was needed was
the occasion.[1] General Wavell, the British Middle East Commander, was not
as enthusiastic for the operation as the Free French, who hoped to win over
the some 30,000 seasoned French troops in the Levant to their cause, which
so far had secured only a few thousand adherents.[2]

The Anglo-Free French attack on land was two-pronged; one force advanced from Palestine toward Beirut and Damascus, the other was launched
two weeks later from bases in Mesopotamia and was directed at the eastern
frontier of Syria. On the sea the British naval and air forces were predominant.

The French troops under General Henri Dentz[3] defended themselves with

---

[1] "I have the honor to transmit to you the enclosed plans for the coming operations
in Syria. . . . The purpose of the operation is to establish at Damascus, and then at
Beirut, a military force capable of ensuring the authority of the High Commissioner
of the Free French. . . ." From General de Gaulle's letter of April 25, 1941, to General
Catroux.

[2] The disappointment of General de Gaulle was such that he refused to recognize
the Franco-British Armistice of Saint Jean d'Acre. In his *Memoirs,* he states: "Instead
of the honest effect which we hoped to exercise on the minds and consciences of the
men . . . so rancorous and humiliating was the atmosphere in which they had been held
that their only desire was to leave, as speedily as possible, the scene of their vain
sacrifices and bitter efforts."

[3] Descendant of an Alsatian family, General Dentz held the dual office of High
Commissioner and Commander in Chief in the Levant. He had already been called
upon to give up a frontline command in order to function as Military Governor of
Paris just before the Germans entered it. In Syria he had the greater anguish of having
to defend his trust against his former allies and his own countrymen. His life ended
on an even more tragic note. Notwithstanding the definite stipulations of the Convention of Saint Jean d'Acre, which ended the fighting in Syria, he was tried by the
French High Court for treason and was condemned to death on April 13, 1945. The
sentence was not carried out, but he died of want and cold in prison the following 18th
of December.

stern discipline even if with no great enthusiasm. During the enemy's assault on Sidon on June 15 they staged a counterattack that nearly threw the British back to their starting points. The losses were heavy on both sides.[4] But General Wilson had all the resources of his Middle East bases to draw on for supplies and reinforcements; General Dentz was completely cut off and could expect no assistance.

The essential problem facing the French Government was whether to let Syria fall to superior numbers or to commit the bulk of the Fleet in order to send reinforcements. One word from Darlan, and fiery Admiral de Laborde, commander of the fleet at Toulon, would have gotten under way for the eastern Mediterranean. But this would undoubtedly have brought on a general engagement with the British, which was something the Navy had always done its best to avoid. Also, with the Lebanon coast 1,600 miles from Toulon and with no suitable bases there, the French Fleet would have had to accept the hospitality of Axis ports in Greece and the Dodecanese. Inevitably this would have meant collaboration and would eventually have led to an alliance with the Axis in place of the former alliance with Britain.

Darlan refused to do this, just as he had rejected the Axis offer to assist with air attack squadrons operating from Rhodes and even from airfields in Syria.

Yet France could not allow the Axis powers to feel that in rejecting their offers of military assistance, she was not seriously trying to defend Syria and Lebanon. If the Axis got any such idea they would immediately have insisted on taking over the defense of Syria and Lebanon themselves, especially as at that time the Wehrmacht was not tied down by the Russian campaign. By undertaking to defend Syria solely with their own forces, the French deprived the Germans of any excuse for joint action in the defense of Africa. However, the French soldiers and sailors on the spot who did not understand the situation, likewise could not understand why the assistance of the German Stukas was refused.

The one thing the French Government could do was to throw a limited part of the Navy into the action. Not a big enough part to bring on a general conflict with the British, but just enough to make some show of defending the French territories. The naval force so sent was to consist of one naval air wing from North Africa and additional ships steaming singly.

At the beginning of hostilities the French naval forces on the Syrian coast consisted of the super-destroyers *Valmy,* commanded by Commander

---

[4] General Dentz's report gave 1,819 dead and missing as the French casualties, of whom 405 were officers or noncommissioned officers. This figure also included those lost on the *Souffleur.* The British gave their casualties as 4,500 killed, wounded, and missing.

Amedée Guiot, and the *Guépard,* with the division commander, Captain Raymond Gervais de Lafond, on board; the submarines *Caïman, Morse,* and *Souffleur;* the sloop *Elan,* the tanker *Adour,* and several sweepers of no military value. This force, under the over-all command of Rear Admiral Pierre Gouton, was based at Beirut, Lebanon, a commercial port with practically no defenses. The Air Force, based inland at Riyaq, consisted only of a few Glenn Martin bombers and a few fighters.

The British forces which were supporting the Anglo-Free French operation were under the command of Vice Admiral E.L.S. King. They consisted of the cruisers *Phoebe, Ajax,* and *Coventry,* plus six destroyers and some submarines. But back of them, in case of need, they had the main British Fleet at Alexandria and the R.A.F. squadrons of the Middle East command.

The very day of the English attack, the *Caïman* barely missed the *Ajax* with a torpedo. The next day, June 9, the super-destroyers carried out orders and fired on enemy columns marching along the coast roads. The bombardment was no great success, as the ships had no antipersonnel projectiles, and no place to get any, since under the armistice conditions no ammunition stocks were allowed at Beirut.

Having fired some 60 rounds, the super-destroyers were on the point of withdrawing when they sighted four British destroyers and, behind them, the masts of cruisers.

The French opened fire first, and within eight minutes the *Guépard* hit the British destroyer *Janus,* bringing her to a stop with her bridge blown up. For fifteen days afterward the *Janus'* commanding officer had a green tinted beard from the dye in the *Guépard's* projectiles. Then, as the British cruisers came up, Captain Gervais de Lafond successfully disengaged and returned to Beirut without any serious damage. But the French Air Force took over and harried the British vessels until they were driven off by British Hurricane fighters.

Admiral Sir Andrew Cunningham, British commander in chief in the Mediterranean, immediately sent reinforcements of six destroyers and the cruiser *Leander.*

On the French side, both the super-destroyers and the Air Force needed ammunition and supplies. While the French Admiralty was struggling with this logistics problem, the British expeditionary corps landed at Sidon on June 12. The defenders were forced to fall back, since the super-destroyers, short of ammunition, could do nothing more than harassing raids.

However, the French Admiralty had sent out the super-destroyer *Chevalier Paul,* with the much needed ammunition. Unfortunately she was torpedoed by a British plane during the night of June 16 some 50 miles off the Syrian coast. The fact that the torpedoed ship also shot down the attacking plane did not compensate for the loss of the ship and the ammunition, but the *Valmy* and *Guépard* arrived in time to save the ship's crew. A second super-destroyer, the *Vauquelin,* managed to slip through from France with ammunition, but she was seriously damaged in Beirut harbor the following day by British bombers.

Beirut was manifestly untenable for the French ships, yet the moment they left the port they were sure to encounter superior British forces. On June 22, in a night engagement with two cruisers and six destroyers, the *Guépard* was raked by a 6-inch shell from the *Leander,* but continued in the fight. On June 25 the submarine *Souffleur* was torpedoed by a British submarine near the Bay of Djounieh. The *Adour,* which carried the entire fuel supply of the French naval forces in the Middle East, had already been seriously damaged by a torpedo plane while at anchor in the roads.

The Navy's Fourth Bomber Group, which the Admiralty had sent out in order to avoid having to accept the Luftwaffe's offer of assistance, arrived at Riyaq, Syria, on June 15, and went into action that same evening against British ships bombarding the French shore defenses at Sidon. Several days later they were sent to take part in the Battle of Palmyra, in the open desert, but without any fighter escort. Consequently they were surprised and lost six planes shot down on June 28 in a battle with 20 English fighters. The survivors boldly bombed Haifa four days later in an attack in which unfortunately their leader, Lieutenant Commander Georges Huber, was lost.

The French fighter squadron which was to complete the aviation reinforcement did not arrive until early July, just in time to engage in a few brushes with the British.

On July 11, all planes capable of flying received orders to return to France, but out of the 13 originally in the bomber group, only 4 remained to fly back.

The super-destroyers *Guépard, Valmy,* and *Vauquelin* had sailed from Syria for Salonika on July 9, there to embark a battalion of troops that had come from France by rail. In order to take them through to Tripoli, they would have had to run the British gauntlet just as the Japanese "Tokyo Express" was to do at Guadalcanal a year later. Two small French freighters also were to try to carry antiaircraft guns, ammunition, and airplane spare parts from Salonika to Syria.

All of these attempts failed. The freighter *Saint-Didier* was sunk by a British torpedo on July 4 off the Anatolian coast. The other freighter, the *Chateau Yquem,* was recalled to save her from the same fate. As for the super-destroyers with the troops, they were discovered by British planes more than 200 miles from the Syrian coast, thus losing all chance of slipping past the British patrols. They accordingly turned about and proceeded to Toulon, in accordance with their instructions. The submarines had already withdrawn to Bizerte. The remaining ships interned themselves in neutral ports.

Ashore, the defenders had slowly succumbed to superior forces. Damascus fell to the British and Free French on June 21. General Dentz, authorized to negotiate, signed an armistice at Saint Jean d'Acre on July 14. Instead of joining the Free French, however, nine-tenths of the French forces elected repatriation with their families and the civil servants in the two mandates, in accordance with the armistice conditions.[5] Part of them were later sent to North Africa, where the memory of their experiences in Lebanon and Syria had much to do with their stubborn resistance when the Allies landed in November, 1942.

Such a resistance without hope of success might seem extravagant folly to some. But it was not really the British against whom France was defending Beirut; in actuality what France was doing was defending Tunisa against occupation by the Axis, which inevitably would have happened had France not made an effort to defend her territories at Syria and Lebanon. For by the protocol which Admiral Darlan had been forced to sign with the Axis on May 27, the way to occupation of Bizerte and other African ports would have been opened to the Germans. Darlan, however, had inserted such conditions in the protocol that he was certain the Germans would never accept them.

The campaign over, the Free French, associated with the British victory, installed themselves in the Levant. But their success was not to be without eventual repercussions, for their spokesman, in order to win the support of the native populations, had promised them independence. As for the British viewpoint, Mr. Churchill stated in the House of Commons, "There is no question of France retaining in Syria the position that was hers before the war." That statement was borne out in the expulsion of France from the Middle East in 1945. It may be asked what historians will think in the future of the benefits obtained either by the British or the Free French from their campaign in the Middle East in June, 1941.

The armistice of June, 1940, had been signed with the expectation that it would bring peace to suffering France. If this was peace, it was certainly a strange peace. From the moment the armistice was signed the French Navy had not been spared fighting in almost every corner of the globe. For instance in Djibouti—French Somaliland.

Here in this isolated territory on the east coast of Africa, some 30,000

---

[5] The repatriations required round trip passages by 21 passenger ships, which carried a total of 33,950 repatriates between Beirut and Marseilles. These figures testify to the loyalty to the Vichy Government of the officers and troops of the Levant. The repatriations required extensive negotiations with the belligerents.

to 40,000 souls looked to France—to the French Navy—for food. And they were shut off from that food by the British blockade.

Why was there any such blockade? The British forces under the brilliant leadership of General Sir Archibald Wavell had already hurled the Italian forces out of Somaliland, Eritrea, and Ethiopia; there could be no possibility of collusion between French Djibouti and nonexistent Axis forces in that region.

At the end of Wavell's campaign, in April, 1941, the Governor of Djibouti, Pierre Nouailhetas, a former Navy man, had already been in secret communication with the British governor of Aden. The British could have no need of Djibouti, except perhaps for the revictualling of British-occupied Ethiopia. And Mr. Nouailhetas would have been glad to lend the use of the Franco-Ethiopian railroad for the revictualling if the British would only drop off a share of the victuals for the use of his own famishing population.

General Wavell was of the same mind. In one of his reports he wrote, "From the point of view of military administration, the obvious policy to follow would be to conclude an agreement with the authorities of Djibouti for the use of the port and the railroad, in exchange for a relaxation of the blockade of the French Somaliland coast."

But Djibouti was an objective of prime importance to the Free French as, rightly or wrongly, General de Gaulle looked upon it as a test of British goodwill toward himself. In their program of extending their control over as much French territory as possible, the Free French, ever since November of 1940, had been planning "Operation Marie," the aim of which was to bring about the accession of French Somaliland. One of their battalions had made the trip across Africa. Two others had gone around the Cape, escorted by the *Savorgnan de Brazza* and the *Commandant Duboc*. They had arrived almost simultaneously at Port Sudan, on the Red Sea—and General Wavell had promptly thrown them, not against Djibouti, but against the real enemy, the Italians.[6] Subsequently those troops had been used in Syria. Apparently all thoughts of action against Djibouti had been abandoned—when suddenly the British broke off the amicable talks with Nouailhetas and rein-

---

[6] Commanding the Free French who proved so valorous at Massawa was General Charles Magrin Vernerey, alias "Montclar," who had fought at Narvik under the orders of General Béthouart. Although originally assigned to participate in the Dakar operation, his brigade was not landed or engaged there. He commanded the 1st Free French Brigade in Eritrea against the Italians, and distinguished himself both at Keren and Massawa, at which latter battle he received the surrender of the Italian commander, Rear Admiral Mario Bonetti.

When the Korean War broke out, General Montclar asked to go with the battalion of French troops which fought with such distinction in the United Nations forces. In order to command this battalion he willingly accepted a reduction in rank to lieutenant colonel.

stituted the blockade of Djibouti, with the added participation of the *Savorgnan de Brazza* and the *Commandant Duboc*. By June, 1941, Djibouti was famished.

It was under these circumstances that Captain Paul Maerten, commanding the French naval forces at Madagascar, down the African coast, received orders to revictual Djibouti.

Apart from the French submarines at Diego Suarez, there were available at Madagascar only half a dozen native sailing craft. But these might slip past the blockade unsuspected, whereas a steamer would certainly be captured. Accordingly these sailing ships were gotten ready in greatest secrecy.

The first to sail was the *Hind,* of 130 tons. Her native crew was officered by two French ensigns and a petty officer, disguised as native seamen and with turbanned heads and walnut stained faces. Ensign Paul Cazalis de Fondouce was the commanding officer. Slipping through the blockade undetected, the *Hind* unloaded 70 tons of food in starving Djibouti. Her evasion of the blockade had been abetted by the submarine *Vengeur,* which had let fly two torpedoes at the blockading *Savorgnan de Brazza*. The *Savorgnan de Brazza* was not hit but she had had such a narrow escape that she quickly departed from the neighborhood, loudly broadcasting a submarine warning.

The second native craft, the *Naram Passa,* commanded by Lieutenant Jean Simonot, also succeeded in running the blockade. But none of the other five was successful, one of them being boarded and captured by British patrols.

The only remaining hope of victualling Djibouti seemed to rest with the submarines, with their limited cargo capacity. Then suddenly the sloop *D'Iberville* put into Diego Suarez, where she was immediately loaded and dispatched to Dijbouti. With her three 138-mm. guns she could laugh at the challenge of the British patrol boats which attempted to stop her. "Stand clear or we open fire!" was *D'Iberville's* reply to the challenge, and she went on to deliver 300 tons of food to Djibouti the day before Christmas.

Next, two submarines went through. And then, in February, 1942, the second *Bougainville,* a converted banana boat, escorted by the submarine *Héros,* delivered 1,300 tons of food to Djibouti in one trip.

The blockade had been thwarted; there was enough food in Djibouti now to last for months. And then suddenly Djibouti learned on May 5, 1942, that Diego Suarez, in Madagascar, the other end of the victual run, had been attacked by the British.

The British stated that they had acted in order to prevent the island falling into the hands of the Japanese. But there had not been a single Japanese attempt against Madagascar, and Admiral Darlan had made a written pledge to Admiral Leahy, the U. S. ambassador at Vichy, to inform him promptly if the Japanese even subjected the French Government to the slightest pressure in that respect.

But Churchill states that the operation—"a model of its kind"—took place at a time "when we sorely needed success." After Malaya and the terrible shock of the loss of the *Repulse* and the *Prince of Wales,* after Singapore and Hong Kong, Diego Suarez promised an easy training ground and an easy victory.

President Roosevelt later represented this affair as a sort of punishment for France's sin in bringing Laval back into power. However, the operation had been planned since December, 1941, months before the "sin" of Laval's return to office. The operation was strictly British, with the United States merely giving it its blessing. The Free French were neither consulted nor invited.

Since the naval base at Diego Suarez dated back to the last century, the defenses could not be considered up to date. The French Navy had some half dozen ships on the station: the auxiliary cruiser *Bougainville* (a converted merchantman), two colonial sloops, four submarines, and a few auxiliary minesweepers. Of that number, the sloop *D'Iberville* and three submarines were not present on the day of the attack.

The attack was a complete surprise. The British forces, under Rear Admiral E. N. Syfret, arrived off Courrier Bay on the night of May 4, planning to take Diego Suarez by land, from the rear. Air support was provided by the aircraft carriers *Illustrious* and *Indomitable,* under Rear Admiral D. W. Boyd.

At 0510 there fell on the sleeping base, simultaneously with torpedoes and bombs, thousands of leaflets containing the British demand for unconditional surrender. In minutes all the planes on the French airfield, as well as the *Bougainville* and the submarine *Béveziers,* were disabled. Only the sloop *D'Entrecasteaux* was fortunate enough to escape the torpedoes and reach the roadstead.

Under these conditions the defenders naturally rejected the demand for unconditional surrender. Captain Maerten and Colonel Edouard Claerebout, commanding the defense, replied to the English admiral by radio, "Diego Suarez will be defended to the end in accordance with the traditions of the French Army, Navy, and Air Force."

The British landings were under way even then in Courrier Bay. However, the minefields cost the British some sweepers and delayed the attacking forces until the defenders reached their posts—some 4,000 men in all, of whom only 800 were Europeans, including the crews of the *Bougainville* and the *Béveziers,* which had joined the defense ashore after the loss of their ships.

The attack was stalled for the whole of May 5, and General R. G. Sturges, commanding the British ground forces, feared that the operation was failing. After a quick visit to the battlefield, he hurried to Admiral Syfret to ask him to eliminate the *D'Entrecasteaux,* whose fire was harassing the landing beaches, and also to create a diversion to the rear of the defenders.

Shelled by the British destroyers and bombed by the *Indomitable's* planes, the *D'Entrecasteaux* had to beach herself, yet she still continued to fire and her crew did not abandon her until after 36 hours of heavy bombardment.

The diversion requested by General Sturges was carried out by the destroyer *Anthony* with an audacity that deserved the good fortune it had. Slipping into the harbor on the night of May 6, it landed some 50 marines from the *Ramillies,* who infiltrated into the defenses and seized several important points. At 2 o'clock the next day the main British attack broke through the defense lines, capturing the French leaders, and several hours later the last coast defense battery surrendered.

There were still the three French submarines to be accounted for, however. The *Héros,* under Lieutenant Rémy Lemaire, was convoying a supply ship to Djibouti when recalled by Captain Maerten. It arrived at Courrier Bay only to be attacked by depth charges from the corvette *Genista,* and then by bombs from the planes of the *Illustrious.* She was blasted to the bottom about 0500 on May 7, taking 24 men with her.

The *Monge,* commanded by Lieutenant Marcel Delort, had also been recalled from escort duty. Reaching the scene of the battle on May 8, she attacked the *Indomitable* with torpedoes, but missed, and was herself sunk by depth charges from the destroyers *Active* and *Panther.*

The only French ships to escape were the *D'Iberville* and the *Glorieux.* Under orders from the French Admiralty these retired to the southern end of Madagascar, and then eventually to Dakar.

Several months later the British completed the conquest of the island by a landing at Majunga against practically no opposition.

The attack on Madagascar, added to the previous ordeals, aroused new feeling throughout the French Navy. That Navy, without approving, could at least discern the reasons behind the attack at Mers-el-Kebir and also behind the British disruption of the sea communications of a France which the enemy partly occupied. But Madagascar was practically without strategic value, and the attack on it would be remembered when stunned men in North Africa were shocked by a similar surprise attack in November, 1942.

And while Madagascar was reeling to the shock of British guns, at the other side of the world the French Antilles were being subjected to another sort of pressure—diplomatic pressure from Washington.

Months earlier, and immediately after the Armistice of June, 1940, an agreement had been made between Admiral Robert, French High Commissioner for the Antilles, and Admiral Greenslade of the U.S. Navy which had fixed the status of the French possessions in the Caribbean. They were to remain loyal to the French Goverment, but were subject to certain restrictions, such as movement of ships and the presence in Martinique of a U.S. naval observer as well as the U.S. consul.

However, the entry of the United States into the war changed its complaisant attitude. Just as the American historian, Samuel E. Morison, wrote candidly, "The Navy looked with covetous eyes on Fort-de-France as the best naval and air base between Puerto Rico and Trinidad."

At any rate, on December 17, 1941, Admiral Frederick J. Horne, U.S.N., arrived at Fort-de-France, bringing new demands. The smiling diplomacy of Admiral Robert succeeded in maintaining the *status quo* simply by giving greater advance notice of men-of-war movements.

But on May 9, 1942, almost at the same time as the attack on Diego Suarez, Vice Admiral John H. Hoover, the new commander of the American forces in the Caribbean, and Samuel Reber, Deputy Director of European Affairs in the State Department at Washington, arrived bringing a sort of ultimatum. It was no less a matter than detaching the Antilles from France and placing them practically under American control, with Admiral Robert being retained at the head of the local administration.

It was a demand that no sovereign government could accede to, especially since at the same time the Americans demanded the transfer of all French merchantmen in the Antilles to them. All of these were directly contrary to the conditions of the armistice—and Germany could be relied upon to scrutinize closely any reply made by Admiral Robert.

Hence negotiations had to be carried on simultaneously with both Germany and the United States before any agreement could be reached. The ultimate solution provided for the complete immobilization on the spot of all the combat ships, merchant ships, and planes at Fort-de-France—as well as the immobilization of the gold stored there. Normal ties between the Antilles and the French Government at Vichy were to continue. Furthermore the Americans were given a key to the secret code so that they, as well as the armistice commissions, could check on the contents of all messages exchanged between Vichy and the Antilles.

Drastic concessions though these were, they were far better than the bloody contests to which France had been subjected elsewhere, and France has always been correspondingly grateful to the Americans.

An incident that occurred during the tensest moments of the negotiations is illustrative of the oddities of the situation.

ON BOARD THE SUBMARINE RUBIS AT DUNDEE, the winter of 1940-41. Admiral Muselier emerging through the hatch. The commanding officer, Lieutenant Commander Cabanier, in the left foreground, stands by with members of his crew.

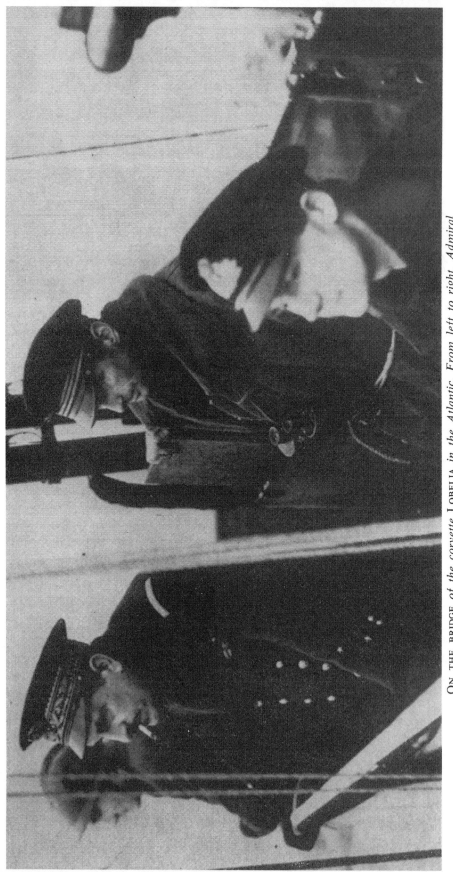

ON THE BRIDGE of the corvette LOBELIA in the Atlantic. From left to right, Admiral Muselier; Lieutenant de Morsier, the commanding officer; and the British liaison officer.

The American destroyer *Blakeley,* whose bow had been blown off by a German torpedo, put into Fort-de-France to get medical attention for its wounded. By coincidence, only a few months before a German submarine had requested permission to land a seriously wounded officer at Fort-de-France. In order to eliminate any possible misunderstanding, Admiral Robert had invited the U.S. naval observer to witness the transfer of the wounded man, which entailed a stay of perhaps half an hour by the U-boat in the port.

This time the American destroyer was able to go alongside the aircraft carrier *Béarn,* transfer the most seriously wounded, have first aid given to the others, and still depart within the specified time.

In both cases the French Navy had conformed to the international conventions which govern the laws of war at sea, and had acted with complete fairness which was recognized by all.

The dispute in the Antilles and the attack on Madagascar created a painful atmosphere between the French Government and the Anglo-Saxon democracies which was brought to an even more critical stage by the new controversy over the French squadron at Alexandria.

As will be recalled, Admiral Godfroy and Admiral Cunningham had entered into a "gentlemen's agreement" as to the status of this French squadron. But that agreement had not taken into account any possibility of Axis forces threatening Alexandria itself.

Now in June of 1942, the rapid advance of the Germans across Libya so threatened the security of this seaport that the British had to give consideration to a possible evacuation. In that eventuality the British fleet would fall back through the Red Sea. But what about Admiral Godfroy's French squadron? Should it follow the British, or should it remain at its moorings and fall, perhaps, into German hands?

The United States was insistent that the French fleet follow the British; even the proposal that the French ships might retire to Bizerte was not satisfactory. The Germans were equally insistent that such an action could become a *casus belli.* The possibility appeared that the French squadron would either be destroyed by the British or have to be scuttled by its own French crews. Fortunately the British victory at El Alamein saved both Alexandria and the French squadron there.

Mers-el-Kebir, Dakar, French Equatorial Africa, Siam, Syria, Madagascar, the Antilles, Alexandria—they were all part of the huge problem the French Navy faced after the armistice. In each case it devoted its best efforts to its duties of feeding France and safeguarding the national heritage overseas. In some cases it was successful, in other cases it was thwarted by superior forces bent on conquest. In some cases these conquests were of definite strategic value, in other cases not. But one may well wonder whether this breaking down of legal ties between the colonies and the home country was not responsible for destroying loyalty, weakening authority, and eventually, with many other political factors, preparing the way for the numerous rebellions that have shaken the world everywhere since the war.

CHAPTER 19

The Anglo-American Landings in North Africa —The Prelude

In the autumn of 1942, the French Government was beginning to look optimistically toward the future.

It had retained the essential part of its overseas possessions. The Germans, while doing their best to derive all possible benefits from the armistice, nevertheless had respected its territorial clauses. The Wehrmacht, deeply engaged in Russia, no longer constituted a threat to Africa. The recovery of the country had begun.

To be sure, the physical existence of France remained difficult: the Government, obliged constantly to compromise with the occupying power, was criticized, even reviled; criminal acts were on the increase, not only against the Germans but against Frenchmen as well.[1]

None of that, however, seriously impaired Marshal Pétain's popularity with the great mass of the French people. His prestige remained great. He was fervently acclaimed whenever he appeared in public. His diplomatic representatives were well received abroad, and one could count on the fingers of one hand the foreign powers who had no representatives accredited to the Vichy Government.

Yet despite the presence of all these diplomats, despite the information

---

[1] A police report for approximately two months in the fall of 1942 gave the following data: 36 criminal attacks on Germans in cafes or in the streets, with several killed, including women; 88 acts of industrial or agricultural sabotage; 100 "ideological" acts of sabotage against buildings occupied by Germans or "collaborators"; 54 acts of sabotage on the railway systems, some of them involving wrecks.

received from French military and naval attachés abroad, the French Government had little exact information on the war effort of the British and the Americans. Essentially this was because the French intelligence services had been wrecked by the armistice. In addition the new military organization set up after the armistice had created a single central intelligence section for all three services which was not nearly as efficient in collecting specialized information.

Yet, from reading the secret bulletins which were routed to the higher echelons at that time, one thing stood out: Germany had failed to win the war in 1942 and would have far less chance to do it now, with the superior American power thrown into the scales. Hence, just as soon as the Allies could assemble the requisite amount of shipping, a "second front" could be expected in Europe. But where? And when?

Laval and his civilian ministers were too much absorbed with everyday problems to try to guess the future. But Marshal Pétain, on the contrary, followed the developing military movements throughout the world with keenly analytical eyes. He conferred on these developments with Admiral Darlan, Commander in Chief of the Armed Forces—ground, sea, and air; with Ministers of State Lucien Romier and Henry Moysset; with Admiral Auphan, Minister of the Navy and Chief of the Naval Staff to Darlan; and with General Jean Bergeret, ex-Minister of the Air Force, and at that time Chief of National Air Defense.

As events turned out, the forecasts of this "brain trust" were entirely erroneous; nevertheless a knowledge of them will make clearer the complete surprise which the Allied landings in North Africa were to the Government at Vichy.

In the first place, it was considered inconceivable that a landing meant to initiate a second front would be made any place else than in Axis-occupied territory. North Africa and the southern part of France had been made neutral territory under the terms of the armistice. It was believed that, without first contacting the French Government, the American Army would never land on territory neutral under international law and which France was morally obligated to defend against all comers. This conception was in line with the reply of S. Pinkney Tuck, U.S. Chargé d'Affaires, to a question which Admiral Auphan put to him on July 1, 1942, as to the possibility of a new attack on Dakar. Said Mr. Tuck, "As long as you have not admitted the Germans to Dakar, we have no reason to intervene there."

It was also assumed that since the Dieppe failure, the Allies would consider it too risky to attack the Wehrmacht in occupied France. Hence the advisers to Marshal Pétain saw only two possibilities: a flanking movement through Norway or the Low Countries, or one through Italy or the Balkans. A movement through the Balkans would have the advantage of perhaps drawing Turkey out of her neutral position and thus open an easier route to Russia than by Murmansk.

The idea of France reentering the war later on was definitely considered, but only if the Allied landings were successful. Although preparing the Army and Navy for that eventuality, Marshal Pétain did not make France's reentry into the war the primary aim of his politics. He considered that France, the first to enter the conflict, had already made enough sacrifices, and that the Allies could well sacrifice themselves a little in turn for her. The essential thing, in Marshal Pétain's eyes, was that the Germans should get out of France. Beyond that, he had a sincere desire for a Franco-German reconciliation. His one obsession was that France, already ravaged by the invasion and now subjected to Allied bombings, should be spared from serving once more as the battlefield of the adversaries.

From its studies the French Admiralty came to the conclusion—rightly or wrongly—that the Allies could not assemble sufficient shipping for a large military operation before 1943. That would give France a few months to sound out the Americans and to prepare the way for an eventual reentry into the war.

Such were French thoughts in the autumn of 1942. But actually, the Anglo-American landings in North Africa were being prepared at that moment.

The Americans on the whole had practiced a friendly policy toward France up until then. Despite diplomatic controversies, the French Government pinned its greatest hopes on the United States. Marshal Pétain found a sympathetic response in Admiral Leahy, U.S. Ambassador at Vichy. On its part the Goverment at Washington had good reason to maintain close diplomatic relations with Vichy; under the pretext of supervising the distribution of American supplies donated to North Africa, it had established there a network of consuls and vice consuls who were in reality intelligence officers studying the military possibilities of the principal African ports. This was even suspected in France, but once again the French Government did not believe that any action would be initiated there without a warning of some sort.

French officers of all services, but especially those of the Army of North Africa, lived in the hope of one day reentering the war against the Germans. At the same time they all—or almost all—were loyal to Marshal Pétain, confident that he would let them know when the proper moment for such action arrived. A certain number of them voluntarily passed on information to the American authorities, but the great majority avoided any such advance communications, believing that this task was the prerogative of the responsible authorities. General Weygand, while making known to the Americans the military needs of North Africa in case the Germans attacked it, was violently angry with two or three subordinate officers who conversed directly with the Americans on that subject.

However, there were Frenchmen who were of the opinion that Marshal Pétain had tied himself too closely to the policies of the armistice, and that he would never launch France back into the war unless he was led to do so by a foreign intervention arranged without his knowledge. They were willing to facilitate that operation. These Frenchmen learned confidentially from American Consul General Murphy that intervention not only was a certainty, but that it was close at hand, and they believed themselves capable of bringing the Army of Africa to join in the operation—or at least not to oppose it.

The guiding spirit of the group was Jacques Lemaigre-Dubreuil, an able industrialist who had large interests in Africa. He had associated with him several others: the astute publicist Jean Rigault, Lieutenant Colonel Louis Jousse, Secretary of Embassy Jacques Tarbé de Saint Hardouin, and Colonel A.S. van Hecke, an officer of the youth organization *Chantiers de Jeunesse*.[2] This group, whom the Americans came to call the "Group of Five," had two or three hundred followers at Algiers with whom they counted on paralyzing the authorities and perhaps even taking over the command. They had a major weakness in this latter aspect, though, in that the group did not include a single high service officer who could sway the armed forces at the decisive moment. They had not dared to contact either General Alphonse Juin, Commander in Chief in North Africa, or General Louis M. Koeltz, commanding the army corps of Algeria. The highest military officer they could enlist was a local division commander, General Charles Mast, who became the chief military adviser of the group. Mast set up a sort of clandestine general staff composed of Colonel Jousse, Major Dartois of the Air Force, and Commander Pierre Barjot of the Navy.

This military directory succeeded in obtaining an effective following among certain elements of the Army and Air Force, mostly at Algiers, but its naval representative, Commander Barjot, carried no weight in the directory and had even less influence with Navy personnel, owing to his having just been discharged from the Navy for insubordinate actions.[3] For

---

[2] The armistice conditions had abolished all military service. However, the French youth in Algeria and in the Free Zone carried out training without arms in camps where they followed an intensive regimen of physical exercise, patriotism, and morale. This organization was known as the *"Chantiers de Jeunesse,"* and was administered by ex-officers of the armed services.

[3] Commander Barjot had been conducting a secret liaison of his own with Allied intelligence agents while serving on active duty on board the *Richelieu* at Dakar, where not a single German was to be seen. His case was just up for review by the Minister of the Navy at Vichy, when Mr. Laval returned to power. The Deputy Chief

that matter, it was evident that the conspirators preferred to leave the Navy out. No high ranking naval officer on active duty had been approached either in Algiers or Morocco, although at the latter place General Béthouart, commander of the Casablanca division, had been admitted to the secret— too late, however, to be able to prepare effectively for the landings.

What the Americans and the Group of Five counted on was that the immense prestige of General Henri Giraud would win over the Army of Africa to their side.

General Giraud had been captured in May, 1940, and had escaped from Germany in April, 1942, under spectacular conditions which had seriously embroiled the Vichy Government with the Germans. Hitler personally demanded the return of the prisoner, whom, since that time, Marshal Pétain had occasionally entertained at lunch.

Giraud refused to surrender, but, because of the agitation involving his name, wrote a personal letter to Marshal Pétain assuring him of his complete loyalty and pledging himself on his honor to do nothing which would embarrass Franco-German relations. Nevertheless, to many officers his name continued to symbolize the spirit of national revival and rejection of defeat.

Contacted by the group at Algiers, General Giraud agreed to support the American intervention, of which he rather naively expected to be given command. He made the proviso, however, that the landings should be made on the Mediterranean coast of southern France, thus insuring its immediate juncture with the French Army and with the French Fleet at Toulon.

The American and English generals were delighted with the accession of Giraud, whose name they regarded as a major trump card, but they regarded the Southern France landings as visionary. They left him in the dark as to their real intentions, merely promising to inform him when the time came.

Actually, as events were to prove, the value of Giraud's name had been overestimated. The French Army was a well-disciplined organization, and one which, despite some Free French infiltration, was bound to obey its legally appointed leaders, of whom Giraud, holding no command, was not one. Furthermore, the Army was not the only force to be considered; there was also the Navy, the first line which any amphibious operation would

---

of Security at Vichy, himself about to be relieved of his post, advised the Minister of the Navy to dispose of the case as quickly as possible before it came to official notice. The punishment assigned was as light as possible: Commander Barjot was discharged from the Navy, given three months' pay and two plane tickets, and sent to North Africa with his wife.

He was recalled to active duty by Admiral Darlan after the American landings, and is today a vice admiral in the French Navy.

encounter. And the commander in chief of the Navy was Darlan—or, more strictly speaking, Auphan, but certainly not Giraud.

No attempt was made, however, to forewarn Darlan or Auphan or any other high ranking naval officer. To be of any value, such a forewarning would have to be given well in advance, and that would have been too great a risk. On the other hand the French defenders of Africa should be given equal tolerance for having carried out their orders strictly when, without any forewarning and without even knowing the circumstances, they were suddenly attacked in the dead of night. The American Army and Navy, with the true chivalry of the brotherhood of arms, was to show such a tolerance. But this attitude did not carry over into the political field— into the relations beween Washington and Vichy and, even more, into the relations between the Frenchmen who followed De Gaulle (but who had not taken the personal oath of allegiance to Marshal Pétain) and those who interpreted strictly their oaths to obey their Government and their duly appointed leaders.

Though the Allied leaders made no attempt to contact him, Darlan on the other hand attempted to discover the Allied plans, with the intention of giving such collaboration as could be discreetly done. This intention was not, as some have alleged, for his own personal interest, but because such action represented the ideas of the military advisers of Marshal Pétain. In the middle of October, 1942, Darlan instructed Colonel Chrétien, chief of military security at Algiers, to establish secret contact with the Americans, under the command of General Dwight D. Eisenhower, U.S.A. Eisenhower's general staff was certainly informed of this approach, because Captain Harry C. Butcher, U.S.N.R., the general's naval aide, refers to it in his book. Captain Butcher also alludes to Churchill's interest in the affair and quotes what he asserts was Churchill's personal retort: "Kiss Darlan's stern if you have to, but get the French Fleet!"[4]

The ranking U.S. representative, Consul General Murphy, was absent at the moment, and it devolved upon Consul General Felix Cole to answer Darlan's representative. Cole consulted the Group of Five and they advised him to reply in the negative. The Group of Five could not understand how the second highest authority in the French Government could deliberately take a position so contrary to that of Marshal Pétain.

In addition the approach came at a highly inopportune time. The Group of Five was just then going through a most critical period. Rigault had recently informed General Giraud that the Allied landings would take place that fall. The General, who had advocated a time no earlier than the spring

---

[4] Captain Harry C. Butcher—*My Three Years With Eisenhower,* page 178a.

of 1943, became violently angry and threatened to throw the whole thing overboard. It was certainly no time to complicate matters by bringing Darlan into the picture.

With that refusal, the last chance for preconcerted action disappeared. With no forewarning to anyone in authority—and, especially, the Navy—blood was bound to flow. Of more serious consequence for the future of France, the Government which up to then had been the rallying point of nine-tenths of France was to be not only by-passed but assailed by its very allies.

For the Allied command, the final definite arrangements were made at a secret meeting at Cherchel, just west of Algiers, between the Group of Five and General Mark Clark, U.S.A., deputy to General Eisenhower, over-all commander of the operation. General Clark had been landed there from a British submarine on October 23, 1942, for the eventful 24-hour conference.

Clark eagerly accepted the military information provided by Mast and his collaborators.[5] "The French were ready with voluminous written information," he wrote,[6] "which later turned out to be accurate in every respect. They gave us locations and strengths of troops and naval units, told us where supplies, including gasoline and ammunition, were stored; supplied details about airports where resistance would be heaviest, and information about where airborne troops could be safely landed."

But in return for this mass of top secret information, the French did not even have the satisfaction of collaborating in the planning of the operation in order to make it less sanguinary. The French believed the operation was still only in the planning stage. "In effect," wrote General Clark in his book, "the advance units of our armada were already at sea." He did not give this information to the French, however. So on the Allied side the conference at Cherchel was not for the purpose of drawing up a peaceful plan of action with the conspirators, but of obtaining from them the few final pieces of important information for a military operation by main force.

This operation carried the code name, "Operation Torch." It had been

---

[5] Among Frenchmen present were General Charles Mast, Lieutenant Colonel Louis Jousse, Commander Pierre Barjot, and Major Dartois of the Air Force. The U.S. representatives were Major General Mark Clark, Brigadier General Lyman Lemnitzer, Colonel Archelaus Hamblen, Colonel Julius Holmes, and Captain Jerauld Wright of the Navy.

[6] General Mark Clark—*Calculated Risk*, pp. 81 and 82.

in the planning stage for some time, and essentially it called for the following program:[7]

(1) An attack on the Moroccan coast by the Western Task Force, entirely American in composition, commanded by Rear Admiral H. Kent Hewitt, U.S.N. The troops to be landed were commanded by Major General George W. Patton, U.S.A.

(2) An attack on Oran by the Center Task Force, a joint Anglo-American group, commanded by Commodore T. A. Troubridge, R.N. The landing troops were commanded by Major General Lloyd P. Fredendall, U.S.A.

(3) An attack on Algiers by the Eastern Task Force, also joint Anglo-American in composition, commanded by Rear Admiral Sir Harold Burrough, R.N. The landing troops were commanded by Major General Charles W. Ryder, U.S.A.

At the time of the Cherchel conference on October 23, the picket submarines for Operation Torch had already been at sea since the 20th; the slow English convoys had sailed on the 22nd, on which day the Western Task Force was departing from American shores; the fast English convoys were to sail on the 26th. An immense military machine had been set in motion, and there could be no question now of making any changes in the operating plan. In vain did General Béthouart urge better chosen landing places in Morocco in order to avoid needless opposition and bloodshed; in vain did Consul General Murphy himself ask for a delay. Nothing now would be heard but the voice of the guns.

Oddly enough, while the American convoys were zigzagging across the Atlantic, Admiral Darlan himself was in Africa, on an inspection trip which took him as far south as Dakar. Vague rumors of Allied movements had led Vichy to believe that Dakar might again be threatened with attack, as it had been in 1940, and in a deliberately widely publicized speech Darlan had warned that Dakar would be harder to swallow than Diego Suarez. But any such subtle warning that France would resist an attack by anyone went unheeded by the Allied leaders, since Operation Torch did not concern Dakar, but North Africa, on which an armada of over 300 ships[8] was now converging. On October 28, Darlan was back in Algiers getting ready to return to Vichy.

There, in Algiers, an abnormal concentration of ships was reported at Gibraltar. But a British aircraft carrier had just gotten under way with its

---

[7] Only a brief outline of Operation Torch is given here. Complete details will be found in Rear Admiral Samuel E. Morison's book, *Operations in North African Waters,* which is Volume II in the series, *History of United States Naval Operations in World War II.*

[8] In his book, *Crusade in Europe,* General Eisenhower mentions "approximately 110 troop and cargo ships and 200 warships."

escort to launch some planes for Malta. Always under such circumstances the French Government had suspended all air and ship traffic between France and Algeria in order to avoid possible incidents. Hence Darlan was stuck at Algiers, where he spent the day conferring with a great many people. Having confidence in the secret advances[9] he had made to the Americans, he could not believe that the abnormal naval activities reported had anything to do with North Africa. In agreement with the Algiers authorities he believed that these ship concentrations were large convoys destined for Malta or Alexandria, or perhaps even a British landing in Tripolitania. The Americans—including Consul General Murphy himself, through an intermediary—had assured him that nothing would take place before 1943. The next day, at Vichy, Darlan was to repeat that assurance to Admiral Auphan.

Only Mast knew otherwise. But that impassive individual, parading his Algiers troops before Admiral Darlan and General Juin that day, did not give so much as a hint of his secret.

Darlan returned to Vichy the following day, and participated in the official ceremonies of All Saints' Day. Behind, in the military hospital at Algiers, he left his only son, who had been stricken with poliomyelitis while on a business trip, and who was now recovering. At a reunion held at Admiral Auphan's house on November 4, Darlan appeared relieved on both his own and the nation's problems, and confidently set forth to the assembled guests his predictions of a "second front" in 1943. But during the night he received news that his son had suddenly taken a dangerous turn for the worse, and he departed by plane for Algiers. It was thus, entirely by chance and without any ulterior motives, that he happened to be in Algiers three days later.

In the meantime, Operation Torch was going inexorably ahead.

Ashore, the French general staffs anxiously followed on the chart the reported progress through the Mediterranean of the convoys that had left Gibraltar (the Atlantic convoys, headed for Morocco, were not even to be suspected until the actual landings). With the eastward progress of the convoys the French staffs, at Vichy and elsewhere, were confirmed in their opinion that the operation was aimed at Tripolitania, to take Rommel's army in the rear. Vice Admiral Jacques Moreau, Commandant of the North Africa Naval District, hastened to check on the defenses of Tunisia. It was he who first realized that the target was Algeria itself, and he hurried back to Algiers to inform Darlan, whom he knew to be there. Darlan

---

[9] Admiral Darlan hoped that the Americans would understand the hints he was trying to give in these secret advances and would realize his real feelings were quite different from the attitude he was forced to take in his official capacity.

refused to believe it, but on the orders of General Juin, Commander in Chief in Africa, a general alert was sent out: all troops were to be at their stations by 8 o'clock on the morning of November 8. The Navy set condition "Danger." In all this the French commanders were doing nothing more than carrying out standing defensive measures already well known to the Americans.

On the German side, the O.K.W.[10] became aroused by the evening of November 6 and informed the French Government's representatives at Wiesbaden that the German Air Forces would fly over French territory in order to take up advance positions in Italy and Sardinia.

And on the Allied side, an English submarine had arrived off the coast of Provence on the night of November 4 to pick up General Giraud. The General had been promised an American submarine, but none being available, a British submarine had been substituted, under the theoretical command of Captain Jerauld Wright, U.S.N.,[11] the U.S. liaison officer at Gibraltar. Giraud was agreeable to this, but not at all to the news that he received when he reached Gibraltar on November 7, having been picked up at sea and transported there by airplane. The bad news was that nothing was going forward as Giraud had advocated, and that, in particular, General Eisenhower, and not Giraud, was to be the commander-in-chief of the expedition.

All the actors in the coming drama were now on the scene. All that remained was for the curtain to rise.

---

[10] O.K.W. *(Oberkommando der Wehrmacht)*—Supreme Command of the Armed Forces.

[11] Later an admiral, Commander in Chief, U.S. Atlantic Fleet (CincLant) and Supreme Allied Commander, Atlantic (SacLant).

CHAPTER 20

The Anglo-American Landings in North Africa —Tragedy and Turning Point

At Vichy, the curtain rose that night of November 7 on an avalanche of confused information pouring in from all points. It was variously surmised that Algiers, or Oran, or Casablanca, or Rabat were the targets of either an external attack or of a *putsch* from inside. The Navy's communication system eventually made the matter clear, and any further doubts were dispelled by the American broadcasts themselves. Over the radio, even before being transmitted by the normal diplomatic channels, came a message from President Roosevelt to Marshal Pétain stating, "Germany and Italy intend to invade and occupy French North Africa," and, consequently, "the intervention of American armed forces has been decided upon."

It was much the same allegation that had been made by the Germans for occupying Norway in 1940, and by the British at Dakar and Madagascar, but the French leaders felt certain that no Axis invasion of French North Africa was in prospect. But had there been any real private understanding between the French and the Allies, the Germans could easily have been tricked into a false move that would have given genuine cause for intervention. But, regrettably, as stated before, no such approach had been made by the Allies.

Hence the reply that Marshal Pétain made, on being awakened to receive the message, was practically spontaneous:

> It is with amazement and sorrow that I learned this night of the aggression of your troops. . . . I have read your message. You invoke pretexts which nothing justifies. You attribute to your enemies intentions which have never been translated into action. France and her honor are at stake. We are attacked; we will defend ourselves. It is the order that I am giving.

Actually any order that Marshal Pétain gave now could only serve to ratify the automatic measures already taken by military and naval units attacked without warning. Even before Pétain's order reached the military forces, many French soldiers and sailors had already been killed. What-

219

ever were the innermost feelings of the French leaders and the good intentions of the American chiefs, war had been brought by the latter to French territory. It was certainly not France that made war on the United States.

Such action automatically broke off diplomatic relations; what was necessary now was to mend them again. Providentially Darlan was on the spot. He was better placed than anyone else to determine whether this was a mere hit-and-run raid, like Dieppe, in which case for France to participate would have been fatal, or whether the landing was a major Allied operation made before France had anticipated it. Under these conditions, the best thing the French Government could do was to approve in advance any measures that Darlan might take, and to prevent by all possible means any conflict between local forces and the Allies from spreading.

Such were Admiral Auphan's ideas for handling the situation. In this he was supported by General Weygand, who, without official position during the past year, had been called into consultation by Marshal Pétain.

Two problems arose simultaneously. One was to delay the appearance of the Luftwaffe in African skies. For, just as in the case of Syria, the Germans had hastened to offer their help in repelling the invasion. The Minister of the Navy, Admiral Auphan, promptly replied to the German offer by suggesting that they might bomb the invading transports off Algiers by planes from the airfields of Sicily or Sardinia—something for which they manifestly needed no permission.

The Germans retorted to this impertinent suggestion by demanding bases in Africa itself. To play for time, Auphan requested the opinion of the local commanders in Africa—which he knew in advance would be negative. Thus the Germans never obtained use of any airfields in Algeria, though on November 9, as will be detailed later, they managed to extort from Laval his permission to enter Tunisia.

The second problem was to avoid embroiling the French naval forces at Toulon in the action. This was relatively simple, as Laval himself was opposed to it, and the shortage of fuel oil was ample excuse against Axis importunities.

There was no question of sending the Toulon Fleet to join the Allies, either, as long as French ships already in North Africa were being made targets for the British and American gunners and as long as a legitimate truce had not clarified the situation. Moreover, in his memoirs Admiral A. B. Cunningham has made no secret of the welcome he would have given Admiral de Laborde if the Toulon Fleet had gotten under way on November 8 to meet with the Anglo-Americans. Cunningham had ordered the British Force H out of Gibraltar to cover the landings, and he subsequently wrote, "The complaisant attitude of the Italian Fleet and the inactivity of the French main fleet unfortunately gave Force H no scope for action."[1]

Had the French Fleet appeared off the North African battlefield undoubtedly it would have been greeted as an adversary; on the other hand, its joining with the Anglo-Americans would have constituted an act of war against the Axis, the consequences of which would have been immediate and grave.

Just as in the crisis of June, 1940, it was not the prerogative of the Navy to adopt a unilateral policy. What was important was that it proceed in accordance with the national policy, and strive first of all for a cessation of hostilities in North Africa if these turned out to be more than a mere commando raid.

Hence the first action under this policy was a broadcast announcement informing the public that Admiral Darlan was at Algiers. This fact was as much of a surprise to the French, who happily saw in it a carefully planned affair to cooperate with the Allies, as it was to the Germans, who likewise saw in it an aspect of collusion and hence were correspondingly angry. The broadcast quoted several phrases which Marshal Pétain, the Chief of State, had addressed to Darlan: "I am pleased to know that you are on the spot. You are able to act and keep me informed. You know that I have complete confidence in you."

Strengthened by that confidence, Admiral Darlan announced the same evening that he had concluded an armistice for Algiers, and that he was meeting the next day with American General Ryder in order to conclude a treaty valid for all Africa.

It was a good beginning. But when Auphan brought this message to Marshal Pétain the morning of November 9, he found that Laval had already been summoned by Hitler and was leaving for Germany immediately. Laval protested that such negotiations could not be carried on during his absence. When this information was transmitted to Darlan, he contented himself with replying that he simply wished "to listen and to report." Marshal Pétain, for the time being, asked for nothing more.

The curtain that rose that night at Algiers was of a different hue, a blood-red hue, though, compared to what was taking place at other ports, the affair at Algiers was but a skirmish.[2]

Algiers was the military headquarters for French North Africa as well as for the Algeria-Tunisia naval district, yet the city itself was only a large commercial port, protected by a few old, half disarmed coastal batteries.

---

[1] Sir Andrew B. Cunningham's report, 30 March 1943—*Cf Supplement to London Gazette* of Tuesday, March 22, 1949. Page 1511.

[2] French dead at Algiers numbered 20, of whom 11 belonged to the Navy.

Its naval forces that night consisted of two submarines, one submarine chaser, and an old sloop.

The Allied landings at Algiers took place at three different points. The American 168th Regimental Combat Team (R.C.T.) landed in the Bay of Sidi Ferruch, the same place where the French had originally landed in 1830; the British 11th and 36th Brigades landed to the northeast of Castiglione; and the American 39th R.C.T. landed on the beaches to the east of Cape Matifou. The entire landing force totalled 23,000 British and 10,000 American troops.[3]

Thanks to the orders issued by General Mast, the landing at Sidi Ferruch took place without a shot being fired; in fact the French troops there greeted the Americans cordially. This was fortunate, since the inexperienced Americans lost 98 landing craft out of 104 in the surf.

But the French sailors, not having been informed in advance, were not a party to the welcome, and Battery Duperré, consisting of three 194-mm. guns under Warrant Officer Joseph Larvor, put up a stubborn resistance. Using one-third of his 45 men as a crew for one of the guns, Larvor set the remainder to defending the works foot by foot, hand to hand, against the swarming invaders, and, despite repeated air attacks, continued firing until the middle of the afternoon.

The same thing happened at Battery Lazaret, to the east of Cape Matifou. The battery, commanded by Lieutenant Jean Beghelli, contained four guns of 194-mm., but was manned by only 36 sailors. Nevertheless Beghelli, though repeatedly bombarded from the sea and the air, rejected all ultimatums and held out until evening.

It was in the harbor that the most serious clash took place. Two British destroyers, the *Malcolm* and the *Broke,* had been assigned the mission of crashing the harbor boom and landing a picked force of American rangers on the docks within. Leading the attempt at 0330, the *Malcolm* was severely pounded by the guns on the northern pierhead and had to withdraw under fire. At morning twilight the *Broke* charged the southern boom under cover of a furious fire from all its guns. At a speed of 26 knots it burst through the boom and managed to pull alongside a quay on which no battery bore. But a detachment of French sailors manned an old casemate battery on the waterfront and blasted away a section of old wall which screened the destroyer from the battery guns. Then they shelled the *Broke* so heavily that she too broke off the action, but so seriously damaged that she sank off the coast the following morning. The 200 Americans of the landing party were rounded up from the various parts of the city into which they had infiltrated, and were disarmed.

The two French submarines—*Caïman,* under Lieutenant Commander Paul Mertz, and *Marsouin,* commanded by Lieutenant Emile Mine—had put

---

[3] Samuel E. Morison—*Operations in North African Waters.*

to sea to engage the invasion ships, but the *Broke* had sighted them and given advance warning over her radio. Vigorously pursued and depth charged the whole day, as well as bombed from the air, the submarines had no chance to attack the transports. The *Caïman* was seriously damaged, but both submarines eventually succeeded in reaching Toulon.[4]

Meanwhile, ever since midnight, some several hundred partisans affiliated with the Group of Five had been cutting telephone wires. They surrounded the residences of the military leaders and occupied several public buildings. They actually had in their hands for a short time General Juin, Admiral Darlan, and even Consul General Murphy, but not knowing what to do with them, they let them go! Cutting the telephone wires had little effect, since the military command had its own private lines and communications. Military personnel are always indoctrinated, anyway, to carry out standing orders even if they are cut off from their leaders, and in this case, perhaps, the local commanders carried out their orders even more vigorously since in this *putsch* from within they detected some of the elements of civil war.

Nevertheless the action of the Group of Five created some confusion in the city and in the vicinity of the airfields, where Allied planes had been able to land as early as 1030 on November 8. The partisans hoped to see General Giraud swoop down from the skies and seize the reins of power, just as had been planned. In fact, Lemaigre-Dubreuil waited in lieutenant colonel's uniform to welcome him. But Giraud was still back at Gibraltar, fuming, because the Americans, having learned that Admiral Darlan was in Algiers, had begun negotiating with *him*.

Back in Algiers, Admiral Darlan had been awakened in the middle of the night, like the others in high command, and had been asked to meet at General Juin's residence. There he also met U.S. Consul General Murphy. He informed Darlan that a great amphibious landing was actually taking place, whereupon the Admiral of the Fleet seemed about to explode. Then he gave it a second thought, his eyes inscrutable behind his blue-tinted glasses. He must have foreseen the opportunity that now presented itself.

He would agree to negotiate, he stated, if Marshal Pétain assented, but with the strict proviso that no "rebel Frenchmen"—and he included Giraud as well as De Gaulle—should interpose between him and the Americans.

A few hours later the city was surrounded. Darlan authorized General Juin to sign for the surrender of the city, and then, as stated earlier in this chapter, notified Marshal Pétain that he was negotiating next day with the Americans.

---

[4] When the Germans swept into Toulon on November 27, 1942, the *Marsouin* escaped a second time and returned to Algiers. The damaged *Caïman* was still in drydock and unable to get underway, so she was scuttled to keep her from being immediately put to use by the Germans.

Not until that afternoon, November 9, did General Clark, as representative of General Eisenhower, arrive at Algiers to try to force the French commander to put a stop to the resistance, which was now assuming serious proportions everywhere. As a matter of fact, the strength of the Anglo-Americans, which Consul General Murphy had stated was 500,000 men, amounted to little more than 100,000; consequently, they were not anxious to have to fight all North Africa.

General Giraud had also finally arrived by then, but everyone avoided him, as no commander on active service wished to place himself under a man whose only warrant for authority stemmed from the Americans. It was Darlan alone who held the key to the situation.

And Darlan was willing to conclude an armistice, but only with the approval of Marshal Pétain. Consequently, after his conference with General Clark, he sent Marshal Pétain a complete résumé of the discussion.

General Clark did not conceal his impatience. Finally, on the next morning, he threatened to break off negotiations with Admiral Darlan completely, and treat with Giraud instead, if Darlan persisted in waiting for approval from Vichy.

All of the French generals and admirals present were of the opinion that they should not wait any longer for Marshal Pétain's approval before ceasing hostilities against the Anglo-Americans. But it is one thing to have an opinion; it is quite another to make the necessary decision—when one is to be held forever responsible for that decision.

The good fortune of France was that a man like Darlan was present. If the Admiral of the Fleet had one outstanding qualification, it was that of decision. Probably no other member of the French Government would have dared to take the initiative that Darlan took when, at 1120 on November 10, he issued an order to all French forces in North Africa to cease hostilities, and followed this up by immediately informing Marshal Pétain of his action.

Darlan's order was sent out to all forces, but before it reached them, tragic events had taken place elsewhere——as at Oran.

Although not a fortified place, Oran was better defended than Algiers. Its garrison included an artillery regiment in addition to three infantry regiments, one of which had been engaged in the severe fighting in Syria in June, 1941. There was also a motorized cavalry brigade, secretly organized at Mascara without the knowledge of the Axis armistice commissions. This brigade was in position to engage immediately.

The French troops at Oran had not forgotten the tragedy of Mers-el-Kebir, and, though not looking for a fight, they had no intention of welcoming any invading force. General Robert Boissau, commanding the division, had been informed on November 6 by his chief of staff as to the coming events, but had refused to follow General Mast. He had made up his mind to carry out his duties just as though he had heard nothing. But, in so doing, he left in ignorance the one person most vitally interested— Vice Admiral André Rioult, commander of the naval forces at Oran.

Since Oran served as a terminal port for the Atlantic convoys coming through the Strait of Gibraltar, the Navy had a considerable establishment there. Stationed there were three fleet-destroyers, four submarines, five sloops or patrol vessels, and several minesweepers. In the inner harbor were four decommissioned submarines.[5] Also there that night was the super-destroyer *Epervier,* just completing a five-month overhaul. A Naval Air Force bomber group was stationed at Tafaraoui nearby, and a torpedo seaplane group at Arzew. The French Air Force had a mixed group at La Senia.

In the same pattern as at Algiers, the Anglo-Americans planned three landings: one in the city, one on the beach of Andalouses to the west, and the third on the Bay of Arzew to the east. At the same time they planned to seize the airfields by troops landed on them by air.

This time the approaching invaders were discovered ahead of time. At 1 A.M. on November 8, the escort of a small French convoy found itself right in the center of a suspicious group of unknown vessels not far from the port, and it immediately gave the alarm. Then, an hour later, the defending troops at Andalouses reported the landings there, and immediately afterward the troops at Arzew[6] had their first brush with the attackers.

On receiving these reports, Admiral Rioult ordered his ships to raise steam immediately, to reconnoiter the scenes of the reported landings, and, if necessary, to attack the adversary.

Accordingly, the port was completely alerted when, around 3 o'clock in the morning, the British sloops *Walney* and *Hartland,* accompanied by motor boats, arrived in the darkness to force the harbor entrance. At once the patrol vessel on duty and the batteries on the breakwater opened fire.

Under fire from the batteries as well as from the vessels getting under way, the venture of the *Walney* and *Hartland* became not a disaster, but a

---

[5] Ships present at Oran on November 8: super-destroyer *Epervier,* in drydock; destroyers *Tramontane, Typhon* and *Tornade;* submarines in commission, *Actéon, Fresnel* and *Argonaute;* submarines, decommissioned or in drydock, *Ariane, Diane, Cérès, Pallas* and *Danaë;* minesweeper sloop *Surprise;* some 15 patrol vessels, minesweepers and tugs.

[6] The first victim of these Franco-American operations was a gunner of the 68th Algerian Artillery Regiment, killed by an American ranger at Arzew at 0120 on November 8 while standing his guard duty unsuspectingly.

slaughter. Swept by fire everywhere from cannon and machineguns at point-blank range, the *Walney* went down under the impact of more than fifty shells while trying to grapple with the *Epervier,* which was blazing away at her from a distance of 100 feet. The *Hartland,* following in her wake, suffered a similar fate.

Out of the 600 U.S. rangers and British commandos committed to the enterprise, there were only 200 survivors. These were immediately given medical attention by their captors. But Captain F. T. Peters, R.N., commanding the daring attempt, had a bitter complaint to make to Admiral Rioult. Although he had just been attempting to make an armed invasion of a guarded port at night, his complaint was that the French had fired first!

But the disaster was not to be all British and American. For, stimulated by the successful encounter, the French seamen proceeded to launch themselves recklessly into what was to be even greater slaughter.

One of the French ships ordered to sortie was the 600-ton sloop *Surprise,* commanded by Lieutenant Commander Jacques Lavigne. Under construction at the beginning of the war, she still lacked most of her armament, having only one old 100-mm. gun in battery. Reconnoitering the Bay of Andalouses in accordance with her orders, she ran into several British destroyers in the morning twilight, and immediately proceeded to attack. The odds were hopeless. Battered to bits by overwhelming fire from HMS *Brilliant,* she went down quickly, taking with her 51 of her crew and four officers, including her captain.

The three destroyers had been ordered to investigate the Bay of Arzew. Delayed by the fighting with the *Walney* and the *Hartland,* they finally sortied in succession and engaged the attackers "with a bravery worthy of a better cause," as Commodore Troubridge wrote later in his report.

Even before daylight the *Tramontane,* under Commander Adrien de Feraudy, encountered the British cruiser *Aurora,* and bravely engaged her. The cruiser's first salvo swept the bridge of the *Tramontane* and put half her guns out of commission. Low in the water, and with her decks cluttered with the wounded and the dead, among whom was her commanding officer, the desperately injured destroyer ran herself aground under the cliffs of Cape Aiguille, not far from the port.

The *Tornade,* commanded by Lieutenant Commander Raymond Parès, suffered the same fate, after having fired all six of its torpedoes in a vain effort against a force of cruisers and destroyers. Only the *Typhon,* under Lieutenant Commander Georges Abgrall, succeeded in returning to port, with her magazines half empty and one stack shot away.

Of the four submarines in the harbor, only three managed to get under way in order to attack the assault transports offshore. Of these three, two never returned. The *Argonaute,* commanded by Lieutenant Henri Véron, and the *Actéon,* under Lieutenant Commander Jean Clavières, went down under the fire and depth bombs of HMS *Westcott* and HMS *Achates,* respectively. The *Fresnel,* commanded by Lieutenant Georges Saglio, was sighted, depth bombed, and pursued by her adversaries all the way to the limits of Spanish territorial waters. Then, since she received no further orders, she proceeded on her own initiative to Toulon. She arrived there on November 13, and, only 15 days later, scuttled herself in company with the rest of the Toulon Fleet in order to avoid falling into the hands of the Germans overrunning the port.

While these operations were taking place at sea, the air bases of Arzew, Le Senia, and Lartigue were captured, one after the other, by the attackers. The naval battery of Santon had three of its four 194-mm. guns disabled in hot action with the British squadron, which included the battleship *Rodney.* The only remaining threat for the Americans came from the forces in the interior, in particular the motorized brigade of Colonel Jean Touzet du Vigier. By a strong counterattack he succeeded in bringing the captured airfield at Tafaraoui, where the Americans had already based numerous planes, under fire of his artillery. Had it not been for the armistice which Admiral Darlan was negotiating even then, the Americans would have been a long time in conquering the Department of Oran.

Meanwhile the super-destroyer *Epervier,* commanded by Commander Joseph Laurin, with the *Typhon* following, had attempted to fight its way through the barricade of British cruisers and destroyers off the port. After a hot engagement which left her in flames, she had to beach herself under the shelter of the coastal batteries at Cape Aiguille in order to save her crew; even so, she lost 12 killed, 9 missing, and 31 wounded. The *Typhon* was not able to break through the British cordon, either, and had to return to Oran.

As evening came on, Admiral Rioult was falsely informed that the attackers were already forcing their way into the city. Carrying out his standing instructions, he promptly ordered that all ships in the port be scuttled. Accordingly 4 submarines, out of commission and without crews even, plus 7 patrol vessels or minesweepers, and 13 merchant ships were sunk in the channels or alongside the docks. Finding escape impossible, the *Typhon* blew herself up in the fairway.

The port of Oran surrendered the next morning, around 11 o'clock, but fighting in the interior continued until the general order to cease firing came from Algiers, also around 11 A.M.

The fight for Oran had cost the Air Force 10 dead and 13 wounded, and the Army 94 dead and 146 wounded. But the Navy, hardest hit, counted 134 dead and 146 wounded, plus those who went down with the *Argonaute* and the *Actéon*—a total of 347.

At Casablanca the curtain had also risen that night of November 8, which has rightfully been called the "dividing line of the war."

Since the German occupation of the French coast from Dunkirk to Bayonne, Casablanca had become France's principal port on the Atlantic. It served as a way port and replenishment base for convoys sailing from Marseilles and Oran for Dakar and the Antilles, and vice versa.

With its improvised navy yard, Casablanca was France's most important naval base left after Toulon. But it had no radar protection, and, despite the four 194-mm. guns and the four 138-mm. guns in the naval batteries of El Hank, defending the approaches, this city of 500,000 inhabitants was very vulnerable to attacks from the sea.

On the morning of November 8, the French naval forces present at Casablanca consisted of the battleship *Jean Bart* (incompleted and with only one of its quadruple 380-mm. gun turrets capable of firing); the 2nd Light Squadron, consisting of 1 light cruiser, 2 super-destroyers, and 7 destroyers; 8 sloops or patrol vessels; 11 minesweepers; and 11 submarines, of which 5 had arrived only that morning from Dakar on a routine training maneuver. The harbor was crowded with merchant ships. At the naval aviation base at Port Lyautey was one fighter squadron and one bomber squadron. The Air Force had a fighter squadron and a bomber squadron based at Rabat-Salé, and the same at Casablanca.

But Casablanca was not all of Morocco. The country had a total of 8,000,000 inhabitants. It had a regular garrison of six French divisions. Under the jurisdiction of a great administrator, General Noguès, residing at Rabat and next in authority to the Sultan, the country was prosperous, powerful, and loyal to France and to Marshal Pétain. The French naval forces in Morocco were commanded by Vice Admiral Michelier, who also was directly responsible for the general defense of Casablanca. As such he commanded not only the naval and air units, but also the local division led by General Béthouart, who was in the confidence of the Group of Five.

Admiral Michelier's staff, like all the other naval staffs, had kept a continuing plot of the positions of the large convoys which were reported at Gibraltar or entering the Mediterranean, and which apparently were aimed at Tripolitania, or even at Tunisia or Algeria, but never at Morocco. Because of a shortage of aviation gasoline, naval reconnaissance over the sea had been abandoned for some time, especially since there were no logical reasons why they should be continued. No one in Morocco had the slightest suspicion that a powerful American amphibious force was even then approaching the coast.

The first intimation Admiral Michelier received was from General Béthouart's chief of staff, who presented himself in the middle of the night with the surprising news of an American landing near Casablanca. General Béthouart had also sent several documents intended to show why the Americans should be welcomed as friends and not resisted as invaders. However, these documents stated as facts certain things which Admiral Michelier knew were untrue—such as the invasion of Tunisia by the Germans, and Giraud's taking over the government at Algiers.

Admiral Michelier had already noted the secretive actions of a few officers in his command, and he now suspected a trap. He picked up a telephone and called General Noguès personally.

General Noguès was at this moment a prisoner in his own residence, having been surprised in the middle of the night by Béthouart's accomplices. But they either did not know of the General's private telephone wires, or did not know where to cut them. To Michelier's inquiry, General Noguès stated that he knew nothing about an American landing, but then told of his own confinement. He asked Michelier what it was all about.

Admiral Michelier replied that he himself had seen nothing, that no such landing had been reported to him by any other source, and that nothing led him to believe Morocco was being attacked from outside. He and Noguès agreed that they were faced with a Free French *putsch,* combined, perhaps, with some minor operation against the coast, the main purpose of which was to lead Morocco into dissidence, as had happened in many other colonies.

Noguès was able to get in touch with loyal troops, who rescued him and at the same time made a prisoner of Béthouart, who was then taken to Meknès, to be tried before a regular military court. His position was precarious, as public feeling against him was high, but his lawyers managed skillfully to drag out the proceedings for the next few critical days. Furthermore, at the recommendation of Minister of the Navy Auphan, the Vichy Government had sent out orders for moderation in Béthouart's treatment.

Meanwhile, even as Béthouart was being arrested, the 105 transports and warships of the Western Task Force had taken their stations offshore under cover of the darkness. The Americans' plan was simple: 9,000 men were to be landed at Port Lyautey to seize the airfield there and convert it to American use; 18,700 men and 79 light tanks were to be landed at Fedala, to march on Casablanca from the north; and 6,500 men and 100 heavy tanks were to be landed at Safi, to advance on the city from the south. Off the harbor of Casablanca itself, ready to smash anything that attempted to leave the port, was stationed a strong naval force, consisting of the powerful new battleship *Massachusetts* with its 16-inch guns, two aircraft carriers, several heavy cruisers, and numerous destroyers.[7]

---

[7] The Covering Group (T.G. 34.1) under Rear Admiral Robert C. Giffen, U.S.N.,

Béthouart had previously made a few Army officers privy to a limited amount of information about the American landings; they, believing Béthouart operating under official Government orders, were delighted, and agreed to welcome the Americans. But when Rabat did not confirm Béthouart's instructions, and when the real truth came out, along with the news of the highhanded arrest of General Noguès, indignation was high. As a result, except at Fedala, the Army everywhere carried out its standing orders for defense, just as did the Navy. Cannon and machineguns were put at the several landing places, so that the attackers thought they had mistakenly selected the most heavily defended places along the coast at which to land. Despite the unseasonably calm seas, they made good their beachheads much later than their schedule had provided for.

In the port of Casablanca itself, nothing had been seen of any invaders, except a few mysterious leaflets dropped here and there. At 7 A.M., five French submarines got under way for their assigned patrol stations, and planes were being readied for reconnaissance, but the 2nd Light Squadron would require another ninety minutes to get under way.

At that moment, out at sea the U.S. aircraft carriers had just launched their first strike. At 0750 the first contact took place in the skies over Casablanca as French fighters rose to meet those from the U.S. aircraft carrier *Ranger*. In the brief encounter, seven French and five American planes were shot down.

The city itself still slept under the morning haze, until, around 8 o'clock, the French antiaircraft batteries opened fire on what they thought was a hostile torpedo plane, but which in actuality was the American fire control observation plane. Then, at 0804, the battle came to Casablanca with the roar of bursting bombs and the crash of 16-inch shells.

From the very beginning of the surprise, the casualties among the defenders were severe. Three submarines were sunk at their moorings before they could get under way; the others hurriedly sortied under the control of their executive officers, their commanders all having been killed on the dock as they were about to board their ships. Flying bits of stone, blasted from the piers by the bombardment, peppered the ships alongside. In the commercial harbor, it was a massacre: 10 freighters or passenger ships were sunk, with a loss of 40 dead and 60 wounded among their crews (fortunately, the passengers had already been landed). A super-destroyer and two destroyers undergoing major overhaul were seriously damaged.

All of this did not occur without some retaliation. The batteries of El

---

consisted of the USS *Massachusetts,* the heavy cruisers *Tuscaloosa* and *Wichita,* screened by the destroyers *Wainwright, Mayrant, Rhind* and *Jenkins.* The aircraft carrier *Ranger* and the escort carrier *Suwanee,* attached to the Center Attack Group, provided air support.

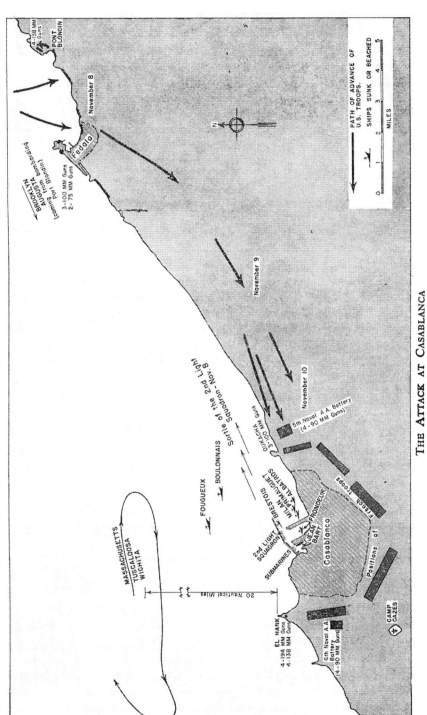

THE ATTACK AT CASABLANCA

Hank were swept with a storm of American bombs and shells of all calibers, but, under the stout leadership of Lieutenant Commander Raoul Bertrand, continued without interruption until the cease fire. The *Jean Bart* opened fire with the single 380-mm. gun turret in operable condition. She was hit several times by 16-inch shells which killed or wounded many of her crew, but she continued the unequal duel until a hostile salvo hurled some wreckage afoul of the turret, preventing its being trained on the targets.

This was around 9 o'clock in the morning. At this time the ships of the 2nd Light Squadron were just getting under way, one after the other, as much to evade the falling shells as to find out what was taking place in the neighborhood of Fedala. The squadron was commanded by Rear Admiral Gervais de Lafond, who had already extricated himself from a similar hornet's nest in the vicinity of Beirut. But here his only chance of escape lay in slipping along close to the shoreline where the rising sun would blind the enemy gunners. Radar, however, made it no longer necessary for a gunner to see in order to shoot straight. Furthermore, Gervais de Lafond was up against an enemy whose superior strength he could never have suspected. But he had no choice except to try; to have remained in the harbor would have inevitably brought him the same fate as the merchant ships sunk at their moorings.

The squadron flagship *Primauguet* found herself held up by machinery undergoing repair, therefore Admiral de Lafond transferred his flag to the super-destroyer *Milan,* and led the squadron out of the harbor. The chaplain, alerted too late to get on board, rushed through the rain of bursting shells to the end of the pier to give his blessing to the ships as they passed on their way out.

Astern of the squadron, the port was disappearing behind the smoke and splashes of the bursting shells. Ahead, the channel was obstructed by a barrage of 8-inch shells. However, all ships succeeded in clearing the channel without damage. But outside, the fury of battle awaited them—a battle of annihilation, which can best be described in three phases.

First of all, the 2nd Light Squadron, which was striving desperately to get into formation to meet the enemy, who had been located on a bearing of 20° True, had its topsides swept by a fierce machinegunning from the Wildcat fighter planes of the USS *Ranger.* This was around 0920. The anti-aircraft battery of the *Brestois* was put out of action. On the *Boulonnais,* Lieutenant Commander Charles Martinant de Preneuf was killed. The gunnery officer of the *Albatros* was severely wounded. On the bridge of the *Milan,* practically everyone was wounded, including Admiral Gervais de Lafond; the only one spared by the bullets was Commander François Costet. The damage and casualties from that first raking fire were to have serious effects on the subsequent shooting of the squadron.

The ships with which the squadron soon became engaged were the American vessels covering the Fedala landing. The French gunners scored hits on the U.S. destroyer *Ludlow* and some of the landing craft, but it was not enough. Against the 2nd Light Squadron, which had now been joined by the *Primauguet,* there poured a rain of shells from the U.S. cruisers *Augusta* and *Brooklyn* and their escorting destroyers to the northeast, as well as from the *Massachusetts* and two American heavy cruisers to the northwest!

And so began the second phase—the scourging.

It began at 1040, when the *Fougueux,* commanded by Lieutenant Commander Louis Sticca, went down under the shattering impact of 16-inch shells from the battleship *Massachusetts* and the 8-inch shells of the U.S. cruiser *Tuscaloosa.* The next victim was the *Milan,* which, with its bow crushed by a 16-inch shell, had to beach itself. The *Albatros* and the *Primauguet* reeled from the impact of the first heavy salvos. The *Boulonnais* died at noon from eight 6-inch shells striking her in the midst of an attempted torpedo attack. A shell from the *Massachusetts* landed just in time to mark with its green splash the place where the destroyer had just gone down with its dead and dying.

In the third phase, only four ships of the squadron remained fit for action. While attempting rescue operations for her stricken companions, the *Primauguet* was hit just below the waterline, forcing her to anchor not far from the *Milan.* The *Albatros* received a 16-inch shell hit forward. The *Frondeur,* hit aft and with her engineroom flooded but with her propellers still turning slowly, limped back into the port—only to capsize the following night. The *Brestois* tied up to the main pier with a 20-degree list from battle damage, and she too capsized there.

It was too uneven to be called a battle. Yet early that afternoon the firing began again when the sloops and the *Alcyon,* the only destroyer left undamaged, cleared the channel in order to pick up the survivors of the *Fougueux.* Against them and the damaged *Albatros* and *Primauguet,* the American Admiral Hewitt threw the full force of the *Massachusetts,* two cruisers, and the planes of the carrier *Ranger.*

The *Albatros* was put out of action; the *Primauguet* hit again. When evening came, she had difficulty even transferring her 90 dead and 200 wounded to shore.

The 2nd Light Squadron had been stricken from the French Navy list. But it had not gone out to its destruction in order to remain in the service of Hitler, as an American Order of the Day stated—a statement which its author must often have regretted later. It had suffered its martyrdom purely because of those higher values without which no country can continue to exist—loyalty, discipline, patriotism, respect for national unity.

When night fell, the port presented a desolate sight, a graveyard of sunken ships. The *Primauguet* was burning in the outer harbor. From the remaining ships capable of turning a propeller, Admiral Gervais de Lafond, though wounded and having lost both his flagships, the *Milan* and the *Prigmauguet,* tried to form another combatant group. Those surviving sailors who no longer had a ship to fight in were handed guns with which to continue the battle in the trenches.

Several such "naval landing forces" were assigned to man a 90-mm. naval antiaircraft battery installed at Aïn Sebaa, in the northeast outskirts of Casablanca. There they took up positions even in advance of the regular garrison regiments. When, on the next morning, November 10, the Americans coming from Fedala attacked them, they fought back fiercely despite heavy losses. Two small sloops—just about all that remained in the harbor—risked themselves outside the breakwater in order to shell the attackers.

Admiral Hewitt believed that the two sloops were the leaders of another sortie by the 2nd Light Squadron, whose battle losses he did not know. He ordered in the *Augusta* and four destroyers to meet the expected attack.

This was an opportunity for the *Jean Bart,* whose crew had worked secretly and feverishly to repair the damaged turret. It opened fire on the *Augusta,* Admiral Hewitt's flagship, and drenched it with the splashes of its heavy shells. It thus saved the two sloops, but drew upon itself the retaliation of all the American planes. Everyone within radio range heard the plain language order from the *Augusta,* "The *Jean Bart* is camouflaged yellow like the adjacent buildings. . . . Silence the *Jean Bart* and destroy any enemy found outside the harbor!"

All this tragedy was happening hours after the "cease fire" had been negotiated at Algiers. The news of this order reached Admiral Michelier in Casablanca at 3 o'clock in the afternoon, in the form of a telegram from Admiral Darlan. Admiral Michelier knew Darlan well enough to realize that such an order by the Admiral of the Fleet must be fully justified. However, at almost that identical moment, Vichy broadcast a message from Marshal Pétain, in plain language, ordering that the fight be continued.

One of the messages must be false, or at least a mistake. But *which* one? Had the Americans, or perhaps the conspirators at Algiers, managed to get hold of the Navy's secret codes?

Admiral Michelier tried to get in touch with General Noguès, but was unable to do so. He thereupon sent a coded message to the French Admiralty at Vichy, asking for a clarification of the matter.

The American commander off Casablanca should have known what was happening at Algiers. But perhaps there had been a break in his communication system. At any rate, in answer to the flagship's message a flight of

American bombers came over at 1600 to chastise the *Jean Bart* with 1,000-pound bombs. The battleship's upper works were severely damaged, but the armored decks held fast and the guns could still fire. And the morale of the defenders was not impaired.

By then Admiral Michelier had not only ascertained the validity of Darlan's message through private channels, but he had also received from the French Admiralty that evening the clarifying message he had sought.

It said, "The order of the Marshal is to continue hostilities *as long as that is still possible."*

Now the order as originally written had not contained that last phrase. Those words, with their highly meaningful reservation, had been especially added by Admiral Auphan at Vichy, under the very eyes of the Marshal himself. Michelier understood what was meant. Resistance was no longer possible—anyone could see that. All means of resistance had been exhausted. He took action accordingly, and informed the Admiralty. At daybreak the next morning, even while the tanks of the wrathful Germans were pouring into the Free Zone of France, a message arrived from the French Admiralty approving his decision.

The tragedy at Casablanca was over for most of the French Navy participants—but not for all. There were still the submarines to be accounted for.

As mentioned before, out of the 11 submarines present in Casablanca harbor, five had gotten under way before the bombardment began on November 8 to take station in their patrol sectors. Of these, the *Sibylle,* operating off Fedala, never returned.[8] The *Méduse, Antiope,* and *Amazone* made torpedo attacks on large American transports, but without success; in fact, they found themselves attacked in turn with shells, bombs, and depth charges, from which they barely escaped.

Back in the harbor the terrific American bombardment of 9 o'clock had sunk three of the remaining submarines on the spot. The *Oréade, Amphitrite,* and *Psyché* were all lost, the commanding officers of two of them being killed and the third badly wounded. The other three submarines got under way and took evasive action. They even tried to take on their armament of torpedoes which had been put ashore while they were undergoing overhaul. In so doing, the *Sidi-Ferruch* was bombed and machine-gunned on the surface, and had to flee, submerged, taking her dead and wounded with her. She hoped to reach either Dakar or Madeira, but she was attacked and sunk on November 11, off Casablanca, by three planes from the U.S. escort carrier *Suwanee.*

---

[8] The *Sibylle* was commanded by Lieutenant Commander Henri Kraut. Her operating area was along the coast between Fedala and Casablanca. The circumstances surrounding her disappearance have never been definitely determined.

The *Méduse* also had been hunted and blasted by sea and air. Half crippled, she beached herself under Cape Blanc on the morning of November 10 in order to save her crew.

The *Conquérant* had been undergoing repairs, high and dry in a floating dock, when the attack began. There was not even a pair of field glasses aboard. But she succeeded in getting afloat, and, without torpedoes or even a periscope, attempted to reach Dakar. Her attempt was hopeless. She was sunk on November 13, off Villa Cisneros, by Catalinas en route from Bathurst to Morocco.

The death struggle of the *Tonnant* lasted until November 15. Though hunted and depth charged for two days without a break, she managed to make a torpedo attack on an American aircraft carrier—probably the *Ranger*—on the 10th, but missed. She then headed for Casablanca, but her commanding officer, Lieutenant Pierre Corre,[9] did not know the state of affairs there, and was determined that his ship should not fall into the hands of the Americans. He accordingly resolved to head for Cadiz, where he hoped to repair his vessel within the 24 hours allotted under international law, and then reach a port in France. But the *Tonnant* became more and more sluggish; her list was increasing. And a British patrol plane was circling in the vicinity. On the morning of November 15 Lieutenant Corre took his beloved ship close to a fishing vessel which could save his crew and, with grief in his heart, scuttled her alongside.

Of all the submarines in the harbor of Casablanca at the time of the American attack on November 8, only three escaped alive. The *Orphée* returned to Casablanca after the battle; the *Antiope* and the *Amazone* managed to make Dakar and rejoin the French naval forces there.

With the death of the *Tonnant,* the tragedy of French North Africa was over. But the losses had been heavy. In killed alone the French Navy had lost 462, the Army 326, and the Air Force 15. The total of the wounded came to over 1,000.

But when one dwells on the suffering, the sacrifices, the fratricidal combats, one wonders if after all this outpouring of blood was necessary.

The answer is to be found in the varying objectives which the combatants were pursuing. On the Anglo-American side the losses suffered were the price paid to gain a foothold in Africa without running the very real risk of complete failure if they had consulted in advance with the French Government.

On the French side, while the French defenders were in intimate agree-

---

[9] Lieutenant Corre had been executive officer of the *Tonnant* on the morning of November 8, but the commanding officer had been killed in the first rain of bombs and shells. Lieutenant Corre had promptly assumed command and continued as captain until the end of the *Tonnant*.

ment with their attackers about taking up arms once more against the Axis, they were equally convinced that any such agreement should have been made through the proper authorities, and not through any secret group of subordinates and civilians. It was because of this that the French Navy fought the very people whom they would most have preferred as friends.

There were those even then who understood. Such a one was that American general who, two and a half years after the tragedy, was decorating a French naval officer with the Bronze Star Medal he had won on the Royan front while serving under the general's command. Before pinning on the decoration, the general made it a point to tell the recipient of the high regard he had had for him ever since their first contact at Casablanca, when they had been on opposite sides.[10]

---

[10] The general was Carl C. Bank, commander of the 13th U.S. Field Artillery Brigade; the French officer was Commander Charles Touraille, at that time commanding the 1st Regiment of Naval Gunners, but formerly the fire control officer of the *Jean Bart*.

CHAPTER 21

France Totally Occupied

At the very moment on November 10 when Admiral Darlan, at Algiers, issued his "cease fire" order to all the French Forces in North Africa, it was eleven thirty in the morning back at Vichy. In Marshal Pétain's office, General Weygand and Admiral Auphan, the Minister of the Navy, were studying the previous message from Admiral Darlan in which he asked what reply he should make to the American proposals for an armistice. They were preparing to tell him to temporize, but with favorable implications, when Admiral Auphan's private secretary dashed in with Darlan's "cease fire" order, which the French Admiralty had just received.

Immediately all faces lighted up. In stopping a fight that could do no good to France, Darlan had proved worthy of the confidence placed in him. Now all that needed to be done was to inform Laval so that he would not hear it first from the Germans.

As will be remembered, Laval was then at Munich, where Hitler had summoned him to negotiate a life-and-death alliance between the two countries. Laval had refused this offer, but now when he was told over the telephone of Darlan's initiative, he replied that if Darlan's action was approved, he, Laval, would have to submit his resignation immediately.

Everyone was aware of Hitler's interest in keeping Laval in the Government, and equally aware that an infuriated Hitler could vastly increase the martyrdom which France was already suffering. There arose a heated discussion in Pétain's office, Weygand and Auphan arguing for the approval of Darlan's action, the friends and collaborators of Laval taking the opposite extreme. Finally, in order not to bring on an outright break with the Germans, Marshal Pétain sent out the plain language message previously mentioned, instructing Darlan to continue the hostilities. (This was the message that had so troubled Michelier at Casablanca.) At the same time Pétain, at the suggestion of Auphan, let Darlan know by private, top secret code, that he still had confidence in the Admiral of the Fleet, and that the orders he was sending him publicly were primarily a means to gain time. A secret channel, independent of governmental communications, was

GENERAL DE GAULLE presiding at a meeting of the Free French Committee in 1941. At his right are Admiral Muselier, Mr. Diethelm, and Mr. Déjean; at his left are Professor Cassin, Mr. Pléven, and General Valin.

January 1942. *The corvette* Mimosa *at Saint Pierre Island.*

thus established between Marshal Pétain and the Minister of the Navy, in Vichy, and the Admiral of the Fleet, in Algiers.[1]

The great misfortune was that only these official disapprovals of Darlan which were published in the press became known to the general public and to the Armed Forces, both in Africa and in France.

But even the public disapproval of Darlan and the negotiations carried on by Laval in Munich did not long prevent what everyone had feared since the British and their allies had gained a foothold in the French territories neutralized by the 1940 armistice: the invasion of Tunisia and the Free Zone of France by the Germans.

This was, perhaps, the reason why the Anglo-Americans had confined Operation Torch to Algiers on the east. However, it was unthinkable that Tunisia would remain unoccupied by one or the other of the two adversaries. When the Anglo-Americans did not land there, it was equivalent to handing it over to the Germans, regardless of political considerations, since the French no longer had the material means with which to defend it.

As a matter of fact, on the night of November 8, the moment the news from Africa reached them, the German armistice commission at Wiesbaden notified the French delegation that "within one hour the French Government must give its assent to the use of the Tunisian airfields by the Axis." Laval yielded to an ultimatum which he could not oppose. During the next two days 100 Axis planes landed on the airfield of El Aouina, near Tunis. However, using police reasons as a pretext, the local garrison kept the Germans parked on the airfield.

The Wehrmacht reacted swiftly. On the evening of the 10th, Laval telephoned to his office from Munich that he had had to give way to new German demands. What these demands were was made clear four hours later by the terse German announcement that Axis forces would land in Tunisia "to prevent further Anglo-American attacks on French territories." Without the assurance of immediate American support, it was impossible for the French troops in Tunisia to resist. That same day, the Government of the Reich, having settled the Tunisian question, notified the French Government that it had decided also to send troops into the Free Zone of France.

Hitler's pretext for this action was that, as a result of the landing of the Anglo-Americans, the whole French Mediterranean coast was threatened, and that he could not rely for its defense on French generals who did not keep their word—meaning by the latter, of course, Giraud. The German

---

[1] These secret messages, in a code which despite armistice conditions had never been given to the Germans, were sent by special channels—first, over private land wires to Marseilles, and then by submarine cable to Algiers.

occupation of the coastal regions, Hitler's letter said, would be accompanied without interfering with French administration and would not affect the judicial status of the armistice—that is to say, there would be no acts of hostility against French troops, there would be no additional imprisonment of French military personnel, etc.

The possibility of such an action by the Germans had already been studied by Marshal Pétain, General Weygand, the Minister for the Army, and the Army Chief of Staff. Some were for fighting simply for the sake of honor, no matter what the result, but all were finally agreed that France had no means with which to fight, and that plunging the country into war again under these conditions would be suicidal.

Marshal Pétain accordingly decided to make no military resistance at the line of demarcation, limiting himself to a solemn protest over the radio. There was nothing, therefore, to prevent the German tanks, supported by the Luftwaffe, from driving peacefully toward Toulon the morning of November 11. This brought the Navy face to face with the immediate problem of what to do with the Toulon Fleet, where the main seapower of France had been assembled since the attack on Mers-el-Kebir.

It was intolerable that the ships should remain in a naval base whose land areas would be occupied by the Wehrmacht. Yet, judicially, despite the incursion of the German troops into the Free Zone, the fiction of the armistice remained. If the High Seas Squadron at Toulon got under way to join forces with the Anglo-Americans, that fiction would obviously be terminated. But it was not the prerogative of the Navy to initiate an action which would have such grave results for the entire country. Lastly, since the disapproval of Darlan's action on the day before, hostilities were theoretically still in force against the Anglo-Americans.

The legitimate solution would have been the cancellation of the disavowal of Darlan's action which Laval had forced from the Government in order to appease Hitler. After all, the Germans had assented to the Franco-British armistice which had terminated the hostilities in Syria and Lebanon the year before. The Navy Minister now argued with Marshal Pétain that the similar armistice Darlan had just made with the Americans should be approved and proceeded with in the same manner. But Laval's supporters demanded that nothing should be done until Laval's return. Although of the same opinion as Auphan, Marshal Pétain felt that his constitutional obligations to Laval required him to wait.

The hours sped by. Vichy was not occupied, out of consideration of its position as the seat of the French Government. But, in the remainder of the southern zone, the advance of the German tanks could be followed over the telephone.

Around one o'clock in the afternoon, Laval, Ambassador Abetz of Germany, and their retinue arrived in Vichy to the accompaniment of the throbbing engines of the Luftwaffe planes. Then followed lunch, a visit to the Chief of State, Marshal Pétain, and endless talking. A decision could not be hoped for before the meeting of the Council of Ministers that evening.

In order to gain time, Admiral Auphan took it upon himself to send off a message by teletype to Grand Admiral Erich Raeder, Commander in Chief of the German Navy, asking that the status of the French Navy be respected. "There are things we cannot do," he said in concluding his letter, "but we can both follow alike the paths of honor and of loyalty to our respective countries." At the same time he ordered the naval authorities at Toulon to parley with the Germans, if they arrived on the scene, in order to prevent them invading the navy yard or the ships. And in fulfillment of the promise he and Darlan had made the British at Bordeaux, he called the attention of all ships to the long standing order that the crews should scuttle their vessels rather than let them fall into the hands of the Germans.

It was five o'clock in the afternoon before the Council of Ministers met. Marshal Pétain had promised Auphan that obtaining the decision they both wanted would be a mere formality. But Laval seized the floor with an account of his complete failure at Munich: Hitler would not consent to enter into any commitments with France.

Seizing on this opportunity, Minister of the Navy Auphan tried to obtain a change of policy that he secretly hoped would result in getting the Fleet away from Toulon. And it was necessary at all costs, he declared, "to end the hostilities in Africa, because France lacks the military means to continue them."[2]

But the Ministers seated around the council table let their emotions make the decision, rather than their judgment. They were exasperated by Giraud's failure to abide by his promise, and angry at Darlan, whom they accused of laying down his arms too soon. Many, completely lacking in the ability to analyze the military situation, still believed in German supremacy. The majority were fascinated by Laval's oratory.

Worn out by the long crisis, Marshal Pétain remained woebegone and silent. The Minister of the Navy found himself alone in his views. The discussion resulted in a communique, immediately broadcast by the newspapers and the radio, that the council "honored the Army of Africa for its

---

[2] In his biography of Pierre Laval, Alfred Mallet quotes this statement, and then adds a remark evidently heard outside the Council room, "Laval cannot expect admirals to be diplomats."

loyalty, and counted on it to continue the fight to the limit of its strength in the interests of France and of the empire."

This was sheer lunacy. Auphan did not hide his feeling that somebody else should be put in charge of the Navy to carry out such unrealistic policies. But a captain does not abandon the bridge of the ship at the height of a storm. After all, the communique was little more than political verbiage, and while it prevented the French Fleet from joining forces with the Americans, it at least did not send it out to operate against them.

By then it was the morning of November 11. And, around 8 o'clock, General Noguès'[3] private courier, Commander Gaston Bataille, arrived by plane to confer briefly with Admiral Auphan and then with Marshal Pétain. Noguès wanted to know just what *was* wanted of him, what with Darlan's order to cease fire and Vichy's instructions to keep fighting. Furthermore, was Darlan acting as a free agent, or was he held under duress by the Americans?

The officer courier departed immediately on his return trip, carrying Marshal Pétain's private instructions. Believing Darlan a prisoner, the Marshal had appointed General Noguès as his sole representative in Africa, and now instructed him to negotiate the best possible arrangement with the Americans—one that would preserve the French empire overseas.

At the same time Pétain informed Darlan, by way of the Navy's secret communication channel through Marseilles, that he, Darlan, was being relieved soley because he was believed to be a prisoner, otherwise he would have been entrusted with the task of negotiating an armistice with the Americans.

That same evening Noguès acknowledged receipt of the instructions and announced that Darlan—who evidently was no longer a prisoner—had summoned him to Algiers the next day in order to confer on the armistice terms and the new status of North Africa. Noguès also let it be understood that, in accordance with the private instructions given to Commander Bataille that morning at Vichy, he would hand over all his powers to Darlan, if the Americans did not object, so that the Admiral of the Fleet could handle the negotiations in the name of Marshal Pétain.

If affairs seemed confusing in Vichy, they were even more so in North Africa. Rumors were going around that General Giraud was to be the Supreme Commander under the new arrangement—something intolerable to the armed services. At Algiers, Darlan had an American sentry posted at his door, but visitors came and went as freely as if the sentry had been French. In fact, the Anglo-American commanders quickly noted that Darlan

---

[3] General Noguès was Governor General and Commander in Chief in Morocco.

was obeyed while Giraud was not, and they were already preparing to use his influence.

Darlan himself, now that he had received the secret message informing him why the authority had been transferred to Noguès, was his confident self again. But before leading Africa back into the war, as the Americans were urging, he was resolved to wait until the next day so that he could act in concert with Noguès. However, during the afternoon of November 11—the very moment that Minister of the Navy Auphan at Vichy was working for the same objective—he sent a message to Admiral de Laborde, at Toulon, "inviting" him to bring the Fleet to Dakar.

Basing his appeal on the official protest which the French Government was making of the German invasion of the Free Zone, Darlan assured de Laborde that by moving the Fleet to Dakar he would be carrying out the unexpressed wishes of Marshal Pétain, and that the Allied naval forces would not oppose its passage. Unfortunately, he sent his coded message directly to Toulon,[4] instead of routing it through the French Admiralty at Vichy, as would normally have been done. By so doing he gave the message the appearance of bypassing the Government—of inciting dissidence, the particular aversion of the Navy. Furthermore, the "invitation" arrived the day after the Government's disavowal of the Algiers negotiations and its broadcast of the directive for a continuation of the hostilities against the Americans. Finally, what assurance did the commander of the Toulon Fleet have that, in the chaos prevailing at Algiers, some outsider had not got possession of the Navy's secret codes and so have sent out a forged message?

That was Admiral de Laborde's reaction, evidently, for he replied to Darlan by referring to the message sent by Commander Quièvrecourt at Noumeau, in September, 1940—a message consisting of a five-letter word expressive of the greatest derision,[5] and comparable only to General Anthony C. McAuliffe's famous reply to the Germans at Bastogne.

Admiral Auphan became aware of this exchange of amenities only after they had occurred. Admiral de Laborde was well known for his violent temper, and Darlan received his comment with amusement. In fact his whole attitude indicated that he had never expected the Toulon Fleet to take his "invitation" seriously.

---

[4] The Admiral of the Fleet could also communicate secretly with his principal Fleet commanders by employing a private code that had not been given to the Germans.

[5] Translator's Note: This five-letter word is reputed to have been the reply given by General Pierre Cambronne, commanding one of the squares of the Old Guard at Waterloo, when called upon to surrender. A direct translation in English is not in decent use, but the essential sense is the same as General Anthony C. McAuliffe's alleged reply of "NUTS!" at Bastogne to the German demand that he surrender.

For one thing, he knew that the Toulon Fleet would obey no orders but those of Marshal Pétain. For another, he knew that he himself had been publicly disavowed by Pétain the day before, and, to the Navy at least, was no longer Commander in Chief. If he had really been serious, he would have routed his "invitation" through his secret communication channel with Auphan. He had not done this. Why?

The logical explanation would seem that he issued his pseudo "invitation" in order to gain more time and perhaps a better bargaining position with the Americans, with whom he was to negotiate next day.

Whatever the reasons, his bypassing of the Minister of the Navy and the correct naval channels did not assist Minister of the Navy Auphan in his own effort to secure a shift in the Government's political alignment.

And events were moving quickly. On the night of November 11 the German High Command demanded of Vice Admiral Marquis, Commandant of the Toulon Naval District, and Admiral de Laborde, Commander in Chief of the High Seas Squadron, whether or not they pledged themselves to defend the Toulon naval establishment against all attacks either by the Anglo-Americans or by "dissidents." If the answer was "yes," the Toulon base and the Fleet would be spared by the Wehrmacht. Otherwise?

Actually the only other choice left was to scuttle the Fleet, inasmuch as Toulon was already surrounded, and any attempt to get the partly immobilized vessels under way, without air cover, without Anglo-American support, and against official orders could only end in disaster.

With the explicit agreement of the Minister of the Navy, the pledge was given immediately. It was far better to keep the Fleet for future use than to scuttle it before it was absolutely necessary. The time to take further action would be for the Government to decide.

Furthermore, this arrangement with the Germans created a small "free zone" around Toulon and the Fleet, and the Army even sent a number of their regiments there, since these were now useless in a country overrun everywhere else by the Germans.

But the obligation taken by the Navy at Toulon did not go beyond that of "defending itself against all comers"—and this had always been the general policy anyway with regard to the territories neutralized by the armistice. But that would not prevent the French Navy from taking every precaution against that pledge ever having to be put into effect. So, even though the German troops occupied all coastal telegraphic centers, the French Admiralty kept the secret of its private cable connections with Algiers, and Auphan and Darlan continued to exchange messages in their own private code with no one ever suspecting. In the same message in which the Minister of the Navy informed Darlan of the pledge relating to Toulon, he also stated that it was his intention never to order the Fleet to sea for any aggressive purpose.

But at this moment another disturbing complication appeared. In answer to Admiral Auphan's request, Grand Admiral Raeder explicitly confirmed the agreement on Toulon, but his extremely courteous telegram was open to misunderstanding since it ended with the hope that "in the future our two navies will accomplish their common duties in close and loyal cooperation."

This hope, oddly enough, anticipated the very kind of Europe that is being attempted today. But at that time, at the strategic turning point of the war, the Minister of the Navy remained more than ever opposed to all forms of co-belligerence, which, in his eyes, would have inevitably caused civil war in France. And any "close and loyal cooperation" was impossible in the atmosphere being created by the total occupation of France and by the deportation to Germany of Jews and French workmen.

The Minister of the Navy therefore sent a note to the German authorities specifying, "The engagement to defend Toulon will not include offensive operations on the high seas by the French Fleet in order to take part in any hostilities between the Axis powers and their enemies, or in participation in the common defense of those parts of the French coast occupied by the troops of the Axis."

Thus the French position was clearly defined: Toulon would be defended by the French, but nothing more; for their part the Germans, reiterating the solemn engagement of the 1940 armistice, pledged themselves to respect the Toulon Fleet and base.

The same day that this Franco-German agreement was being drawn up in France, a Franco-American agreement was being drawn up at Algiers.

General Noguès had arrived at Algiers absolutely opposed to Giraud, as were all the leaders who had had to fight against the American landings. But he quickly agreed with Darlan that, regardless of their feelings, the appointment of Giraud to an important position was necessary if any agreement was to be achieved. And an early armistice was absolutely necessary. General Clark was threatening to imprison every French leader loyal to Pétain who would not join forces with the Americans against the Axis. With Marshal Pétain's directive for continuation of the hostilities still standing, any unilateral action by important leaders toward collaboration with the Americans would have, as General Juin stated, created an appalling muddle.

A compromise was therefore arranged by which Giraud accepted command of the French armies subordinate to Darlan. Noguès returned to

Darlan the powers delegated to Noguès when Darlan had been believed a prisoner. Darlan, by general consent, assumed the title of High Commissioner of France in Africa "in the name of the Marshal under duress." The governors of the territories, the military cadres, and the whole French administration remained in their normal order in the new era of Franco-American collaboration which was now beginning.

On November 13, General Dwight D. Eisenhower and Admiral Andrew B. Cunningham arrived in person in Algiers in order to ratify that arrangement for the Americans and British.

But for this agreement to have full effect, with no impairment to French unity, the approval of Marshal Pétain was necessary, for only with the concurrence of the Chief of State could the African empire reenter the war legitimately. The Admiral of the Fleet and the Governor General of Morocco therefore sent a joint report to Vichy, setting forth the terms of the agreement they had negotiated for the best interests of France, and asked for Marshal Pétain's explicit approval.

The message arrived during the night of November 12, and Minister of the Navy Auphan personally took it to the Marshal at 9 o'clock the next morning. The Chief of State was already indignant at the Germans for having summarily arrested General Weygand the day before and driven him off to Germany. He therefore immediately gave his approval to the agreement negotiated with the Americans; but, being obliged to consider German reactions, he requested the Minister of the Navy to obtain the approval of the Chief of Government also.

Laval was already in touch with the occupation authorities over the matter of Weygand's arrest. When he read the terms of the agreement telegraphed from Algiers, he promptly telephoned German Ambassadoı Otto Abetz, at Paris. He read out the agreement word by word to Abetz, and added that he was inclined to approve it, but did not wish to do so without the assent of Berlin. He requested Admiral Auphan to wait for that assent before replying.

The rest of the morning dragged by in suspense. The Minister of the Navy at Vichy and Admiral Darlan at Algiers were impatient to broadcast the word that Marshal Pétain had approved, which would have smoothed out differences of opinion in France as well as in Algiers. Several times during the day, Admiral Auphan communicated with Darlan, counseling patience. Finally, at around 3 o'clock in the afternoon, he took it upon himself to send Darlan the following message in their secret code: "Confidential agreement of the Marshal and of Laval has been received. But cannot answer you officially until after occupation authorities have been consulted."

At Algiers, Admiral Darlan was nervously puffing on his pipe and reading over his chief secretary's shoulder as the latter decoded the message. When the first sentence was decoded, Darlan straightened up and gleefully announced, "We have the Old Man's agreement!"

A few moments later Radio Algiers broadcast the first proclamation of the new High Commissioner, who, to the slogan of "Long live Marshal Pétain!", announced his own assumption of the responsibility for French interests in Africa and for the defense of the territories "in agreement with the American authorities." The following day another broadcast assured the officers and civil servants who had taken the oath of allegiance to Marshal Pétain as Chief of State that they would be complying loyally with that oath by obeying the orders which he, Darlan, would give in Marshal Pétain's place. Similar public declarations by Noguès and Giraud confirmed that broadcast. Under the direction of the Admiral of the Fleet, French Africa was reentering the war on the side of the Allies!

These orders of the day, however, made it impossible that this "confidential agreement" of Marshal Pétain would ever get the official approval of the Government or the Germans. The latter never even replied to the request of Laval, and as a consequence the French Government never replied by either a "Yes" or a "No" to the important messages received from Algiers on the night of November 12. It was on the "confidential agreement" message, and the known restrictions placed on the Marshal by the Germans, that Darlan—for two years the designated successor of the Marshal—founded the legitimacy of his powers. No one at Algiers questioned it. The French Army, Navy, and Air Force would resume the war against the Axis which they had begun in 1939.

The Government at Vichy, subject to German pressure, could do nothing else but react. To protect his political position and to soften adverse reaction, Laval was compelled to disavow the action at Algiers. But in this he was far behind the fanatical collaborators, who fierily demanded nothing less than the reconquest of French Africa with the assistance of the Axis.[6] Darlan, Giraud, Noguès, and all the other principal French leaders in Africa were stripped of their French nationality and publicly stigmatized for having negotiated with the Americans instead of continuing to fight them.

It was not at Algiers that the denunciations of the collaborationists did the most harm. Darlan was prepared for this, and, if he had lived, European France and her empire overseas would have combined again on the day of victory without rancor on either side. It was in European France that the

---

[6] For some reasons never explained, the emotional Laval decided on November 23 to create an "African phalanx" in order "to deliver North Africa from the yoke of the Anglo-Saxons."

official propaganda worked havoc. Public opinion was deceived by the epithets of "traitor" and "felon" which the Government's pronouncements were levying against the leaders of Algiers. Their ears assailed by contradictory radio broadcasts from Vichy and from abroad, the mass of the people no longer knew what to believe.

Only Marshal Pétain and Minister of the Navy Auphan knew the truth. But the Marshal had pledged Admiral Auphan to absolute secrecy concerning the series of personal messages which had guided Darlan; he himself, through fear of German reactions, never alluded to them in the slightest.

But the collaborationist circles in the Government suspected plenty. The naval officer at Vichy who had coded Admiral Auphan's private messages was arrested and interrogated for days by the internal security police of the Ministry of the Interior. Later a very thorough investigation, in which the armistice commissions themselves participated, was made of all the messages exchanged between France and Algiers during the period of the crisis. But the precautions of the French Admiralty had been thorough, and the secret was never discovered.

In those tense days the position of the Minister of the Navy, well known to be opposed to the policies adopted by the Council of Ministers on November 11, was becoming more and more difficult. He personally felt that, for the time being at least, he had placed the High Seas Squadron in security, and he had contributed toward the reentry into the war of the French forces overseas. When, on November 15, Laval talked at a Cabinet meeting of continuing the fight against the Americans in collaboration with the Germans, Admiral Auphan declared that he could no longer have his name associated with such a policy. He submitted his resignation on the spot. If he had had any qualms about deserting Marshal Pétain in doing so, he was relieved of those feelings by the next action of the Marshal himself. Acting under German pressure, the Chief of State now delegated to Laval all his own powers, except that of revising the Constitution, and thenceforth separated himself from all active conduct of politics.

Admiral Auphan returned to his regular rank of rear admiral,[7] and was replaced as Minister of the Navy by Admiral Abrial, idolized by the people for his valor at Dunkirk and the reputation he had later made as Governor General of Algeria.

While these changes were occurring at Vichy, other things were occurring in Tunisia, the link between the France of Vichy and that of Algiers— changes that would be of vital import in the coming all-out battle there between the forces of the Axis and those of the Allies.

---

[7] Admiral Auphan had no further active duty during the war, but was retained on full pay. He was permitted to return to his home at Villefranche de Rouergue.

The Resident Governor General at Tunis was Admiral Esteva, the former Admiral, South. The senior Army commander in Tunis was General Georges Barré; the commander of the naval forces was Vice Admiral Derrien.

The disarmament which the Italians had required at Bizerte, the principal naval base in Tunis, was much greater than at Algiers. Admiral Derrien had under his orders only three 600-ton torpedo boats, two minesweeping sloops, and nine decommissioned submarines with no crews aboard. The majority of the coast defense batteries had been put out of service. To defend and police the whole extensive Bizerte area, there were only three battalions of troops, when the actual requirement was nineteen. In addition Derrien had reached the age for retirement and was due to be relieved the next month.[8]

On November 7 Derrien received a visit from an old friend, General Bergeret. General Bergeret had received confidential information in France of the impending American landings and had rushed from Vichy to take part in them. On his way through Algiers he had tried by hints to let General Juin and Admiral Darlan into the secret, but they had preferred to trust Consul General Murphy's statement that there would be no American landings before 1943. Now that the American transports were almost off the coast, General Bergeret risked confiding in Admiral Derrien, who immediately became very enthusiastic over the news. Consequently the admiral was not surprised when he received a telephone call from Admiral Esteva that night.

Admiral Esteva had just received a call from U.S. Consul Hooker A. Doolittle, bearing a message from President Roosevelt not only confirming the landings but announcing that they had already begun. While warning Consul Doolittle that he himself would faithfully obey any orders from his chiefs, Esteva was personally so sympathetic with Allied plans for the landings that he urged the "the Allies hurry up, as the Germans will be here within 48 hours!"

Everything favored the Allies. If American ships had arrived at Bizerte the morning of November 8, they would probably have been received with welcoming arms rather than with gunfire.

Tragically, not a ship appeared. Even a token detachment landed there would have enabled Admiral Darlan to have included Tunisia also in the armistice he negotiated two days later. But an armistice is a "cessation of

---

[8] In anticipation of retirement, Admiral Derrien had made an official request of the Germans—the only request he ever made of them in his entire life. He had asked for the privilege of taking his sword with him. There was delicate irony in this request, for the German authorities had forbidden anyone to possess arms in the Occupied Zone—even anything as useless for a weapon as the sword of a naval officer.

hostilities between opposing forces." And at Tunisia, despite the notice given by Doolittle, no troops appeared, hence there were no "opposing forces" and there could be no "hostilities." Furthermore, the absence of American troops aroused serious doubts as to the strength of the Allied landing forces. Worse still, the American radio announced that the President's notes had been delivered to the Resident Governor General and to the Bey of Tunis, thus tipping off the Germans far enough in advance to permit them to reach Tunisia first.

However, on November 8, Derrien sank three cargo vessels in the canal leading into the Bizerte harbor, but without effectually blocking the entrance. He had done this in compliance with orders from Algiers, but it is not known even today whether this was a precautionary measure against the Anglo-Americans, or against the Axis, or simply to show the admiral's resolution to defend Bizerte and thus give Admiral Auphan, in France, an excuse against having to send the Toulon Fleet out to help defend Tunisia.

However, the Germans were already proceeding with their own measures. In accordance with their announcement at Wiesbaden, the German Air Force began rushing planes to Tunisia, and by the next morning 104 Luftwaffe planes had landed on El Aouina airfield, outside Tunis. Under orders, the French garrison permitted them to land, but barred any advance into the countryside.

It was at noon on November 10 that Derrien, like all the other French commanders in North Africa, received Darlan's "cease fire" order, putting an end to hostilities with the Anglo-Americans. Although there had been no hostilities in Tunisia, and although orders disavowing Darlan's action came from Vichy shortly afterward, Admiral Derrien broadcast the "cease fire" order, still hoping that some of Doolittle's promised Americans would appear.

Instead, the very opposite occurred. That evening the French Admiralty informed him that at any moment the Wehrmacht would land at Bizerte and Tunis. "I am fully aware," said Admiral Auphan in his message, "of the repercussions of this. But be assured that I, like you, am thinking only of the final good of France."

In accordance with this new directive, Derrien ordered his men to allow the German troops to pass through the naval base, and to avoid any contacts with them in their passage. General Barré, for the same reason, withdrew his French troops from the coast to the interior, to the heights known as the "Tunisian backbone." Thus a gap was beginning to open up between the Navy, tied to the navy yards and the ports, and the Army, preparing to retreat to the mountainous Algerian frontier.

The news of the German invasion of the Free Zone of France, which reached Bizerte on November 11, created great confusion there. "Whom are we fighting, the Germans or the British and Americans?" Admiral Derrien inquired of the French Admiralty.

That was the day the crisis was reaching its peak at Vichy. Auphan sent back word that his personal advice was to remain neutral toward both, but that a meeting of the Council of Ministers would decide that evening.

For his part, Admiral Esteva called Darlan at Algiers directly on the telephone. The two had always been intimate friends.

"Hello. Is it you, Jean Pierre?" answered Darlan. "This is François speaking. Would you like to become an American?"

"Why, certainly," answered Jean Pierre Esteva. "But they had better hurry up, those Americans."

At the same time General Juin was telephoning to Barré, "We are going to smack the Boches!"[9]

The phrase circulated back to Bizerte. "May I tell my men?" asked Derrien. "Yes," said Esteva.

Enthusiastically the commander of the naval forces at Bizerte seized his pen and sent the following order of the day to his subordinates:

> After two days of talk and confusion, the order has just reached me explicitly designating the enemy against whom you are to fight. That enemy is the Germans and the Italians. Soldiers, sailors, airmen of the Bizerte defenses, you now have your orders—blaze away with all your heart against the foe of 1940! We have a reckoning coming. Long live France!

The broadcasting of that message in the late afternoon caused general rejoicing both aboard ship and ashore. The crews sang the "Marseillaise." The officers on some ships toasted the news in champagne. But the bottles had not even been emptied when an amazing counterorder came, cancelling the previous one and directing that all copies of it be withdrawn and destroyed.

What was happening?

The main thing was that Derrien had read his order of the day over the telephone to Esteva. Esteva gasped. When you prepare to turn on an enemy and strike him, it is not customary to inform him in advance. Next, the November 11 communique of the Council of Ministers, just received, had directed that hostilities continue against the Anglo-Americans. Lastly, these had never shown up to join in the new arrangement promised Esteva by U.S. Consul Doolittle. At midnight Derrien despairingly cancelled his order of the day and prescribed an attitude of strict neutrality toward all belligerents. The sudden reversal chilled the hot enthusiasm of the crews.

That next morning German planes began landing at the naval air base of

---

[9] "Boches" was the insulting epithet applied to Germans by the French during the First World War.

Sidi Ahmed. During the afternoon, five Italian torpedo boats, two small cargo ships, and a few motor boats entered the channel and anchored in Sebra Bay, near Bizerte, to establish a base there.

Derrien had no desire to be remembered as "the admiral who turned over Bizerte to the Germans." He considered driving them out with gunfire, and asked General Barré for reinforcements for that purpose. But Barré was already retreating toward the interior; he not only refused to send more troops, but even asked Derrien to return the three battalions he already had. The fate of Bizerte was sealed.

From Algiers came telephone calls from Darlan and Moreau, asking Derrien, their comrade, to join with them and the Anglo-Americans. From the French Admiralty at Vichy came the official Government disavowal of Darlan and directions that Derrien was no longer to take orders from his former superior.

Unlike Darlan, Derrien had no understanding of politics and the things that lie concealed under public attitudes. He was only a bluff, gruff old sea dog. In the telephone calls from Algiers he perceived what he thought was a conspiracy against the legitimate government, and so informed the French Admiralty.

Admiral Auphan was still Minister of the Navy then. Despite the critical situation he himself was in, he tried to guide Derrien by his reply, sent on the evening of November 12: "Take your orders from General Noguès, who is at Algiers and who has the directives and confidence of the Marshal."

Nothing, however, could change the course of events. The fate of Bizerte could not be separated from that of Tunisia. And Governor General Esteva, directly under the orders of Laval, now saw arriving, one after the other, as if to watch his every move, the German Minister Rudolf Rahn and Vice Admiral Platon, Minister without Portfolio to Laval. In their wake trailed a number of others noted for their interest in close Franco-German collaboration.

Platon, in addition to having been at Dunkirk, had been Secretary of State for the Colonies during the attacks on Dakar and Gabon. Ever since those occurrences he had harbored strong resentment against the English and also against all forms of dissidence. His martinet character made him an admirer of the German characteristics of orderliness, discipline, and machine efficiency. If he was no longer convinced of German victory, he saw little to choose between them and the Allied democracies as to purity of cause. Uncompromising, he considered it a sacred duty, and not just a political maneuver, as did Laval, to continue resistance in Africa to the Anglo-American attacks, even if he had to do so with German collaboration, and regardless of how the conflict might end. He was one of those who, at Vichy, had declaimed the loudest to Marshal Pétain against the "traitors" of Algiers.

Despite the advice of Auphan, Laval had decided to send Platon to Tunis, to make it appear to the Germans that something was being done at least to defend French territory against the Allied landings.

The trip across the Mediterranean was dangerous—just the sort to delight the old warrior. He visited all the leading personalities in Tunisia, preaching discipline and loyalty to Marshal Pétain. It was a language that always had appeal. And profiting from the general confusion, the Germans quickly infiltrated everywhere, and then consolidated their positions.

From the land side all the Germans had in front of them was Barré's 12,000 men, unsupported by a single American. These men, withdrawn to the heights behind, looked grimly down at the Germans, neither side attempting to force the issue.

In Bizerte the Navy, completely encircled and isolated, guarded its installations without paying any attention to the German troops passing through. After all, when the first German plane had been allowed to land untroubled, the last chance for a successful resistance at Bizerte had disappeared.

It was not until November 19 that the first Allied elements from Algeria arrived at the heights of Medjez el Bab, where the French troops were posted. And these first elements were so few was to constitute only a token assistance: two 37-mm. antitank guns, two 75-mm. guns, one antiaircraft gun, and 140 British paratroopers. Against these and Barré's small force, the Germans already had in Tunisia 35,000 men, 140 light and heavy tanks, considerable artillery, and a powerful air force.

The first shots were fired by the American antiaircraft gun against German planes flying over the French lines at 8 o'clock in the morning. The shots were so scattering that the German commander thought they were accidental, and he merely ordered the French to disperse. When the French stood their ground, they were violently attacked by waves of Stukas, followed by paratroopers. General Barré's men defended their position stoutly. And thus it was that the French Army of Africa, neutralized since 1940, took up the war where they had left it—on the side of the Allies.

Belatedly the Allies tried to save the day. A British division, supported by tanks, fought its way as far as Jefna on the road to Bizerte, and as far as Djedeida on the way to Tunis. But, lacking air support, the Allies suffered severe losses before falling back in December to their starting points.

At the time of this offensive, the newly organized French command at Algiers had sent a messenger to Admiral Derrien, urging him to attack the Germans from the rear. But Derrien was by now physically worn out, mentally confused, unable to take the responsibility of breaking the bonds which tied him to Tunis and to Vichy. Even had he wished to do so, he had not the forces at his disposal to do anything. The only thing that could have saved Tunisia from the very beginning was for the Allies to have gotten there first, or else to have come with such force that they could have thrown the Germans back into the sea before they consolidated their positions. Shackled to his navy yard and to the installations which he could not abandon, the unfortunate Admiral Derrien was as much a victim of the dilatory policy of the Allies as he was of the ebb and flow of politics.

And out of all this confusion in North Africa, out of all this dilatory conduct on the part of the Allies, the Germans were to learn of the conspiracy organized by Giraud, of Darlan's dealings at Algiers, and of the French Army's turning against them despite all the orders apparently issued by Marshal Pétain. And, learning, they inevitably took the measures that were to lead to the scuttling of the Toulon Fleet on November 27, and to the German seizure of Bizerte and its ships on December 8.

CHAPTER 22

Tragedy at Toulon and Bizerte

Founded in 1589 by King Henry IV—"Henry of Navarre"—Toulon naval base had seen history made throughout the centuries. During the Revolutionary period of 1793, the English and Spaniards had occupied it under chaotic conditions. They had given the officers of the French Navy the hard choice between collaborating with them or surrendering their ships. The matter ended with the navy yard and most of the fleet being burned. A repetition of the circumstances in 1815 was avoided only through skillful negotiations. Since then the roadstead, the navy yard, and the fortified heights protecting it had become the heart of French naval power.

Here the greater part of the French Fleet, escaping the tragedy of Mers-el-Kebir and the threat at Dakar and elsewhere in 1940, had come for protection under the guns of the shore batteries. On June 27, 1940, there had been only 36 men-of-war at Toulon; in November of 1942 there were almost 80 ships there, representing more than half of the total tonnage of the French Fleet—the most modern, the most powerful half. These ships were organized in three distinct groups:

The High Seas Fleet, commanded by Admiral de Laborde, and consisting of one powerful new battleship, three heavy cruisers, two light cruisers, ten super-destroyers, and three destroyers.[1]

Ships in commission under Vice Admiral Marquis, Commandant of the Toulon Naval District, consisting of one old battleship, one seaplane tender, two destroyers, four torpedo boats, and ten submarines.[2]

Ships decommissioned under the armistice, and having only skeleton

---

[1] Battleship *Strasbourg;* heavy cruisers *Algérie, Dupleix, Colbert;* light cruisers *Marseillaise* and *Jean de Vienne;* super-destroyers *Guépard, Verdun, Tartu, Volta, Vauquelin, Kersaint, Indomptable, Gerfaut, Vautour,* and *Cassard;* destroyer *Bordelais, Mars,* and *Palme.*

[2] Battleship *Provence* (flagship of the training division); seaplane tender *Commandant Teste;* destroyers *Mameluk* and *Casque;* torpedo boats *Adroit, Baliste, Bayonnaise, Poursuivante;* submarines *Fresnel, Caïman, Marsouin* (returned from North Africa after the Allied landings), *Casabianca, Redoutable, Aurore, Iris, Venus, Diamant,* and *Glorieux.*

255

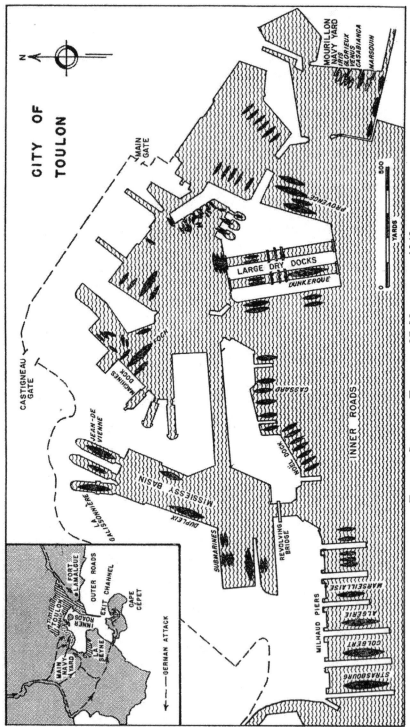

FRENCH SHIPS AT TOULON, 27 NOVEMBER 1942

crews. These included one damaged battleship, two cruisers, eight super-destroyers, six destroyers, and ten submarines.[3]

In addition there were present, on November 14, the usual collection of small light craft to be found in any large naval base—sloops, submarine chasers, patrol vessels, etc.

The rapidly shifting situations following the Allied landings on November 8 had naturally caused great concern at Toulon. The fact that the landings had been made by force, and without any advance notice, recalled to many the British and Free French attacks at Dakar, in Syria, and at Diego Suarez, with their heavy toll of French lives. Also, advance news had already been received of the severe losses at Casablanca.

One of the things that disturbed everybody was Admiral Darlan's sudden and surprising turnabout, followed as it was by the series of confusing disavowals at Vichy.

On the other hand the news, when it came, of the German invasion of the hitherto free southern zone aroused emotions in the Toulon Fleet to the highest degree. Anything was preferable to the German yoke. Anti-German demonstrations broke out on several ships and had to be quelled by the officers.

The agreement guaranteeing the neutrality of the Toulon base was only superficially encouraging. The unusual manner in which it had been negotiated—directly between the Germans and the senior French naval officers at Toulon rather than through usual Government channels—also was disquieting. Finally, Admiral de Laborde had required each officer in his command to take a special oath of allegiance to the Government—something which would inevitably torture the souls of many on the cross of conscience.

Toulon was not only crowded with naval personnel, but also with a flood of refugees fleeing ahead of the German advance into the Free Zone. It was also full of fantastic rumors. One sloop on patrol offshore even reported that it had sunk an Allied submarine off the port with depth charges.

The Army regiments which had arrived to help garrison the base were full of resentment against the Germans; on the other hand, the Navy was more fearful of another Mers-el-Kebir at the hands of the Allies. The high command at Toulon simply prepared to defend the base against all comers, thus taking out insurance against any German claims that their troops were needed to help defend against Allied attacks.

One of the first things done was to bring up to date the standing orders of the Admiralty that the Fleet was to be scuttled before allowing it to fall

---

[3] Battleship *Dunkerque;* cruisers *Foch* and *La Galissonnière;* super-destroyers *Tigre, Lynx, Panthère, Lion, Valmy, Aigle, Vauban, Mogador;* destroyers *Lansquenet, Hardi, Foudroyant, Siroco, Bison, Trombe;* submarines *Espoir, Vengeur, Achéron, Henri Poincaré, Pascal, Galatée, Naïade, Sirène, Thétis,* and *Eurydice.*

into alien hands. The next day, November 15, Admiral de Laborde made a flying trip to Vichy, where he conferred with Admiral Auphan, whose resignation was practically already written out, and with Chief of State Pétain and Laval. Immediately thereafter he broadcast an order of the day to his Fleet, telling the crews that the security of Toulon lay in their hands.

"At a time," he concluded, "when some of the highest ranking officers are losing their sense of duty, you must show that devotion is not measured by the number of stripes or stars. Strict discipline and the highest type of military conduct are absolute requisites for everyone. I have today given the Marshal my guarantee of your faithfulness and he has instructed me to tell you that he is counting on you to save the unity and honor of France."

During the days that followed, the tension at Toulon increased with the successive shocks of Marshal Pétain's withdrawal from all connection with political affairs, Admiral Auphan's resignation as Minister of the Navy, and the increasing Government tirades directed at the French leaders in Africa. Next, the Germans required the withdrawal of the French troops which had entered the Toulon area in order to help with its defense. Finally, the Germans demanded the removal of all air units stationed in the Toulon area.

The new Minister of the Navy, Admiral Abrial, attempted to restore confidence by making a personal visit to Toulon on November 23. However, all the explanations he gave consisted of generalities, when the Fleet would have liked to know specific facts so that they might understand the situation. Further, Admiral Abrial directed that if some day the ships had to be scuttled, they must be sunk right side up, without capsizing, giving the impression that the idea was to sink them so that they could be readily raised—for whose use, it was not made clear. Lastly, Admiral Abrial approved the measures taken for the defense of the port and Fleet in cooperation with Axis troops, against attacks coming from the sea—a direction from which only Allied attacks could come.

The new Minister of the Navy had intended to go next to Marseilles to meet with the French Merchant Marine Services there. Immediately after the Allied landings in North Africa, the Germans had demanded the chartering to them of the entire remaining French merchant fleet,[4] since this

---

[4] Vichy did not learn of this demand until 4 P.M. on November 20, at which time a telegram was received from Mr. Louis Nicol, Chief of the French Merchant Marine Subcommittee at Wiesbaden. Two hours later Mr. Laval issued orders that the most pressing German demands were to be met. Even before receiving that reply, General Johan Casper, Commanding the German troops at Marseilles, had announced his intention of placing an armed guard on all French merchant ships.

Pursuant to the Laval-Kaufmann agreement of November 22, the 5th of December was the specified date on which the Germans were to take over the ships. Several days later the German Government made the amazing demand that the French Government pay the operating expenses of these ships, arguing that they had been made available to the Germans in order that these might help fight the Americans in North Africa, and against Communism!

would no longer be needed for transportation between European France and North Africa. On November 22, Laval had agreed to cede to Gauleiter Kaufmann, Commissioner of the German Merchant Marine, all French merchant vessels except some 18 ships of 50,000 tons total, which France was to retain for her own special needs. The ships thus ceded amounted to the number of 158, with a total tonnage of 646,000.

Admiral Abrial's purpose in going to Marseilles was to draw up a suitable program for the transfer, but he was recalled to Vichy, instead, by the news that French West Africa, with the ships and base at Dakar, had joined forces with the Americans and British. Before doing so, Governor General Boisson, High Commissioner at Dakar, had sent a trusted representative to Algiers to verify the authenticity of the private secret messages that had been exchanged between Admiral Auphan and Admiral of the Fleet Darlan. Once convinced of the reality of Marshal Pétain's "confidential agreement" in connection with Darlan's actions, Boisson had placed himself under the orders of Darlan, while at the same time sending assurances to Marshal Pétain at Vichy that he "continued faithful to the Marshal's policies, which had also always been his own."

The Commander of the French naval forces at Dakar was Vice Admiral Collinet. When called upon to explain his dissidence, Admiral Collinet had replied that he was "in complete agreement with the views of the other general and flag officers of the three services, not one of whom had been able to figure out any other solution to the situation facing them."

That had been November 23. The next day, in France, German troops carried out night raids on a few French merchantmen at Sète and Port Vendres. Simultaneously German engineer troops occupied the French naval air base of Palyvestre, at Hyères, within the zone of the fortified Toulon base itself.

The German naval officers assigned to liaison duties at Toulon were sure that these occurrences were merely mistakes on the part of some local commanders and would be quickly rectified. Actually these two occurrences, contrary to Germany's most solemn pledges, were merely premature movements in an over-all plan, long prepared, for seizure by surprise of what remained of the French Fleet.

Ever since December 10, 1940, there had existed in the files of the German staffs a certain Directive No. 19. This file was so secret that the Italians were not even allowed to suspect its existence. The directive was explicit:

> In case any uprising should occur in French Africa, the territory of European France not yet occupied is to be seized immediately. At the same time, the French Fleet and Air Force must be seized, or at least prevented from going over to the enemy. The Kriegsmarine and the Luftwaffe, in liaison with the land forces, will jointly plan the measures through which the Fleet can be most readily seized and the ports occupied. . . .

The code name for this movement was "Operation Attila."

The first part of this detailed plan—that providing for the occupation of the Free Zone—was carried out on November 11. Supported by the Luftwaffe, the German motorized columns crossed the line of demarcation, occupied the valleys of the Rhône and the Garonne, and pushed forward to the Mediterranean coast. Any hope that the new special neutrality zone at Toulon would be respected was doomed. On November 19 Hitler ordered that on the 27th the second part of Operation Attila should be carried out. This part—"Operation Anton"—provided for the occupation of the forts and naval base at Toulon, the seizure of the French Fleet there, and the disarming of what remained of the French Army in the southern zone.

The German excuse for Operation Attila was that the French had brought it on themselves by their Army of Africa turning against the Axis under the orders of leaders like Giraud, whose name was anathema across the Rhine, or like Darlan. Hitler and his chiefs could never forgive themselves for having had confidence in Darlan for so long.

But there was more to it than that. There was, in particular, that famous note of November 14 in which Admiral Auphan had served notice that French collaboration with the Germans for the defense of the European coast of France would not go beyond that single sector of Toulon. For example, the French Admiralty refused the German request that it put back into service the coast defense batteries in the German occupied sector along the Gulf of Lyons; and it even more tersely refused to undertake any warlike operation on the high seas.

The Germans had hoped for far more collaboration. From the moment that the French Navy refused to play the Germans' game, it was doomed.

In all fairness, it must be said that, as we know definitely today, the senior officers in the German Navy attempted to have Operation Anton cancelled —partly because they believed it violated their plighted word, and partly because they were sure that it would never be successful. The officers of the Kriegsmarine knew the officers of the French Navy too well to believe for one second that they would allow their ships to be put to German use any more than they themselves, after World War I, had allowed their own Fleet to remain in English hands at Scapa Flow.[4a] But the German Army was determined not only to disarm the remaining French troops but also to eliminate the neutralized naval establishment at Toulon, which they regarded as a dangerous foreign body in the middle of their battlelines.

[4a] That was precisely the opinion of Commander Hugo Heydel, the Kriegsmarine liaison officer to the SS general charged with carrying out Operation Anton. When the general asked him what he considered the chances for success were, Heydel replied: "None, as, in my opinion, the French have already prepared a Scapa Flow, just as we ourselves would have done!" (Heydel letter to Mordal, January 19, 1958.)

It was for this reason that the operation against Toulon was carried out almost entirely by troops of the Wehrmacht, with the German Navy limiting themselves to action later, and only after Toulon had already been taken over by the Army. As a result, the Army troops advancing on Toulon were without those naval specialists who might have prevented, or at least cut down, the amount of destruction that eventually transpired.

Yet even so, the reliance of Vichy and Toulon on the German promises was so great that the Germans came within a hair's breadth of succeeding.

Under Operation Anton, two German armored columns were to invade the Toulon area simultaneously. One, from the east, was to occupy Fort Lamalgue, the command post of the Naval District Commandant, and the navy yard at Mourillon. The other, coming from the west, was to enter the main navy yard, where the larger ships lay, and was to send a detachment to seize the fortified positions of the Cépet Peninsula, which commanded the exit channel from the yard to the outer roads. To prevent any French ship's getting away, the Luftwaffe was to seal off the harbor by laying mines in the exit channel.

The operation was planned to coincide exactly with a diplomatic notice served on Laval around 4:30 in the morning, by which time it was expected that the German soldiers would already have boarded the French ships. As a result, the alerting messages which were sent immediately from Vichy to Toulon upon receipt of the German notification arrived too late to alert the defenders in time to do anything to change the outcome.

Moreover, the consideration with which the Toulon base and Fleet had been treated by the Germans had allayed French suspicions to the point where, for the first time since November 8, part of the crews (one-eighth) had been given overnight liberty.

To prevent the alarm being given, the Germans had sent out advance guards, who seized all the French police posts on the roads their tanks were taking, and who cut all telephone wires. One of these posts did manage to get off a mounted motorcycle policeman, but he barely beat the Germans to the main navy yard gate.

It was therefore a complete surprise when, at 0425, the first German tanks showed up at Fort Lamalgue. This was a fort in name only, being a mere barracks without fortifications of any kind. Admiral Marquis, Commandant of the Toulon Naval District, was captured in his bed without being able to get out one word of warning.

But the Germans were not able to locate the district's communication center immediately, and while they were looking for it, Rear Admiral Marcel Robin and duty officer Lieutenant Commander Paul Le Nabec managed to telephone Rear Admiral Gérard Dornon. Admiral Dornon, the Assistant

Commandant, always slept at his post at the main navy yard. Admiral Robin instructed Admiral Dornon to notify Admiral de Laborde immediately on his flagship, the *Strasbourg*. Admiral Dornon did this, and asked for instructions regarding the scuttling of the ships under the orders of the District Commandant.

Admiral de Laborde, Commander in Chief of the High Seas Fleet, at first refused to believe the Germans could be guilty of such a breach of faith. He accordingly directed that the crews on all the ships be awakened, the boilers lighted off,[5] and all hands sent to their stations for scuttling, but that no further action was to be taken without direct orders from him.

Meantime reports were pouring into the Assistant Commandant's post from the Castigneau gate to the west and the Mourillon gate to the east, that the Germans were hammering at the closed gates and even trying to scale the walls. Admiral Dornon ordered that those Germans climbing the walls be treated like ordinary hoodlums, and fired upon, and that those at the gates be held off by parleys for as long a time as possible. But by 0520 the Germans had managed to enter the Mourillon navy yard. Five minutes later the Castigneau gate was burst in by German tanks. Upon this information, Admiral de Laborde, on the *Strasbourg,* directed that the general order for scuttling be broadcast immediately over the radio to all ships. This order the signalmen also repeated over and over from the signal blinkers on the yardarms: "Scuttle! Scuttle! Scuttle!"

It was still dark at that time, and the German tanks lost their way in the maze of docks, wharves, and shops of the immense navy yard. They did not arrive at the Milhaud piers, where the larger ships lay, until about six o'clock. They did not reach the Machines dock until about 0620, or the other docks until an hour later. By then they were too late.

Aboard the *Strasbourg* the lines had been cast off and the crews were all at their abandon ship stations when the first German tank smashed in the gate leading to the ramparts at about six o'clock. Whether by accident or by design, she fired one of her 88-mm. guns. The shell burst inside one of the ship's secondary battery turrets, mortally wounding Lieutenant Dominique Fay, who was supervising the sabotage of the guns. The shell fragments also wounded six of the turret crew.

The heavy machineguns on the *Strasbourg* immediately fired back, but Admiral de Laborde ordered them to cease firing.

It was still dark. German infantrymen appeared on the wharf, and voices hailed the *Strasbourg*.

"Admiral, my commanding officer sends word that you must hand over your ship undamaged."

---

[5] It should be pointed out that it takes five or six hours after boilers are lighted off before a naval force can get under way and put to sea.

Admiral de Laborde himself answered. "It has already been scuttled."

There was a brief discussion ashore. Then the German voice called out again.

"Admiral, my commanding officer sends word that you have his greatest respect!"

It was a dialogue worthy of Homer's *Iliad.* But during this time Admiral de Laborde's flag captain had already made certain that all the below decks spaces had been cleared. Now he sounded the siren as the signal for execution.

Explosions sounded all over the ship, as gun after gun was blown up. The reduction gears on the turbines had been cut with an oxyacetylene torch, and other important machinery parts blasted with hand grenades. The sea cocks were opened, and the *Strasbourg,* which drew 10 meters, settled on an even keel until her top decks were four meters under.

The same destruction was going on aboard the cruiser *Algérie,* flagship of Vice Admiral Lacroix, one or two piers over. By the time the first German officer appeared and hailed her, she already had 2,500 tons of water in her and was on the point of sinking. All of the guns had been blown up except for the after turret, and these just waited for the lighting of the fuse. Admiral Lacroix and his flag captain went down onto the pier to meet the newcomers.

"We have come to take over your ship," announced the Germans.

"You are a little late," replied Admiral Lacroix. "It is already sinking."

"Will it blow up?"

"No."

"In that case," said the Germans, "we will go aboard."

"In that case," replied Admiral Lacroix, "it will blow up."

As a matter of fact, even at that moment a column of flame shot up, forward, where the plotting room had been set afire. Simultaneously the crew of the after turret set fire to their fuse.

The Germans stepped back, alarmed; by the light of the flames terror could be seen spreading over the face of the French-speaking German. Then the Germans moved forward to surround Admiral Lacroix and his staff and to inform them that they were all prisoners.

With added flames fed by a drifting oil barge, the *Algérie* burned for two days, punctuating the air from time to time by exploding torpedoes or ammunition. The *Marseillaise,* which had gone down with a 30-degree list, burned for almost a week.

At the pier where the *Colbert* was moored, the Germans, who were attempting to climb aboard, found themselves all mixed up with the French, who were abandoning her, as they crowded together behind any possible shelter in order to avoid the heavy fragments bombarding them from the explosions on all sides. The *Colbert's* senior aviation officer himself set fire to his plane on its catapult. On board the cruiser *Dupleix,* in the Missiessy basin, the Germans were actually climbing aboard when the fuses and combustibles were set afire. The cruiser sank with a heavy list. The magazines blew up at 0830, and the torpedoes a couple of hours later.

On board the old *Provence,* the commanding officer, Captain Jacques Le Merdy, had been very much troubled ever since 0545, when he had received a mystifying telephone message from the office of the Assistant Commandant of the yard: "Orders have been received from Monsieur Laval that all incidents are to be avoided."

This call from Vichy had been the result of a hot stream of messages that had been exchanged between Vichy and Toulon ever since the first appearance of the Germans. Captain Le Merdy had sent an officer across the yard on foot to inquire just what the order meant. The officer returned, surrounded by armed Germans who had intercepted him. This was something far more enlightening than any telephone messages. Captain Le Merdy had stalled for time by arguing with the Germans while, below, the *Provence's* crew hurried to carry out the scuttling orders received over the radio. By the time the Germans woke up, the deck was already listing under their feet. Captain Le Merdy and the division's commanding officer, Rear Admiral Marcel Jarry, were promptly made prisoners.

The ships undergoing major overhaul or else in "caretaker" status, with only skeleton crews aboard, were naturally unable to carry out sabotage to the same degree of destructiveness as their companion ships in full commission. It was only for this reason that three super-destroyers and one destroyer, aboard which there had been time to do very little damage, were later salvaged, repaired, and put into commission by the Italians. On the *Dunkerque,* in drydock where she was still being repaired after the heavy damage she had received at Mers-el-Kebir, the crew succeeded only at the last moment in blowing up the guns and in sabotaging the turbines, range finders, and communication and combat centers.

Of the some 15 destroyers and super-destroyers[6] in commission and moored side by side at the Noël dock, not a single ship remained afloat when the Germans came up. All had blown themselves up and gone down with their battle flags still flying. They lay on the bottom in one chaotic

---

[6] Super-destroyers *Lion, Tigre, Panthère,* and destroyer *Trombe* were towed to Italy and put back in condition during the first quarter of 1943. But out of the 220 days they served under the Italian flag they were actually at sea only from 20 to 40 days on the average. At the time of the Italian armistice in 1943, the *Lion* and the *Panthère* were scuttled at La Spezia. The *Tigre* and the *Trombe* were returned to the French at Bizerte in October, 1943. These last two ships were the only ones of the original Toulon Fleet that were ever recovered by France.

heap—guns blasted to pieces, masts lying in all directions, ships listing at a dozen different angles. The signal halyards of the *Cassard* still flew the unnecessary signal: "The admiral's orders have been carried out."

The various submarines had been moored in both navy yards. With electric propulsion, these ships could have got under way at a moment's notice. But, in the main navy yard, the great majority of them were either undergoing repairs or were in decommissioned status. Moreover, a revolving bridge blocked their passage to the exit channel. All of these had to scuttle themselves.

There were nine submarines in the Mourillon navy yard. Awakened by the gunfire as the German tanks crashed through the gates, their crews had rushed to their battle stations. The five able to get under way smashed the boom across their basin with their bows and headed for the exit channel—the *Venus, Casabianca, Marsouin, Iris,* and *Glorieux*.[7] The *Glorieux* had gotten away only under a hail of German bullets, to which the commanding officer, Lieutenant Commander Robert Meynier, replied with shots from his own automatic pistol, fired over the top of the conning tower hatch.

The Luftwaffe roared through the skies overhead, showering the escaping submarines with depth charges and bombs. The net tender at the heavy antisubmarine net at the harbor entrance was very slow in opening it. Owing to shallow depth inside the harbor, it would be impossible to submerge until the submarines were outside the jetty.

The exit channel had been mined, and the submarines were finding it hard going under the rain of bombs from above and of shells from the German tanks on the waterfront.

"Where are you going?" called out the captain of the *Venus* to the commanding officer of the *Iris,* which was passing him at the end of the channel.

"To the gates of hell!" replied the *Iris's* captain. "Are you coming too?"

But the *Venus* was not to make it. She had only part of her crew aboard, and had been severely damaged by near misses. Therefore, in accordance with standing orders, her captain scuttled her in the outer roads where her crew could be easily rescued.

The *Iris,* however, succeeded in escaping and reached Spain, where she was interned at Cartagena until the end of the war.

---

[7] The *Venus* was commanded by Lieutenant Pierre Crescent, who had already fought the English when they tried to take over the *Surcouf* in Portsmouth, England, harbor on July 3, 1940. The *Casabianca's* commander was Lieutenant Commander Jean L'Herminier. The *Marsouin* was commanded by Lieutenant Mine, who had escaped from Algiers during British depth charge attacks only twenty days before. The *Iris* was commanded by Lieutenant Louis Dégé, ordinarily her executive officer but at this time substituting for her regular captain, who was absent. Captain of the *Glorieux* was Lieutenant Commander Robert Meynier.

Only the *Glorieux, Marsouin,* and *Casabianca* came through the ordeal unhurt, and managed to reach ports in Algeria.

It was finished. The sacrifice of the Fleet had been made. The Germans were everywhere—but with empty hands. Coming to take over in the wake of the Army and Luftwaffe, all that the sailors of the Kriegsmarine could do was to turn around and go back home.

As for the French officers and crews, they were interned in a guarded camp ashore for a few days while the disappointed Germans determined what was to be done with them. Their hearts were sick at the thought of the beloved ships, sunk by their own hands, but their heads were high. And the French Government at Vichy stoutly held that they could not be made prisoners of war since the scuttling of the Fleet had not been in any way an act of hostility against the Germans, but merely destruction of French naval ships recognized as their own in the original terms of the 1940 armistice. And to that the Germans eventually had to agree.

As for Admiral de Laborde, instead of defending himself against German accusations, he stood on the deck of the *Strasbourg* demanding to know why the Germans had not kept their sacred oath in regard to the neutralization of Toulon. Disconcerted in the face of so much righteous indignation, the German commander did not dare to use force to remove the doughty old warrior from his post. de Laborde had curtly declared that he would not leave his ship except on direct orders from his Chief of State, Marshal Pétain. Eventually the Germans managed to reach Vichy and secure the necessary authority by direct radio to de Laborde:

"I learn at this instant that your ship is sinking. I order you to leave it without delay. Philippe Pétain."

It was that extraordinary message, intercepted at Algiers, that gave the French naval forces in Africa their first intimation of what had occurred at Toulon.

It was at Bordeaux, on June 18, 1940, that Admiral Darlan, his assistant, Admiral Auphan, and the other French naval leaders had given their plighted word to the Royal Navy that they would never permit their ships to fall into the hands of the Germans. They had carried out their promise at Toulon by scuttling 77 of France's most powerful naval units: 3 battleships, 7 cruisers, 32 destroyers of all types, 16 submarines, 1 seaplane tender, and 18 sloops or smaller craft.[8]

---

[8] Battleships *Strasbourg, Dunkerque,* and *Provence;* cruisers *Algérie, Dupleix, Foch, Colbert, La Galissonnière, Marseillaise,* and *Jean de Vienne;* destroyers *Aigle, Baliste, Bayonnaise, Bison, Bordelais, Casque, Cassard, Foudroyant, Gerfaut, Guépard, Hardi, Indomptable, Kersaint, Lansquenet, Lynx, Mameluk, Mars, Mogador, Palme, Poursuivante, Siroco, Tartu, Valmy, Vauban, Vauquelin, Vautour, Verdun, Volta* (incompletely scuttled because of not having a crew aboard), *Lion, Panthère, Tigre,* and

But France gained something, too, in the tragedy. She preserved the sanctity of her oath—first, to the Germans, in the armistice, and, secondly, to the British at Bordeaux. In the ultimate moment of decision, her Navy's officers and men had remained steadfast in obedience and loyalty, the twin pillars of strength without which no military or naval organization can exist. As one able historian has said, "If, at Toulon, the French Navy amputated one of its limbs, in doing so it saved its soul and laid the foundations for its renaissance."[9]

The scuttling of the Toulon Fleet caused a great stir throughout the world. Imaginative reporters built up stories about it. False press reports led the world to believe that there had been many casualties, and commemorative services were held at numerous places in the Western world. As a matter of fact, the losses were almost entirely on the material side, yet, such as they were,[10] they expressed the stern determination of occupied France to resist.

The clandestine Communist newspaper, *L'Humanité,* at first labelled the scuttling as "an act of sublime patriotism," but two or three years later it insinuated that the officers had had their hands forced by their crews.

The London *Times,* on November 30, 1942, said, in effect, "Even those who believe that the French Fleet could have served more usefully in the liberation of France, by joining forces with the Allies, cannot refuse to render profound homage to the French Squadron for the manner in which it kept its plighted word."[11]

It has been asked why the Germans did not plan to seize Bizerte and the French ships there on the same day that they occupied Toulon. General Barré's greatly inferior force, even when reinforced by a small token Allied detachment, could not hope to hold off the 35,000 Germans, supported by artillery and the Luftwaffe, which had entered at Bizerte. The answer probably is that the Germans felt their rear was poorly secured. In fact Marshal Albert Kesselring declared, later, that it was hard to believe they had ever succeeded in establishing a beachhead.

Even so, German diplomat Rahn, in Tunis, hoped to cause a division in Barré's troops. He asked Laval to dismiss Barré, and he tried to get Ad-

---

Trombe; submarines *Acheron, Aurore, Caïman, Diamant, Espoir, Eurydice, Fresnel, Galatée, Henri Poincaré, Naïade, Pascal, Redoubtable, Sirène, Thétis, Vengeur,* and *Venus;* seaplane tender *Commandant Teste.*

[9] Pierre Varillon, *La Sabordage de la Flotte—(The Scuttling of the Fleet).*

[10] In addition to Lieutenant Fay, killed on board the *Strasbourg,* some sailors were killed or wounded, and all of these were casualties resulting from the explosion of a mine dropped on the end of the jetty, near an antiaircraft battery.

[11] Pierre Varillon, *Le Sabordage de la Flotte—(The Scuttling of the Fleet).*

miral Esteva to have planes drop leaflets to the French troops ordering them to disobey Barré's orders. However, Esteva had reached an understanding with Barré, and he refused Rahn's request. This had all occurred prior to the German operation against Toulon on November 27.

On that day the German Admiral Eberhard Weichold called on Admiral Derrien, commanding the French naval forces at Bizerte, and informed him that the Wehrmacht was in the process of occupying Toulon in order to prevent any of the Toulon Fleet from leaving the harbor. He did not mention the scuttling by the ships' crews; in fact he may not even have known of it at that time. But what he was anxious to obtain from Admiral Derrien was a commitment that the French ships at Bizerte would not attempt to escape.

Considering the fact that apart from nine old decommissioned submarines, without crews, the French naval forces at Bizerte consisted of only three 600-ton torpedo boats and two minesweeper sloops, the Germans' anxiety would seem to have been exaggerated—especially since the Germans held all the approaches to the harbor where the ships were moored. Consequently Admiral Derrien could give the requested assurance without any qualms.

The commanding officers of the ships themselves had fully recognized their helplessness, and had asked Admiral Derrien what action they should take if the Germans attempted to seize their vessels.

"That eventuality will never arise; it is not even worth considering," replied the admiral, still confident that the Germans would faithfully comply with the terms of the 1940 armistice.

The next day the harbor of Bizerte was severely bombed—by Allied planes. In order to avoid useless bloodshed, Admiral Derrien had the three torpedo boats placed out of commission and removed to the safer area of the lake, which was connected to the main harbor. Only a scuttling detail of six men was left on each ship. Advance preparations were made for sabotaging the turbines by placing wedges so that they would shear off the turbine blades at the first attempt to operate the engines. Only the two sloops were kept in commission so that they could evacuate the families of naval personnel from Bizerte, if necessary.

The bulk of all the ships' crews were stationed at a fort, where, it was hoped, they would be available for use some day.

The German commander at Bizerte also took advantage of every occurrence at Vichy to overawe Admiral Derrien. For on December 5 Marshal Pétain, bowing to the inevitable, had grudgingly acceded to the disbandment of all French troops everywhere. The new German commander at Bizerte, General Alfred Gause, waited only two days before summoning Admiral Derrien to appear at German headquarters on the morning of the 8th.

At the appointed hour Admiral Derrien, along with his deputy, General Maurice Dauphin, and their two chiefs of staff, appeared at General Gause's tent during a torrential downpour. German planes in great numbers constantly circled overhead. Evidence of overwhelming force was visible on all sides.

Without preliminaries, General Gause handed Admiral Derrien an ultimatum demanding the immediate surrender to the Germans of all ships, fortifications, depots, radio stations, and other installations at Bizerte. Failure to do so would bring the following immediate consequences:

First, all ships and troop encampments would be attacked and bombed without cessation until destroyed;

Second, ships' crews would be slain to the last officer and man;

Third, no quarter whatever would be given, as any resistance on the part of the French garrison at Bizerte "after the French forces had been dissolved by Marshal Pétain" would result in those troops being considered no longer as regular soldiers and entitled to the protection of the laws of war.

The French commander was given exactly thirty minutes to comply with this ultimatum, and no opportunity to consult with his various subordinates. Admiral Derrien was a brave man, but living in the atmosphere of the armistice for almost three years had accustomed him to compromise each time that resistance seemed useless. Furthermore, rightly or wrongly, he was convinced that the Germans would carry out their threat.

"I did not have the right," he said later, "to send hundreds of brave people to their deaths simply to save my personal reputation."

Accordingly he yielded to the ultimatum and sent the following message to the units under his orders:

> I have just learned from the German authorities that total demobilization has been ordered in France. In accordance with the terms of this order, the ships, batteries, depots, harbor installations, radio stations, and other military installations, as well as all small arms, must be turned over intact to the German and Italian troops. The troops of the Axis have taken all necessary measures to suppress forcibly and without mercy all attempts to resist, or to destroy, or to scuttle. I ask all officers, petty officers, soldiers, and sailors to obey this distressing demand in order to avoid useless bloodshed. This order is to be carried out without delay. 0950 8 December.

Several hours later the occupation of Bizerte became an accomplished fact. During the ensuing days 3,500 soldiers and approximately 6,000 sailors were demobilized; among these, 2,500, of which 50 were officers, were relieved from all further duty and returned to France.

Admiral Derrien, worn out and ill, would have preferred to be relieved, but the Government at Vichy requested him to remain at his post. Thereafter he devoted himself to the welfare of the population—in particular the working class, who were threatened with deportation to Germany. Also he managed to preserve, intact, a great many valuable installations which were of great service to the Allied troops when they arrived there, six months later.

The thing most distressing to the sailors was the German seizure of their ships. There were those who said that Admiral Derrien should have taken measures in advance to insure their destruction the moment it became evident that the ships could not escape. But Admiral Derrien had reason to hope that he could secure for them the same status as Force X had received from the British at Alexandria. Premature destruction of the ships under those circumstances would have been a grave dereliction of duty.

In actuality, all that the Axis acquired were a few old, worn out submarines, five small surface vessels, a badly damaged super-destroyer, a small tanker and an antiquated minelayer.[12]

Of the submarines, two were eventually to be sunk at Bizerte by the Allied aerial bombardment of January 30, 1943, and two others were scuttled there on May 6, 1943, just ahead of the Allied entry. Three others were towed to Italian ports where, without ever having been made serviceable, they were destroyed by the Germans at the time of the Italian armistice. Only one, the *Phoque,* ever served under the enemy flag. Recommissioned as the *FR-111,* she sailed for Lampedusa Island on February 27, 1943, but turned back shortly because of defective machinery. In this state she was sunk by Allied planes the next day, ten miles off the coast of Sicily.

As for the surface ships, the five of them carried a total of only eight 100-mm. guns—far less firepower than the battalion of tanks which the combat command of U.S. General Lunsford E. Oliver abandoned in the mud, intact, on December 10, after the unsuccessful Allied offensive against Tunis. It is very probable that these tanks, put to service by the enemy, did far greater harm to the Allies than the French surface ships taken over by the Germans at Bizerte.

For, records show that of the sloops, one was sunk by Allied planes at Leghorn in May, 1943, and the other, taken over by the Germans at the time of the Italian armistice, was scuttled by them at Genoa, in April, 1945. Of the three torpedo boats, all were sunk or scuttled, one after the other, under the German flag, after having contributed practically no military service under the Italian flag: the *Pomone* and *Iphigénie* were de-

---

[12] Submarines *Requin, Dauphin, Phoque, Espadon, Nautilus, Circé, Calypso, Saphir,* and *Turquoise;* surface ships (torpedo boats and sloops) *Commandant Rivière, Batailleuse, Pomone, Bombarde,* and *Iphigénie;* super-destroyer *Audacieux;* tanker *Tarn;* and minelayer *Castor.*

TOULON, NOVEMBER 1942. *The wrecked forward turrets of the cruiser* COLBERT.

Toulon, November 1942. *Scuttled sloops in the old harbor.*

stroyed in the Dodecanese, and the *Bombarde*—rechristened the *TA-9*— at Toulon on August 23, 1944.

But the Bizerte units were almost negligible in importance compared to the Toulon Fleet, which the French Navy sacrificed to honor its sacred promise. For two and a half years that Fleet had been the great, almost the only, symbol of national sovereignty. For two and a half years it had been the principal tie between France and the empire, and it had protected both against threatened starvation. And in the moment of its immolation it had passed on the torch of French liberty to the African naval forces that were in themselves to constitute the reincarnation of France as an ally of the democracies in the final victories of the war.

CHAPTER 23

Rejoining the Allies

The best half of the French Fleet disappeared at Toulon. The other half was scattered all over the world: 136,000 tons of warships in French Africa; 66,000 tons at Alexandria; 34,000 tons in the Antilles; and 16,200 tons in Indochina.[1] As compared to this quarter of a million tons of fighting craft, the total tonnage in the Free French Naval Forces amounted to only 31,000, mostly in small ships.[2]

To reorganize these ships so that they could keep in company with the other Allies was a major problem. There were no technical services, since all administrative work had previously been handled in European France. There were no spare parts, no navy yards, very little ammunition and few torpedoes, and only a limited number of trained reserves for replacements. Finally all the ships were in sore need of modernization. Except for a few ships in the F.F.N.F., all the vessels had been constructed prior to 1939, which meant that they lacked airpower, antiaircraft defenses, radar, sonar and other new antisubmarine weapons—all the new developments that had so changed the technique of naval war since 1939.

---

[1] (NAVAL FORCES OF AFRICA). Battleships (both needing repairs) *Richelieu* and *Jean Bart;* cruisers *Georges Leygues, Gloire, Montcalm;* super-destroyers *Fantasque, Malin, Terrible;* destroyers *Simoun, Tempête, Alcyon;* Colonial sloops *La Grandière, Dumont d'Urville;* minesweeper sloops *Boudeuse, Commandant Delage, Commandant Bory, Annamite, Gazelle, Gracieuse;* submarines *Centaure, Archimède, Argo, Glorieux, Casabianca, Marsouin, Atalante, Orphée, Amazone, Antiope, Vestale, Sultane, Aréthuse, Perle.*

(FORCE X, at Alexandria). Battleship *Lorraine;* cruisers *Duquesne, Tourville, Suffren, Duguay-Trouin;* detroyers *Basque, Forbin, Fortuné;* submarine *Protée.*

(NAVAL FORCES OF THE ANTILLES). Aircraft carrier *Béarn;* cruisers *Emile Bertin, Jeanne d'Arc.*

(NAVAL FORCES IN INDOCHINA). Cruiser *Lamotte-Picquet;* Colonial sloop *Amiral Charner;* sloops *Marne, Tahure;* submarine *Pégase;* hydrographic ship *Lapérouse;* plus small river gunboats.

[2] (FREE FRENCH NAVAL FORCES). Super-destroyers *Léopard, Triomphant;* Colonial sloop *Savorgnan de Brazza;* corvettes *Roselys, Aconit, Lobelia, Renoncule, Commandant Detroyat, Commandant d'Estienne d'Orves, Commandant Drogou;* minesweeper sloops *Chevreuil, Moqueuse, Commandant Duboc, Commandant Dominé;* submarines *Rubis, Junon, Minerve;* plus MTBs, minesweepers, and submarine chasers.

But these were small problems compared to those of a political and spiritual nature. Since the 1940 armistice these ships had been dispersed around the globe, subject to the most contrasting climates—moral as well as physical. Of the personnel, those in European France, who were still to contribute in surprising manner, had decided viewpoints. Allied to them in spirit were the sailors of North Africa, who, despite the events of November, 1942, still retained their loyalty to the established government as represented in Marshal Pétain. They recognized that the Marshal was to all purposes a prisoner of the Germans, and hence they had consented to accept Admiral Darlan in North Africa and Governor General Boisson in French West Africa as representing what the Marshal would have directed if he had been a free agent, and they still kept his portrait in the place of honor on all ships.

Then there were the sailors of Force X. Isolated for over two years, plagued by all sorts of propaganda, the squadron at Alexandria had nevertheless remained an example of unswerving loyalty. It would not agree to break officially with the new Laval-dominated government at Vichy without first making certain that the homeland would not suffer too long an additional martyrdom if they should rejoin the Allies. In addition, new animosities had developed there out of the action of the British in drawing up batteries of field artillery with muzzles aimed at the Force X ships on the night of the Allied landings, just as they had done on the preceding July 3 when Rommel's advance had reached its nearest approach to the city.

Not too different were the feelings of the men on the ships immobilized in the Antilles, where American pressure had merely resulted in firming their attachment to the mother country.

Then there were the sailors at Djibouti, completely isolated from the war and yet still closely blockaded by the British. There were the loyal sailors at Gabon, incarcerated in a Free French concentration camp, and those at Diego Suarez, whom the British had not yet released. And there were the sailors in Indochina, isolated from all the rest of the world, living only by tolerance of the Japanese and paying by daily compromises and personal suffering for the honor of keeping Indochina in the empire.

And, on the other hand, there were those who prided themselves on never having given up the struggle—the sailors of the F.F.N.F. With only the smallest nucleus of career officers who had graduated from the Naval Academy, they were a heterogenous group whose patriotic fervor was matched only by their political attachment to the person of General de Gaulle. Few of them probably really believed in their accusations of treason against the sailors loyal to Vichy, but they took pleasure in flaunting their feeling of superiority over them. This did not endear them to the sailors of

French North Africa, who were equally proud of their own loyalty to the Government, and who had not too high an opinion of F.F.N.F. discipline.[3]

As was to be expected, the first contacts between those with such variegated sentiments were difficult. At Gibraltar, there was a noticeable absence of cordiality at the meeting, on March 27, 1943, between the F.F.N.F. sloop *Savorgnan de Brazza* and her sister ship of the North African naval forces, *La Grandière*. Even so, there was every evidence of a latent good will which had only to be nourished.

And this was the first task to which Admiral Darlan set his hand, for he knew that in order to reorganize the Navy into a single, unified service, it was necessary first of all to unify the French. At the same time that he had called upon the French to take up arms once more against the Axis, he had assumed the title of High Commissioner of France in Africa. As assistant, he took General Jean Bergeret, of the Air Force, an exceptionally talented leader whose personality had so impressed the Allies that they had entrusted him in advance with the secret of the Allied landings. Around these two was formed an Imperial Committee, composed of all the Governors and Governors General of the African colonies, as well as General Giraud, Commander in Chief of the Army and the Air Force. This was the political organization of the new Government; policy decisions made here and routine administrative business would be carried out by administrative assistants.[4]

Admiral Darlan retained the Navy under his personal orders, administering it through Admiral Michelier. Admiral Michelier at the same time retained his own departmental command in Morocco. Preparations were made to send a naval mission to the United States under Admiral Raymond Fenard. A similar mission was planned for London, but it would have to wait until the rival movement of De Gaulle was merged into the new Government. Meantime a liaison officer was assigned at Gibraltar.

The civilian departments of Finances, Production, and Commerce were coordinated under Delegate General Alfred Pose, an eminent economist who succeeded in changing the dollar rate of exchange from the previous 75 francs to the American dollar to the far more favorable figure of 50 to the dollar. The administrative functions of the new Government were car-

---

[3] Admiral Auboyneau, in his *Instructions 29 FFNFI* of 13 January 1943, wrote: "The discipline of the personnel of the F.F.N.F. is actually not satisfactory, and it is necessary to improve it with the least possible delay."

[4] Admiral Darlan did not wish to appoint either Ministers or Secretaries of State to administer the various departments of the Government. He simply appointed competent civil servants to carry out this work. Not having ministerial rank, they were not qualified to sit with the Imperial Committee and therefore had no voice in making Government policies.

ried on by no more than 700 persons, from the admiral down to the last orderly, and the capitol building was no more than a requisitioned schoolhouse. The first budget set was 22 billion francs, but of this only 4 per cent represented civil government expenses, all the rest being devoted to the war effort.[5] Paid for out of the military part of the budget was the Army of North Africa, which rapidly grew to a strength of more than 300,000 men. From these men were formed General Juin's expeditionary corps for the campaign in Italy, and General Jean de Lattre de Tassigny's First French Army, divisions of which were to operate in Provence, on the Rhine, and on the Danube.

To unify the French sections and to facilitate liaison with the Americans, members of the Group of Five or their friends were assigned to important posts. Jean Rigault was given the Department of the Interior, with Henri d'Astier de la Vigerie heading the Police, under him; Jacques Tarbé de Saint-Hardouin became head of Foreign Affairs.

The laws under the new Government were the regular laws of France, toned down in certain cases to facilitate the work of reconciliation between the divergent groups. There was a particular problem in regard to the political prisoners in the concentration camps, as most of these had been sent there as undesirable deportees from European France—such political prisoners, for instance, as Spanish Reds, agitators of all sorts, or Communist-minded supporters of De Gaulle in opposition to the established government. All who could prove their actions had resulted from honest patriotism were released after individual hearings, but the majority of the Communists were kept in detention. Among these latter were 27 members of the French Chamber of Deputies, who had been deported to African internment by the Deladier government in the autumn of 1939 because of their subversive activities.

Darlan's greatest problem was to live down the reputation he had acquired for his Anglophobe speeches and the agreements he had made with the Axis while he was a Minister under Marshal Pétain. In fact President Roosevelt felt that he had to justify to the American public his dealings with Darlan, and he declared that these were only a "temporary expedient." Thereupon Darlan wrote the following letter to General Mark Clark, deputy to General Eisenhower:

> I am, perhaps, only a lemon which the Americans intend to throw away after squeezing it. Insofar as the individual is concerned, I do not count.

---

[5] (ORDINARY BUDGET). Civilian expenses: 850 million francs for the public debt and 350 million francs for the High Commissioner's Office. Military expenses (personnel): Army, 4,790 million francs; Air Force, 863 million francs; Navy, 884 million francs; Colonies, 775 million francs.
(EXTRAORDINARY BUDGET). War expenses: 13,926 million francs.

When the restoration of French sovereignty shall have become an accomplished fact, I will return to civil life. If this is what President Roosevelt means by "temporary expedient," then I am in complete agreement. But under existing conditions it is only around such men as Giraud, Noguès, Boisson, and Michelier that the French in Africa can unite in confident cooperation with the Allied armies and with the people of European France to achieve the final victory. The task of accomplishing this union will be made more difficult if the Allies themselves create doubt among the French.

On December 4 he wrote to Prime Minister Churchill also, this time on the subject of radio attacks on his government emanating from London and from Brazzaville:

I would never have attained this objective—relaunching Africa into the war—if I had simply presented myself as a dissident, instead of operating under the aegis of Marshal Pétain. I am convinced that the French who are fighting Germany, *each in his own way,* will eventually join forces, but I believe that for the time being they must continue their separate ways. Certain resentments, particularly in French West Africa, are too deep rooted to make it possible to do more. As you can see for yourself, I am going about my business without attacking anyone. I request the same treatment in return.

Less than a month later, and only a few hours before his death, Admiral Darlan concluded an interview broadcast over Radio Algiers with the words:

Uniting the French is the matter of first importance. If it takes place around me, so much the better. But my person is of little consequence; that it takes place is in itself the essential thing.

But such language had no effect on his political opponents. The Free French would accept the union, but only under the leadership of General de Gaulle. A number of the participants of November 8 were disappointed at noting that, in the end, the spirit and leaders of Vichy still held their place. Constant passage of emissaries between London and Algiers aroused local passions. Leaflets, articles in the papers, small posters pasted on walls —they all constituted disguised appeals for agitation, if not actually for assassination.

Confident in his destiny and preoccupied with the preparations for war, Darlan took no precautions. A detachment of sailors was being organized as his personal guard, but the blow fell before it was detailed. The day before Christmas, Darlan went to his office to meet Pierre Bourdan, of the British Broadcasting Corporation, who had made a special trip from London in a sincere effort to promote union between his countrymen. Arriving around 1500, ahead of his guest, Admiral Darlan found in the outer office a young man who had gained access through some trivial pretext. Drawing a pistol, the young civilian fired two shots at pointblank range.

The desperately hurt man was rushed to the nearest hospital, but nothing that could be done was of any avail. Within only a few minutes the Admiral of the Fleet breathed his last.

Despite the conspiratorial atmosphere prevalent in Algiers for several weeks past, Admiral Darlan's funeral was most impressive. French, British, and American troops rendered full honors. General Eisenhower hastened from his headquarters to be present and to assure General Bergeret that if the investigation revealed the slightest American or British complicity, he would ask to be relieved of his command, as such misconceived associations would be fatal to joint military operations. His naval deputy, Admiral Sir Andrew Cunningham, Royal Navy, was at his side in the front rank of the funeral cortege. It is difficult to reconcile these marks of respect with Winston Churchill's reference later to Admiral Darlan's "dishonored grave."[6]

The assassin, Fernand Bonnier de la Chapelle, who fanatically believed that he had performed a glorious deed, was immediately tried and executed. It was evident that he was but a tool of more important individuals. But who, in the higher places, had put the weapon in his hand?

All of the facts in the murder case have not been—perhaps may never be—brought to light. It would leave the case too incomplete to present here the clues gathered by the police from the moment of the shooting up until the day the case was definitely closed after the arrival of General de Gaulle. But because of the reams that have been written about them, it is impossible to pass over the reconciliation which took place with the arrival of the Count of Paris, pretender to the throne of France, or of the arrests over a period of weeks of persons in close contact with the former Group of Five. At the time, the most varied accusations were made: against the Germans—against the Free French—against the Allies, even.[7] The only thing that can be definitely said is that time has not yet produced a satisfactory solution to the puzzle. The only Admiral of the Fleet that the French Navy has ever had sleeps his eternal sleep under that Navy's reverent guard, in a casemate of the Admiralty at Algiers.

---

[6] Winston Churchill, *The Second World War*, Vol. II. "The fame and power which he ardently desired were in his grasp. Instead, he went forward through two years of worrying and ignominious office to a violent death, a dishonoured grave, and a name long to be execrated by the French Navy and the nation he had hitherto served so well."

[7] General de Gaulle, in his memoirs, employs a mystifying phrase to accuse "a policy resolved to liquidate a 'temporary expedient' after having utilized it." The expression "temporary expedient" was used by President Roosevelt with reference to the use of Darlan in securing North Africa's adherence to the Allies.

Perhaps because of a premonition, or because of his concern that the Government should function without interruption, Admiral Darlan had designated General Noguès as his successor in case of a short disability, and had given a mandate to the Imperial Committee to elect his successor in case of a permanent disability. Under the circumstances the Imperial Committee voted on the very evening of the funeral. U.S. Consul General Murphy had let it be known that the name of Giraud, very popular in America, would be welcome. In fact Giraud was generally considered—wrongly, as it turned out later—to be the individual best situated to secure a concord with De Gaulle because he was the one least compromised with Vichy.

General Giraud was unanimously elected—and did not delay in revealing his feelings toward the Navy. On his very first visit to the Algiers Naval District he pointedly observed to the Commandant, "I do not like vice admirals!"

And that was only the beginning.

It would be beyond the scope of this book to elaborate on the many incidents, progressively worse, which ultimately led to the political downfall of General Giraud. It might be simply mentioned, as an example, that in a speech in March, 1943, he repudiated all French laws enacted subsequent to June 22, 1940, as having been enacted under duress. Furthermore he thought it good policy to free all militant Communists.

Such blunders made possible the entry of General de Gaulle into the Government at Algiers, though, at General Eisenhower's insistence, his installation did not take place until after the liberation of Tunis. It was not until May 30, 1943, that the leader of the Free French arrived at Algiers.

Changes immediately began to occur. Within the first week General Jean Bergeret was placed under arrest in his quarters, which he left only for the confinement of a prison for twenty-two months; Governor General Boisson was dismissed from his post, and then placed under arrest; General Noguès had to seek political asylum in Portugal to avoid a similar fate. Jean Rigault himself was prosecuted.

None of these things recommended themselves to the Navy High Command.

Within four days after his arrival, General de Gaulle reached an agreement with Giraud for the establishment, under their co-chairmanship, of a French Committee of National Liberation. This committee, according to the wording of the agreement, was to constitute "a single central authority." As such, it "assumed authority over the territories and over the forces of the Army, Navy, and Air Force, which, until then, had come under the jurisdiction of either the National French Committee of London or of the 'Civilian and Military Commander in Chief' of Algiers."

This was certainly a decisive step toward a political union of the French outside European France. But a spiritual union was far from the result. Algiers remained a hotbed of intrigue, with the various cliques squabbling for influence and position.

Admiral Muselier, creator of the F.F.N.F., who had left De Gaulle because of differences with him in England, had returned to service in Africa and had been entrusted by Giraud with functions similar to those of a Chief Police Commissioner. He found his hands full trying to prevent the Free French from inciting the troops to desert and reenlist in the ranks of their own legions. To put an end to such destructive practices, Muselier, who shied at nothing, considered having De Gaulle arrested. In fact he even went so far as having restrictive quarters prepared for De Gaulle on the yacht *Girundia II,* anchored in Algiers harbor. But Giraud did not dare give his consent, and it was Giraud who, in November, 1943, found himself removed from office and placed definitely on the retired list, and who came close to being assassinated.

The new French Committee of National Liberation had immediately taken over the naval forces, but by then Admiral Michelier, as Darlan's appointed naval deputy, had had six months to work with the ships and commanders. It had been a busy six months.

First, he had had to repair the damages of the November fighting, to salvage all material possible, to take stock generally, and to establish a lend-lease program with the United States. He had also had to guard against the encroachments of the Allies, who seemed to regard the African ports somewhat as in the nature of conquered territory, to be used by themselves without much thought of the needs of the French. However, at Algiers, the chivalrous courtesy of Admiral A. B. Cunningham and his chief of staff, Commodore Royer M. Dick, greatly facilitated matters, and French sovereignty was quickly and completely respected. In Morocco, Rear Admiral John L. Hall, Jr., Admiral Hewitt's former chief of staff, was equally cooperative. Everything there was pooled: the French naval shops worked in liaison with the American salvage groups; the antiaircraft defense was American, the coast defense batteries French.

The U. S. Navy was quick to appreciate that it was to its advantage to trust the French Navy, which was far better acquainted with the possibilities and the drawbacks of the port of Casablanca. However, for quite some time the U. S. Navy was less trustful in the matter of letting the French Navy have the location of the minefields they had laid off Casablanca. As a result, the French trawler *Poitou* was sunk by a German U-boat on

December 17, 1942, off the port while waiting for more than 24 hours for an American pilot to steer her through the minefield. Such incidents were infrequent, however, and were quickly adjusted.

At Dakar, there were no problems at all. The American admiral, William A. Glassford, Jr., a personal representative of President Roosevelt, regarded himself purely and simply as a guest of Admiral Collinet.

One odd occurrence is worth mentioning. On two separate occasions—January 9 and February 12, 1943—President Roosevelt offered in great secrecy to provide the funds for the entire payroll of the French Navy.[8] Admiral Michelier refused, but requested instead that this generosity be expressed by transfer of materials and of destroyers and escort vessels.

During these six months the Merchant Marine in Africa had functioned under the administration of the Navy, just as it did in France. The supervisor was Rear Admiral André Lemonnier, promoted to that rank by Admiral Darlan on November 21, 1942. The first thing he had to do was to regain the use of the merchant ships which, under the armistice agreements with the Americans on November 10, had been practically placed at the disposal of the American command.[9] A new agreement was negotiated between Admiral Darlan and General Mark Clark on November 22, by which 9 passenger liners, 20 cargo ships, and 2 tankers, totaling 268,000 tons in all, were assigned to the pool for the use of the Allies. The remaining 10 passenger and 51 cargo ships—the oldest and slowest of the merchant fleet, and totaling 193,000 tons in all—were returned to the French command for the carrying trade and for transportation of troops between French West Africa and the Mediterranean. It was hoped that this fleet could be increased by 400,000 or 500,000 tons if Britain could be persuaded to return the French ships which she had seized from the time of the armistice up to the North African landings.

---

[8] The offers were transmitted confidentially: the first time, on January 9, to Admiral Michelier alone; the second time, on February 12, at Algiers, to Admirals Michelier and Moreau jointly, by Rear Admiral John L. Hall, Jr., U.S.N., Commanding the Sea Frontier Forces, Northwest African Waters. Admiral Hall was accompanied by Captain Jerauld Wright, U.S.N., a member of General Eisenhower's staff. No similar offer was made to take over the payroll of the Army.

These offers came at a time when the English, who were subsidizing the Free French Forces, were considering cutting off the food supplies to Force X at Alexandria. The French gained the impression that the American President was teasing his friend, the British Premier.

[9] Article 8: "The officers and crews of all French merchant vessels now in the harbors of Algeria, French Zone of Morocco, Tunisia, will disembark as may be required by the Commanding General, U.S. Army. They can then make free choice whether to work for the United (Allied) Nations; in case of volunteering, pay and pensions will be guaranteed from the date of volunteering."

Resumption of ocean traffic meant more escort vessels were needed—vessels to defend against attacks by Axis planes and submarines now that France was back in the war. The proof of this occurred on the first day of the new status of belligerency, November 13, when the Luftwaffe staged a slaughter in the harbor of Boogie. There they sank the merchantmen *Alaina, Koutoubia,* and *Florida,* and damaged a number of others, as well as several British vessels.[10]

The 50 or 60 potential escort vessels which were available all needed guns—their armaments had been completely removed in compliance with the armistice terms. The Allies supplied the necessary 20-mm. Oerlikons, the twin-mount machineguns, the rocket mounts, etc., and by the end of the year some 20 ships had been rearmed and work was proceeding rapidly on the others. At the same time the bombed or scuttled ships in Casablanca harbor were being raised through the assistance of powerful American salvage gear. By December 31, 1942, some 15 such ships had been salvaged or were in process of being raised.

At first, most French merchant ships—in fact all ships fast enough to keep up—were incorporated into the large Allied convoys, but the French Navy attempted itself to escort the slower, less important ships, even with manifestly insufficient means. As a result, the cargo ship *Mascot,* escorted by the small, weakly armed patrol vessel *Goëland,* was sunk by an Italian plane on December 9. Although things gradually improved during the first six months of the renewed hostilities, enemy submarines sank the patrol ship *Sergent Gouarne* off Alborán Island, on March 25, 1943, and some seven or eight merchantmen. Of these latter the *Sidi bel Abbès,* previously salvaged at Oran and now torpedoed by the *U-565* on April 20, 1943, just west of Oran, was the most disastrous. She was transporting a battalion of Senegalese infantrymen at the time, and 567 of them went down with the ship.

Almost from the first the cruisers at Dakar had begun relieving the British cruisers searching for German raiders and blockade-runners in the broad Atlantic. The *Georges Leygues, Gloire,* and *Montcalm*—and, later, the cruisers of Force X—took part in these long, tedious patrols, in the

---

[10] The eastern Algerian harbors were constantly attacked by Axis planes during the Tunisian campaign. Bône was bombed 33 times between November 10 and December 31. Bougie was attacked almost daily during November.

To the west, Algiers was attacked a dozen times during November. Except for the Allied attack on November 8, Casablanca was bombed only once, by a few long-range German Condor planes on the night of December 30.

A bold attack was made at Algiers on December 12, 1942, by Italian "frogmen" from the submarine *Ambra,* who sank two large freighters and damaged four others. Sixteen Italian frogmen were made prisoners after this raid.

course of which the *Georges Leygues* found and sank the blockade-runner *Portland.*

Meantime, the battleship *Richelieu* and the latest French cruisers and super-destroyers departed for American shipyards to be repaired or modernized;[11] the destroyers, torpedo boats, and escort crafts went to Bermuda for the same purpose. When the *Richelieu* and the *Montcalm* got under way from Dakar on January 30, 1943, under escort of four U.S. destroyers, it was the first time that French men-of-war had operated with American naval ships in time of war. The French communication officers felt at first that they had not been given all the information necessary for them to be completely familiar with American communication procedures, but that was soon remedied.

The super-destroyers *Fantasque* and *Terrible* left on February 21 for Boston, to be followed in June and July by the *Malin,* the *Georges Leygues,* and the *Gloire.* On their return, the successful alterations which had been effected in a few weeks by the American workmen, especially in the antiaircraft department, aroused the enthusiasm of all hands.

However, the warmth with which the French naval ships and sailors were received in the fighting fleets overseas was not duplicated in American and British home ports and in places in North Africa. The officers of the *Richelieu,* under repair in the Brooklyn navy yard preparatory to joining the British Home Fleet at Scapa Flow, were assailed by the American press as "Germanophiles" because they still displayed the portrait of Marshal Pétain aboard, and the French vessels were even labeled the "French Nazi Fleet." Both here and in British ports, ardent partisans of the Free French endeavored, with little success, to entice the crews of French ships to desert and enroll in the Free French ranks. The recruiters managed to persuade less than 100 of the *Richelieu's* entire crew to shift allegiance.

In North Africa, the cooperation of some British military authorities with the Free French recruiters brought an indignant message from Admiral A. B. Cunningham to the British Admiralty, denouncing "the stupidity of these things." In the United States, at two press conferences in March of 1943, Secretary of the Navy Frank Knox similarly denounced the recruiting efforts.

Nevertheless, in his memoirs, General de Gaulle defended these procedures and spoke of enlisting 300 deserters from the *Richelieu*—which was an exaggeration of almost 400 per cent.

There is no doubt that ill-advised practices of this nature, observed also at Algiers, in the Antilles, and at Alexandria, seriously affected discipline

[11] The amount of work involved in repairing and completing the *Jean Bart* was so great that there was little probability it could be finished in time for the ship to participate in the war. She was therefore completed after the war, in France.

and compromised the ability of the ships to engage in combat after they were refitted. It was a deplorable situation, coming at a time when a merger of the naval forces of France was being discussed.

In the Mediterranean itself, the Navy's most immediate objective was the reconquest of the Tunisian ports, particularly Bizerte. As far back as November of 1942, General Giraud had sent forward 60,000 men to the Tunisian front—all the troops he had available. They could only compensate for their inferior equipment by their courage, but even so they managed to hold their part of the Allied line of battle. Without this embryo army, preserved by Vichy, the Allies might have been much harder pressed by the German offensive. To this force the Navy furnished a battalion of seamen and a semimobile battery of 155-mm. guns taken from Nemours.

In the spring the reinforced British and Americans attacked simultaneously in southern Tunisia, where General Leclerc's column had joined up with the British Eighth Army, and on the Algerian-Tunisian frontier. The Germans were beaten back everywhere, and by May 7 the Americans had entered Bizerte and the British had retaken Tunis, where General Barré made a dramatic reentry.[12]

Cut off by land and sea and air, the Axis troops laid down their arms. The Allies captured several thousand self-propelled vehicles, 250 tanks, 1,000 guns, and 250,000 prisoners, of whom 40,000 fell into the hands of the French Army of Africa. The Germans, who had taken advantage of the Allies' delay to beat them into Bizerte, had been crushed in their own trap. Unfortunately the French who had lived through the German occupation were likewise crushed there.

The Bey of Tunis, who had been loyal to France despite the defeat, was dismissed like any minor civil servant, simply because his loyalty had been to the France of Marshal Pétain. Later his death in exile was to have repercussions disastrous to France.

The Governor General, Admiral Esteva, had remained during the German occupation to protect the empire, and particularly to protect the 80,000 Israelites who lived in the country. He had continued to pay the allowances to the families of service personnel who had gone over to the Allies with General Barré. Of him, German Ambassador Rahn had said, "Esteva plays the piano in order to lull us to sleep. He will pay for that!"

Forcibly removed from his office by the Germans before the recapture of the city, and expelled to France, he was arrested in 1944, after the liberation of France, and was tried by the High Court of Justice. On

---

[12] Barré had the distinction of being the first general of the Army of Africa to take up arms against the Axis after the armistice. He also had the distinction of being the first general to be excluded from the Regular Army by the French Committee of National Liberation, just after the final victory in Tunis.

March 15, 1945, he was condemned to dismissal from the Navy and to imprisonment for life. Wasted by grief and illness, he was released in 1950 just in time to prevent his dying in prison.

Throughout the German occupation of Bizerte and the Allied bombardments and siege, French naval personnel in the city had maintained law and order, had safeguarded lives and property, and had prevented last minute destruction by the Germans of essential machinery, the magazines, the fuel stocks, the water mains, and other vital installations. All these they turned over to the entering Allies, practically ready for use; they even had set up a secret, underground workshop. In all of Tunisia the only electric power station left in operating condition was that of the Navy. Within bare days after the recapture of the city, the machinery of the Navy yard was running for the benefit of the Allied fleets assembling there for the coming invasion of Sicily.[13]

The Navy tried to regain possession of everything belonging to it, so that it might be transferred from the old government to the new with no dislocation of the established order. Thus, by an odd chance, Captain Maerten, former commandant of the Navy at Madagascar and just recently released by the British, was the first to enter Ferryville, where he substituted the French national flag for the Cross of Lorraine which someone had hoisted there. At Sfax, the Royal Navy specifically asked for the services of Commander Xavier Chevillotte, the former commandant there, whom the Italians had supplanted because of his opposition to them. But Commander Chevillotte had been denounced as a "collaborator," and even though Admiral A. B. Cunningham himself offered to guarantee his "integrity," he was not allowed to return to his post.

The most unfortunate victim of the "purge" was Vice Admiral Derrien. General Giraud accused him—unjustly, as was proved—of having deliberately refused to return General Barré's three battalions of troops to that general when he retreated into the interior on November 11. A preliminary board of investigation, which included two deputies, one of them a Communist, remanded him for regular trial. Under the Naval Code of Justice his case should have been tried by a full court of admirals. Instead, on May 12, 1944, he was eventually tried in closed court by an "Army Tribunal" consisting of two civilian judges, two generals, and one rear ad-

---

[13] Well in advance of the German occupation of the Sidi Abdallah navy yard, French naval personnel had taken important security measures against their coming. During the night of November 10, 1942, all secret technical documents and plans of possible interest to an invader were secretly buried in a cave and the entrance walled up. The next night, all documents on pyrotechnics had been similarly hidden. On the night of the 12th, the servo-motors of all torpedoes and the delicate control mechanisms of all submarine mines were also concealed.

miral. He was absolved of the charge of surrendering Bizerte to the Germans, but was held responsible for not having scuttled the ships under his command. His sentence was dismissal from the Navy and imprisonment for life.

At first he was confined in chains in the Maison Carrée Prison, along with natives condemned for common felony. In deteriorating health and with blindness threatening, he was finally released on suspended sentence on May 9, 1946, just twelve days before he died. Then—he was buried with full military honors.

While at Bizerte and elsewhere the deficiency in officers and men was being made up with new replacements, the status of Force X, at Alexandria, was finally being resolved.

From the moment Admiral Darlan had brought French North Africa back into the war on the side of the Allies, every effort had been made to persuade Admiral Godfroy and his officers of Force X to join the alliance. Officer envoys had been sent to Egypt, first by Darlan, then by Giraud, and finally by Michelier, but Godfroy's loyalty to what he regarded as the legitimate government of France was unshakable. The British almost jeopardized the discussions by threatening to cut off the food supplies of the inactivated squadron. Godfroy demanded certain assurances before consenting to change his stand.

On May 15, General Giraud finally gave those assurances:

> Union between our forces is advantageous to France. It must be a loyal union, and that is why I would never subscribe to the domination of a single party, or of a single faction, or of a single individual. It must be generous, and I will not agree to Frenchmen being unjustly reproached because of having obeyed the country's laws or the orders of their superior officers. It must be sincere, it must be tolerant. . . .

The assurances were perfectly clear. On May 17, 1943, Admiral Godfroy radioed Admiral Michelier that he was joining up with the Naval Forces of Africa. He was equally prompt to inform the Admiralty at Vichy of that fact.

In reply he received a message signed by Laval personally, ordering him to scuttle his ships. The head of the Government personally signing a naval order evidenced that the Germans were monitoring every communication to the Admiralty. Admiral Godfroy politely answered that his commitment had already been made, and thenceforth refused to communicate further.

A detachment of 2,000 French sailors from Algiers was sent to bring the partly demobilized ships of Force X up to complement. Some of these were tragically lost when the British transport carrying them—the *Yoma* —was torpedoed on June 17, some forty miles off Derna.

Of the Force X ships, the submarine *Protée* and the destroyers *Basque, Fortuné* and *Forbin* proceeded directly through the Mediterranean for the ports of Algeria. The battleship *Lorraine* and the cruisers *Duquesne, Tourville, Suffren,* and *Duguay-Trouin* made the long trip around Africa to reach their destination at Dakar—a noteworthy performance, considering their three-year inactivation.[14]

On arrival at Dakar, Admiral Godfroy was relieved of his command. He was not assigned another. And on December 9, 1943, he learned—through the newspapers—that he had been "compulsorily retired as a disciplinary measure."

The winning over of the men-of-war and the merchant ships in the Mediterranean was far easier, however, than doing that same thing in the Antilles. There the naval commander, Admiral Robert, was not only Commander in Chief of the Naval Forces but also High Commissioner of the Antilles, a political office. Under his administration the islands existed not only under the 1940 armistice and subsequent agreements with the Germans but also in accord with a *modus vivendi* entered into with the United States. This agreement covered not only the French men-of-war and merchant ships in the Antilles, but also the hundred planes stored there and the 300 tons of gold which had been brought there for security when the Germans had overrun the mother country. Under the agreement with the United States, the Antilles administration had promised the Americans that they would send neither ships nor planes nor gold back to Europe, and they had equally bound themselves to the Germans to destroy all this rather than let any of it be seized by the Americans. Through these negotiated agreements, the Antilles not only obtained food to keep body and soul together, but they remained a recognized part of the French empire.

The Allied landings in North Africa and the immediately ensuing changes there aroused varying emotions in the Antilles. The Army garrison, inspired by the name of Giraud, was ready to join the new Government in Algiers, as were the civilian public, long since wearied of the American blockade. The Navy, however, was loathe to forswear its traditional allegiance to the established government, and yet equally disinclined to scuttle its ships out of any love for the Reich.

On their part, the Americans, having broken off diplomatic relations with the Antilles administration, were quite candid about their intention of eliminating these "Vichyite" enclaves if they did not agree to join with the new pro-Allied group at Algiers. And in the background, agitating against

---

[14] The cruisers arrived at Dakar on August 18. The *Lorraine*, delayed by damages at Durban, joined at Dakar a few weeks later.

both the "Vichyites" and the pro-Allies, was a so-called "Martinique Liberation Committee," presided over by a Communist.

There was serious danger in the Antilles, not only of aggressive operations from without, but of civil war from within.

Ever since May of 1943, Admiral Robert had been bombarded with messages from Laval, ordering him to scuttle all his ships—to destroy all the planes—to take the gold out of Fort-de-France and to sink it far at sea. Admiral Robert pointed out that not only was it physically impossible to carry out these measures, being under the constant surveillance of the Americans, but that any attempt to carry them out would start an immediate revolution in the islands. When the orders were reiterated by Vichy, Admiral Robert replied that if the government insisted on their being carried out, he would be forced to hand in his resignation.

Matters in this tense situation were not relieved by the careless action of a naval censor in clearing for newspaper publication a spiteful article attacking the leaders of the Army of Africa. The rift between the Army and the Navy widened. A riot broke out in the public square in Fort-de-France on the anniversary of the armistice. On May 29 a detachment of the Colonial Army quartered nearby at Balata announced over the radio that they were joining the Free French.

There could be no question of using the Navy against the colonial troops to enforce their obedience. Even on board ship, feelings were running high. The situation was becoming impossible.

On June 30, the High Commissioner sent a radio message to Admiral Hoover, the U.S. representative in Antilles matters, requesting him to ask the American Government to send a plenipotentiary to arrange the conditions for a "change of jurisdiction" and a resumption of imports. One requisite set by Admiral Robert for any arrangement was that it must contain a solemn guarantee that French sovereignty over the islands would be maintained. Admiral Robert informed the Government at Vichy of his communication the very day after it was sent.

In consequence of the proceedings thus set in motion, the administrator, Henri Hoppenot, designated by the new Government in Algiers, arrived at Fort-de-France aboard the super-destroyer *Terrible,* on July 14, 1943. To him Admiral Robert handed over the sacred trust of the islands and all the Government property they contained,[15] which he had managed to safeguard against all the dangers of war, either from outside or from inside.

With the transfer of the Government, there automatically went the small

---

[15] The most valuable "property" was probably 8,766 boxes containing gold to a total of 306.8 tons. It was this gold that later served as France's contribution to the International Monetary Fund created in the Bretton Woods agreements.

naval force that had been immobilized in the Antilles ever since the armistice. Not a moment was lost in getting the ships fit for service. The *Béarn* was sent directly to New Orleans to be converted for service as a plane ferry. The *Jeanne d'Arc* was given a quick overhaul in Puerto Rico and then returned to the Mediterranean, where she arrived just in time to take part in the Allied operation against Corsica. The *Emile Bertin* was sent to Philadelphia for modernization and repairs similar to those carried out on the other 7,000-ton French cruisers.

In spite of storm and stress Admiral Robert had brought his ship of state—the French Antilles—safe into port. American courtesy permitted him to return to Vichy to give an account of his stewardship. There is no doubt that he received the commendation of Marshal Pétain for his faithful performance. But at the time of the liberation he was placed under arrest. After 18 months in prison he was condemned by the High Court of Justice and sentenced, on March 6, 1946, to 10 years of forced labor. However, no one dared to try to put the sentence into effect, with the result that he was only "disgraced"—or "honored"—according to the personal beliefs of the individual.

At Reunion Island, the *Léopard* had the painful privilege of exchanging the last shots fired at each other by Frenchmen during the war. On December 30, 1942, Dijibouti, under command of General Edmond Dupont, who had been appointed as successor to Governor Nouailhetas, accepted the course of joining the Allies. Indochina was cut off from the West by the intervening sweep of the war in the Pacific, and would not be liberated until the surrender of Japan. With the accession of the Antilles, the regrouping of the empire and its reentry into the war became an accomplished fact. The advent of General de Gaulle's government at Algiers would automatically bring about in some manner or other the fusion of the Free French Naval Forces with those of the empire, to reconstitute the National Navy.

But it would be another year before that National Navy would again have the use of its normal bases in European France.

CHAPTER 24

French Naval Operations, 1943-1944

One of the first things the French Committee of National Liberation did after it took office in June, 1943, was to eliminate the naval leaders in power at the time of the Allied landings. Admiral Michelier at Casablanca and Admiral Moreau at Algiers were relieved of their commands. Admiral Michelier was placed on the inactive list at half pay; Admiral Moreau was retired in accordance with the age limits set under a new decree expressly issued for the occasion.[1] In their places the Committee selected two officers to jointly head the new National Navy, Vice Admiral Collinet, commander of the naval forces in French West Africa, and Rear Admiral Auboyneau, commander of the F.F.N.F.

Vice Admiral Collinet was an excellent choice, but he refused the position despite the urging of both De Gaulle and Giraud, and preferred to retain his command at Dakar. So the choice fell on Rear Admiral Lemonnier, who up to then had headed the merchant marine service. He was appointed Chief of Naval Operations, with Auboyneau as his deputy. The separate naval headquarters that had been maintained at Casablanca and London were merged into a single headquarters at Algiers. The senior French naval officer remaining in England became simply the Commander of the Naval Forces in Great Britain, or C.N.F.G.B. On November 9, 1943, the Government—that is to say, the French Committee of National Liberation—created a "Commissionership of the Navy," or Ministry of the Navy. Louis Jacquinot became the first holder of that office. The Navy was fast returning to its traditional organization.

The total strength of the new National Navy at that time was some 40,000 men, of whom about 2,000 were officers. Some 2,000 of the seamen were natives of the colonies, from 5,000 to 6,000 came from the F.F.N.F., 2,000 from Force X, 1,500 from the Antilles, and some 475 from the former Madagascar forces, of whom 45 were officers, after an intervening period of detention in British prisons. The remainder, approximately 30,000,

---

[1] This decree of August 12, 1943, also eliminated Vice Admiral Rioult, commanding the naval forces at Oran, Vice Admiral Godfroy, commanding Force X, Rear Admiral Robert Leloup, of the Antilles naval forces, and other senior officers—in all, some 30% of all the flag officers on active duty.

came from the Naval Forces of Africa. At the time of the Allied landings in France, a year later, the Navy's strength had risen to around 50,000 men, of whom 3,400 were officers and 7,000 were native seamen from the colonies. Some 6,500 reserves had been recalled to active duty. Also 1,600 men, including 190 officers or student officers, had joined from the 10,000 or so escapees to Spain in 1943.

It took a certain length of time to bring the regulations of the F.F.N.F. into accord with the traditional regulations of the Navy and to incorporate changes required by the dependence of the new Navy on the armies and navies of the other Allies. The most important matter, that of a common promotion system, was resolved and became effective on January 1, 1944.[2]

At the time Mr. Jacquinot assumed office as Navy Commissioner, the French Naval Forces consisted of 3 battleships, 1 airplane tender, 3 heavy cruisers, 6 light cruisers, 13 destroyers and super-destroyers, 19 submarines, 1 frigate, 7 corvettes, and 87 miscellaneous ships, such as sloops, patrol craft, minesweepers, motor torpedo boats, etc.[3] With the exception of some 10 ships coming from the F.F.N.F., all of these units were French naval units and had been built before the war.

Naval aviation, already partly modernized, thanks to Allied contributions, included one bomber squadron (16 Wellingtons) and one patrol squadron (9 Sunderlands and 2 French seaplanes) at Dakar; one bomber squadron, consisting of 9 old Glenn Martin planes, even then being replaced by Catalinas, at Agadir, and one fighter squadron of 15 Dewoitines and two squadrons of Latécoère or Walrus observation planes in the Mediterranean.

Not to be forgotten was one commando regiment of Marines, stemming

---

[2] Promotions under the regular rules had been carried out in the naval forces of Africa, but in the F.F.N.F. there had been some notable departures from the straight rules for advancement. For instance, Thierry d'Argenlieu, although at the time a captain, temporary rank, was promoted "Rear Admiral, *pro forma,*" on August 12, 1941. It required three separate decrees from General de Gaulle, all issued on the same day, November 3, 1943, but made retroactive to June 1, 1942, to promote d'Argenlieu to rear admiral in the reserves, with temporary rank.

Naturally, when the F.F.N.F. and the Naval Forces of Africa were merged, all ranks held at the time by either were confirmed.

[3] Battleships *Richelieu, Jean Bart,* and *Lorraine;* airplane transport *Béarn;* heavy cruisers *Suffren, Duquesne,* and *Tourville,* all armed with 203-mm. guns; light cruisers *Duguay-Trouin* and *Jeanne d'Arc,* armed with 155-mm. guns, and *Emile Bertin, Georges Leygues, Gloire,* and *Montcalm,* armed with 152-mm. guns; super-destroyers or destroyers *Fantasque, Terrible, Malin, Triomphant, Fortuné, Combattante, Alcyon, Tigre, Tempête, Trombe, Simoun, Basque,* and *Forbin* (the super-destroyers of the *Fantasque* class were at this time redesignated as light cruisers, but they will retain their original classification in this text); submarines *Glorieux, Centaure, Perle, Sultane, Vestale, Casabianca, Marsouin, Archimède, Argo, Orphée, Curie, Rubis, Minerve, Amazone, Antiope, Aréthuse, Atalante, Protée,* and *Junon.*

from the F.F.N.F. Marine battalion, and one group of naval gunners.

The collapse of Italy in September of 1943 and the now overwhelming superiority of the Allied navies changed the character of the war. The main work of the Allied navies hereafter would consist of escorting convoys, hunting down the few last German U-boats, and staging amphibious operations on the continent. In order to participate in this work the French Navy obtained from the Americans and British, on loan or transfer, a large number of small ships,[4] which gave it the rather nondescript aspect it was to have at the end of the conflict.

Naturally the French naval contribution represented but a small proportion of the immense forces involved in the amphibious assaults on Europe. The main contribution the French Navy made was the springboard of its harbors and bases in North Africa, which constituted a strategic asset of incalculable value. Moreover, the operations mounted in common with the Allies showed that the officers and men of the French Navy had not lost their traditional virtues.

Among the first French ships to participate in Allied operations was the *Richelieu*. After quick repairs in America, she joined the British Home Fleet, under Admiral Sir Bruce Fraser, on November 20, 1943. Her training was still incomplete when the German battleship *Scharnhorst* sortied in December, so that she missed the exciting hunt for that vessel. However, Admiral Fraser personally gave the *Richelieu's* captain his regrets that he had had to leave her out of that operation, and later took the occasion to address the ship's entire crew in French. In February, he incorporated the *Richelieu* in the raiding force he took to the Norwegian coast. The middle of the following month the *Richelieu* left Scapa Flow to join the Eastern Fleet at Trincomalee, for the war's final operations against Japan in the Indian Ocean.

One by one, the French 7,000-ton cruisers took up patrol duties in the central Atlantic as quickly as their repairs made them available. In addition to watching for enemy raiders and blockade-runners, they had to stop and search certain neutral vessels for contraband cargo or passenger suspects traveling between Spain and South America. The cruisers of Force X were similarly employed as soon as they reached Dakar. They were also em-

---

[4] From the United States: 6 destroyer escorts (*Sénégalais* class), 32 escort vessels of 355 tons (P.C. type), 50 submarine chasers (S.C. type), 31 minesweepers, some 40 tugs or harbor craft, and about 50 landing craft. From Great Britain: 1 destroyer, *Combattante* (*Hunt* class), 6 frigates of 1,325 tons (*Découverte* class), 9 corvettes, under the assistance program for the F.F.N.F., 4 submarines (one of them an ex-Italian), 14 motor minesweepers (M.M.S. type), 21 harbor defense motor launches (H.D.M.L. type), 8 motor torpedo boats (M.T.B. type), 7 light motor launches (M.L. type), and some miscellaneous harbor craft.

ployed as fast transports, conveying 28,000 men from West Africa to the Mediterranean without a loss. They were soon given the duty of patrolling the entire mid-Atlantic, between 21° and 29° west longitude, and 3° and 10° north latitude—an expanse of over 200,000 square miles, to cover which they had only the additional assistance of British long-range Liberator planes based at Gambia, West Africa.

In November of 1943, however, after Marshal Pietro Badoglio's new Italian Government had entered the war on the side of the Allies, the two Italian cruisers *Duca degli Abruzzi* and *Duca d'Aosta* came to assist in the patrol. Two alternating patrols were thereupon established, one consisting of the *Duca degli Abruzzi* and the French cruisers *Montcalm* and *Georges Leygues,* and the other of the *Duca d'Aosta* and the French cruisers *Gloire* and *Suffren.* The shorter ranged French cruisers *Duquesne* and *Tourville* were used as emergency reliefs on this patrol.

The Italian cruisers were based at Freetown, British Sierra Leone. This was perhaps just as well, because although Italy was now accepted as a full ally, there were Frenchmen who could not forget her unprovoked attack on a helpless France in June, 1940. In those first meetings of French and Italian crews ashore, sharp rejoinders and even blows were exchanged.[5]

However, at sea everything went smoothly, and the patrols went without a hitch. The last blockade-runners were now sunk or returned to the fold.[6] Only a few months more, and the French ships would head north to participate in the liberation of France.

In the eastern Mediterranean, though, hostilities had not died away, even though Italy had changed sides. The Germans still clung to the Italian Dodecanese Islands, throwing off British troops landed in Kos and Leros, and the Aegean Sea remained a danger area until the very end. Operating in this area was the small French naval division of the Levant, consisting

---

[5] In March, 1944, the Italian cruiser *Giuseppe Garibaldi* was in Gibraltar at the same time as three ex-F.F.N.F. corvettes. One of these, the *Aconit,* was just celebrating the anniversary of its double victory against two German U-boats the year before. Some of the French sailors, overstimulated, had the bright idea of painting the Cross of Lorraine on the *Garibaldi's* bow, and at the same time seizing her admiral's flag from his barge while it was standing by to take him on an official call. Naturally, this created quite a furor. Admiral Burrough, commanding at Gibraltar, was beside himself; the Italian admiral insisted on apologies; but the French liaison officer, who had rushed to Admiral Burrough to express his regrets over the incident, had no intention of thus humiliating himself before the Italians. Fortunately the British commander was an understanding person, and the matter was smoothed over without further complications.

[6] In a 30-day period beginning December 26, 1943, five German blockade-runners were sunk: three in the South Atlantic, one in the North Atlantic, and one in the Pas-de-Calais itself.

of the sloops *Moqueuse, Commandant Duboc, Commandant Dominé,* and the patrol vessel *Reine des Flots.* This ship, assigned to the defense of Castellorizo, repelled two attacks by German Junker 88s on October 24, and four days later shot down one, and perhaps two planes of a squadron of 12 Stukas which had just attacked a British convoy.

In addition to the French ships based in the Levant, the super-destroyers *Fantasque* and *Terrible,* from Alexandria, covered the evacuation of the English garrison of Leros on November 19 and 20.

The convoy activities of the French Navy increased in proportion to the growth of that Navy. In 1943, French escort ships carried out more than 700 missions and the naval air force totaled some 2,400 hours of flight in protection of convoys—these figures being exclusive of activities during the operation against Corsica.

By now the greatest enemy threat came from bombers, torpedo planes, and glide bombs. The few U-boats that remained had little chance against the powerful antisubmarine groups ranged against them. In one such engagement, near Djidjelli, Algeria, on May 4, 1944, the French destroyer *Sénégalais,* under command of Lieutenant Commander Pierre Poncet, had a major part in sinking the *U-371.* But before her last plunge, the U-boat got off a torpedo which blew off the stern of the *Sénégalais* and killed 14 men. For his part in the action Lieutenant Commander Poncet was personally decorated by U.S. Admiral Hewitt.

During these last 18 months of the war the French submarines were divided into two groups. The oldest ones were assigned training duties. The newest ones—*Casabianca, Protée, Archimède, Perle, Curie, Aréthuse, Orphée, and Sultane*—operated in the Mediterranean, carrying out 45 patrols. They sank eight enemy vessels, of which three were credited to the *Casabianca* alone. Some submarines engaged in special missions off the coasts of Provence and Spain. The minelaying submarine *Rubis* continued its dangerous task in the North Sea and Bay of Biscay, where, in early 1944, it celebrated the 500th mine laid by it in enemy waters.

Nor were these submarine operations without casualties. On April 19, 1943, the *Vestale,* commanded by Lieutenant Commander Raymond Attané, was mistakenly attacked by HMS *Wishart,* and an ensign aboard her was mortally wounded. The next day the *Aréthuse,* though in a specially designated submarine training area, was fired on by an Allied convoy. The *Casabianca* was next, and then in October the *Minerve* was bombed by a British plane while getting under way from Portsmouth, and had to return to port with two men killed, plus serious material damage. Worst of all, on July 8, 1944, the *Perle,* commanded by Lieutenant Marcel Tachin, was sunk through error. There was only one survivor.

Only one French submarine was lost to the enemy during these patrols. During the month of October, 1943, the *Protée* failed to return from a patrol off the coast of enemy-held Provence.

French merchant ship losses from November, 1942, until the capitulation of Germany, amounted to only thirteen cargo ships and two trawlers.

The first really important operation for the new Navy was the recapture of Corsica, the first French territory in Europe to be liberated. And it was recaptured entirely by French means, as at that time the Allies were devoting all their forces to the landings at Salerno.

The island of Corsica, formerly part of the Free Zone of France, had been occupied by the Axis on November 11, 1942, only three days after the Allied landings in North Africa. Eighty thousand Italian troops were garrisoned there, and additional detachments of German troops occasionally occupied positions on the east coast. Despite the demobilization of all French armed forces decreed by the German Government on November 27, Captain J. Quédec, former commander of the French naval forces on the island, managed to retain a post as local director of the merchant marine. With a few officers and sailors he thus continued to carry out naval duties, although in a civilian status. Small cargo vessels connected the island with Marseilles by semiweekly sailings, two of them being lost to Allied submarines during the 10 months of Axis occupation. Keeping the island supplied with food was difficult, but the Corsicans were both frugal and resourceful, and there was less privation in the back areas than in many cities in France.

Just as everywhere else, the occupation of the island had brought into existence underground resistance groups, and gradually a "National Front" was formed, in which the Communists took considerable part. The Allied secret strategic services formed contacts with this network and smuggled arms to it. English submarines took part in these secret missions, but it was the French submarine *Casabianca,* commanded by Lieutenant Commander L'Herminier, which made the most runs.

The *Casabianca* had been detailed to this duty by Admiral Darlan personally. Immediately upon arrival in Algiers, following her escape from Toulon, her captain had been sent by Darlan to Colonel William Eddy, U.S.M.C., head of the O.S.S., who explained what was wanted of him. This was to land secret agents[7] in Corsica on the nights of December 14 and 15,

---

[7] Special mention must be made of the leader of this group, Sergeant Major Griffi. For eight months he directed the operations of the Maquis, during which time he handled 286 secret messages, as well as bringing about the torpedoing of the Italian passenger ship *Francesco Crispi.* Caught at last in Ajaccio, in August, 1943, he was tried, condemned, and executed on the eve of the Italian armistice.

in order to set up secret wireless connections. Following this mission, the *Casabianca* completed half a dozen similar ones by August, 1943, carrying sometimes 20 tons of guns and ammunition on a single trip.

When the Italian Army suddenly laid down its arms on September 9, 1943, the Germans promptly occupied Bastia, the principal port in the north of Corsica, in order to safeguard the withdrawal of their troops from Sardinia. They thus evacuated two divisions of troops, which later gave the Allies a great deal of trouble on the Italian front. Unfortunately neither the French nor the Anglo-Americans were able to prevent the evacuation at this time. To avoid all incidents, the Italians had withdrawn into the interior, whereupon the National Front took over the administration buildings of Ajaccio without firing a shot. But the population feared that the Germans might return, and put out a call via secret radio to Algiers for help.

General Giraud would have been glad to send troops to Corsica immediately, but no transports were available. All Allied shipping was tied up at Salerno, where a powerful German counterattack was under way. Furthermore, some of the best French naval units in the area were also participating in the Salerno operation in support of the Allied landings. These units were the super-destroyers *Fantasque,* commanded by Commander Charles Perzo, and *Terrible,* commanded by Commander Pierre Lancelot. On August 22 they had carried out a raid in the Gulf of Gaeta, where they had battled with fast enemy motor torpedo boats and had bombarded a German headquarters in Scalea. A few days later they were operating with the British 12th Cruiser Squadron,[8] under the orders of Sir Algernon Willis, commanding Force H,[9] which was protecting the aircraft carriers assigned to the Salerno operation.

The super-destroyers had been off the Italian coast for two days, heavily engaged with the German bombers, when they received sudden orders to proceed to Algiers at top speed. Arrived there, they were immediately set to embarking the equipment and personnel of a battalion of shock troops, whom they transported to Corsica at an average speed of almost 30 knots.

Off Ajaccio they were met on the night of September 13 by the *Casabianca,* which had preceded them with another 109 men crammed into every nook and cranny of the submarine. Waiting on the dock in his proper uniform again was Captain Quédec. Captain Quédec had not only persuaded the Italians to provide him with pilot service, but they had even

---

[8] The British 12th Cruiser Squadron was commanded by Commodore W. G. Agnew, R.N., who had made himself famous by the raids of his Force K on Italian convoys during the Axis siege of Malta.

[9] Force H included six battleships, two aircraft carriers, the 12th Cruiser Squadron, and three flotillas of destroyers.

turned over to him the coastal batteries guarding the entrance to the Bay of Ajaccio. They were unanimous in protesting that they had never had but one enemy, and that was the Germans!

On the return trip to Algiers, the *Terrible* had a turbine failure that laid her up for six weeks. But the *Fantasque* immediately embarked 275 men, and with the destroyers *Tempête* and *Alcyon,* each of which carried 100 men and 10 tons of equipment, she promptly turned about for the trip back to Ajaccio. All three ships arrived at Ajaccio the night of September 16, with no incident other than two submarine alerts and a pattern of depth charges dropped by the *Alcyon,* without result.

The Navy was scraping the barrel everywhere for ships to take part in the recapture of Corsica. The submarines *Perle* and *Aréthuse* took on three tons of flour and five tons of ammunition. The *Jeanne d'Arc,* just arrived at Casablanca after overhaul in Bermuda, was sent to Gibraltar to bring back six 40-mm. Bofors and 20 Oerlikon machineguns, which the U.S. repair ship *Vulcan* installed within 36 hours after their arrival at Algiers. Thus armed against enemy aircraft, the *Jeanne d'Arc* was able to take part in the fourth trip to Corsica, which landed 1,200 men and 110 tons of equipment and supplies.

The *Montcalm,* recalled from Dakar, reached Algiers on September 21, after four days steaming, and left for Ajaccio in company with the *Fantasque* the next day, the two ships together taking in 1,500 men and 200 tons of equipment. During this trip the *Fantasque* ran aground, and the *Montcalm* barely avoided following her as the pilots erred. The *Fantasque* was stranded for four days, but pulled off with minor damage and without being bombed by enemy planes while in her helpless position. In fact the German reaction to the reoccupation of Ajaccio did not occur until September 30, when they destroyed a British LST with glide bombs in Ajaccio harbor.

By October 1, some 6,800 men with 20 guns and 30 tanks were ashore and heading over the mountains toward Bastia. By October 4, the Germans were evacuating. Total French losses were 72 killed and 270 wounded among the French regulars, and 150 casualties among the Maquis who participated. General de Gaulle came to Ajaccio on October 9 to celebrate the liberation of the island, and in his speech he did not fail to condemn the Government at Vichy.

Between September 12, 1943, and October 1, 1944, by which time the Mediterranean had been freed of the enemy, 99 convoys had sailed from North Africa to Corsica, carrying 62,700 men, 110,000 tons of supplies and equipment, and 6,400 vehicles. The only losses suffered were the small minesweeper *Marie Mad,* lost with all hands by a mine off Ajaccio on November 24, 1943, and the passenger steamer *El Biar,* sunk by enemy air attack on April 20, 1944, with only one survivor.

Corsica in French hands was a valuable Allied asset. It provided space for 17 airfields, accommodating 2,000 Allied planes. It provided the springboard from which the Allied landings in Provence were later launched. And it was the birthplace of the Naval Assault Group of Corsica, which, after training by raids on the islands of Pianosa and Elba, was to have the honor of being the first to set foot on the soil of Provence in the final landings of the liberation.

Had the Allies been less preoccupied with Salerno and the strengthening of Ajaccio, they might well have turned Bastia into a second Tunis for the Germans. Had there been more forces to throw across the German line of retreat, they might have turned that retreat into a catastrophe. As it was, only a few British submarines and one Polish submarine harassed the retreating Germans, sinking one or two German transports.[10]

Once Corsica was pretty well secured, the 10th Division of superdestroyers, composed of the *Fantasque* and *Terrible,* found themselves involved in even more strenuous adventures. They had now become reclassified as the 10th Division of light cruisers, since the term "destroyer" was generally applied by the friendly navies to designate much smaller ships. After going out into the Atlantic to meet and escort the rejuvenated *Richelieu* to Algiers, the two vessels proceeded to Alexandria to join in the British operations against the Dodecanese. After withstanding an enemy air attack in company with HMS *Phoebe,* they assisted in sweeping the channel between Crete and Rhodes clear of all enemy vessels.

Back to the western Mediterranean, on December 24 the *Fantasque* intercepted the German freighter *Nicoline Maesk,* which she forced onto the beach southwest of Tortosa, Spain. One week later she was at Horta, in the Azores Islands, where, in company with the *Malin,* she spent 15 days in a vain search for German raiders.

The *Terrible* was still undergoing engine repairs, so the *Fantasque,* under a new commanding officer, Captain Antoine Sala, now teamed up with the *Malin.* From January 21 to 25, the two ships alternated in bombarding the Italian coast near Civitavecchia, Formia, and Terracina, the main purpose being to distract the enemy from the new Allied landing at Anzio.[11] They next became fast troop transports, ferrying 500 men per ship from North Africa to Naples, after which they shifted to newly captured bases in southern Italy for raids in the Adriatic.

The *Terrible* had now returned to action, and she and the *Fantasque* fell on a German convoy between Pola and the Piraeus on February 29, 1944, sinking the German freighter *Kapitan Diedrichsen,* of 6,500 tons, and the

---

[10] One of the vessels sunk was the former French ship *Champagne,* seized by the Germans in November, 1942, and which was now flying the German flag.

[11] The cruiser *Gloire,* participating in this action, emptied her entire magazines in the bombardment and had to be replenished by planes.

corvette *UJ-201,* and damaging the torpedo boats *TA-37, TA-36,* and *UJ-205.* On March 4 they bombarded the Istrian coast, and repeated at the Island of Zante three days later. Another week found them off the Dalmatian coast, and a day or two later they surprised a group of 5 German landing barges ferrying troops and war materials to Navarino, in the Peloponnesus. Two of these, the Siebel ferries *SF-273* and *SF-274,* were sunk in the initial attack. The other three were badly damaged and were sunk the next day by Allied planes. In the action the *Fantasque* received six 20-mm. hits, and the *Terrible* three, which wounded several men.

With a new division commander, Captain Lancelot, and a new captain, Commander Charles Géli, in the *Fantasque,* the two ships and the *Malin* returned to the eastern Mediterranean. During the next eight or ten weeks, they operated all the way to Crete, bombarded Kos, and swung back to raid in the Gulf of Quarnero, where on the night of June 16 they sank the small tanker *Guiliana* and put two of her minesweeper escorts out of action. They were readying themselves for the great days of August, when, with other French naval units, they would share in the landings in Provence and the recapture of Toulon.

There they would be reunited with their comrades who, less fortunate, had had for four years to resist the German invader underground.

CHAPTER 25

The Navy in Occupied France

It was peculiarly fortunate that the first Germans to arrive in the ports and along the coasts of the Channel and the Atlantic in June of 1940 were the soldiers of the Wehrmacht, and not Germany's excellent sailors. For soldiers, of whatever nationality, have never been quite comfortable in situations concerning the sea.

Thus, at Cherbourg as well as at Brest, the soldiers of Generals Rommel and von Hartlieb did not know exactly what to do while they waited for the men of the Kriegsmarine, who were coming along behind on the highways. Knowing nothing of the huge personnel requirements of a naval base, they were astounded at the large number of prisoners on their hands. In particular they did not know what to do with the large number of officer prisoners.

At Cherbourg, all officers except the medical officers of the naval hospital were placed under strict guard. At Lorient, one observing German noted that certain officers—the naval line officers—had no velvet borders to their stripes;[1] thereupon all officers lacking velvet borders to their stripes were imprisoned, and all the others released. At Rochefort, the catch was even more extraordinary; it was no longer stripes, but stars, with which the conqueror was encumbered. For it was here that all the departments of the Ministry of the Navy—administration, personnel, research, supplies, etc.— had stopped in the course of the retreat, and the number of flag officers captured would have formed complete platoons. The first thing the armistice commission did was to release outright all these encumbering hostages.

At Brest it so happened that the German admiral designated to take over the naval command was Admiral Lothär von Arnaud de la Périère. A French name, and rightfully his, because, a century and a half earlier, his ancestors had emigrated from France into Germany during the French Revolution. During the First World War he had distinguished himself in command of a submarine. Whether it was out of sympathy for another

---

[1] The officers of the different corps of the Navy are distinguished by the color of a velvet border to their strips—violet for the engineers, black for the naval constructors, red for the medical corps, etc. The officers of the line are the only ones who do not have a velvet border to their stripes.

submariner, or whether it was merely to facilitate his own task, he proposed to Captain Jean Le Normand, who was on shore duty at Brest, that he remain at the head of several noncombatant departments of the base—tugs, lighters, harbor pilots, etc. Under French naval personnel these would be maintained during the occupation, thus forming a sort of French enclave in the navy yard.

The armistice had just been signed, and Captain Le Normand asked for time to think it over. He was lucky enough to be able to get in touch with Admiral Darlan, who immediately sent back word for him to seize this opportunity to hang on to his post, and to remain there to protect French interests as long as possible.

This precedent, with its paradoxical organization, was adopted by the Germans at all the large French ports in the Occupied Zone. Within a few months all these French naval officers, theoretically prisoners of war, were carrying on the duties they normally would have been doing—and under the orders of the French Admiralty! Likewise, the workmen and other civilian employees continued in their workshops or offices, under their own engineers and supervisors, and were paid and directed by the French Admiralty at Vichy. In accordance with international convention, they were required to do industrial, but not military, work for the conquerors —though, it is needless to say, this was done with little zeal. However, they worked with tireless energy at building shelters for the civilian population and at repairing the damages caused by the war's bombardments or by sabotage before the armistice.

Being on the spot, the naval officers so engaged were able to keep close watch on French Government property, they prevented the workmen from being deported to Germany, and they saw to it that the families of absent sailors—even those in the F.F.N.F. in England—were properly supported. Furthermore they kept the French Admiralty informed of all that was going on. And quite a few, of their own initiative but sure of the approval of their superiors, who even gave them hints to that effect, made secret contacts with the Allied intelligence networks which mushroomed in the Occupied Zone. Through them the Allies received invaluable information.

At first the calm of national mourning settled over the Occupied Zone. The Germans were making preparations to invade England, and the full efforts of the Royal Air Force were directed against enemy-held airfields and the areas where the landing craft were being concentrated. But all that changed as soon as the first German men-of-war appeared to make use of the French ports—U-boats at Lorient, surface ships at Brest. Cherbourg, being too close to the English coast, never harbored more than a few German light craft or blockade-runners in transit to and from the Atlantic.

But from the day, December 28, 1940, that the German cruiser *Admiral Hipper* took refuge in Brest after its first cruise in the Atlantic, this port became acquainted with systematic Allied bombing. The attacks increased in intensity with the arrival of the battleships *Scharnhorst* and *Gneisenau*. Unfortunately it was the city that suffered, more than the naval base. Protected by concentrated antiaircraft batteries, and camouflaged as well as screened by artificial fog, the German ships suffered very little, though civilian casualties were heavy.

"Your English planes aim very badly!" was the word sent out by Lieutenant Jean Philippon, former executive officer of the submarine *Ouessant,* who had remained on duty at Brest after scuttling his ship, and who had made connections with the Allied intelligence network.[2] "You will never get these ships by horizontal bombing!"

As a matter of fact, before they caused any appreciable damage to the German ships, the R.A.F. had destroyed 250 houses and killed 200 civilians and wounded 500 others, all within a few months.

The exciting chase of the *Bismarck,* as well as the escape of the *Scharnhorst, Gneisenau,* and *Prinz Eugen,* in February, 1942, gave French naval officers at Brest an opportunity to furnish the Allies with useful information. As early as May, 1941, Philippon had observed the preparations of the Kriegsmarine to anchor mooring buoys in the roadstead for a very large ship. This, along with other information he succeeded in getting to London, and which the British Admiralty acknowledged after the war, helped the British to make their dispositions to intercept the *Bismarck,* just 400 miles short of Brest, after she had sunk the *Hood* and then evaded detection in the North Atlantic.

A few weeks later, Petty Officer Bernard Anquetil, a radio operator, was tracked down while he was riskily trying to transmit to the British a lengthy message giving in detail the results of an R.A.F. attack on the *Scharnhorst.* Like many other French sailors in Occupied France, he paid with his life for his devotion to duty.

In February, 1942, the preparations for the famous "Channel dash" of the German Squadron from Brest to Germany were reported by secret

---

[2] In addition to his more professional duties, Lieutenant Philippon had charge of the vegetable gardens in the area which the French sailors of Brest cultivated with a passion in order to improve their fare. Seeing no harm in this, the Germans permitted him to travel about at will—which greatly facilitated his intelligence activities. In 1952, when one of the authors of this history was collaborating in the preparation of a book on the *Scharnhorst,* he brought the story of Philippon and the vegetable gardens to the attention of Admiral Kurt Hoffmann, former commanding officer of the German battle cruiser. Admiral Hoffmann, a chivalrous opponent, asked if it would be possible to meet his ingenious adversary. Unfortunately Philippon, then a Commander, was away from Paris and the meeting could not be arranged.

French naval observers in time for interception by the British had not several things gone unexpectedly wrong.[3]

Information like this was possible only because French naval personnel had succeeded in placing themselves in all the occupied ports where they could observe every movement of the Kriegsmarine. But their very presence there was often wrongfully interpreted by their own countrymen. A number of officers were accused of collaborating with the enemy. At Lorient, Jacques Stosskopf, a French naval constructor, appeared to the workmen to be an inhuman wretch, a traitor ingratiating himself with the conquerors by bullying his own people. But this severity was only a cloak behind which he defended his workers, even at the cost, as it proved, of his own life. For German counterespionage agents finally solved his secret, and he was executed in 1944 by a firing squad at the reprisal camp of Strüthof.

But these things could not be told then, and, under the strain of the occupation, grudges and hatreds were developing. On March 26, 1944, Rear Admiral Le Normand, who had just left his post after holding it for forty-two months, was assassinated in his own home. Many of his officers suffered the worst of insults at the time of the liberation of Brest, until positive proof of their secret heroism and patriotism was revealed to the public.

Le Normand's successor, Rear Admiral Négadelle, also met a tragic end. He had been designated by the French Admiralty to take Admiral Le Normand's place at Brest, with orders to protect the naval installations in every way possible, so that they would be available for use by the Allies in the landings which were expected. He carried out his mission so well that the Germans several times endeavored to have him replaced. They were rid of him finally. On August 27, 1944, he was killed at his headquarters by an Allied bomb in one of the most violent air attacks ever made on the city. His aide-de-camp, Naval Constructor René Ravaud, was severely wounded by the same bomb.

The story of Brest was repeated at Lorient, which was for two years the base of Admiral Karl Dönitz and his German submarines, and which became acquainted with British bombs as soon as it harbored its first U-boat. Attacked occasionally during the first two years, it was bombed heavily from the beginning of 1943, and on January 15 was practically wiped off the map. But even the ruins continued under attack, until life became impossible there, and the city had to be almost completely evacuated. But the large German U-boat base at the fishing port of Keroman

---

[3] Translator's Note: While naval attaché at the American Embassy in Vichy at this time, I informed Washington by radio code of the activities surrounding these German ships, all indicating their imminent departure. From what I have learned since the war, I am of the opinion that the information I sent originated with Philippon's organization.

TOULON, NOVEMBER 1942. *1800-ton destroyers resting on the bottom.*

TOULON, NOVEMBER 1942—*Top left: The heavy cruiser* ALGÉRIE *resting on the bottom and burning. Top right and bottom: Two views of the scuttled battleship* STRASBOURG.

nearby was practically untouched under its tremendously thick reinforced concrete protection overhead. In the pens here, which had held only 10 submarines in 1940 and 20 in 1942, some 28 could be securely sheltered in 1943.

But, as at Brest, the French naval personnel remained at their posts under their German masters with a patriotism that was as effective as it was ingenious. In fact when Commander Adrien Charrier, formerly with the F.F.N.F., took over his duties as commanding officer at Lorient after its liberation, he reported that under Stosskopf the navy yard had produced for the Germans only one-tenth of what it produced when the Germans supervised it themselves.

A typical example of the French ingenuity was the case of the cruiser *De Grasse*. This ship had been only 28 per cent completed when, along with the navy yard, it fell into the hands of the Germans in 1940. Representing no value to the Germans, it blocked the building ways for other work which they wished done, and they directed that it be made sufficiently watertight and buoyant so that it could be towed away.

Construction was resumed toward that end, but Chief Naval Constructor Henri Antoine[4] saw to it that progress was not too rapid. One witness wrote, "the workmen put in their time mostly in making a lot of noise, and in wrecking one week the work they had done the week before. In addition they stole and hid away in the double bottoms of the *De Grasse* a large quantity of tools and equipment so that it would be available on the day of liberation."

Even in the straight commercial harbors, the Navy, working under the cloak of its traditional responsibility for supervising the merchant marine, established a strong naval nucleus everywhere. It not only set up detachments of naval police—whom the workmen called "Darlans"—but it also set up groups of naval firemen.[5] As a result, from Dunkirk to Bayonne, the Germans could do nothing without its being promptly reported to the officers of the French Navy. The firemen, too, were invaluable with their heroic work in rescuing the injured and checking the conflagrations in

---

[4] French commandants at Lorient, up to the time of liberation, included Naval Constructor Henri Antoine (up to August 15, 1942); Captain Jean Bécam (August 15, 1942, to November, 1942); Rear Admiral Urvoy de Porzamparc (November, 1942, to July 5, 1943); Rear Admiral Pierre Rouyer (July 5, 1943, to May 15, 1944); and Captain Corentin Le Floch (May 15, 1944, until the liberation.)

[5] Naval firemen were nothing new. The conflagration occurring at Marseilles in 1938 had emphasized the inefficiency of the local units as compared to the worth of the disciplined naval firemen brought from Toulon. Thereupon France's largest commercial port had been assigned a battalion of naval firemen, under a commander, just as at Paris there is a regiment of military firemen commanded by a colonel. Beginning with 1942, the Navy had sought to establish similar units in all the principal commercial ports.

civilian areas during the devastating aerial bombardments of Boulogne, Le Havre, Nantes, Bordeaux, Marseilles, and other places preliminary to the Allied landings.[6]

When, after the liberation, Admiral Thierry d'Argenlieu, one of the earliest associates of General de Gaulle, inspected the bases that had been taken care of by the "Navy of Vichy," he was met by naval personnel who under four years of bombing had guarded the Government's property, hiding what they could not remove. The mechanics at Lorient pulled out from the double bottoms of the *De Grasse* quantities of irreplaceable tools, the supply officers at Brest unearthed from their hiding places kilometers of cloth and stocks of provisions beyond price at that time and place. All these constituted ways of fighting the Germans by men who most certainly would have preferred to do that fighting at sea, in their own ships.

It is a matter of record that the naval personnel who in 1943 remained on duty in the Occupied Zone, along the English Channel and the Atlantic seaboard, numbered 3,053. To these must be added 124 medical and supply officers, on duty either in the ports or assigned to various liaison organizations with the occupying authorities. In all there were approximately 3,200 officers and men who thus, "for the good of the service," accepted the label of "collaborator" which the uninformed public was so quick to bestow upon them.

Not only did the seamen of the Navy thus continue their duty to the country, but the seamen of the fishing fleets were in no way behind. Some thirty trawlers and sailing craft, caught by the armistice off the fishing banks of Newfoundland, sailed to Africa to continue their duty of feeding the population of France.[7] The fishermen of the Occupied Zone were permitted by the Germans to continue their fishing, but only in small vessels with small crews, and restricted to areas just a few miles off the coast. A German patrol boat generally kept guard over the fishermen, though sometimes a squad of German soldiers would take passage on the fastest boat in the fleet to maintain its surveillance from there. Nor was the Kriegsmarine wrong in distrusting the fishermen of France. Often a fishing boat, slipping past the German patrols at tremendous risk, would carry to England a load of young Frenchmen anxious to reenter the war, or Allied aviators shot down over France, or—even more dangerous cargo—secret intelligence agents!

---

[6] Not a single major bombing attack on these ports occurred without bringing death to the ranks of the naval firemen. For example, 4 were killed at Bordeaux on August 9, 1944, and 8 at Marseilles during the great air attack of May 27, 1944, which killed over 900 of the civilian population.

[7] Thirteen of these vessels arrived at Casablanca in November and December. Captured by the British on the way were the *Orage, Gémeaux, Joseph Duhamel, Sénateur Duhamel,* and *Urania.*

As early as June 24, 1940, some 133 men of the Island of Sein, constituting almost the entire male population, had escaped to England in fishing boats just before the arrival of the Germans. Eighty service-age men had escaped to Britain from Guernsey at the same time; a similar thing occurred at Douarnenez and Camaret, in Brittany. The Douarnenez boats *Emigrant* and *Petite Anna* established the first liaisons between the British and Breton intelligence agents in the latter part of 1940. A crew from Guilvinec crossed the Channel nineteen times in war work. The *Véai Vad* carried four agents to a rendezvous with a British submarine off the Glénan Islands. In April, 1943, the *Dale'h Mad,* of Tréboul, landed 18 evacuees in England, one of them a squadron leader in the R.A.F. The *Suzanne René* and the *Breis Yzel* repatriated 34 Allied aviators.

The seamen of the merchant marine were just as patriotic. The *Val de la Haye,* a small 350-ton cargo ship chartered by the Germans, took French leave of its charterers and joined the British at Gibraltar, to later become one of the most dependable participants in the Corsican convoys of 1943-1944. But even more dramatic was the story of the *Roz-Bras,* formerly the Dutch coaster *Baltic,* which had been seized by the Germans in 1940 and put to carrying cargo, under the German flag but with a Spanish crew, between Bilbao and France. One night in June it was boldly stolen by a former captain of the French merchant marine who had escaped from Bayonne by signing on a vessel as an ordinary seaman.

Not only had the French merchant captain stolen the ship, through the complicity of the British consul, but he had made arrangements for it to be met and taken over by a British man-of-war. The British ship did not show up, but the Free French sloop *Dumont d'Urville* did, and took it over herself. The new captor changed the *Baltic's* name to *Roz-Bras,* and placed his own prize crew aboard.

Legally, the French merchant captain was no more than a common pirate; in addition he was also a deserter from the freighter on which he had originally signed. To add to the complications, the Dutch consul demanded the return of the ship to the Netherlands. The captain of the *Dumont d'Urville* insisted that the ship was a prize taken on the high seas in a legal manner.

The British were the worst embarrassed of all because their consul at Bilbao had been involved in the affair, contrary to diplomatic privileges. The affair was eventually hushed up without becoming an international matter.

But the successful voyages of French fishermen and other vessels to England on clandestine business were not the whole story; there were many other vessels which failed, or else which made port bullet-riddled and with dead and wounded on their decks. For the battles between the adversaries off the French coasts, at sea or in the air, spared no one.

Thus the *Notre Dame du Châtelet* was sunk by a British submarine off the entrance to the Gironde on May 15, 1941, with only two survivors. Death or destruction came in a similar manner to the *Donibane,* of Lorient, the *Saint Pierre d'Alcantara,* the *Slack,* lost with all hands, the *Equille,* machinegunned off Tréport, and the *Saint Bernard,* sunk in May, 1942, off Douarnenez. Three months later planes of the R.A.F. shot up a flotilla of sixty fishing boats, sending them back to their harbors riddled with bullets and with three men dead and fifteen wounded.

To these losses, continuing through 1943 and 1944, there must be added the losses resulting from mines. The mines were twice as dangerous as bullets to trawlers, for these risked not only running into the mines, but also catching them in their nets where the mines would explode when hauled in. Such was the fate of the *Tiens Bon,* off Brest, in December, 1942, and the *Jeannine,* of Boulogne, off Gravelines in March, 1943. By November of 1942 the number of fishermen killed or missing amounted to 160, and grew to several times that before the end of the war.

The landings of the Allies in North Africa in November, 1942, and the incidents brought on by that landing, made a definite change in the history of the personnel of the French Navy who had remained in France. The break with the empire, the invasion of the Free Zone, the scuttling of the only vessels remaining in the home country, and the suppression by Hitler of French armed forces everywhere should have brought about the end of the naval establishment. But there was work to do, plenty of it. There was the Government property in the shipyards and bases to be preserved, and, most particularly, there were the personnel of the Navy and their families to protect and subsist. There were thousands of demobilized seamen scattered throughout the country who had to be cared for; there were thousands of seamen of the merchant marine without employment, due to the seizure or the destruction of their ships; there were the sailors of the F.F.N.F., fighting overseas, whose dependents had to be kept from starvation. Lastly there were the docks, shops, and naval installations everywhere which must be kept in serviceable order against the time when they would be needed upon the return of the Allies to France.

All these tasks were undertaken by the French Navy, under the supervision at Vichy of Admiral Abrial, and, later, his successor, Rear Admiral Henri Bléhaut, who held the office of Minister of the Navy and Secretary of the Colonies from March, 1943, until the liberation of France.

The magnitude of the subsistence and employment task may be appreciated from the fact that the German attack on Toulon, and the resultant scuttling, threw 1,166 naval officers and 30,823 enlisted men back onto the rolls of the unemployed. This figure did not include medical and supply officers.

Approximately 4,000 officers and men remained in uniform in the southern zone of France, employed in administrative or social welfare work, in the naval police or fire fighting groups, or as maintenance men. The merchant marine administrative office also employed a certain number, part of whose work was to make studies for reviving the merchant fleet as quickly as possible after the war.

The Minister of the Navy also succeeded in maintaining a few naval schools, with their staffs: the naval orphans training school (*Pupilles de la Marine*) at Cahors, and the Naval Academy at Clairac. The social services absorbed some 120 officers, the Ministry of Post and Telegraph some 40, with an additional 60 for communication work with the merchant marine.

The administrative and auxiliary services of the Navy were increased to the utmost possible. For instance, all of the personnel of the old Third Bureau of the Admiralty were retained by camouflaging them into the Historical Section, which, with the Central Hydrographic Office, absorbed 60, with an additional 30 being distributed among various Government organizations. Two hundred young officers were enrolled in the civilian technical institutions still functioning—the Advanced School of Electricity, the School of Mines, the School of Optics, the School of Political Science, etc. Moreover, in 1943 alone, positions in industry, some of them important, were obtained for officers separated from the Navy.

One of the objectives of all this was to safeguard naval personnel from being deported to forced labor in Germany. But the foremost idea in the minds of many was to work toward a transfer to Africa to reenter the war there, or else to form a connection with the underground resistance organizations that were growing up everywhere.

For the attitude of the Navy's personnel had changed a great deal since the days of 1940. Marshal Pétain's retirement from politics and Pierre Laval's policies of increased appeasement of Germany had alienated many. Germany's violation of its agreement with respect to the Navy had been the final straw.

But it was not a matter of the officers and men on active duty abandoning their posts, for there they could render their greatest services. But those who had been demobilized, those who had no obligation except to themselves, had many opportunities to choose from. Unfortunately certain resistance organizations were tinged with communism and held out the prospect of civil war. Yet, amid the conflicting propaganda, it was difficult to know which organization was good, and which was questionable.

Every man had to make his own decision, according to his own temperament and according to the position he had reached. Many, at the head of factories or of important public services, considered that from both the social and the patriotic point of view they had no right to abandon the employees under them.

For others, it was not easy to escape and join the Allies. The frontiers everywhere were closely guarded by the Axis. A few fortunate ones managed to escape in English planes taking off from secret landing fields in France, or else by submarine from the coast of Provence. But the majority had no such opportunities or never had the necessary contacts to acquire them. For them, the only road to Algiers was by smugglers' paths over the Pyrenees to Spain, which carried with it the almost certain internment in the Spanish camp of Miranda. Even so, by January of 1944, over 1,600 men of the Navy, of whom 190 were officers or student officers, had taken that route.

But all of the naval personnel who thus left France, as well as those serving in North Africa at the time of the Allied landings, were faced with the distressing problem of how to support their families in France. The French Admiralty at Vichy had already provided for the support of the dependents of the men fighting in the ranks of the F.F.N.F., so they applied the same system for those in North Africa who reentered the war there. One of the first things Admiral Bléhaut did, after he had found a way to communicate with Algiers, was to assure the officers and men who had returned to fight that their families would be taken care of. In June, 1943, a message was sent to Admiral Lemonnier, via the French naval attaché in Madrid, which concluded with these words: "Do not be worried about your families, as we are looking after them with the greatest care." Algiers sent word back through the same channels that the message had been received and the assurance was greatly appreciated. The crews themselves were also informed by an all-Navy message that the subsistence of their families in France was assured.

This carefully devised welfare program almost came to grief, however, when the Government at Vichy, at the demand of the occupying power, was forced to take in some rabid advocates of collaboration with Hitler. Further, the Paris press raged against those wives of Free French admirals who were continuing to draw dependents' allotments.

Mr. Laval wished to set up an interministerial committee to check the list of beneficiaries. Aware that the Germans would certainly have collaborators amid such a committee. Admiral Bléhaut quickly took personal action. At that time he had jurisdiction over 18,000 out of the 19,000 families receiving these allotments, and he had no intention of sharing that task with anyone. He simply refused to consider such a committee, and, up to the very end of hostilities, the families of the men fighting overseas had their material existence assured.

However, the great majority of the demobilized naval personnel, like the rest of the population, could do nothing except remain in France. Some of them joined the local resistance groups and found themselves in the ranks of the Maquis when the final fighting took place. Lieutenant Commander

Jacques du Garreau became the chief of the F.F.I. (French Forces of the Interior) at Sisteron, in the Lower Alps. In central France, Lieutenant Pierre Bordes organized the attacks on many a German road convoy. Lieutenant (junior grade) Jacques Farnarier, with the F.F.I. of Finistère, directed reconnaissance against the Germans in Brest at the time of the siege. Lieutenant Commander Pierre Bugard, of the Medical Corps, organized the health service of the F.F.I. of Dunkirk. These officers are mentioned only as examples; it would be impossible to compile the complete list of all those who served in the Resistance.

Some men put their maritime experience to particular use. The merchant marine units and the network of naval police and firemen constituted the framework for an ideal intelligence organization which expanded tremendously during 1943. They kept track daily of every change in the German coastal defenses, of the movements of all ships, and of the results of air attacks, and transmitted them to the Allies by various means. In this they were assisted by practically the entire maritime population, who watched and reported what they saw to the men they knew they could trust: administrative officers of the naval recruiting service, naval medical officers on detached duty in seaports, etc.

In every grade, the naval personnel assigned to the Ministry of Post and Telegraph knew how to take full opportunity of the possibilities afforded by their positions. For example, Chief Radioman Jean Morvan, in his position of tester and trouble man at the post office of Lagny, listened in on enemy telephone communications for the benefit of the F.F.I. He also, when occasion required, disrupted the German communication lines.

As the time for liberation approached, countersabotage groups were organized all along the coast to prevent damage and destruction to installations by the Germans in their retreat. At Dieppe, the port captain was able to prevent the departing Germans from blocking the entrances to the wet docks, thus making them serviceable immediately the Allies entered. At Sète, the French themselves so ingeniously carried out, beforehand, an apparently thorough destruction of harbor installations and equipment that the Germans thought these were completely useless, whereas only a little work and care were needed to repair the superficial damage.

Whatever had been their choice during the days of the occupation, when the opportunity to fight again presented itself, the men of the Navy, whether on active duty or not, thought only of serving their country to the best of their ability.[7a]

[7a] Translator's Note: The armistice terms forbade the French from collecting information on the Axis powers. Nevertheless, certain Ministries at Vichy and the intelligence units of the three military services continued to do so in great secrecy. The Germans would have imposed harsh penalties if they had obtained proof of these

But individual men were not required to depend upon their own initiative alone. The French Admiralty at Vichy had arranged to maintain contact with all demobilized regular Navy personnel throughout the country, as well as with all the reserves. After Toulon, the excess personnel were given three months leave with pay, and then placed on "armistice leave" (*congé*

---

officially-sanctioned prohibited activities. It was for this reason that the officers engaged in intelligence work were extremely cautious in passing such information to Allied or neutral representatives unless they were reasonably certain that their actions met with the approval, explicitly stated or implied, of their superior officer. It was not until Admiral Auphan became Minister of the Navy, that I (U.S. Naval Attaché at Vichy) began receiving information on the Axis from French Naval Intelligence—and then not directly but by a devious channel.

After his retirement in November, 1942, Admiral Auphan endeavored to establish contact with General Giraud. When he was unable to do this, he formed and maintained steady secret contacts with General Georges Revers, leader of the underground Resistance Organization of the Army. As liberation approached, Auphan busied himself with planning measures which would limit the destruction the Germans would not fail to attempt before retreating from France. German counterintelligence finally became aware of the admiral's activities and he had to go in hiding for some time. He was hidden by his parish priest. Shortly after the liberation of Paris, Admiral Auphan made contact with Commander Thomas G. Cassady, U.S.N., the former Assistant Naval Attaché at Vichy and at that time with the O.S.S. I have it from Comdr. Cassady that the admiral and Captain Pierre Samson, ex-Chief of Naval Intelligence at Vichy, were always most cooperative and on several occasions were of great assistance to him in carrying out his intelligence duties.

Jacques Mordal, who had served as one of Admiral Auphan's confidential assistants for six months while the latter was Minister of the Navy, requested to be returned to his regular duties as a medical officer when the admiral resigned. After the scuttling of the Fleet at Toulon, Mordal was assigned as medical officer to the personnel of the merchant and fishing fleets on the Channel coast from Dunkirk to Le Havre. "It was a golden opportunity to carry out intelligence work," he once told me, "and it would have been a pity not to have taken advantage of the opportunity. I travelled constantly—naturally with a German *aussweiss* (pass)—and everywhere I went I received the utmost assistance from the personnel of the Navy, and of the merchant and fishing fleets. The German officer who renewed my *aussweiss* each week never failed to impress on me the necessity of obeying promptly all challenges by sentries. And he would add 'We would be distressed if anything should happen to you!'"

Apparently the Germans did not suspect Mordal. However, one day in January, 1944, he thought his end had come. While returning from clandestinely inspecting some new German works at Cape Antifer (near Le Havre), he was arrested by a German soldier and taken to an officer for questioning. At the end of two hours the officer informed him that he had been reported for asking directions in French—French with a pronounced English accent. In spite of his precarious situation—he carried compromising papers on his person—Mordal burst out laughing. He asked the German officer if he would not give him a written statement to that effect so that it could be sent to his English professor who, in yesteryears at college, had dispaired of his lamentable accent. In his turn the German laughed too and released Mordal—without having him searched.

d'armistice) with half pay, but under conditions that enabled the Director of Personnel of the Fleet to recall them at any moment. A special service, the S.S.P.D. (Statistical Service for Demobilized Personnel) was set up at Lyons, presumably merely to assemble statistics on personnel separated from the service; in reality it was a clandestine mobilization center working in close liaison with all the S.L.O.M. groups (local Navy relief groups).

The S.L.O.M. had been created in 1940 to assist sailors and their families in adjusting themselves to the difficult new conditions of life. By 1944 it had greatly expanded, and reported to a central headquarters at Vichy. Extending all over France, in the northern zone as well as in the southern, and carefully concealing its activities under a label of social welfare, it formed an organization ready-made for effective work when the moment came.

Admiral Bléhaut not only knew of, and officially approved, all these activities, but had his administrative officer, Captain Charles Jacquinet, serve as coordinator. Any cooperation of this kind was extremely dangerous, as the German police were eternally vigilant.

Arrests were on the increase. At Vichy, officers of the naval intelligence were arrested in their hotel. What the Germans were after was to locate all former Alsatian naval personnel in order to induct them forcibly into the Kriegsmarine. The French Navy had foreseen this, and had protected the Alsatian sailors by giving them false papers.

At the same time, with every day that the war continued, the number of ex-Navy men attempting to escape to North Africa or to join the resistance groups was increasing. And only too many of them fell victims to the German police. Some were deported to German concentration camps, from which many did not return; some fell under the bullets of firing squads. Among those who thus joined the Valhalla into which d'Estienne d'Orves, de Saussine, Petty Officer Anquetil, and Engineer Stosskopf had already entered, were Commander Henri Vaillant, Chief of Naval Security at Vichy, arrested on January 12, 1944, and Lieutenant Henri de Pimodan, arrested on February 3, neither of whom ever returned. Also Petty Officer Pierre Briout, who parachuted into France on several occasions and was killed in his last mission; Captain Jacques Trolley de Prévaux, who disappeared on August 19, and whose wife was executed on the same day. Also Lieutenant (junior grade) Richard, arrested and executed while he was organizing countersabotage groups to protect the merchant ships at anchor in the Berre Pond; and Lieutenant Charles Bonal, captured and executed just as he was about to slip across the Spanish border. All these—and how many others!

More fortunate was Commander Louis Pothuau, arrested on November 26, 1943, while trying to escape by submarine to Algeria; he lived to return from deportation and ended his career as a vice admiral and Deputy Chief of Naval Operations. And Commander Edouard Jozan, arrested the first time by the Gestapo at Bizerte in December, 1942, then released, only to be rearrested in France at Luchon in March, 1943, and interned at Oranienburg; he lived to become vice admiral in command of the Mediterranean Squadron. And Admiral de Penfentenyo de Kervéréguin, of Lorient fame, who was arrested merely for giving a lecture, but was fortunate enough to escape the consequences.

Yet it was not only personnel problems with which the Navy was concerned. There were the ships at Toulon—scuttled ships, yet still objects of prime importance.

The harbor of Toulon was shallow, and to be sunk there did not imply permanent destruction. The hulls were barely submerged, the masts and spars of many extending above the water. It was more than a possibility that the ships which had not been completely wrecked by fire or explosion would be raised and repaired by the Axis. To carry out the promise that had been made to the British at Bordeaux—that the French Fleet would never be allowed to fall into the hands of the Germans—something would have to be done.

That was the problem which Admiral Abrial and Admiral Bléhaut, one after the other, worked on—not merely to prevent the Germans from utilizing salvaged ships, but also to save them for France as the nucleus of the new French Navy-to-be.

With that in mind, a naval command was maintained at Toulon. Rear Admiral Henri Danbé was well endowed with what the English call "devotion to service" to accept that command under such desperate circumstances.

At the time of the invasion of the Free Zone, the French coastal region up to the Rhone River had been placed under the jurisdiction of Italian Admiral Vincenzo De Féo, who was replaced on December 15 by Admiral Vittorio Tur. But under the secret schedule for Operation Attila, which had been rigidly held from the Italians' knowledge, the German Navy had reserved for itself the Toulon navy yard as a German enclave, under the command of Rear Admiral Reinhardt Scheer. This officer was later replaced by a naval constructor, Dr. Graeber, who, in addition to the navy yard, had supervision of the private shipyard at La Seyne. This state of affairs continued until the Italian armistice on September 9, 1943, at which time the Wehrmacht extended its hold to include the entire coastal region.

As was pointed out earlier, the German Navy had had no part in the attack on Toulon, whose prime mover was Marshal Keitel. In fact, Admiral Raeder had been opposed to it from the first, and Admirals Karl Hoffmann and Paul Wever and Lieutenant Commander Ruault-Frappart, the German Navy's representatives at Wiesbaden and Toulon, requested to be relieved of their duties immediately after the invasion of November 27, 1942. As a matter of fact the German Navy was interested in the Toulon Fleet only to the extent that they did not want it to join the Allies. As to utilizing it themselves, they knew full well that even if they managed to lay their hands on it, it would take them months to put it into shape where it could be used.

But if the German Navy did not want the sunken ships for themselves, the Italians did—not so much to increase the strength of their own fleet as to prevent them becoming the nucleus of a resurrected French Navy after the war.

They lost no moment in taking advantage of the situation. Profiting by the pronouncement by the Germans on December 3 that "all ships of war belonging to the French State are confiscated," they appropriated to themselves the lion's share of the sunken fleet. Out of 70 scuttled ships of a total tonnage of 237,049, they modestly reserved for themselves 212,559 tons, leaving their German partners only 24,490 tons of small units.

A swarm of Italian engineers descended on Toulon. *L'Ente Recuperi Italiani a Tolone* (The Italian Salvage Company at Toulon), headed by Chief Naval Constructor Odourdo Giannelli, quickly brought the pick of the personnel and equipment of all the Italian salvage companies to the job. On December 22, the Italian Navy appointed a captain to the command of the few ships that could be quickly salvaged. And in early January, 1943, despite the protests of the French Admiralty against this flagrant violation of the armistice terms of 1940, they took over the super-destroyers *Lion,* *Tigre,* and *Panthère,* and the destroyer *Trombe.*[8]

Working with the greatest energy, by June the Italian engineers had either afloat or in drydock three cruisers, seven super-destroyers, and the seaplane tender *Commandant Teste.* Three months later, at the time of the Italian armistice, the number of ships they had raised numbered thirty. This number did not include four minesweeping sloops and three small torpedo boats which had been salvaged by the Germans, or those other vessels, not fit for repair, which were being marked for scrapping. From these ships went shiploads and trainloads of equipment and scrap metal to Italy—the aircraft catapults, the superstructure and the armor plate of one turret from the *Strasbourg,* the conning tower and interior fittings of the *Dunkerque,* and everything removable from the waterline up in the 10,000-ton cruisers.

Even the downfall of Benito Mussolini on July 25, 1943, did not stop this seizure. Despite French protests, the Italians, who had already taken over the destroyer *Siroco* in June, added to it the destroyers *Lansquenet* and *Hardi* and the submarine *Henri Poincaré* in August and September.

---

[8] These were ships which, because of the absence of crews aboard, it had been impossible to properly destroy.

These dates are significant. Ever since August 1, the Badoglio Government had been preparing to treat with the Allies. Actual negotiations began at Lisbon on August 19. At the time the *Hardi* was towed away from Toulon during the night of September 6, three days had already gone by since the armistice had been signed, although it was not to be announced until the 9th. Thus it was that the *Hardi,* scuttled and then raised at Toulon, was scuttled again only a few days later, this time by the Italians themselves, at Savona, to keep it from falling into the hands of the Germans.

Without a doubt the General Staff of the Italian Navy could honestly say that they had no knowledge of these top secret armistice negotiations. They could also argue that by towing the ships to Italy they were taking them out of reach of the Germans at Toulon. But since so many of the salvaged ships were to fall into the hands of the Germans again at Genoa and Imperia, in the long run it did not make much difference. But one can readily see why the French Navy, at the treaty of 1947 with Italy, insisted on that country turning over to France two light cruisers and four super-destroyers as just compensation for those French naval ships which had been confiscated by the Italians.

Immediately the Italian negotiations with the Allies were known, the Germans seized and interned all the Italians engaged in the salvaging operations at Toulon. Admiral Bléhaut, at Vichy, seized this opportunity to send a note to the Germans, via Laval, calling to their attention that he had always considered the squadron at Toulon was to serve as the nucleus of the future French Fleet. He therefore requested that the French Navy be permitted to place shipkeepers on board all ships that had been refloated, in order to guard and preserve them for this purpose.

The negotiations were skillfully conducted at Wiesbaden by Captain Jean Estienne, Chief of the Naval Sub-Commission for the French Delegation, and were supported at Toulon through the good offices of Lieutenant Commander Ruault-Frappart of the German Navy.[9]

These negotiations with the Germans encountered quite a different atmosphere from those attempted with the Italians. For one thing the Kriegsmarine realized that, except for submarines, the war at sea was practically

---

[9] Ruault-Frappart said to a French officer, in August, 1944, "I tried to save the Fleet by attempting to dissuade the Wehrmacht from attacking Toulon. I failed in that. However, I did succeed in concluding negotiations that were favorable to your Fleet. If I fail now in this attempt to take care of your ports and your ships, I will be driven to despair." He had previously said to another officer, "If ever two German officers have merited the Legion of Honor, they would be Commander Pezold and myself." Commander Gustav Pezold was one of the members of the German Naval Commission at Wiesbaden.

over in the Mediterranean. As to the future, it did not have the same feeling of rivalry toward the French Navy that the Italians had,[10] though it was concerned with the half dozen small craft and 600-ton torpedo boats which it had raised and which it claimed were no longer covered by Article 8 of the 1940 armistice.[11]

Consequently, on September 25, 1943, the Germans admitted as a matter of principle that all the other wrecks at Toulon were the property of the French Navy. They held, however, that the French ships they had seized at Bizerte on December 8, 1942, had been acquired under quite different circumstances and were therefore legally theirs. Nevertheless, when the French refused to give them the builders' plans for the sloops *Commandant Rivière* and *Batailleuse,* of the Bizerte fleet, they did not insist on obtaining these plans.

Agreement was finally reached on the whole matter on April 1, 1944. By it, the Kriegsmarine permitted the French Navy the right of taking preservation measures in the case of ships sufficiently salvagable to have military value: the battleships *Strasbourg* and *Dunkerque,* the seaplane tender *Com-*

---

[10] The understanding attitude of the members of the Naval Sub-Committee of the German Armistice Commission at Wiesbaden has already been described. But the following incident is even more characteristic of the chivalrous attitude that still seems to typify the warriors of the sea, enemies though they may be.

On September 12, 1942, the submarine *U-156* torpedoed the British ship *Laconia* off the Gulf of Guinea. The *Laconia* had aboard 3,800 persons, including 1,800 Italian prisoners. When he learned this, the captain of the *U-156* alerted all Axis submarines in the area, while the German Armistice Commission at Wiesbaden asked the French Admiralty to order out ships by radio from Dakar. The French cruiser *Gloire* and the sloops *Dumont d'Urville* and *Annamite* participated in this rescue, which was without precedent in the annals of submarine warfare, and brought back 1,083 survivors, of whom 415 were Italians.

The grateful enemy asked the crews of the rescuing ships for the names of relatives or friends who were prisoners in Germany, with the idea of releasing an equivalent number. The requested lists had not been in their hands fifteen days when the French ships involved reentered the war against the Axis. For the Germans to keep their word under these circumstances required the height of magnanimity, especially since there were those of Hitler's entourage who were not so punctilious. The locating of the imprisoned relatives and friends took a long time, and in fact was not completed until six weeks after the Allied landings in Normandy and at a time when already the whole of France was rising against the invaders. Nevertheless, on July 10, 1944, some 358 French prisoners were thus delivered by the Germans at Compiègne, to be freed —only 57 short of the 415 Italians who had been rescued from the sinking *Laconia.* There was never time enough to fill out the full number for parity.

[11] This was the article by which Germany engaged herself not to put forward any claims on the French Fleet, either during hostilities or at the conclusion of peace. One of the legal advisers of the Germans argued that this article applied only to an intact fleet, and not to a scuttled fleet.

mandant Teste, the cruiser *La Galissonnière,* and four 1,800-ton destroyers, the *Foudroyant, Adroit, Casque,* and *Mameluk.*[12]

The old battleships *Provence* and *Océan* were too decrepit to be worth repairing; in addition the *Océan* had been used as a target ship for testing underwater explosives.[13]

The cruisers *Colbert, Foch, Dupleix, Algérie,* and *Marseillaise* were also considered beyond repair and were marked for scrapping.

The command of the ships to be salvaged and eventually repaired for re-incorporation in the French Navy was entrusted to Captain Emile Rosset,[14] who assembled a working force of 150 or 200 carefully chosen sailors. To remove the *Strasbourg* and *La Galissonnière* from their dangerous proximity to the Germans, and hence liability to Allied bombings, he had slips dug for them in the banks of the Bay of Lazaret, quite apart from the Toulon roads.

Toulon had not suffered as much from the earlier Allied bombings as Brest and Lorient. However, after the Italian armistice the attacks on Toulon began in earnest, and in the great Allied air raid of November 24, 1943, a dozen or more ships which the Italians had previously raised, were sent to the bottom a second time or else seriously damaged.[15] Other heavy Allied attacks occurred during the first half of 1944. In the raid of March 11, 1944, the naval district headquarters were destroyed, many buildings in the yard wrecked, and another half dozen refloated ships were sunk for a second time. By August, only some 20 ships remained afloat out of the 35 or more that had been refloated. And all of these would disappear under the bombs of the Allies when the final battle for Toulon occurred.

Such spectacular results cannot be attributed solely to the skill of the Allied bombers. Actually, these were aiming at the German submarines in Toulon. Furthermore, the raised ships had no crews, no effective antiaircraft defense, no firefighting groups nor damage control installations to extinguish fires and maintain watertight conditions.

---

[12] The *Adroit* had formerly been the *Epée,* and the *Foudroyant,* the *Fleuret,* but had been rechristened to honor two 1,500-ton destroyers lost during the Dunkirk evacuation.

[13] The *Dunkerque* was in such poor condition it was scarcely believed that she could be repaired. The Germans requested that her bow be removed so that the rest of her could be floated out of drydock, which they wished to use for their own ships.

[14] Later a vice admiral and Deputy Chief of Naval Operations.

[15] The combat ships thus sent to the bottom a second time, on November 24, 1943, were the *Aigle, Baliste, Chamois, Naïade, Bayonnaise,* and *Jean de Vienne* (capsized and gutted while lying in the dock). Ships damaged were *La Galissonnière, Volta, Mogador,* and *Dédaigneuse.*

Sunk in February, 1944, were the *Vautour* and the *Sirène,* and on March 23, 1944, the *Caïman, Gerfaut, Guépard, Pascal,* and *Redoutable,* and the salvaged wreck of the *Dupleix.*

Another threat, equally great or even greater than the Allied air attacks, hung over the coast of France. Even before the Allied landings in southern France, the Germans had made preparations for, and had actually begun, the systematic destruction of all harbor installations on the French Mediterranean coast. The French protested immediately and vigorously. On June 28, 1944, Admiral Bléhaut wrote an urgent letter of protest to Admiral Theodor Krancke, commanding the Kriegsmarine in France. The matter was referred to Admiral Dönitz, who very generously, though unsuccessfully, protested personally to the Army General Headquarters (O.K.W.) against these destructions, which he considered both senseless and useless. At Toulon, Admiral Heinrich Ruhfus was sympathetic, but stated that he was under strict orders from above.

Already the German engineers were placing the depth charges. The Cronstadt Quay—the famous "Quay of the Port"—was threatened with destruction. Worse still, preparations were being made to blow up the ancient main gate of the navy yard, a thing of no military importance, but of great historical value.

Admiral Danbé sent Captain Gilles de Maupéou to the German admiral's headquarters with a personal plea that this venerable and inoffensive landmark be preserved.

Admiral Ruhfus relented. "But I am going beyond my instructions," he declared to Captain de Maupéou. "You will have to feed me when I am sent to the galleys!"

Three hours later the blasting charges were removed from the gate. Saved also was the Lazaret Quay, near which were anchored the ships of Captain Rosset's group. But all the remaining installations of the great Toulon base were destroyed.

CHAPTER 26

Normandy and the Beginning of the Liberation

It was June of 1944. Four long years since the tragic spring of 1940. Four years that the enemy had been garrisoned in France, twenty months since he had occupied the whole country.

How much longer? How much longer before liberation?

That liberation was approaching, was almost there, but the only awareness France had was of the sufferings incidental to the gigantic Allied air attacks which had been taking place for weeks over the whole coast, over the communication centers, over the railway lines and the marshalling yards. The railway between Paris and Le Havre had been cut in fourteen places. Between Paris and the sea there remained not one bridge standing over the Seine. The last to go, the ones at Rouen, had been blasted away—but only after twenty mass bomber raids spread out over what is still called "the red week of Rouen." Close to 3,000 civilians lost their lives in that week.

Gifted seers might have detected in all these attacks some definite pattern, some definite strategic purpose. But what that purpose was—what direction it would take—was difficult for those in France to see at that time, particularly since the Normandy coast was not the only target of the Allied bombers. They spread their destruction almost without distinction—in the most unexpected places—at Boulogne as at Annecy. Some even believed that the Allies had given up the idea of a landing at all, confident that their airpower alone would bring Germany to her knees.

Yet the hour of liberation was approaching.

On April 14, 1944, the cruisers *Montcalm,* commanded by Captain Joseph Laurin, and *Georges Leygues,* under Captain Edouard Deprez, left

Mers-el-Kebir for an unknown destination. All they knew was that their division commander was Rear Admiral Robert Jaujard; that new propellers had been installed in the *Montcalm;* that they had received new 152-mm. shells, manufactured in America; that they had completed a strenuous series of target practices. But, off Gibraltar, as they headed north, morale began to soar. They suddenly realized that this time they were bound for the *great adventure.*

That adventure led them first to the River Clyde, to wait for D-day. Behind them the *Gloire* sulkily remained in the Mediterranean. She was busy ferrying the 9th Colonial Infantry Division to Corsica, where it would jump off on the operation to recapture Elba.

But no naval officers represented France on the general staff which had been drawing up the plans for "Operation Neptune," the naval part of the Normandy landings. True, the limited resources of the French Navy permitted it to make only a modest contribution to this gigantic undertaking, but it would surely have been to the advantage of the Allies to make use of a few of the experienced officers who had served, before or during the war, on the Channel coast. In particular it would have helped them in assessing the enormous mass of miscellaneous information that flowed in from the 35 or 40 intelligence networks that were operating along the coast. And even more useful could have been that splendid corps, the Pilots of the Fleet. These especially trained petty officers, veritable walking editions of the *Pilotage Instructions,* had over the years acquired a most complete knowledge of the French Atlantic and Channel ports. There were numbers of them serving even then in North Africa, and others could have been recruited even closer from the Occupied Zone.

Regardless of other things, the Allies planned on employing only Anglo-American troops for the assault landings. As Admiral Hewitt was to remark to General de Lattre de Tassigny, when similar dispositions were made later for the landings in Provence, amphibious operations were complicated enough without adding to them the difficulties inherent in language differences. Only a few French commandoes went in with the assault waves. The first large French unit, the 2nd French Armored Division of General Leclerc, did not land in Normandy until August 2, fifty-seven days after D-day.

Language differences were not such a drawback in naval operations, however, so the French cruisers and smaller units were included in the supporting forces.

The battleships of the French Navy did not participate in the Normandy landings, nor did the heavy cruisers, because these were considered insufficiently protected against air attacks. However, the heavy cruiser *Duquesne* served as a supply ship for Admiral Jaujard's division. Other than the *Montcalm* and the *Georges Leygues,* the only French ships participating in

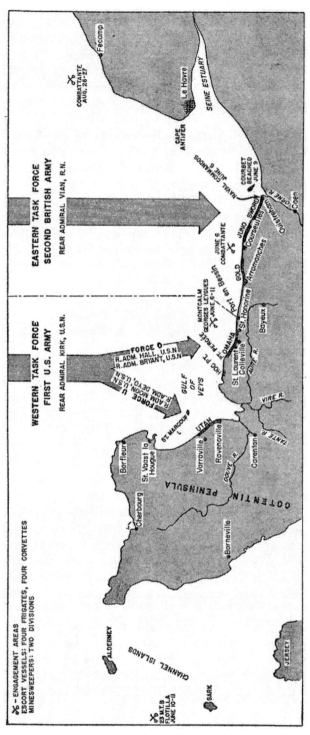

The Landings in Normandy

the Normandy landings were one destroyer, four frigates, four corvettes, one flotilla of MTBs, and two divisions of minesweepers.[1]

The two cruisers formed part of the actual fire support for the assault, the corvettes and frigates acted as escorts to convoy the assault troops across the Channel. The minesweepers operated at the beginning along the English coast, and then later in the Arromanches sector off the French coast.

The beaches chosen for the landings extended along the Bay of the Seine from Caen, at the mouth of the Orne River, on the east, to the Cotentin Peninsula, on the west. The British sector extended from the Orne to Port-en-Bessin, the American sector along the Gulf of Veys, that indentation formed by the estuary of the four rivers flowing into the Channel east of the Cotentin.

The naval part of the undertaking was under the command of Admiral Sir Bertram Ramsay—the same Admiral Ramsay who had played such a prominent part in the evacuation of Dunkirk. It was only poetic justice that now he should again have the leading role in the operation that would bring those same troops back victoriously to the coast from which they had been driven.

Under Admiral Ramsay, Rear Admiral Sir Philip Vian, R.N., commanded the Eastern Task Force, whose mission was to land the Second British Army between Arromanches and the Orne River. The Western Task Force,[2] under the command of Rear Admiral Alan G. Kirk, U.S.N., had as its mission the landing of the First American Army at locations east and west of Carentan, which would henceforth be historically known as Omaha and Utah Beaches.

There will be no attempt to give here more than the barest outline of Operation Neptune, the naval part of the over-all "Operation Overlord." More than 4,000 ships took part in this operation, the detailed plans of which alone exceeded 1,100 printed pages.

It was June 3, at 2:30 in the morning, that Admiral Jaujard's two cruisers got under way from Belfast, to join Rear Admiral Carleton F. Bryant,

---

[1] Destroyer *Combattante* (Lieutenant Commander André Patou); frigates *Aventure* (Commander Jean Querville), *Escarmouche* (Lieutenant Commander Jacques de Lesquen), *Découverte* (Lieutenant Commander Jean Récher), and *Surprise* (Lieutenant Commander Jean Levasseur); corvettes *Roselys* (Lieutenant Commander René Kolb-Bernard), *Aconit* (Lieutenant Charles Le Millier), *Renoncule* (Lieutenant Raymond Mithois), and *Commandant d'Estienne d'Orves* (Lieutenant Georges Sabouret); 23 M.T.B. Flotilla (Lieutenant Pierre Iehlé).

[2] The Western Task Force consisted of Force U (Utah Beach), Rear Admiral Don P. Moon, U.S.N., with Support Group under Rear Admiral Morton L. Deyo, U.S.N.; and Force O (Omaha Beach), Rear Admiral John L. Hall, Jr., U.S.N., with Support Group under Rear Admiral Carleton F. Bryant, U.S.N.

U.S.N., commanding the Support Force for Omaha Beach. This force consisted of the U.S. battleships *Texas* and *Arkansas,* the British cruisers *Glasgow* and *Bellona,* the French cruisers *Montcalm* and *Georges Leygues,* and a screen of a dozen British and American destroyers.

The group was off Plymouth at 7:30 the next morning, when orders were received delaying the operation for twelve hours. But that evening the *Texas* sent a message to the *Georges Leygues,*[3] "I believe the outlook for tomorrow is favorable." The prediction proved accurate, for an order was shortly received to resume course for the landing beaches.

After a miraculous feat of navigation,[4] considering the mass of ships crowded together in those narrow waters, the Omaha Support Force arrived at the set hour off the French coast. Already the explosions of the prelanding aerial bombardment were resounding along the whole coast. At five o'clock in the morning the *Arkansas, Montcalm,* and *Georges Leygues* anchored off Port-en-Bessin, at the eastern end of the American sector, at ranges from 6,000 to 9,000 meters from the shore. They were not scheduled to open fire until 5:50, but fifteen minutes before that time they were taken under fire by a battery of four 155-mm. guns installed at Longue, whereupon they opened fire in return and soon silenced it temporarily.

After that, the scheduled bombardment was carried out according to plan. The *Georges Leygues* and the British destroyer *Tanatside* had assigned as their target the heights of Saint-Laurent. The *Montcalm* fired for ten minutes at the slopes of Sainte-Honorine, and then shifted fire to Port-en-Bessin.

At the beginning the landings seemed to be progressing everywhere in a most satisfactory manner. But the German heavy batteries were far from being permanently neutralized. On several occasions the battery at Longue, as well as another battery of 170-mm. guns which appeared to be placed somewhere near the tip of Hoc Point,[5] opened fire on the beaches and the ships. There were several very critical moments, especially when the guns at Longue opened up just as the landing craft of the second assault wave

---

[3] The nickname which the American signalmen gave the *Georges Leygues* was "George's legs."

[4] "I can but express my admiration for the manner in which the many convoys navigated and maneuvered. At least a good thousand ships of all types and all sizes must have steamed through swept channels No. 3 and No. 4. In approximately two hours that large group took their stations in the transport zone without, so far as I know, a single collision taking place." *Report of Admiral Jaujard.*

[5] Actually there was no battery on the tip of Point Hoc, and the Americans could have spared themselves the effort of the heroic and glorious expedition of Colonel James E. Rudder's Rangers, who scaled the cliff in broad daylight—only to find that the guns were wooden dummies! The real guns had been moved back to the rear several days previously.

were approaching the beach. The *Arkansas* and *Georges Leygues* immediately took them under counterbattery fire and succeeded in definitely silencing that obstinate battery.[6]

The night following that exciting day was relatively quiet except for an enemy air raid, during which the French cruisers shot down one of the attacking planes. In the days that followed, the cruisers gave fire support as requested, until the Anglo-American troops they supported had advanced inland beyond the range of their 152-mm. guns. On the two days of June 7 and 8 alone, the *Montcalm* fired a total of 369 shells, and the *Georges Leygues* 211. On June 15, Admiral Jaujard's division was sent back to Milford Haven to replenish its ammunition, fuel, and supplies before leaving for the Mediterranean—and a similar role in the Provence landings to come.

But the ten days of operations off Port-en-Bessin had given the *Georges Leygues* the opportunity to make the first contact with a liberated French village. Finding that an English commando group had arrived at Port-en-Bessin, Captain Laurin sent a boat in. He had the satisfaction of learning then that the gunfire of the Allied ships had caused no casualties among the inhabitants. But some sixty cows *had* been killed, and the village mayor, not at all pleased, wanted to know who was going to pay for the damages!

At the opposite end of the sector the destroyer *Combattante* had operated on the right flank of the British Force J during the assault on the beaches west of Courseulles. Part of a group including four British ships, it silenced an enemy battery during the first day, at cost of one man wounded by an enemy shell fragment.

Returning to Portsmouth after a brief stay on the firing line, the *Combattante* went again to Courseulles on June 14 in order to permit General de Gaulle to visit the liberated sector. After that she was engaged mostly in patrol duty between the English coast and Barfleur and Cape Antifer.

It was in the British sector, also, that the only French actually to participate in the first assault were engaged. These men were part of the naval commandos previously organized within the F.F.N.F. in England under the command of Lieutenant Jean Kieffer. At 7 A.M. on June 6, these commandos, 171 in number, landed in front of Ouistreham, which they captured from the Germans at a cost of 15 killed and 30 wounded—a good quarter of their strength.

The frigates and corvettes, which had been assigned to escort duty, were active from the opening day. Some of them made as many as eighteen trips

---

[6] The gunners of the *Georges Leygues* visited this battery later and were gratified to find shell fragments from their own projectiles which had entered the casemates through the embrasures.

per month between England and the beaches of Omaha, Saint-Vaast-la-Hougue, and elsewhere. On June 10, the *Surprise* struck a mine in the vicinity of Point Percée and had to be towed back to Portsmouth. During the night of the 22nd, Commander Jean Querville's 108th Independent Escort Group, composed of the *Aventure, Escarmouche, Aconit,* and *Renoncule,* had to fight off a squadron of German JU-88s, with one of the attackers being shot down by the *Aventure.* In addition there were several submarine warnings. The Group followed up these with depth charge attacks, but without result.

After August 11, the *Découverte* was engaged in ferrying supplies to the Third U.S. Army, which, after seizing Saint-Malo, was plunging westward along the shores of Brittany. A little later, the *Combattante* was sent in to block the Germans, who were trying to evacuate Le Havre at night by sea. Despite the covering fire of the German coast defense batteries at Fécamp, she sank or damaged three or four of the evacuation craft.

Even the old battleship, *Courbet,* commanded by Captain Roger Wietzel, had a part in the proceedings. Stripped of everything useful, she was towed to Ouistreham and sunk there in shallow water, along with several other old ships, to form a protective breakwater for the steady flow of men and supplies into France.

Throughout the entire operation the MTBs of the 23rd Flotilla were constantly on reconnaissance in the Channel. On the night of June 10 they had a stiff brush with three enemy light craft off Guernsey. *MTB 98* got in a torpedo hit, but in turn received answering fire that wounded two officers —one of them her commander, Lieutenant (junior grade) Roger Lagersie. After the entire summer in this business, they were shifted to Brittany to be ready for the attack on Brest.

Meantime the objective of the American forces landed at Utah Beach had shifted from getting a toehold ashore to the capture of Cherbourg itself. The two Allied artificial harbors at Arromanches and Saint-Laurent had sufficed for the first couple of weeks of the landings, but the steady supplying of the ever increasing armies ashore required regular harbor facilities— especially after the American harbor at Saint-Laurent had been destroyed by the great storm of June 19.

The port of Cherbourg fell to the American land attack on June 27, but only after severe fighting. The Germans' main objective in this resistance was to gain time to destroy the port facilities in order to render them unusable by the Allies. Everything was methodically dynamited, so that the roadstead and harbor were left cluttered with 110 wrecks, not to mention hundreds of artfully placed mines. But the salvage crews of Commodore William A. Sullivan, U.S.N., worked so efficiently that the harbor was quickly cleared and, during the next three months, 2,137 large ships docked there to unload 2,827,000 tons of munitions, food, and other supplies for the armies moving inland. This was exclusive of the vast amount of gasoline delivered by the underwater pipeline which had been laid from England to France.[7]

Allied planning had not provided for any French contribution to the actual assault on Cherbourg, but when the Americans entered the port they found at their posts in the naval base approximately 500 officers and men of the French Navy, who, through the whole four years of German occupation, had devotedly watched over the French Government property there. Now, under the command of Captain Pierre de Robien, who had helped defend Cherbourg to the last in 1940, these officers and men went to work for the Allies. They recovered and repaired everything that could be of use—the naval hospital, the submarine repair shop, parts of the supply department, etc. For the time being, the Americans kept control of everything concerned with operations, such as the naval air bases of Chentereyne and Querqueville, but, from November on, the French naval command gradually took over the direction of all the services at Cherbourg.

With the additional facilities provided by the unloading installations at Cherbourg, the Allied armies continued their sweep inland, liberating the western coasts of France almost as rapidly as they had been overrun by the Germans in 1940. With the Third American Army advancing rapidly in Brittany, it was expected that Brest, at the extremity of the Breton Peninsula, would be recaptured within the matter of days.

But, faithful to his principle of defending fortified places to the end, and furious at the fall of Cherbourg, Hitler had issued "no surrender" orders to his commanders everywhere on the coast. In accordance with these orders 45,000 Germans dug in behind the massive fortifications of Saint-Malo, Brest, Lorient, and Saint-Nazaire.

The German commanders who received these orders were as skillful as they were obstinate. They would render many of the western harbors unusable for the Allies, whether completely destroyed, like Le Havre, desperately defended, like La Pallice, or blocked, like Bordeaux or Antwerp. Antwerp, though captured on September 4, did not receive its first Allied convoy until November 28. Bordeaux, liberated on August 28, 1944, was blocked to Allied shipping until the German strong points at Royan and Pointe de Grave, preventing access from the sea, were liquidated near the end of April, 1945. The lack of harbors for unloading was to be responsible for halting General Patton's offensive in Lorraine, when he was stopped, not on account of enemy resistance, but for lack of ammunition and gasoline to keep his tanks moving.

---

[7] This was the famous PLUTO (Pipe Line Under the Ocean).

It would have been desirable to liquidate these pockets of German resistance in the rear of the Allied lines as quickly as possible. But in those first months the Allies could not land sufficient forces and supplies in France to do this and at the same time press hot on the heels of the German armies withdrawing toward the German frontiers. Choice had to be made between opening the ports as quickly as possible to speed up the supply of personnel and material, or driving to the Rhine with whatever was then available, at the risk of being faced with a shortage of ammunition, gasoline, and food.

Under the circumstances the Allies determined to direct their drive toward the east, and leave the strongly garrisoned ports of the Gulf of Gascony for later operations. This procedure would liberate the greatest part of French territory in the least possible time, but at the cost of giving the newly appointed German commander, Field Marshal Walther von Model, time to reestablish the German front in the west. This, in turn, would make possible the dangerous German counteroffensive in the Ardennes, in December, 1944, better known to Americans as the "Battle of the Bulge."

No one, however, anticipated any great difficulty in recapturing Brest, as its garrison, in addition to the naval personnel and the antiaircraft batteries, consisted only of three battalions of infantry and a few units of fortress artillery under the command of Colonel Hans von der Mosel, who was in turn responsible to General Wilhelm Farmabacher, commanding the German XXV Army Corps in Brittany. These thinly spread garrison troops took up defensive positions in a semicircle around the city and facing inland.

Meantime the Americans advanced rapidly until, on August 7, the head of their 6th Armored Division reached Guipavas, only eight kilometers east of Brest.

It was then, with the first American shells already falling in the city, that the 2nd Parachute Division of General Hermann Ramcke, veteran of Crete and the Afrika Korps, rushed to the assistance of the defenders. Simultaneously, from the north, General Karl Spang's 266th Infantry Division fell back through the suburbs to the northwest.

Despite the efforts of the U.S. 6th Armored Division, half of General Spang's 266th Infantry succeeded in joining forces with the defenders of Brest. More serious, General Ramcke's Parachute Division took advantage of the diversion to cross the bridge at Plougastel and enter Brest with forces practically intact. Further time was gained by the defenders through the decision of the Allied command to divert the 6th Armored Division temporarily toward Lorient. As a result it took the Allies four weeks to capture the city.

Beginning with August 22, the Allies pounded the defenders with 32 batteries of heavy artillery, aided by massed formations of bombers. Even the old British battleship *Warspite* took position at the entrance to the channel in order to add the weight of its 15-inch projectiles to the thundering bombardment.

It is still a question as to which did the greater damage to Brest—the pulverizing bombardments of the Allies or the fires deliberately set by the defenders under their "scorched earth" policy. But it is a fact that when the first American patrols, led by French Navy supply officer Raymond Deshaies and his sailors, entered the port, there was nothing left of the "old city" of Brest but smoking ruins and blasted rubble.

It was during the course of this tragic siege that Admiral Négadelle, commander of the French installations in the port, perished on August 25. Two weeks later, 400 Frenchmen, in addition to 600 German soldiers, were killed by a single tremendous explosion that blasted their underground shelter in the heart of the city. These 400 were the bravest, those who had remainder at their posts to the very end—first aid volunteers, doctors, nurses, and the Mayor of Brest, Mr. Euzen.

But in contrast, another member of the French Navy who had remained at his painful post during the occupation, Commander Jean Pont, had the honor of hoisting the first French flag over the wreckage of the naval headquarters building. It was not an ordinary flag; it was the identical one which had been lowered by Commander Pont when the Germans took the city in 1940, and which ever since had been carefully hidden and reverently guarded by the naval personnel of the Captain of the Port's office.

As the siege neared its end, Captain Charles Lucas, of the French naval reserves, who had been appointed the port's commandant when it was captured, organized a company of infantry from the naval personnel who had gathered outside the city. This company, together with a similar one from Quimper, participated under American command in the operations against Brest. Afterward they were organized into the Infantry Battalion of Finistère, and took part in the siege of Lorient. On October 5, 1944, this battalion was integrated with the 4th Regiment of Naval Infantry in order to bring together all personnel of the Navy who had served with the F.F.I. (French Forces of the Interior). In December they were placed under command of the Commanding General of the French Forces of the Department of Morbihan.

CHAPTER 27

The Provence Landings and Toulon

Originally the hope had been to make landings in southern France simultaneously with those in Normandy. But a great many things interfered: opposing political concepts on the part of the Allied leaders, technical limitations, and the unexpectedly slow and difficult campaign in Italy. Since the Normandy operation had been given priority, the Provence operation would have to make use of what was left over. And there was so little left over, that it was necessary to wait for Operation Neptune-Overlord to get under way before it could possibly be determined what material would be available. It was not until June 7 that a date for the Provence landing was officially set—and then it was somewhat vague: "A day as close as possible to August 15."

For the French Navy the landing in Provence had a special sentimental appeal. It was not merely to create a diversion for the northern landings and to catch the enemy between two fires; its aim was also to liberate the great commerical port of Marseilles, and to recapture Toulon. Marseilles was needed to supply the armies in their final drive into Germany. But Toulon—Toulon was the base from which the cruisers and super-destroyers had left in 1940 for Dakar, and to which they were now returning in the van of the battleline. Toulon was the port which up to November, 1942, had constituted the sole tie between France and the empire, and which had enabled France to stick it out. Toulon was the place where the Navy had made the supreme sacrifice of scuttling half of its own strength in compliance with a pledge it had made to its allies. Only a return in force to Toulon could efface the bitter memories of that tragic period.

It is not necessary to describe in detail the enthusiasm with which the French forces in Africa entered into the undertaking. For one thing, France, both as to her Army and Navy, would have a far greater share in the operation than in any previous one. Ever since February, four French officers representing all three services had met with the Allied staffs in the college building just outside Algiers where the plans were prepared in the greatest secrecy. The French naval representative was Commander (soon to be Captain) Yann Le Hagre.[1] He would be joined later by a considerable staff.[2]

---

[1] Today a vice admiral and Commandant of the Cherbourg Naval District.

With the experience of many similar operations, the Allied services had formulated definite principles for amphibious landings. However, the French had the advantage of intimate knowledge of the terrain where the fighting would take place. As a result the French representatives were accorded a voice far out of proportion to the strength of the French forces that would be involved—especially on the naval side, where France could contribute but 50 ships. On land, though, the French Army would be on an equal footing with the American forces. Because of language difficulties, the Allied command had decided to use, in the early landing waves, only troops speaking a common language, English. However, General de Lattre de Tassigny's troops would follow immediately on their heels.

Over-all commander, since the operation was in the Mediterranean, was British General Sir Henry Maitland Wilson, with Admiral Sir John Cunningham, R.N., in over-all control of the naval operations. However, the on-the-spot commander was Vice Admiral Kent Hewitt, U.S.N., commanding the Western Task Force. General Alexander M. Patch, U.S.A., commanded the Seventh U.S. Army,[3] and Brigadier General Gordon Saville, U.S.A.A.F., the air forces.

The French Mediterranean coast extends approximately the same distance on each side of the Rhône delta, but the terrain of the two sections differs vastly. The coast of Provence, to the east, is jagged and abrupt, with steep hills rising immediately to the rear; at first sight, it appears far less inviting than the western section. There Languedoc, with its long beaches and great plains stretching inland, seems readymade for amphibious operations. But the enemy had strewn those deceptive beaches and plains with innumerable minefields, tank traps, and obstacles of all sorts.

Furthermore, ships can safely navigate almost up to the very shores of Provence, whereas the shallows extending far off the Languedoc coast are ideal for underwater mines as well as being full of sandbars. Lastly, it was in Provence that all the desirable large ports were located; Sète and Port Vendres, in Languedoc, had only limited capacity.

Provence having been selected as the general location, the choice of the specific beaches was governed by the enemy defenses—particularly the

---

[2] The staff members were Captain Robert Morin, charged with preparation of plans for restoration of the ports of Marseilles and Toulon; Lieutenant Commander Raymond Payan, preparation for naval gunfire support; Lieutenant Olivier de Rodellec, intelligence; Lieutenant Jean Ollivier, radio communications. Later on additional officers were assigned to act as guides for the American beaches and as liaison officers with the shore fire control parties.

[3] General de Tassigny's force, originally known as the "Detachment of Army B," was attached to the U.S. Seventh Army, where it was designated as the French First Army. Both it and the U.S. Seventh Army were placed under the orders of General Jacob L. Devers, U.S.A., commanding the Sixth Army Group.

340-mm. gun battery at Cape Cépet, on the Saint-Mandrier Peninsula which guards the Toulon roadstead to the south.

At the time of the construction of this battery by the French Navy in 1932, it had been one of the most powerful coast defenses in the world, dominating 80 kilometers of coastline, from La Ciotat in the west to Lavandou in the east. If it was in serviceable condition, it could render useless all the beaches in this vicinity—a fact well known to Captain Le Hagre, since he had been personally concerned with the work of installing the battery.

It was reasonable to believe that this battery, like the rest of the Toulon defenses, had been "scuttled" by its garrison on November 27, 1942. As a matter of fact, its two twin-mount turrets had been dynamited at that time. In one turret the sabotage charges had been exploded in the muzzles, splitting the barrels for more than a meter and a half, making them completely unserviceable.

But in the other, the charges had been placed in the much stronger powder chambers, putting the guns out of condition for some months but not damaging them beyond repair. Moreover, the Germans had succeeded in salvaging two 340-mm. guns from the scuttled battleship *Provence,* in Toulon harbor, and had used these to replace the two that had been definitely destroyed. At the time of the Allied landings all four guns would have been as good as ever, if courageous employees of the Toulon navy yard had not managed secretly to damage one in a second act of sabotage.[4] The preliminary air attacks of the Allies put the other turret out of action early, so that when the Allied squadrons eventually took station to silence the battery, only a single 340-mm. gun was in condition to fire.

None of this was known, of course, to the Allies at the time the operation was planned. For that matter, a single 340-mm. gun, so placed, would have been enough to work havoc in the landing areas. Consequently the planners were all agreed that the landings should be made to the east of Cape Nègre, out of reach of the Saint-Mandrier battery.

Even so, the western part of the chosen beaches lay supposedly within range of a battery of 164-mm. guns, which the Americans located at Titan. This battery was believed to be on the extreme eastern end of Levant Island, one of the Hyères group. Actually there was no longer a battery there. It had been sabotaged by the French in November, 1942, then repaired, and later shifted by the Germans to San Salvadour, on the Gulf of Giens. In its place the Germans had substituted four beautiful dummy guns of wood, which the Allied reconnaissance planes photographed so realistically that even contrary evidence by the submarine *Casabianca* had

---

[4] For his leading part in this sabotage, Foreman Richelme was afterward awarded a decoration.

no effect. In making this reconnaissance, on the night of June 8, 1944, the *Casabianca* had closed to within 10,000 meters of the supposed battery, and had dueled with a German patrol vessel for 13 minutes, without receiving one answering shot from Titan.[5]

Despite this, the American command consented to use the beautiful beach of Cavalaire only on condition that a commando raid be made on Levant Island beforehand in order to silence the battery. Two similar commando assaults were mounted at the two extremities of the assault beaches —Cape Nègre in the west and Le Trayas in the east—to prevent the enemy bringing up reinforcements to the threatened beaches.

The Provence operation, whose code name was "Anvil-Dragoon," thus took on the following form:

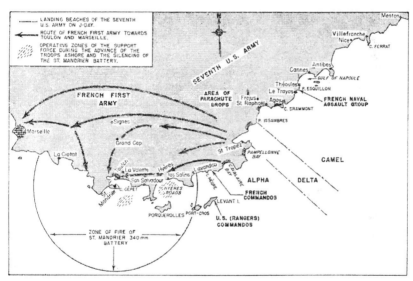

THE LANDINGS IN PROVENCE

A. Three landing forces: Force Alpha, to assault between Cavalaire and Saint-Tropez; Force Delta, to land on the beach at Nartelle, to the east of Saint-Tropez; and Force Camel, to strike between Agay and Saint-Raphaël.

B. A supporting force—Force Sitka. In addition to the French commando raid at Cape Nègre and the American ranger raid on Levant Island, this force was to put ashore at Le Trayas a commando force made up of

---

[5] The *Casabianca's* surface opponent was probably the *UJ-6078*, formerly the French *Havraise*, scuttled on November 27, 1942, later refloated by the Italians, and then seized by the Germans on September 9, 1943. She was never heard from again after her report from a position off La Ciotat on June 8, 1944.

the Naval Assault Group of Corsica, transported in American MTB's.

Admiral Hewitt flew his flag in the U.S. amphibious command ship *Catoctin*. This ship not only carried the usual amphibious communications circuits, but in addition a command center for the land-based Allied planes, operating from Corsica, which for the first time would act in direct liaison with the naval forces. The supporting carrier forces consisted of seven British and two American escort carriers under the command of Rear Admiral Thomas Troubridge, R.N.

It is no more possible to give the full details of the landings in Provence than could be done in the case of Normandy. At best only an outline will be attempted of Operation Dragoon, as far as the French naval forces were concerned. Essentially these forces were assigned two separate missions: fire support for the initial landings, and protection for the convoys carrying the French First Army. Then, as soon as the beachhead was secure, all ships would combine with the U.S. and British men-of-war in the battle for Toulon.

Two divisions of French cruisers took part in the operations of the Support Force: the 4th Cruiser Division, commanded by Rear Admiral Jaujard, consisting of the *Georges Leygues, Montcalm,* and *Gloire,* and the 3rd Cruiser Division, under Rear Admiral Auboyneau, consisting of the *Emile Bertin* and the *Duguay-Trouin*.[6] Also included in this gunfire support group were the former super-destroyers *Fantasque, Terrible,* and *Malin,* which had now been reclassified as the 10th Light Cruiser Division. The old battleship *Lorraine* would also be used in the bombardment of the heavy battery on Saint-Mandrier Peninsula.

Fifteen French destroyers, destroyer escorts, and sloops would be engaged in convoying the troops of the French First Army. Assisting them in this escort duty would be half a dozen ships of the patrol craft type which had been generously loaned by the U. S. Navy at the beginning of the year.

The commander of the Support Forces, who would also direct the attack against Saint-Mandrier, was Rear Admiral C. A. Davidson, U.S.N. Admiral Davidson had been in command of the assault on Safi during the Allied landings in North Africa, in November of 1942. But since then the relations between him and the officers and men of the French Navy had been far more amicable. He had supervised the training exercises of the French cruisers for the coming operation, and had made lengthy visits to a number of them, including 48 hours spent on the *Emile Bertin*. He had expressed his astonishment at the rapidity with which the French ships adapted them-

---

[6] The *Jeanne d'Arc,* third ship in the 3rd Cruiser Division, did not participate actively in the operations, being detached to transport members of the Provisional Government to Cherbourg at the end of August.

selves to Interallied methods, and had recommended them strongly for participation in the coming operation.

The beginning of Operation Dragoon was the departure, on August 10, of the slowest convoys: Convoy T.M. 1, from Taranto, carrying the equipment of the French II Army Corps, and Convoy A.M. 1, from Oran, made up of LSTs carrying the assault forces themselves. The ships of the Support Force, including the French contingent, left Taranto and Malta on August 11. The next day the minesweepers entered the Strait of Bonifacio. That same day Admiral Lemonnier, at the invitation of Admiral Hewitt, boarded the flagship to watch the operations from there. The ship was literally swarming with American generals and admirals, among whom one civilian in khaki, with no insignia whatsoever, shared a modest stateroom with three other persons. He was James V. Forrestal, Secretary of the Navy of the United States!

Off Ajaccio, on August 14, the forces rendezvoused—an immense armada of 1,200 ships, manned by more than 100,000 sailors, converging from Oran, Algiers, Bizerte, Palermo, Taranto, Naples, and Malta. That night over 5,000 paratroopers, in 396 planes and gliders, took off from airfields near Rome to drop behind the beachheads and block all the roads leading to them. And at midnight, the same night, the landing craft carrying the French commandos arrived off Cape Nègre and Le Trayas.

At Cape Nègre, everything went off as planned. Captain Ducourneau's company of 40 men took the battery and the gunners by surprise. But the commandos of the Naval Assault Group led by Commander Roland Seriot ran into trouble.

Coming from Bastia, Corsica, aboard U.S. MTBs commanded by Lieutenant Commander R. J. Dressling, U.S.N., they arrived on time off Point Esquillon, between LeTrayas and Théoule. Here they were landed by means of rubber liferafts, and then divided up into two sections to seal the roads leading from Fréjus and Saint-Raphaël.

The first section of 30 or more men, under Lieutenant Charles Letonturier, made out well enough. But the second section, under Lieutenant Commander Louis Marche, ran into a minefield a little way back from the shore, and three officers and 14 petty officers were blown to pieces or disabled. Engineer Officer Lucien Chaffiotte, the only officer unwounded, realized the impossibility of proceeding, and withdrew the surviving men to the shore with all the wounded they could carry. But no sooner had they reembarked in their rubber boats than they were strafed through mistake by British Mosquito planes. There was nothing to do but to swim back to the beach—and into the waiting hands of the Germans.

It was a bad start, and left the roads open to German reinforcements. As it happened, the Germans had no reserve forces to bring up, so the failure of the commandos was without bad effects. Furthermore, the men who were captured were almost all liberated the following day by U.S. soldiers and the Maquis.

The American rangers assigned to capture the battery at Titan, on Levant Island, were more than surprised; they were happily dumbfounded. The supposedly powerful battery turned out to have only wooden guns and no defenders.

As a result of all this, the landing beaches were pretty well cut off from the rest of the world, and all the assault forces would have to do would be to overcome the local defenses.

The assault waves went in at the appointed hour, but before that, from 0530 to 0730, the Allied bombers had blasted the defenses, and after that the warships offshore took over the bombardment for another half hour. Then, preceded by minesweepers, ahead of which again were radio-controlled "drone boats" loaded with explosives to blow up any underwater obstacles, the first waves of the assault forces moved in.

At the beaches of Cavalaire and Pampelonne, to the west, everything went so well that there was hardly any need for naval gunfire support. The same was true at Delta beach, where Admiral Bryant had concentrated his most powerful ships, the U.S. battleships *Arkansas* and *Texas,* the U.S. cruiser *Philadelphia,* and the French cruisers *Georges Leygues, Montcalm,*[7] *Fantasque, Terrible,* and *Malin.*

But the Camel beaches, to the east, from the tip of Issambres to the Gulf of Napoule, were something else again. Neither the air attacks nor the shells of the U.S. cruisers *Tuscaloosa* and *Brooklyn,* the British *Argonaut,* and the French *Duguay-Trouin* and *Emile Bertin* had destroyed the German defenses at Saint-Raphaël. So these beaches were simply bypassed, the assault forces being landed at Nartelle, Agay, and Cape Drammont instead, where they captured Saint-Raphaël from the rear the next day. There, as at Fréjus, they found many French sailors evacuated from Toulon and concealed under various disguises all along the coast.

By August 17, there were no enemy targets left within range of the warships' guns, and the American troops were spreading out from the beaches all along the coast to the east, or were pushing inland directly toward Grenoble. The next act on the program was the scheduled liberation of Toulon by the French Army, supported by the Allied naval and air forces.

---

[7] The third ship of the 4th Cruiser Division, the *Gloire,* had been assigned to the support force for Alpha beaches, under the command of Rear Admiral J. M. Mansfield, R.N.

THE BATTLESHIP JEAN BART *alongside the dock at Casablanca on November 11, 1942, shortly after the fight. Note the extensive structural damage to the stern.*

THE UNDAMAGED GUNS *of the El Hank battery at Casablanca after the Allied bombardment, delivered in November 1942.*

ALGERIA, NORTH AFRICA, *December 1, 1942. General Eisenhower, Admiral Darlan and Admiral A. B. Cunningham salute the Tomb of the Unknown Soldier.*

VIEW OF THE DRYDOCKS AT TOULON *in August 1944. In the foreground, can be seen the wreckage of the battleship* DUNKERQUE.

The Toulon undertaking had been entrusted to General de Lattre de Tassigny's French First Army—more specifically the 3rd North African Infantry Division, commanded by General de Monsabert, and the 1st Motorized Infantry Division, formerly the 1st Free French Division, commanded by General Diego Brosset, to which the 1st Naval Infantry Regiment belonged.

These divisions had left Taranto on August 13, and their equipment had left Oran three days earlier, both convoys being largely escorted by French naval vessels.[8] After one submarine alert[9] which proved groundless, they arrived at the landing places on the evening of August 16 and immediately began disembarking. General Brosset's division landed at Cavalaire, and General de Monsabert's troops at La Foux, at the upper end of the Gulf of Saint-Tropez. Here the dying Luftwaffe's last attack caused 80 casualties among General de Monsabert's men.

Four days later the remainder of General de Tassigny's Army, the 9th Colonial Infantry Division arrived under the command of General Pierre Magnan. Everything was ready for the march on Toulon.

Captain Le Hagre, who was intimately acquainted with the terrain, strongly recommended that Toulon be attacked from the rear by means of roundabout roads over the plateau of Grand Cap and the waste land of Signes. Accordingly General de Tassigny adopted the following plan of battle:

---

[8] The escorts for the Troop Convoy were commanded by Commander Fernand Lamorte, who was also captain of the *Hova* and commander of the 5th Destroyer Escort Division. It included the 5th D.E. Division, consisting of the *Hova, Algérien* (Lieutenant Commander Louis Pinel), and *Marocain* (Commander Melchior Monick); the 3rd Destroyer Division, consisting of *Fortuné* (Commander Joseph Bosvieux), *Forbin* (Lieutenant Commander Robert Barthélémy), and *Simoun* (Lieutenant Commander Jean Spitz); and the USS *Hilary P. Jones* (Lieutenant Commander F. M. Stiesberg, U.S.N.).

The escorts for Convoy T.M. 1 were commanded by Commander André Morazzani, who was also captain of the *Tempête* and commander of the 6th Destroyer Division. The escorts included the 6th Destroyer Division, consisting of the *Tempête* and *Alcyon* (Commander Victor Marchal); the 2nd D.E. Division, consisting of the *Somali* (Lieutenant Commander Maurice Delaire) and *Tunisien* (Lieutenant Commander Michel Burin des Roziers); the sloops *Gracieuse* (Commander Paul Mestre), *Moqueuse* (Commander Louis Ploix), *Boudeuse* (Lieutenant Commander Guy Lafargue), *Commandant Delage* (Lieutenant Commander Jean Beau), and *Commandant Dominé* (Lieutenant Commander Jean Cornault); the British corvettes *Aubrietia* and *Columbine,* and the destroyer *Farndale.*

[9] The 29th German Submarine Flotilla, based on Toulon, had lost the *U-462, U-952, U-471,* and *U-969* in the Allied air attacks of August 6, 1944. On August 16, the remaining three ships left port, the *U-230* to cruise off Toulon, and the *U-466* and *U-967* to patrol between Cannes and Cape Bénat. In compliance with orders, their crews scuttled them, August 19 to 21.

First, a feint against the eastern side of Toulon, over the Hyères plain, in order to draw the defenders to that side;

Then, the main attack, by surprise, from the hills in the rear, which would permit flanking the fortress from the west.

The Navy and the Air Force were to silence the enemy's coastal batteries and provide direct fire support for the frontlines. The *Georges Leygues* and the *Montcalm* had already been at this since the day before, but now, in order to place their shells where most needed, they had to shift to new stations in the Hyères Roads. This was in the target zone of the famous 340-mm. battery on the Saint-Mandrier Peninsula. As a precautionary measure the French battleship *Lorraine* and the U.S. battleship *Nevada* and cruiser *Augusta* had pounded Saint-Mandrier a good part of the previous day without any answer from the battery.

On the morning of August 20, the *Lorraine, Georges Leygues,* and *Montcalm* swung into position and were warmly greeted by the enemy's 138-mm. and 164-mm. batteries on the peninsula, which they promptly engaged with a smothering fire. There was still no sign of life from the 340-mm. battery, and everyone was happily thinking that it had been definitely put out of action, when at two o'clock in the afternoon an enormous geyser of water, followed by the distant *boom,* proved that this was not so.

Only one gun appeared to be in action, but that was enough to be dangerous. Admiral Davidson considered throwing the Naval Assault Group of Corsica against it in a commando action, but a week's bombardment finally silenced the battery.

Levant Island had already been captured but the remaining Hyères Islands still barred use of the Salins-Hyères roadstead. Port Cros, the next island in the group, was attacked also, but was firmly defended by Germans who had dug themselves in at the old fort there. It required 36 hours of heavy shelling by the USS *Augusta* and the British battleship *Ramillies* before the Germans would give up.

The German batteries on the third island, Porquerolles, also were very active. They drove the first minesweepers out of Hyères roadstead. The battery on San Salvadour dropped a shell on the *Fantasque* which wounded several men. It took a considerable landing force from the U.S. cruiser *Omaha* and the U.S. destroyer *Eberle* to compel the island's surrender on August 21.

That day the *Montcalm* entered Hyères roadstead behind a group of minesweepers and began bombarding the German lines east of Toulon. The next day the *Georges Leygues* took over the work, and the following day all three French cruisers of the 4th Cruiser Division fired on the batteries of Cépet and San Salvadour.

Meanwhile the position of the Germans ashore was anything but good. Owing to the critical situation of the German armies, facing defeat in the north, General Johannes von Blaskowitz, commanding Army Group G and responsible for the immense sector from the Loire River to the Italian frontier, could send no help to General Friedrich Wiese, commanding the German Nineteenth Army, which defended the Mediterranean coast. Not only that, but General Weise had had to send five of his thirteen divisions to reinforce the line in Normandy. Of the remaining eight divisions, only the 242nd, holding the line from Agay to Toulon, was up to full strength. At the end of forty-eight hours it found itself facing three American and two French divisions. The Luftwaffe in that area had only 175 planes left at the beginning of the landings, and their airfields had been effaced by the opening Allied air attacks.

So deep had the advance American troops driven inland toward Grenoble and the Rhône valley by the time the French First Army invested Toulon, that Hitler had already given Von Blaskowitz orders to leave only one division to defend Toulon and Marseilles, and to withdraw all his other troops for a junction with Army Group B. At the same time Admiral Ernst von Scheurlen, commanding the southern French coast in the Mediterranean, had ordered Admiral Heinrich Ruhfus, German Navy commandant at Toulon, to scuttle all ships there which could not be removed, and to destroy all installations.

German tugs came to tow away the *Strasbourg* and *La Galissonnière,* in order to sink them as block ships in the southern channel, just as had been done with the tanker *Garonne* in the northern channel. But Captain Rosset had already forestalled that endeavor by sinking barges in such manner as to prevent the shifting of either ship. However, thirty-six B-25 bombers of the American Air Force partly executed the German mission by blasting the *Strasbourg* and *La Galissonnière* to the bottom in the course of sinking a few small German craft. At the same time Toulon itself received the lethal visit of 130 B-26 planes.

The three remaining German U-boats, finding themselves unable to get within range of an Allied target, scuttled themselves during the next few days, as did the remaining vessels of the 6th Patrol Craft Flotilla. The crews of these ships joined their comrades ashore in the frontlines for the last futile defense against the overwhelming Allied forces.

To make the case even more hopeless, French naval personnel still on harbor service duty, along with demobilized personnel in the area, had been secretly preparing to reenter the conflict. Liaison with the Allied armada had been established by several officers of the Navy in Algiers who had been dropped by parachute behind the German lines. This group included Lieutenant Commander Léon Allain, and Lieutenants (junior grade) Ronald Midoux, Antoine Sanguinetti, Maxime Arnault de la Ménardière, and François Granry.[10] One of these officers later made his way through the German lines to guide General de Tassigny's troops over the mountainous terrain behind the city to strike the Germans from the rear.

Meanwhile the French feint from the east was becoming an actual threat to such an extent that Admiral Ruhfus abandoned his headquarters at Boudouvin[11] to fall back on the Saint-Mandrier Peninsula. Fort-du-Coudon, last German stronghold to the east of Toulon, had already been taken by Captain Ducourneau's commandos, who scaled a height supposedly impregnable. La Valette fell on August 23. The German defenders of Toulon itself were driven back into isolated strong points at Mourillon, Malbousquet, Six Fours, and Saint-Mandrier.

Of these, Saint-Mandrier was the strongest, and to this the Allies gave their first attention. The guns of the old *Lorraine* had been bombarding it for five days without pause—a bombardment that was augmented by other ships as they took position. But their fire and the bombs of the attacking planes were still answered by numerous antiaircraft guns, one 164-mm. gun of the Croix des Signaux battery—and "Big Willie," as the Americans had nicknamed the remaining giant 340-mm. gun on Saint Mandrier.

Admiral Davidson took new measures to meet the situation. On August 25 the *Lorraine* fired seventy 340-mm. shells at "Big Willie," while the American cruiser *Augusta* and the British *Sirius* blasted the Croix des Signaux battery, and the *Montcalm* shelled the 90-mm. antiaircraft guns of Saint-Elme. The enemy appeared beaten into silence—and then "Big Willie" opened up again, and the Allied bombardment had to be renewed in full force the next day.

But human flesh and blood can endure just so much. Overwhelmed by the deluge of bombs and shells,[12] Admiral Ruhfus surrendered the last 1,800 German defenders of Toulon on August 28. The last defenders, because the Naval Infantry, after hard fights at Hyères and La Crau, had entered the city itself, along with the land forces, on the 25th, and the newly appointed District Commandant, Rear Admiral Roger Lambert, had taken over the base on the 26th.

---

[10] Lieutenant (junior grade) Jean Ayrel was killed during this mission.

[11] The Boudouvin estate, six kilometers outside of Toulon, had been acquired by the Navy in 1942. An underground command post with an excellent communications network had been installed there. It is still the residence of the Naval District Commandant at Toulon.

[12] Between August 13 and 20, the Saint-Mandrier Peninsula received an estimated 785 tons of bombs; during the following week it was struck by 8,698 projectiles of all sizes.

But the return of the French Navy itself to Toulon was not yet possible. The entrance channels were still osbtructed in places, and not until the minesweepers had thoroughly done their work would it be safe for ships to enter. Admiral Lemonnier himself had arrived at Saint-Tropez early to handle the indispensable liaisons between ship and shore and the various Allied groups, as well as to serve as advance command for the Navy general staff in Algiers. First French naval ship to enter the harbor was the transport *Quercy*,[13] on September 3, but "the day of glory" waited until the 13th, when, for the first time since the scuttling of the Fleet, a French squadron anchored in the roads, battle flags flying and action pennants trailing far astern.[14]

The price of the whole operation to the French Navy was small: 27 dead in the Naval Assault Group and 15 in the 1st Naval Infantry Regiment, plus some 60 wounded. At sea, there had been no deaths. Apart from the men wounded on the *Fantasque* on the 19th, only the *Georges Leygues* had several casualties in a 40-mm. antiaircraft battery, and these were not fatal.

Marseilles could not hold off the French First Army any longer than Toulon had. The whole coast of Languedoc fell without a fight, with the patrol craft *Sabre* landing a military security group on August 29 to take over at Port Vendres, last outpost before the Spanish frontier.

In the east the liberation of the rest of the Provence coast was equally swift. The U.S. forces landed on the Provence beaches on the morning of August 15, had swept over Cannes by the 24th, and on to Nice. Here the French cruisers were again in action, with the *Emile Bertin* giving the *coup de grâce* to the grounded French freighter *Condé*, which it was feared the Germans would free and then sink as a block ship in the port's entrance. The *Emile Bertin* then proceeded, on August 25, to silence a German battery that dominated Villefranche. The *Terrible,* which had assisted the *Emile Bertin,* shelled enemy radar installations on Cape Ferrat and Mount Boron on the same day, and then on the 26th it attacked targets beyond Antibes, last enemy holdout west of the Monacan border. By the 1st of September the Mediterranean coast from Spain to Monaco was again in French hands.

In the north, the race for Germany had already begun. By the 11th of September General Patch's army of the Provence beaches had joined forces with the Allied armies driving south from Normandy. The race was now

---

[13] The transports *Quercy* and *Barfleur* served as ammunition ships; the *Elorn, Var,* and *Mékong* were the tankers.

[14] In the French Navy it is the custom for ships returning from a campaign to fly an "action pennant" which is one meter long for each month the ship has been away. Each of the French ships entering Toulon on September 13 had been away from France for more than four years.

for the Rhine, and it seemed only fitting that the first force to reach it was the French First Army. It arrived on the Rhine bank at Rosenau, just north of Basel, Switzerland, on November 19.

Final victory would not come until May 8 of 1945, but it was inevitable now. And to provide the sinews of that great victory drive up from the southern beaches there poured through the ports of Marseilles, Toulon, and Port de Bouc 4,123,794 tons of material and 905,512 men, not to mention the 306,000 tons of material and the 380,000 men that had been landed initially across the beaches themselves.

As the American historian Samuel E. Morison says, these figures were enough to justify the soundness of the decision to invade southern France in the face of so many divergent opinions concerning it.

CHAPTER 28

Paris—And the Last Winter

When the 2nd Armored Regiment of Marines, wearing their sailor hats with red pompons, led the liberating troops into Paris on August 24, 1944, it marked the return of the Navy of France to its native country. The City Hall was reoccupied that night at 10 o'clock to the clamor of bells announcing the news from every belfry. But the German troops still held several blocks of buildings in the heart of the city, and well into the middle of the next afternoon a piece of white bunting quartered with a black cross flew over the building that was the traditional home of the Ministry of the Navy, just off the Place de la Concorde. The flag was the personal emblem of the German Naval Command in France—"Admiral, Frankreich."

However, for days the building had been under the secret surveillance of a group of men lurking in the adjoining buildings. These were all officers and men of the French Navy who, under the command of Commander Paul Hébrard, had organized a secret Navy headquarters in the city. With them were a number of ordinary seamen who had spontaneously collected around the French Navy group and who were identified by the makeshift uniform of blue and white striped jerseys which they wore under their jackets.

The object of their surveillance was the old Ministry of the Navy building in the Rue Royale.

Below, in the Place de la Concorde, General Leclerc's tanks opened fire on the German admiral's headquarters around three o'clock in the afternoon of the 25th. Under cover of this diversion, Commander Hébrard and his companions crossed over by a precarious temporary footbridge thrown across from the neighboring building, and infiltrated into the headquarters of the unsuspecting defenders. Within two hours the battle was over and the flag of France once more flew over the historic Ministry of the Navy. Hastily the Navy captors threw a guard around the premises, so that they might turn the building over, intact, to the new leaders when they should arrive.

The first of these was Admiral Thierry d'Argenlieu, who had been appointed Vice Chief of Naval Operations at the beginning of the month.

Landing in Normandy with General de Gaulle, the admiral had accompanied De Gaulle on his entry into Paris on the 26th, when the admiral took command of all naval establishments in the liberated regions of the north.

On receipt of the news that Paris had been liberated, the members of the Provisional Government, along with the officers of the Consultative Assembly and a few other high officials, had embarked on the cruiser *Jeanne d'Arc* at Algiers on August 29, to make the passage to Cherbourg. On September 2, the Commissioner of the Navy, Louis Jacquinot, installed himself at the Rue Royale headquarters, where he was joined in a few days by Rear Admiral Lemonnier, coming by plane from the naval front in Provence.

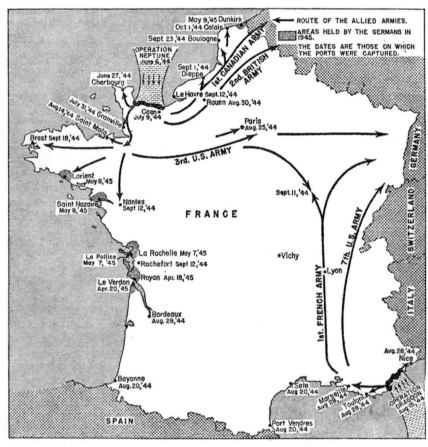

THE LIBERATION OF THE FRENCH PORTS

But even while Paris and southern France were being liberated and the great inland drives of the Allies from Normandy and Provence were starting, the movement had begun to clear the invader from the Channel and North Atlantic ports also.

North of the Seine estuary, the Canadian First Army, under General H. D. G. Crerar, headed a drive along the coast to the north and east. Rouen was liberated on August 31, and Dieppe fell the next day without a fight.[1]

After Cherbourg, Dieppe was the first French port to be reopened to Allied shipping. Though the Germans here, as elsewhere, had tried to destroy the installations, the French Captain of the Port had ingeniously prevented the sabotage from being effective. Three days after Dieppe had passed into Canadian hands, the Allies were unloading 6,000 tons of military supplies there daily.

The small port of Fécamp was also taken by the Allies without a fight. But stern fighting lay ahead at Le Havre, Boulogne, and Calais in the north, and even bloodier fighting for the ports of the Bay of Biscay, to the south.

The capture of Le Havre was almost a repetition of the assault on Brest. Throughout the Normandy campaign the port had served as a base for a small flotilla of German torpedo boat destroyers, which, along with the *Schnell Boote* of Cherbourg, harassed the invasion fleet like hornets until they were finally blasted to the bottom, one after another. To capture Le Havre required nine days of heavy fighting, supported by more than 10,000 tons of heavy bombs and the powerful guns of HMS *Warspite* and the

---

[1] The French Captain of the Port at Dieppe, Mr. Quesnel, had succeeded in convincing the German harbormaster that, in times of alert, the drawbridge which straddled the entrance to the wet basins should always be left open. Then, when the Germans were about to depart, he wrecked the bridge machinery while the bridge was in the open position, with its ends resting on the dock, so that when the Germans came along to blow it up in the entrance channel, they were unable to do so.

At Dieppe, also, the French intelligence network to which one of the authors of this book belonged had made contact with a young French woman for whom the German general commanding the division at Dieppe entertained very warm feelings. In accordance with instructions she constantly preached to her admirer on the uselessness of trying to defend Dieppe. Whether the general was convinced, or whether his instructions were different from those issued to other German commanders along the coast, the fact remains that Dieppe was abandoned without a fight, although pretty strong defenses had been erected there.

The Mayor of Dieppe was very indignant that this woman, who had publicly consorted with the enemy, was being protected by a prominent member of the Resistance from the harsh treatment that was given to other women who had shown a weakness for the enemy. He was amazed when the author pointed out to him that it was due to her that he still had his roof over his head, instead of lying under its debris, like his colleagues in other less fortunate cities.

British monitor *Erebus*. Almost 9,000 civilians paid the penalty for being caught in a city blasted by bombs from planes of friends.

The British had other and even more important reasons for a quick capture of Boulogne and Calais. First of all, these fortresses protected the several German V-1 launching sites in the vicinity—and these long-range flying bombs were causing serious damage and casualties in the English capital. Next, here and there about Cape Gris-Nez were the large German guns that not only menaced all passage through the Strait of Dover, but also threw shells into Dover roads as well.

Boulogne had been cut off from the rest of German-held territory by September 7, but it was not until ten days later that the heavy siege guns which had been used in taking Le Havre arrived and were emplaced. The assault lasted six days and ended with the surrender of the 10,000 German soldiers garrisoning the port. Calais fell on September 30, and the first troops entering the city were guided in by Engineer Officer Robert Levert and his Boulogne detachment of naval firemen.

The rest of the story of the liberation of the north and northwest of France belongs largely to the armies, except in part for those warriors of both sea and land, the Marines. For, when General Leclerc's 2nd Armored Division landed at Omaha Beach on August 2, to help drive the Germans back to the Rhine and beyond, his forces included the 2nd Armored Regiment of Marines, equipped with tank destroyer weapons, each of which had been christened with the name of a former French destroyer. Clad in British battle dress, but still obstinately wearing their sailor hats with red pompons, they participated, under the command of Captain Raymond Maggiar, in the pursuit of the retreating Germans. They distinguished themselves at the capture of Alençon. They were the first to march by the Arch of Triumph in Paris. It was in one of the closing engagements on the outskirts of the Bois de Boulogne that Lieutenant (junior grade) Michel Vassal fell. He had been one of the survivors of the tragedy which had befallen the French submarines in Morocco, two years earlier, at the time of the American landings. And it was still another Marine crew that manned the first French tank to reenter Strasbourg, on November 22, 1944.

But the war was far from over.

"We have found again the France of victory, but we do not forget that the war continues," wisely declared the Chief of Naval Operations of the French Navy.

Still ahead were some of Germany's most deadly surprises: on land, the great offensive in the Ardennes, the "Battle of the Bulge"; at sea, the advent of the snorkel and the Walther hydrogen peroxide engine which would give a new lease on life to the U-boat warfare; in the air, vastly increased airplane production (3,031 fighter planes in September as compared to 1,016

the preceding February) and the appearance of the revolutionary jet pro-
pelled Messerschmidt 262—"the most sensational fighter plane ever produced up until now."[2]

The French Navy's job in this final period was tremendous. There were
captive ports still to be liberated; there were construction and repair jobs
to be done in those already freed; there was liaison to be maintained with
the empire; there were already omens of the coming trouble in Indochina;
and, last but not least, there was the clearing of mines along the coasts.

Of all the Navy's tasks this was the most thankless, yet the one that
required the most men and ships; the least spectacular, yet the one most
arduous and urgent. During the whole past four years the shallows, the
harbor entrances, and the estuaries had been crammed with mines, laid
by the Allies as well as by the Germans. So enormous was the task that,
even with the assistance of the Allies, it would be impossible to clear the
whole coast immediately. Accordingly certain "red zones," forbidden to
shipping, were left alone and every effort given to clearing, on a priority
basis, the shipping lanes most urgently needed for the war effort and the
civilian subsistence.

In the Mediterranean, the shores of Sète were swept between October
22, 1944, and February 12, 1945—at the cost of the French minesweeper
D-202. Port Vendres was tackled next; that took from December 4 to
March 28, and resulted in the severe damage of the *D-252* by an acoustic
mine. Other French sweepers were operating in the region of La Ciotat
and Sanary, and in still unsafe corners of the Toulon roadstead.

All the Mediterranean sweeps were accomplished with equipment furnished by the Allies. But in the northern zone—the Atlantic and the Channel
—there were available some nine old sweepers of the 1940 fleet, returned
by the British but with their machinery well worn out. The Allies, however,
agreed to sweep the entrances of the ports north of Brest, while the French
undertook to clear those of Bayonne and Saint-Jean-de-Luz, although to
do so they had to call in some of the sweepers from the Mediterranean.

In addition there was convoy escort duty, which had to be kept up as
long as the enemy had U-boats at sea. In this duty the *Enjoué* (ex-*P.C.
482*), commanded by Lieutenant Georges Decugis, was sunk with all hands
by the *U-870* off Cape Spartel on January 9, 1945. Twenty-two days later
the *Ardent* (ex-*P.C. 473*) went down in collision with a British freighter
off Casablanca, but fortunately without loss of life. Another two months
saw the destroyer *Combattante* blown up on a mine off the entrance to

---

[2] This was the opinion of the French aviator, Pierre Closterman. General Carl A.
Spaatz, Chief of the U.S. Army Air Forces in Europe, had been warning America
against this plane ever since July, and had pressed for early delivery of American jet
planes to counter it.

the River Humber, with a loss of 68 killed or missing out of a crew of 185.

But while the French Navy was defending against enemy submarines in the Channel and the Atlantic, its own submarines were operating against whatever German ships could still be found anywhere. In the eastern Mediterranean, the *Curie,* commanded by Lieutenant Pierre Chailley, sank two German transports of 2,000 tons on October 2, 1944. Off the Norwegian coast the *Rubis* closed its glorious career by laying four minefields between September 24 and December 9, 1944. These reaped a harvest of seven victories, bringing the total of the *Rubis'* victims to fifteen.

On land, the French naval infantrymen, even if they did not have ships' decks under them, had no cause to complain of lack of action. Lieutenant Commander Kieffer's battalion, which had been engaged at Ouistreham, continued its operations with the British 1st Brigade of Commandos, and distinguished itself at the taking of Walcheren Island, blocking the mouth of the Scheldt, in November, 1944, and in raids on the companion island of Schouwen in December. The Naval Armored Regiment, forming part of the French 2nd Armored Division, participated in the drive to the Rhine. By February 9, 1945, they had destroyed 57 enemy tanks, 11 half-tracks, 27 armored vehicles, and caused numerous enemy casualties, at a cost to themselves of only 5 tanks, and 51 men killed and 215 wounded.[3]

The 1st Naval Infantry Regiment, after its operations at Toulon, participated in the hard fighting in Alsace at the end of the year, and finally ended its activities in the Aution Mountains in the Italian theater. The 4th Naval Infantry Regiment was occupied in keeping the Germans shut up in Lorient. The 3rd and 5th Regiments were just being organized in the region of Arcachon, and would become the nucleus of the future Brigade of the Far East.

Although the Germans had been driven out of southern France they still held strong positions in northern Italy, where they remained a constant menace to Provence. After the American Army had driven north from the Provence beaches toward the Rhine, the only troops left to meet any eruption of the Germans were General Paul Doyen's force, which was largely infantry, with practically no artillery and only a very small air force. What he needed badly was the support of naval ships.

Up until October 16, 1944, that support was provided by Rear Admiral Davidson's Task Force 86. On that date Rear Admiral Auboyneau succeeded Admiral Davidson in command of the force, which was now largely made up of French ships. Less than three weeks later the force was re-

---

[3] After being recalled westward for the Royan operation, the Naval Armored Regiment returned to the eastern front and was in on the taking of Berchtesgaden on May 5, 1945.

organized and redesignated the Flank Force with a new commander,[4] Rear Admiral Jaujard, flying his flag in the *Montcalm*. Although the composition of the force varied from time to time, it usually included 4 or 5 French cruisers, half a dozen French destroyers, and a number of escort ships, patrol craft, and minesweepers.[5] In addition to the French ships, the Flank Force at the beginning included 4 destroyers, 12 minesweepers, some escort ships, and a flotilla of MTBs from the U.S. Navy.

The cruisers, based on Toulon, constituted the bombardment group. The destroyers making up the support force also operated from Toulon. All ships of the force cruised continually, during daylight hours, some ten miles off the coast, between Ventimiglia and Cape di Nola. At night the destroyers took over the job of blockading the Gulf of Genoa.

At Cannes there was based a patrol group consisting, on the average, of four escort vessels and submarine chasers. This group was particularly effective against the floating mines which the enemy released in the westward current in the hope that they would interfere with the traffic out of Toulon.[6]

Finally, the MTBs based at Golfe Juan, near Cannes, carried out night raids along the Italian coast.

It would be useless to try to describe all the various occasions on which the Flank Force fired against German batteries, communication centers, amunition dumps, and other such targets in support of the Allied armies operating ashore. The figure of 3,766 shells fired by the cruisers and 6,392 by the destroyers will give some idea of their activities.

But one of the most useful activities of the patrol craft of the Flank Force was the interception of "human torpedoes," which made their appearance off the Provence coast subsequent to the landings. Three of these torpedoes, ridden and steered by enemy swimmers, were sunk on September 5, 1944, by the U.S. destroyer *Ludlow* and the French *Malin*. The *Cimeterre* also sank a human torpedo, and in December and January the *Sabre* and the *Fortuné* destroyed three Italian MTBs of the 10th MAS.[7]

---

[4] Admiral Auboyneau had left on the *Emile Bertin* on a mission to Greece and the eastern Mediterranean.

[5] French ships that served at one time or other with the Flank Force included the cruisers *Montcalm, Georges Leygues, Gloire, Emile Bertin, Jeanne d'Arc,* and *Duguay-Trouin;* the super-destroyer *Tigre,* and the destroyers *Alcyon, Basque, Fortuné, Simoun, Tempête,* and *Trombe.*

[6] Sometimes as many as 40 of these mines were destroyed in a single day; in all, 430 were destroyed in the approaches to Toulon.

[7] This flotilla was a part of the small fraction of the Italian Navy which remained loyal to the Fascist Republic created by Mussolini in the brief period after his spectacular liberation from the Gran Sasso on September 12, 1943.

The *Javelot,* the *Cimeterre,* and subchaser *No. 105* each sank an explosive-laden motorboat also.

After February of 1945, when Germany's situation was becoming rapidly worse, the Flank Force had to redouble its activities in order to check any last minute acts of desperation on the part of the Germans. The cruisers stepped up their bombardments, the destroyers worked in closer to the shore. Three more enemy MTBs were sunk—one by the *Lansquenet* on March 15, another by subchaser *No. 25* on April 11, and the third by the *Trombe* on April 16. But in the engagement the *Trombe* was struck by a torpedo from the enemy MTB which killed 19 men, probably the last casualties to be suffered by the French Navy at sea during the war. Eight days later the subchasers *No. 112* and *No. 122* and the *Lansquenet* sent six more MTBs to the bottom. Three others (two Italian and one German), which had left San Remo to carry out a raid on the Corsican coast, scuttled themselves in the Gulf of Porto on April 24, with all the crews being made prisoners. The war was nearing its end for Hitler's forces in Italy as well as elsewhere, but, before evacuating the Italian Riviera, the Germans sank the last of the French ships scuttled at Toulon and later refloated by the Italians and towed to Genoa or La Spezia.

But before the Flank Force was dissolved on May 13, 1945, it had had to log one major disaster to its forces, and that was not caused by enemy action. On Christmas, 1944, the *Terrible* and the *Malin,* of the 10th Light Cruiser Division, were in collision during exercises off Naples. The *Malin* lost its bow as far back as No. 1 gun.[8] The *Terrible* had one fireroom flooded and her superstructure razed from the after stack to No. 3 gun. After the collision, 69 men were reported dead or missing, of whom 61 were from the *Malin.*

By now the dread German war machine that had once swept over most of Europe had been pushed back completely out of France except for strongly fortified pockets along the Channel coast south of Brest. Here they were hemmed in by 80,000 French fighting men coming for the most part from the former French Forces of the Interior (F.F.I.). But the improvised armaments of these besiegers would not permit their taking the offensive against an enemy so well entrenched, so well provided with artillery, and constantly in touch with its homeland by air.[9] Furthermore, the welfare of the hundreds of thousands of French civilians had to be considered. They were, in effect, hostages in these German-held cities.

---

[8] The *Malin* was repaired by replacing the damaged section with the bow of the *Indomptable,* which had been scuttled at Toulon on November 27, 1942.

[9] These communication lines were kept open by planes taking off at night from the base at Friedrichshafen, on Lake Constance.

The cost of taking such grimly defended fortresses, only to win a wrecked city and an unusable port, had been only too well learned at Brest. That was the reason besiegers had refrained from assaulting Lorient, Saint-Nazaire, La Pallice, and La Rochelle.

Bordeaux, as described before, had fallen, intact, to the F.F.I. on August 28, 1944. But lying almost 100 kilometers up a river easy to mine, the port had never been used by the Kriegsmarine other than as an entry port for blockade-runners and, from September, 1940, to September, 1943, as a base for Italian submarines operating in the Atlantic.[10] This last activity had brought down on the city some heavy Allied air attacks, one of which, on May 17, 1943, had caused the death of 172 civilians. The Allied bombs had destroyed the locks to the drydocks, leaving five Italian submarines stranded, and halting use of the harbor by the Axis for several months.

When General von Blaskowitz had received the order from Hitler's headquarters to withdraw his forces on August 17 and to regroup them where needed, he had given General Albert Nake, commanding in the Bordeaux region, the order to destroy all the harbor installations before leaving. But after negotiations with the encircling F.F.I., General Nake had agreed not to carry out this destruction in exchange for the pledged promise of the F.F.I. not to harry his troops in their retreat. The Germans probably thought that the obstructions they had already placed in the Gironde below the town[11] would effectively prevent its use by the Allies. The F.F.I. promise had been kept, the Germans had moved out, and the national flag of France had again been run up over the city hall by Lieutenant Commander René Jalabert, who at the time was serving with the Maquis of Dordogne.

Even without the obstructions, the harbor of Bordeaux would have been unusable by the Allies as an unloading port, because the Germans still

---

[10] To avoid the dangerous passage of the Strait of Gibraltar after each patrol, the Italian Navy had obtained permission from the Germans to establish an Italian submarine base (Betasom) at Bordeaux. Twenty-seven Italian submarines from the Mediterranean were based here, as well as three others which joined from the Red Sea after General Wavell had captured their bases in Eritrea. Of these 30 submarines, three were sent as cargo carriers to Japan or the Indian Ocean, a few returned to Italy, and 16 were lost while on patrol. At the time of the Italian armistice there were only two at Bordeaux, both undergoing major overhaul.

It was from Bordeaux that Lieutenant Commander Prince Valerio Borghese, in the *Leonardo da Vinci,* carried out the trials of a small "pocket" submarine, which was to be carried on the deck of a large submarine to the entrance of the Hudson River in order to attack the ships in New York harbor. The trials were completely successful but the sudden turn of the war in Italy prevented the project ever being carried out.

[11] These obstructions consisted of seven ships, varying between 40 and 140 meters in length, sunk in two parallel rows across the axis of the channel. Although the work of clearing them away was begun in late 1944, it was not completed until February of 1946.

had strong garrisons heavily dug in at Point de Grave and around Royan, on both banks of the Gironde near its mouth.

Had not the ports of Cherbourg and Dieppe in the north been available to the Allies for supplying their armies as they drove inland, there might have been good reason for giving first priority to recapturing some of the large ports on the Atlantic coast of France. But thousands of tons of cargo could be poured in through those two channel ports alone every day, and, in addition, Marseilles was rapidly being restored to usefulness. Hence, despite the impatience manifested in some Government circles for "reasons of prestige," the Allies had wisely decided to make the attack toward the Rhine their first concern, and leave the recapture of the Atlantic ports until more forces were available.

With the end of the land campaign on the Provence and Languedoc coasts, it seemed as though that time had come. The Moroccan 1st Infantry Division, from De Lattre de Tassigny's Army, and the 1st Naval Infantry Regiment were detached for that purpose and ordered to the southwest front on December 18.

Then, within less than 24 hours, the Germans had erupted in that desperate winter offense in the Ardennes, with its ensuing threat against the pivot point of Strasbourg. The 1st Naval Infantry Regiment was immediately recalled to the threatened eastern front, and the projected attack against the coastal ports had to be postponed, even though an actual date— January 10—had been set for its beginning.

Through some error never explained, the air attacks which the Allies had been asked to make as preliminary bombardments on the Gironde pockets were never cancelled. On January 5, 1945, some 175 British bombers came over as originally planned, and dropped tons of bombs— not on the German pockets, but on Royan itself, which was destroyed from top to bottom, with 1,000 of its inhabitants dead in the ruins.

The French naval forces, not being able to do anything about the battles in the Ardennes and at Strasbourg, continued to plan for the eventual campaign against the German-held strong points on the coast. On the Gironde front, ever since October of 1944, there had been the 1st Regiment of Naval Gunners, commanded by Commander Charles Touraille.[12] For air support there was Naval Air Group No. 2, commanded by Commander François Lainé, which had been organized in November, 1942, by combining Lieutenant Félix Ortolan's Fighter Squadron 3F with Lieutenant Raymond Béhic's Fighter Squadron 4F.[13]

---

[12] Originating as a battery of four 155-mm. guns, and designated as the 1st Battery of Naval Gunners, it received an addition of four 90-mm. batteries after the Italian campaign and had been redesignated the 1st Regiment of Naval Gunners.

[13] From December 9, 1944, until May 8, 1945, this air group carried out 1,108 sorties

For the projected attack on the Atlantic pockets, the Navy had organized a French Naval Task Force (F.N.T.F.) on December 15, 1944, and had placed it under the orders of Rear Admiral Joseph Rue, flying his flag in the *Lorraine*. While waiting to take its part in the final assault operations, the F.N.T.F. had the responsibility of blockading the German pockets to prevent the Germans from bringing in supplies—often in neutral ships— or of escaping after destroying everything.[14]

The F.N.T.F. had assembled at Cherbourg in December, when first organized. It consisted at that time of the *Lorraine, Duquesne, Gloire,* some 1,500-ton destroyers, and a group of minesweepers that had just come from the Mediterranean. But the German Christmas offensive had so disrupted the original plans that the *Gloire* and the destroyers had to rush back to the Mediterranean.

An attempt to begin operations on a limited scale in December had turned out badly also. The objective had been the recapture of the small islands of Houat and Hoedic, off the mouth of the Loire River. But the French armed trawler *Abel Alain,* with a small assault force of sailors, had run unto a flotilla of Germans who were on their way to Houat with a much larger body of reinforcements. The encounter, which had been brought about by a fog, resulted in the *Abel Alain* being beached, its commanding officer killed, and some 30 French sailors captured.

Later, an attempt by the *Duquesne,* with the destroyer escorts *Hova* and *Somali,* to bombard the German defenses of Belle Isle was thwarted by another fog. For the time being, the only activities continued were the duels between the batteries of the 1st Regiment of Naval Gunners and the German antiaircraft guns on Point de Grave and in the La Rochelle-Royan region.

During this lull in the hostilities along the coast, the local French commanders and the German leaders of the garrisoned pockets—Vice Admiral

---

and dropped 532 tons of bombs. Its missions varied from reconnaissance and patrols over the lines and at sea to bombing the German defenses in the pockets. It lost altogether eight planes and four crews, but among its losses was Warrant Officer Paul Goffeny, who had already distinguished himself in Syria. On New Year's Day of 1945 he and his whole plane crew were lost in the resulting explosion when he bombed a German tanker off Point Coubre at almost masthead height.

His name was honored by being given to the ex-German aircraft tender *Max Stinsky,* which had escaped from one of these German pockets and was interned in Spain until it was eventually turned over to France in 1946. As the *Paul Goffeny* it took an important part in the war in Indochina, and is today still in commission.

[14] In a letter dated February 5, 1945, Admiral d'Argenlieu called attention to the constant traffic between the German pockets and the Spanish ports. He stressed the strength of the German force of 8 submarines, based at Saint-Nazaire and La Pallice, plus numerous armed trawlers and minesweepers, as compared to the French force of only 8 MTBs at Brest, plus a few submarine chasers and armed trawlers.

Ernst Schirlitz at La Rochelle, and Colonel Hartwig Pohlmann and Rear Admiral Hans Michaellis at Royan—had made agreements aimed at reducing the suffering caused by the sieges. These agreements provided for the exchange of many prisoners, the evacuation of the civilian population who wished to leave the cities, and the preservation of La Rochelle and La Pallice from the destruction that had been visited upon other French cities by their German defenders.

This state of affairs, in which the Germans were being hemmed into their fortifications without loss of lives, could just as well have continued right up to the capitulation of Germany, of which many unmistakable signs were beginning to appear. Nevertheless, on April 13, at a time when the American armies were within 100 kilometers of Berlin and the Russians less than 50, General de Larminat, commander of the French forces in that sector, launched "Operation Vénérable," intended to clear the entrance to the Gironde. And, 15 days later and only one week before Germany's capitulation, he ordered the attack on the Ile d'Oléron designated as "Operation Jupiter."

Although not in favor of these operations, the Navy carried out its commitments. The *Lorraine* and the *Duquesne* made up the bombardment group of the F.N.T.F., along with the destroyers *Fortuné, Basque, Alcyon,* the destroyer escort *Hova,* the frigates *Aventure, Découverte,* and *Surprise,* and the sloop *Amiral Mouchez,* plus eight French and a dozen British minesweepers. A squadron of seaplanes based on Hourtin and Lieutenant Béhic's 4F Squadron from Cognac also played a prominent role in the operations.

The blockade of the German positions which had been carried out by light craft from Brest was augmented each night by the 23rd Flotilla of MTBs. Armed pinnaces patrolled the mouth of the Gironde. Fourteen enemy vessels which attempted to evade this blockade were captured, and only five slipped through to Spain.

On the night of April 5, the *Surprise* drove two German Class M minesweepers to shelter behind the German minefields, and on the following night the pinnace *Coccinelle* captured an enemy picket boat with two officers. On April 10 the *Fortuné* and the *Hova* captured the German-manned trawler *Hasard* off Les Sables d'Olonne. Another German trawler was captured by one of the French seaplanes, and six other ships were intercepted on April 18. The only active reply from the Germans was a very accurate salvo from the German batteries on the Ile de Ré which made the *Surprise* draw off to safer distance.

For Operation Vénérable, General de Larminat had considerable forces: 42 infantry battalions, 23 artillery groups, the equivalent of 4 armored regiments, and 2 engineer battalions—a total of 50,000 men, 300 tanks, and 280 guns, of which 190 were larger than 75-mm. In the artillery was the 1st Regiment of Naval Gunners with four batteries of 155-mm. guns. For air support there were 100 French planes plus innumerable Allied planes so that on certain days there were "more friendly airmen in the skies than there were enemy troops in the defenses below."[15] Altogether these planes made 5,400 sorties, during the course of which they dropped 10,000 tons of bombs!

To prepare for the assault, the minesweepers had swept and bouyed the firing stations of the large ships on the night of April 14.[16] The bombardment force, departing from Plymouth, arrived on station at 0745 on the 15th, and at 0800 the *Lorraine, Duquesne,* and the destroyers opened fire on Point de Grave. One of the main reasons for this bombardment was to draw the defenders' attention to the Point de Grave side while the land troops assailed the Royan area. For two days the bombardment group kept up their fire without the slightest response from the enemy—no enemy planes, no submarines, no enemy shellfire, even. Then, informed that they were no longer needed, the F.N.T.F. returned to Brest, lighter by several hundred tons of powder and shells!

The defenders of the Royan pocket surrendered on the evening of April 17, Admiral Michaellis being captured in his own command post at Pontaillac. But on Point de Grave the fighting continued until the 20th. There a German lieutenant commander, commanding the Narvik Battalion, refused to surrender, and it became necessary to blast him out with one-ton bombs and tank destroyers.

Four thousand and six hundred Germans were captured at Royan, of whom 150 were officers. At Point de Grave the prisoners numbered 3,500. But the price paid for the victory was high—369 men killed and over 1,500 wounded, to say nothing of the obliteration of the communities and the casualties in the civilian population. And all of this was done simply to open, 15 days ahead of VE-day, a river which was so obstructed that it could not be cleared for traffic until the following year!

Although equally useless, Operation Jupiter, begun on April 29, at least had the merit of being less costly. The *Lorraine's* big guns were not deemed necessary, so Admiral Rue had shifted his flag to the *Duquesne.* While covering the landing of the troops on the southern end of the Ile d'Oléron,

---

[15] Such was the case on April 14 and 15, when the Royan pocket, with a total of only 4,600 defenders, was assailed by 1,000 Flying Fortresses carrying altogether some 8,000 men.

[16] Seven magnetic or acoustic mines were swept from the stations which the bombardment ships were to occupy.

the *Duquesne* expended five hundred and fifty 8-inch shells on the German batteries, and the destroyers fired 100 shots each. The following day, May 1, 1945, Oléron capitulated.

At La Rochelle, at Saint-Nazaire, and at Lorient, the French commanders had the intelligence to sit tight and wait for the end of the war when Germany as a whole would capitulate and these cities could be regained without bloodshed and without mass destruction.

Dunkirk also capitulated in the same manner, though here things were somewhat different. Whereas elsewhere the German defenders had remained within their fortifications and waited to be attacked there, Admiral Friederich Frisius, commander at Dunkirk, was a man of another caliber. He had formerly been the commander of the German naval forces on the Pas-de-Calais coast. When he had been forced to fall back to Dunkirk in September of 1944, he had drawn to himself all the German units on the Belgian coast which had been unable to withdraw to the Breskens pocket or to escape across the Scheldt. Now, during the closing days of hostilities, he enlivened matters by making audacious sorties that aroused quite a commotion in that region.

For instance, on April 9, he sent out a strong raiding party to disturb the sleep of the Allied troops. At that time the low lands behind Dunkirk were all inundated, as the Germans had blown up the dykes in order to have the additional protection of the flooded areas. The ground beyond was held by the siege lines made up of a Czech brigade, a few elements of British artillery, and three French battalions, formerly of the F.F.I.

Coming down a canal silently in rubber boats, the Germans scattered two companies of newly arrived besiegers and penetrated several miles inside the Allied positions. In the panic of surprise the English engineers blew up several bridges at Gravelines. Seasoned reinforcements had to be hurried up; these were found in a group of naval infantrymen whom the Commandant of the Navy at Boulogne had organized. Even so, the besiegers never did manage to dislodge the Germans from the strong positions they had taken, regardless of how many bombs the Allied planes rained upon them.

Admiral Frisius caused more troubles to the Allies than did his colleagues at Lorient and La Rochelle put together. In a way, it may be said that he never surrendered. When, in Germany, Marshal Alfred Gustav Jodl signed a capitulation on May 7, 1945, for all the armed forces of Germany everywhere, the redoubtable Admiral Frisius consented to quit fighting—two days later.

CHAPTER 29

The Navy in Indochina

The concessions which in 1940 Governor General Decoux had had to grant the Japanese—air bases for their operations against Malaya and the Dutch East Indies, and the stationing of troops in Indochina—had at least gained for the French a measure of security. The French administration continued to function, the authority of the Governor General was recognized, and a diplomatic mission headed by a courteous and moderate man, Ambassador Yoshizawa, was accredited to Admiral Decoux. The French flag still flew from the border of China to the Gulf of Siam, and the French armed forces continued to exist.

That existence, it is true, was considerably restricted, and, after the Japanese attack on Pearl Harbor on December 7, 1941, it rapidly became worse.

For one thing, this Far Eastern part of the empire was definitely isolated from the mother country. The last maritime contact beween Indochina and France was the tanker *Nivose,* which had left for Saigon in November of 1941 to take on a cargo of fuel oil for Dakar. It did not reach Dakar until August, 1942, after having steamed all the way through the South Pacific and around Cape Horn. Since then—no more mail service, no more replacements for the armed services, no medical supplies, no manufactured products. Nothing but brief radiograms, and those few and far between.

However, Indochina was not without resources, and it did its utmost to exist.

In this struggle for life, the Navy had an important role. Tonkin, the northern section, did not grow enough rice to support its own population; on the other hand Saigon, capital of Cochin China in the south, needed the coal of Tonkin to keep its electric power stations going. It was necessary to carry north the rice which Cochin China raised in abundance, and bring back south the coal from Hon Gay. This could be done only by sea, as the single track Trans-Indochinese Railroad did not have sufficient capacity —even when General Claire Chennault's "Flying Tigers"[1] did not keep the line cut.

---

[1] In 1937 Major Claire Chennault of the U.S. Army Air Force was about to be

355

Indochina's merchant fleet of 130,000 tons could easily have handled this traffic if no one had interfered with it. But in April, 1942, the Japanese had forcibly requisitioned eleven of the best ships in this fleet. In addition, American planes and submarines were soon operating along the entire Indochina coast, sinking all Japanese vessels they encountered—and not a few Indochinese ships as well.

There is a record for the years of 1942, 1943, 1944, of some 30 attacks on Indochinese warships or merchantment by American planes or submarines—either directly by bombs or torpedoes, or indirectly by mines. These attacks resulted in the loss of eight merchantmen and five warships,[2] not to mention the extensive damages and loss of human life on other ships that were attacked but not sunk.

It was undoubtedly difficult for the submarine commanders as well as Chennault's pilots to distinguish, in the waters off Indochina, the French flag from the Japanese. It is equally true that in comparison to the 420,000 tons of Japanese ships thus sunk between December, 1941, and June, 1945, the French tonnage sunk represented but a small percentage. Nevertheless it is certain that at times these attacks were not cases of mistaken identity. For instance, the French Indochinese gunboat *Francis Garnier,* attacked by planes, had fired back in self-protection, and had brought down or damaged one of the attackers. Thereafter, during numerous attacks, the pilots of the China Air Task Force could be heard calling to each other over their intercommunication phones that here was a chance to get even.

However, the excuse of mistaken identity must have been true in the case of the pilots who dropped tons of bombs on a string of bamboo rafts being towed by a tug at two knots in Along Bay, for the next day the Allied communique announced the attack as resulting in the destruction of a Japanese aircraft carrier.

---

retired for age when Madam Chiang Kai-shek invited him to supervise the organization of an Air Force for China. Nicknamed the "Flying Tigers," his organization, consisting at first mostly of American volunteers, made a great reputation against the Japanese. In July, 1942, it was incorporated into the U.S. Army Air Force, initially as the China Air Task Force, and later as the XIV U.S. Air Force.

[2] The ships lost were the liner *Khaï Dinh* (ex-*Lamartine*), sunk by planes in Along Bay on November 22, 1942; the freighter *Canton,* destroyed off the coast of Annam, on November 30, 1942, by a mine laid by the USS *Tautog;* the *Gouverneur Général Pasquier,* blown up by a mine off Haiphong on May 7, 1943; the freighter *Gouverneur Général van Vollenhoven,* torpedoed off the Annam coast by the USS *Bowfin* on November 25, 1943—the patrol vessel *Béryl,* escorting it, was also lost with all hands that same night; the freighter *Françis Garnier,* blown up by a mine on February 20, 1944; the freighters *Kai Pinh* and *Ping Sang,* sunk by planes on January 15, 1944; the hydrographic ship *Astrolabe* and the minesweeper *Picanon,* sunk by planes on February 26, 1944; and the freighter *Song Giang* and escort sloop *Tahure,* sunk off Cape Varela by the USS *Flasher,* on April 29, 1944.

Whatever the case, the Commandant of the French Naval Forces in Indochina saw his merchant ships and escort vessels disappearing little by little. All possible means were taken to replace the sunker coasters. The navy yard at Saigon began the construction of a number of large wooden junks. For psychological reasons primarily, because the resulting armament was totally inadequate, the merchant ships were armed with some antiquated 47-mm. or 65-mm. guns and a couple of old machineguns manned by men from the cruiser *Lamotte-Picquet,* which had been decommissioned in early 1942. However, before the war ended, the Navy in Indochina had to run truck convoys to Haiphong to bring back food and other supplies for its own needs. During the final months of the Japanese occupation, when all shipping had come to a complete halt, the population of Tonkin came to the thin edge of starvation.

Apart from the American planes and submarines, the war came visibly to Indochina only on January 3, 1945, when for the first time in three years an American squadron appeared in the South China Sea. It was one of the task groups of Vice Admiral John C. McCain's Fast Carrier Task Force 58. Coming from the American landings in Luzon, it swept the entire coast from Camranh Bay to Cape Saint-Jacques and Saigon, sinking everything that floated. In this one raid of January 12, the Japanese lost 127,000 tons of shipping, including one heavy cruiser, nine escort ships, and a dozen tankers. Unfortunately the French Navy was not spared, either; it lost three freighters and a patrol vessel at Saigon.

Not far away was moored the decommissioned *Lamotte-Picquet,* now serving as a training ship for native seamen apprentices. The markings of its nationality were plainly visible, yet it was set on fire and sunk by the American planes, and one of its officers was mortally wounded. The only reply its commanding officer, Lieutenant Commander Jean Mottez, made was a burst of machinegun fire to protect his men as they abandoned ship.

This, however, was the last blow struck at the French Navy of Indochina by the United States Forces. The blows that came after were struck by the Japanese Army.

When, on November 13, 1942, Admiral Darlan had led the French Forces of Africa back into the war against the Axis, he had not deemed it advisable to embroil Indochina by extending the hostilities to Japan. On the other hand, General de Gaulle's Free French Government had been officially at war against Japan since December 8, 1941. It was a rather platonic form of war, however, since no engagements had taken place between the Japanese forces and the Free French Navy in the Pacific. Nevertheless, the French bases in Oceania, taken over by the Free French, had been placed at the disposal of the Allied command for such hostilities.

But with the establishment of General de Gaulle's Government in Algiers in July, 1943, conditions changed.

In mid-March of 1944 the battleship *Richelieu* left Scotland to join Admiral Sir James Somerville's British squadron at Trincomalee, Ceylon, and, shortly after its arrival in the Indian Ocean, it formed part of the protective screen for the British carrier *Illustrious* and the American carrier *Saratoga* in the bombardment of Japanese positions at Sabang, just off the tip of Sumatra. This action was intended as a diversion for the American landings which were being carried out at Hollandia, New Guinea, on the same day. This was the first time a French man-of-war had taken an active part in the Pacific campaign.

The following month, on May 17, the *Richelieu* participated in the bombardment of Surabaya, and in a similar operation against the Andaman Islands in June. In July she was part of an imposing fleet which shelled the Japanese installations on the Island of Pulo-We, at which time she distinguished herself by silencing a coastal battery harassing the screening destroyers at close range. Admiral Somerville sent her captain congratulations on his "efficient fire."

Thereafter, after a long overhaul at Casablanca and Gibraltar, she returned to form part of the 3rd British Battle Squadron, under Vice Admiral Harold T. C. Walker, R.N., for the final few months of the war in the Pacific.

These first actions by French naval ships in early 1944 brought no retaliation against Indochina by the Japanese. As a matter of fact, Indochina still remained under the jurisdiction of the French Government at Vichy, even though that jurisdiction was represented only by a few dispatches. Perhaps the Japanese considered the *Richelieu* and the other units engaged in escort duty in the Pacific as being "dissidents" beyond the control of the Vichy Government, which therefore could not be held accountable for their actions.

But when, on August 21, 1944, the Germans forcibly removed Marshal Pétain and other high government officials to Germany just ahead of the Allied recapture of Paris, the French Government which the Japanese had thus far recognized came to an end. In its place General de Gaulle had installed his provisional government, with its declared state of war with Japan. Under the circumstances it would have been expected that Admiral Decoux, at Hanoi, would have received an ultimatum from Tokyo demanding to know immediately whether or not he recognized the authority of the new regime.

But things are never that simple in the Far East. Officially, no change took place in the relations between the Governor General of Indochina and the Japanese. On his part, General de Gaulle requested Admiral Decoux to continue at his post. At the same time, however, he privately appointed General Eugene Mordant, who had retired as Commanding Officer of the French Army Forces in Indochina a few months earlier, to head the "resistance" movement in Indochina.

The organizing of resistance movements in territories occupied by the Axis powers had long been a strategic policy of the Allies. Such movements had been encouraged and supported in China, France, Czechoslovakia, and elsewhere. Accordingly the Allies now parachuted into Indochina, as well as into Burma, arms and ammunition with which to fight the Japanese. Some of these arms were intended for the regular French Army troops in Indochina, as they had been without supplies from France for so long. Not all these arms fell into the hands of the French regulars, as was evidenced when they were later put in use against Frenchmen and not against Japanese.

For that matter, the organization and arming of resistance forces in Indochina could have been justified only if the Allies had intended to conduct a military campaign against the Japanese in that territory and wished to instigate a general uprising of the public to coincide with that operation.

But the Allied general staffs had no such intention. They had no need for the French bases in Tonkin and Cochin China, and their whole offensive, other than harassing operations, was directed at the Philippines. Once these were recaptured, the Japanese in Indochina would be bypassed, just as at Truk and other Japanese-held islands in the Pacific.

This, in fact, was the strategy that had been agreed upon at the Interallied Conference held in Quebec on August 24, 1943. Indochina had been systematically crossed off the list of future operations in the Pacific, because strategically it was of no use except as a corridor to China. And for such purposes, priority had been given to the Burma Road, the recapture of which was to be undertaken by Admiral Lord Louis Mountbatten, commanding the Southeast Asia theater of operations.

Further decision was made, a few months later, to include Indochina in the Chinese sphere of action, the only modification being a provision that if operations were launched simultaneously from the north by General Chiang Kai-shek and from the south by Lord Mountbatten, the limits of the occupation would be determined by the respective advance of each army.

The French were not consulted at all during this latter arrangement, which was concluded at Chungking on December 8, 1943, at a conference in which General Brehon Somervell, special envoy of President Roosevelt, largely supported Chiang Kai-shek's point of view.

General de Gaulle was not able to interest the Allies in the problem of Indochina any more than Marshal Pétain had been in 1940, when his effort to send reinforcements from Djibouti to Indochina had been checked by the British as well as by the Germans.

The Japanese, on their part, were concerned with Indochina not so much because of the political situation, but because of the security of their troops stationed there. A change of Government at Paris would not affect this, but the American landings in the Philippines and a British offensive from Burma most certainly would.

With Allied forces so menacingly close, the Japanese also had to consider the possibility, small as it was, of a sudden attack by the French troops which were still under arms in Indochina. A little loose talk as well as a few imprudent actions by men of the resistance group did not tend to allay the Japanese worries any.

The first disquieting indication of a change in Japanese attitude came at the end of November, 1944, when Ambassador Yoshizawa asked to be relieved of his post to avoid participation in any action contrary to the peaceful policies he had advocated during the past three years. But before leaving for Japan he gave Mr. de Boisanger, Admiral Decoux's diplomatic adviser, a thinly veiled warning, "If the Americans occupy Manila, a new situation will arise which cannot fail to lead the Government of Tokyo to revise its attitude with respect to Indochina."

The warning was as sound as it was well intentioned. Manila fell to the U.S. forces on February 24, 1945. Not two weeks later, Schunichi Matsumoto, the new Japanese Ambassador at Saigon, brought Admiral Decoux an ultimatum[2a] at seven o'clock in the evening. The ultimatum expired two hours later, and promptly upon its expiration the Governor General was made a prisoner, along with Admiral Bérenger, commander of the French Naval Forces in Indochina. Military operations were already under way elsewhere, and at 9:30 the Japanese launched a general attack on all the military installations at Saigon.

At the Francis Garnier barracks, naval headquarters at Saigon, Lieutenant Louis Larroque resisted for two hours with only 50 men. Three sailors were killed at the gates of the navy yard while holding off the attackers to allow time for the destruction of the more important installations. The majority of the officers were captured in their own homes or while trying to reach their commands at the navy yard or in the river. Only one company of sailors, under Lieutenant Commander Paul Morcau, managed to escape on the gunboat *Tourane* to Tan-uyen, on the Donnaï River, where it joined the Maquis for a three months' fight before falling into the hands of the Japanese.

[2a] The ultimatum demanded that Admiral Decoux, in order to give proof of his determination to defend Indochina to the end in close collaboration with Japan, place the French armed forces, the police, the administration and all means of transport and communication directly under the orders of the Japanese military. Failing which, a serious situation might develop, as the Japanese then would be obliged to operate without consideration for the fate of the 40,000 French in Indochina. The admiral indignantly refused to sign the dishonoring letter of acceptance presented to him.

At Camranh Bay, a few officers and men from the base took to the jungles and lived at large for some weeks before being captured, one after the other. When the last of these, Lieutenant Edmond Pistre, burning with malaria and weak from starvation, had to surrender on June 1, 1945, he had been in the jungles for 83 days.

Even if they had been warned in time, the ships of the Indochinese Fleet would have had small chance of reaching a friendly port. Practically none of them had the necessary steaming radius. Furthermore, most of them had been immobilized for months, far upstream from the open sea. The *Tourane* had to scuttle herself as soon as she had disembarked Lieutenant Morcau's company at Tan-uyen. The patrol boat *Armand Rousseau* was simultaneously attacked from both sides in the harbor of Saigon.

With a few exceptions, the entire flotilla of Indochina was anchored in the delta of the Mekong River at the time of the Japanese attack. The sloop *Amiral Charner* was at My Tho, along with the gunboats *Mytho* and *Avalanche* and the minesweeper *Paul Bert*. The sloop *Marne* and the patrol vessel *Maurice Long* were at Can Tho. The hydrographic ship *Lapérouse* was at Vinh Long, along with the store ship *Cam Ranh* and the patrol vessel *Capitaine Coulon*. The gunboat *Francis Garnier* was anchored at Kratié, in the middle reaches of the Mekong, 200 kilometers upstream from Phnom Penh and 500 kilometers from the open sea.

In Tonkin, the gunboats *Commandant Bourdais* and *Vigilante* were at Haiphong, and the patrol vessels *Frézouls* and *Crayssac* in Along Bay.

These were all that remained of the French Naval Forces in the Far East.

The *Francis Garnier* was shelled and set on fire in a surprise attack. Three of her men were killed ashore by Japanese bayonets while trying to return to their ship. Scuttled by the watch officer, the last man aboard, the gunboat sank in the Mekong. Her crew took to the jungle, where they kept up the fight until April.

At My Tho, the *Amiral Charner,* which was powered with diesel engines, managed to get away from the dock and anchor in the river. It signalled all the other small ships to send their crews aboard in boats, and then sank the abandoned craft by gunfire. At high tide she got under way in a desperate effort to make the Philippines, but was overtaken by Japanese planes and pounded with bombs. She too had to scuttle herself.

The ships at Vinh Long and Can Tho likewise were destroyed by their own crews when they found escape impossible. Officers and men took to the shore under the command of Lieutenant Commander Jean Mienville, of the *Marne.* In company with a few hundred soldiers, police, and civilian volunteers they fought their way, foot by foot, toward Point Ca Mau, but there was no assistance from any direction, and they too were captured piecemeal before the end of the month. The last to be taken were a small group under Chief Petty Officer Marius Chabert, former master of the *Cam Ranh,* who were overtaken only after they had reached a small island in the Gulf of Siam.

At Haiphong the Japanese had surprised and overpowered the gunboats *Commandant Bourdais* and *Vigilante,* the latter of which was still undergoing major repairs for damage inflicted by the Flying Tigers. Four men escaped by swimming, and later they found a hiding place on an islet in Along Bay.

On the other hand, the *Frézouls* and *Crayssac* managed to elude the Japanese search planes and make their way separately to sea. They met up with each other at Port Wallut, where they also found Captain Charles Commentry, naval commandant in Tonkin, who had escaped from Haiphong with a hundred or more men. The only ships of the Indochinese Fleet to keep the flag of France flying in the Far East, they slowly worked their way toward the Chinese frontier, leaving behind a major in the Medical Corps, Doctor Léon Flottes, to effect the last possible sabotage and then to look after the families they were leaving behind. Doctor Flottes ended his mission, along with his wards, in the nightmare of a Japanese work camp.

The crews of the *Frézouls* and *Crayssac* and the survivors under Captain Commentry encountered conditions little less desperate. Even when they reached Chinese territory they were subjected to extortion, not only from the pirates[3] infesting the seaboard but from the regular Chinese forces themselves, who made them pay for even the water they drank. At long last they made contact with the French Military Mission at Kunming, and on July 17, 1945, Captain Commentry, reduced to a bare shirt and trousers, took off by plane for India, and then Paris, to report to the French Government on what had happened to the Navy in Indochina.

The Army troops there had fared little better. Some of the strongest managed to fight their way through the mountains of Laos until, around the middle of June, they reached the Chinese border. Others, less fortunate, were massacred under the most atrocious conditions. Out of the 12,000 French regulars at the time of the March 9 attack, the Army of Indochina suffered a loss of 2,000 killed, of whom 250 were officers and 500 noncommissioned officers.

Amazingly enough, General Chennault and his Flying Tigers would gladly have assisted the French Army in Tonkin, and were all ready to take off for this purpose, when they received orders from Washington forbidding

---

[3] After the surrender of Japan, the French naval units near the Chinese frontier had to be on guard against their supposed ally, the Chinese; against the Viet-Namese rebels; against the recalcitrant Japanese; and against the native pirates, who were conducting operations on their own private account.

it. "Apparently," wrote General Chennault in his memoirs, "it was American policy then that French Indochina should become a mandated territory after the war, and not be returned to the French. The American Government was interested in seeing the French forcibly ejected from Indochina so that the problem of postwar separation from their colony would be easier."[4]

By this time the war in Europe was over. And while their comrades of Indochina were languishing in the Japanese prisons of Saigon and Hanoi, the crew of the *Richelieu,* newly returned to the Pacific theater, were enjoying the satisfaction of a campaign where one victory quickly succeeded another. In April she sailed with the British battleship *Queen Elizabeth,* two cruisers, five destroyers, and two British escort carriers, to test the Japanese defenses on Sumatra and to intercept enemy coastal shipping between Sabang and Padang. That same month found her, again with the *Queen Elizabeth,* covering the British landings to retake Rangoon. On April 30 she bombarded the Japanese airfield in the Nicobar Islands, and two days later the enemy-held navy yard at Port Blair, in the Andamans. Rangoon fell the next day, and the *Richelieu* reentered Trincomalee harbor just in time to celebrate the victory in Europe.

But hardly had she completed taking on fuel and stores, when she was rushed back to sea again. A Japanese cruiser had been sighted by British submarines and destroyers in the vicinity of Port Blair.

Admiral Walker had divided his forces into two groups, one formed around the *Queen Elizabeth,* and the other around the *Richelieu.*

It was the destroyers of the *Richelieu* group which first relocated the enemy cruiser on the night of May 16. Captain Jean du Vignaux steered to close the range, and the eager crew waited for this opportunity to put their long practiced marksmanship to use.

But then came the devastating message, "Enemy sunk! *Ennemi coulé!"*

It was a message from the 28th Flotilla of British destroyers, who had just sent to the bottom the Japanese cruiser *Haguro* by a skillfully executed torpedo attack almost under the noses of the *Richelieu's* gunners. All that these could do was to exhibit their skill with the antiaircraft guns against the swarming Japanese planes which all that day and the next attempted to get revenge for the *Haguro.*

"The enemy is withdrawing rapidly, but I look forward to sending you out at the first opportunity to intercept him," wrote Admiral Sir Arthur Powers, R.N.,[5] a few days later to Captain du Vignaux.

---

[4] *The Way of a Fighter*—The Memoirs of Major General Claire Lee Chennault, U.S. Army (Retired), page 342.

[5] Vice Admiral Sir Arthur John Powers was Commander in Chief of the East Indies Station.

To be ready for the occasion the *Richelieu* hurried to Durban for dry-docking. She returned to Trincomalee on August 18; the war in the Pacific had ended three days before.

That is, the war in the Pacific with Japan had ended. The war of Indo-china was just beginning.

No one can say, of course, that this war might not have occurred if, the moment the Japanese military power had crumbled, French or friendly forces had moved to reoccupy the principal centers of Indochina and re-turn the control of the government to the French, whom the Japanese had evicted five months earlier. But it is reasonably certain that the extraor-dinary difficulties encountered by the French at Saigon and at Hanoi played a strong part in bringing on the war, which was to last for nine long years.

"Extraordinary" difficulties is the term used because they resulted as much from the acts of friends as of enemies, to say nothing of the errors of the French Govenment. Still, France was fortunate, perhaps, that at the Interallied Potsdam Conference of July, 1945, the agreements made at Chungking in 1943 were modified. Under those agreements the entire territory of Indochina would now have come under Chinese control, since no British or Chinese military operations had taken place in that territory. But it was decided at Potsdam that the southern limit of the Chinese zone of occcupation should be the 16th parallel of north latitude, with the British occupying the lower part of the country up to that parallel.

Admiral Lord Mountbatten was readying his troops for transport to Saigon for that purpose on August 19, when General Douglas MacArthur, of the United States forces, made a momentous decision. He had been desig-nated as Supreme Commander of the Allied Forces for everything con-cerned with the surrender of Japan, and now he forbade the signing of any instrument of surrender or the carrying out of any landings or the reoccupa-tion of any enemy-held territory until he had proceeded in person to Tokyo for the official signing of the document of surrender of the Japanese Empire.

The result of that order was to delay the landing of the first Allied con-tingents at Saigon until September 11, 1945, twenty-eight days after the Japanese defeat. During those twenty-eight days the soldiers and sailors of the French Forces of Indochina had continued to swelter in Japanese con-centration camps, while, outside, the revolution was organizing itself, openly aided and abetted by the Japanese military, who still roamed the land, free and untrammeled—and armed. And it was during those twenty-eight days that the revolution first showed its bloody hand in the massacre of several hundred French people, women and children included, at Saigon —at Hanoi—at Bac-ninh.

The first Frenchman to arrive at Saigon from the outside was Commander Urbain de Riencourt, who parachuted in on August 22. He succeeded in making contact with the imprisoned French sailors, and even obtained the release of Lieutenant Commander François du Boucheron, probably the best informed man available on Navy matters at Saigon. By the end of September a battalion of liberated French Navy men was methodically re-organizing the various naval departments of the government and assisting the British in restoring law and order to the city, where radical elements were running amuck. This small naval group distinguished itself on September 28 by rescuing a troop of Ghurkas of the 20th Indian Division, who had been heavily attacked by the rebels.

"The splendid work of the Navy in arriving swiftly and bringing timely assistance to the English troops," wrote General D. D. Gracey, "promptly relieved the situation."

For the French to assemble troops for the return to Indochina was not difficult; it was the lack of ships to transport them that was troublesome. A small advance contingent was ferried from Ceylon to Saigon by air on September 12, but the main garrison was to be General Leclerc's armored division. A new Governor General, Admiral Thierry d'Argenlieu, had been appointed on August 14.

The new Government in Paris failed to appreciate the advantages of continuing in office the man who had so tenaciously defended Indochina against the Japanese, and whose experience and reputation would have been invaluable in the task of restoring law and order. Instead, Admiral Decoux left his Japanese prison only to reenter another in France as soon as he arrived there.[6] On the trip back, his plane stopped at Calcutta, where Admiral d'Argenlieu was waiting for a plane to Saigon, but the new Governor General made no effort to confer with his predecessor.

Even if the Americans had not grasped the importance of the revolution that was beginning in Southeast Asia, the British had—and they were prompt to give their maximum suport to the French. The reestablishment of French administration in Cochin China and in Annam would undoubtedly have been impossible without the able assistance of Admiral Mountbatten.[7] It was through him that the British steamers *Queen Emma* and *Princess Beatrix* were obtained to transport the first units of General Leclerc's force to Saigon on October 3, 1945. The transports were escorted by the *Richelieu* and the super-destroyer *Triomphant,* which had just been modernized in America. The *Richelieu* was too large to steam up the narrow, winding river channel, but the *Triomphant* proceeded to its moor-

---

[6] On his arrival at Paris, Admiral Decoux was during the next twenty months, kept under surveillance at the military hospital of Val de Grâce, until provisionally placed on liberty. After months of judicial inquiries by the Public Prosecutor of the High Court of Justice, the charges against him were dismissed.

[7] In his book, *Leclerc,* Mr. A. Dansette states that Lord Mountbatten later confided to General Leclerc that if President Roosevelt had not died, the French never would have returned to Indochina.

ings at the foot of Charner Boulevard, where it received an enthusiastic reception as the first French man-of-war to return since the Japanese had occupied the country.

Other ships would soon follow, however, as the Navy was dispatching all available vessels to the Far East. Between October 15 and 27, Indochina saw the arrival of the aircraft carrier *Béarn* with crowded decks, as well as the cruisers *Gloire* and *Suffren,* the light cruiser *Fantasque,* the destroyer escorts *Somali* and *Sénégalais,* the transport *Quercy,* and the sloops *Annamite* and *Gazelle.*

The reoccupation of Cochin China and Annam was primarily a job for the Navy. Before General Leclerc left France, Commander François Jaubert, commanding the Far East Naval Brigade, which was a part of Leclerc's force, had called on his superior to offer his services, but the general did not appear too interested. However, once he had arrived in Indochina, it did not take the new Army Commander in Chief long to discover that the deltas and jungle rivers of that country bore no resemblance whatever to the arid wastes of the Sahara!

In fact, no one could move anywhere except by water. Colonel Massu's armored column, rolling overland from Saigon to the relief of My Tho, found itself bogged down in the traps which the rebels had dug in the main highway. It was the landing party from the *Richelieu* and the Naval Infantry Brigade, going up by river, which relieved the town with the assistance of the sloops *Gazelle* and *Annamite.*

It was the Navy, too, which reoccupied Gô Công and Vinh Long in the delta of the Meking River, and Tan-uyen on the Donnaï. Regrettably, this last operation resulted in the loss of Commander Jaubert, killed in his boat on January 25, 1946, while directing the assault. This was the second tragic blow in a row, as on November 18 a detachment of 19 men proceeding from My Tho to Saigon in a junk had been ambushed and massacred by the rebels.

The British had given hearty assistance in all these early operations. But with the beginning of the New Year they deferred to the French, and on January 15, 1946, General Leclerc assumed full responsibility for all military operations in southern Indochina, under the jurisdiction of High Commissioner Thierry d'Argenlieu.

There still remained Tonkin, the northern part of the country, to be reoccupied if French administration was to return to all of Indochina. Its reoccupation should not have been any more difficult than that of the southern part, and it might have been readily accomplished—had it not been for the Chinese.

Beginning on August 11, 1945, the small patrol vessels *Frézouls* and *Crayssac,* up near the Chinese border, initiated the return by steaming up to

FRENCH TROOPS *landing at Ajaccio, Corsica, from the* TEMPÊTE.

FRENCH REINFORCEMENTS *for the Italian campaign on deck of the cruiser* GLOIRE *entering Naples harbor.*

THE NAVY RETURNS TO TOULON. *French contingent parades on a street in Toulon during a demonstration of the Allies' might after the Provence landings.*

Hon Gay, at the head of Along Bay. By the 15th they were at Haiphong, to be warmly welcomed by the French population. However, Lieutenant Jean Blanchard, who had taken command, failed in his attempt to reach Hanoi via the Bamboo Canal. Instead, he had to fall back, with the *Crayssac* as full of holes from rebel fire as a sieve. It was only by road that he managed to reach the capital of Tonkin, and then under Japanese escort! Furthermore, when he arrived there, he found that all of the French officers who had been made prisoners were still held in the Japanese stockades. It was not until the 5th of October that they were released, at the same time that Chinese armed forces came to replace the Japanese.

Up until that time the American O.S.S. officers had been very quick to help the French in every way possible, but overnight they changed radically. It was, perhaps, coincidence that the Chinese troops took up positions on the 16th parallel of latitude at that very time.

For several months the only French forces in north Indochina were stationed in small, isolated posts in the Fai-Tzi-Long archipelago, where they could be supplied by patrol vessels and armed junks. Between trips, these vessels spent their time running down pirates. On September 3, the *Frézouls* captured a pirate craft by boarding, but on the next day the *Crayssac* was taken in a pirate ambush at Hon Gay, and her commanding officer, Lieutenant Henri Vilar, summarily executed. The Chinese, however, forced the pirates to free the crew, as well as the American O.S.S. officer who had been aboard at the time the ship was captured.

However, in mid-November the arrival of the *Sénégalais*, later relieved by the *Somali*, and then by the *Algérien*, permitted the consolidation of French positions in Along Bay, despite the protests of the local Chinese commander.

If General Chiang Kai-shek had not had troubles in his own country just then, it is to be wondered whether he would ever have permitted the French to reoccupy Haiphong and Hanoi. However, on February 29, 1946, the French Ambassador, Mr. Meyrier, obtained an agreement by which the Chinese Government, in return for material concessions, agreed to French forces relieving the Chinese troops in Tonkin.

All this time the rebels, whose announced desire was for an autonomous state in the French Federation, had been extending their movement in northern Indochina, and had installed a Viet-Namese revolutionary government at Hanoi. The French Government had recognized this "de facto" government, and on March 6, 1946, entered into an agreement by which it acknowledged Viet-Nam to be an independent state, but with membership in the French Federation and the French Union; in return, the Viet-Nam Government agreed to accept the protection of the French troops.

"Operation Bentré"—the reoccupation of Tonkin—was by far the most ambitious amphibious operation the French Navy had ever undertaken with its own personnel and ships. The naval forces, under the command of Vice Admiral Auboyneau, consisted of the cruisers *Emile Bertin, Tourville,* and *Duquesne,* the super-destroyers *Triomphant* and *Fantasque,* the sloops *Savorgnan de Brazza, Chevreuil,* and *Gazelle,* the destroyer escorts *Algérien* and *Sénégalais,* the aircraft carrier *Béarn,* the armed merchant cruiser *Barfleur,* six large transports, and many landing craft of all types.

As so often happened when dealing with the Chinese, the French transports were mistakenly fired on by the troops they were coming to relieve. For over an hour Commander Jubelin, commanding the *Triomphant,* patiently endured a murderous attack before returning the fire in self-defense. With his first salvo, a cloud of white flags broke out over the Chinese fortifications, and the "mistake" was soon remedied.

With the Chinese finally departed, all that remained to be done was to come to an understanding with the young Viet-Namese Republic, first born of the Associated States of the French Union. Ho Chi Minh, leader of the Viet-Namese, received a sovereign's welcome when he arrived at Saigon on his way to France to conclude the final agreements there.

The Navy, reduced to a starvation budget, was recalling and decommissioning its ships one by one. The Army sustained a similar reduction in strength under the national impression that the future political situation would be favorable.

However, this peaceful stage was but a passing moment, prelude to bloodier times. Ho Chi Minh returned from France with only mediocre concessions, and serious rioting began in Haiphong. On November 19, Ho Chi Minh threw off the mask and proclaimed a general insurrection against France.

The details of the Viet-Nam war, which ended only at Geneva, in 1954, with recognition of the complete independence of Viet-Nam, are not within the province of this work. Mention of it is made here only to emphasize the heavy burden which was to face the Navy and to jeopardize its revival after the ordeals of World War II. For nine long years the Navy had to deliver, across a distance of 7,000 miles, all the supplies needed to maintain an expeditionary force of from 120,000 to 150,000 men. It kept open communication lines along the river routes when none existed by land. It supported the Army with the gunfire of its flotillas in places where no tractor guns could have gone. It blockaded the rebel coast, it provided air support to battlefields beyond the range of any land-based planes. It did all this right up to the last tragic hours of the Battle of Dien Bien Phu. For nine years, the Chief of Naval Personnel of the Fleet had to set aside, out of a total of approximately 58,000 men, a full 16,000 for Indochina.

It was a drain, the sacrificial effects of which will continue to be felt for a long time to come.

CHAPTER 30

Bitter Reunion

While their comrades of the merged Free French and Navy of Africa were fighting to liberate them, the officers and men who had remained in France —whether still in service or in civilian life—went through days as full of anguish as of hope. The disruption and ruin resulting from Allied bombing, the unpredictable movements of the German Army and the destruction it left in its wake, the shortage of food, the black market, the terrorism of some of the Maquis and the counter-terrorism of the Militia—all tended to create an atmosphere of civil war. Everyone in France was asking himself how the changeover would be made between the Vichy Government, on which the more destitute depended for sheer existence, and the new authorities who were being installed by the Government of Algiers as fast as new areas were reconquered by the victorious Allies. The essential thing, in everyone's opinion, was just to get rid of the Germans; after that, the readjustment in France would be easy.

It was not the first time that France had known the ebb and flow of wartime politics. More than once the kings or other rulers had had to liberate parts of France from foreigners or dissident groups, like the English and the Burgundians in 1436, or the Spaniards and the Catholic League in 1594. But always, following the liberation, there had been a policy of tolerance, of amnesty, which pacified the violence of partisanship and restored national unity. It was optimistically hoped that the same thing would occur now.

While waiting for the readjustment, the demobilized officers and men everywhere took a leading part in maintaining law and order, protecting the lives and property of the populace, and preventing rash retaliations. Some became the victims of their loyalty to the Government of Vichy.[1] Others, still loyal to the established order, worked in secret for the benefit of the Allied intelligence organizations or else volunteered their services to the

---

[1] Among the few men of the Navy who disappeared in this manner was Vice Admiral Charles Platon, one of the heroes of Dunkirk. But in the next few years, part of which he spent as a Cabinet Minister in Pierre Laval's Government, he had become conspicuous as a partisan of extreme measures. In August, 1944, he fell into the hands of the Maquis of Dordogne and was summarily executed by them.

non-Communist Maquis of the F.F.I. (French Forces of the Interior).

Those who still served their country in uniform in the ports and navy yards were instructed by Marshal Pétain, in a broadcast message on June 6, 1944, to maintain an attitude of neutrality toward both belligerents. Under German duress as he was, and with all of France still at the mercy of Hitler, he could not well have done otherwise. A more audacious proclamation would have been in keeping with public sentiment, but without weapons and without even any knowledge of the Allied plans, to have instigated premature action would have left France open to the same bloody retaliation that was visited upon Warsaw for its abortive uprising. Furthermore the Vichy Government had secret information through Swiss channels that the American command did not ask for more.

Behind the scenes, however, instructions were being issued or actions taken at the various administrative levels which went well beyond the official attitude of passive neutrality. Just before his communication lines had been cut off by both the German retreat and the Allied advance, Rear Admiral Bléhaut, Minister of the Navy, had sent out orders to all naval personnel in France, directing them to rejoin the fight at the side of their comrades from overseas, and to place themselves under the orders of the leaders in Algiers.

The naval headquarters at Algiers were not unaware of these orders. As far back as the spring of 1943, Admiral Bléhaut had established secret communication with Algiers via the French naval attaché in Madrid. Later, officer couriers like Lieutenant Commander Barthélémy had made round trips between the two sections. In addition, the Naval Security Service at Toulon had set up a clandestine radio link with Algiers. It was by this channel that, on August 7, 1944, Admiral Bléhaut sent the following message to Admiral Lemonnier:

> For Lemonnier, from Jack.[2]
> The Navy in Metropolitan France, faithful to the line of conduct followed during the past seventeen months, has remained united and disciplined, aloof from all European influences, police or political. Our personnel in the ports are doing their utmost to prevent confiscation and destruction in the naval establishments, which are being safeguarded with the object of realizing a much desired reunion between the Navies of Algiers and of Metropolitan France.
>
> In case of invasion, the personnel have instructions to place themselves under the orders of the Navy of Algiers while maintaining appearances in order to prevent reprisals against other naval personnel not yet liberated . . .

The message[3] ended with proposals for a procedure to follow in order to establish closer liaison.

---

[2] "Jack" was Captain Charles Jacquinet, administrative officer on the staff of Admiral Bléhaut.

[3] Unnumbered message carrying the date-time group 071800 August.

No reply was ever received to this message. However, four days later, Algiers found a way to send a message related to ordnance material.

"Are there," asked Commander Henri Trautmann, Director of Intelligence at Algiers, "any spare 152-mm. inner liner tubes available to replace those in the guns of cruisers now approaching the limit of wear?"

An answer was immediately sent, informing him that there were some at Toulon, out of reach of the Germans—and that the Allies should take care not to bomb them!

Up to the very end, Vichy maintained this clandestine communication with Algiers, thanks to a secret radio transmitter installed on the roof of the Palace of Chaillot[4] under the supervision of Commander Paul Boulanger, chief of the communications section of the Minister of the Navy.

At the same time other steps were being taken in the political field, toward the same end that Admiral Bléhaut and his associates were seeking in the military field. Marshal Pétain sought the assistance of Admiral Auphan, now living at his home in an inactive status, in establishing a political liaison with General de Gaulle.

More than once, since his resignation, the former Minister of the Navy had spoken to the Marshal on the necessity of establishing a contact with the Government of Algiers and the Allied statesmen in order to prepare for the postwar reunion of the French which Admiral Darlan had initiated at Algiers and which was so much in accord with the national tradition as well as the feeling in the Navy itself. Marshal Pétain had fully intended to promote a transfer of power to whatever legitimate government arose after the liberation, even if it meant his own retirement. But with perhaps excessive prudence he did not wish to set any such movement in progress as long as the Germans possessed the power to retaliate. But on the strength of secret intelligence from Vatican sources, he asked Admiral Auphan to meet him at Vichy on August 11, 1944. At the same time he instructed the Admiral in writing to make contact with the Allied command and with General de Gaulle "for the purpose of finding a solution to the French political problem, at the time of liberation, of such nature as would prevent a civil war and would effect a reconciliation among all Frenchmen of good faith."

Working his way through the mass of retreating Germans, the admiral arrived in Paris that same evening and immediately made his mission known to his contacts in the Resistance, who transmitted the information to Algiers. Again there was no response to this well-intended advance.

In the meantime events were moving rapidly at Vichy. A number of the Government's Ministers here had already been taken, willingly or unwill-

---

[4] This radio was on the roof of the wing which shelters the Naval Museum. The Palace of Chaillot is located in the Place du Trocadéro, on the north bank of the Seine, directly across from the Eiffel Tower.

ingly, to Germany, Admiral Auphan had advised Marshal Pétain to remain in Vichy until he could arrange with the Resistance leaders for the Marshal's trip to Paris, where a public reconciliation with General de Gaulle would have a tremendous moral effect on France. But it was too late. On August 20 the Germans forcibly removed Marshal Pétain from Vichy and took him to Germany. Admiral Bléhaut, loyal to the end, refused to be separated from his chief and accompanied him into captivity.

Informed of this by radio, Admiral Auphan posted on the walls of Paris, and sent to the newspapers for publication, Marshal Pétain's last appeal to the French:

> . . . Once more I call on you to unite. It is not difficult to do one's duty but it is sometimes difficult to know what that duty is. Your duty, however, is simple: Join those who will guarantee to lead you in the path of honor and along the road of order. . . . Obey those who preach for a peaceful society, without which order can never be established. . . .

This last message thus broadcast, the ex-Minister of the Navy had only to wait for the arrival of the first French or Allied authorities in order to carry out the mission Marshal Pétain had entrusted to him.

Meanwhile, with all the political leaders at Vichy having fled or been deported as prisoners, certain members of what had formerly been the French Admiralty had formed, under Captain René Amet, an organization called the "Navy Center." Its purpose was to guard the archives and to insure the subsistence of naval personnel and the safety and welfare of their families. The rest of the Admiralty personnel joined the Maquis. Several days later the archives were turned over to a representative of the general staff of the Navy of Algiers, who personally checked everything.

On August 26, the day after the Allies had entered Paris, Admiral Auphan was informed that General Juin, Chief of Staff of National Defense of the Government of Algiers, had reentered the city along with General de Gaulle. The admiral had had close relations with General Juin during the hectic years of 1941 and 1942, so he promptly informed the general of his mission and requested a meeting.

They met on the afternoon of August 27, at the home of a mutual friend. The rupture of November, 1942, was fully discussed, as well as all the events that had followed the Allied landings and Darlan's resumption of hostilities against the Axis. At the conclusion of the meeting General Juin took with him several documents which the admiral had given him for General de Gaulle, in one of which the admiral asked for a personal interview. Another one in particular pointed out the service that would be rendered to the public in a political reconciliation that would strengthen respect for legitimate government.

This approach, like the previous one, was greeted with utter silence.[5] The new Government showed no intention of having any contacts with the preceding one.

That refusal, with its consequences which still so grievously affect French politics, is not a subject for discussion in this book. All that will be considered here is the consequence of that refusal in the Navy.

For Admiral Auphan, having failed to make contacts on the government level, had determined to see what could be done on the naval level. It did not occur to him that his juniors, his comrades, his close friends of the period before November, 1942, would deliberately avoid meeting him. Yet such was the case. The officer he sent to the new Chief of Naval Operations, requesting an interview, was told on September 3 that there could be no question of such a meeting—that it would be far too dangerous "for him and for me."

It soon became evident that in the new regime—and especially among the civilian appointees—there were those who considered that to have supported the Vichy Government was, *ipso facto,* an act of treason against the country. Under the shadow of this grim idealogy, the Navy's new leaders found it expedient to allow the public to forget, as quickly as possible, the loyalty with which the Navy had carried out its traditional obligation of obedience to the civil government, regardless of party or politics. Hence the dissociation between some of the higher echelons of the new Navy and those in command during the critical days of the armistice. Some officers who merely by chance had happened to be in North Africa in November, 1942, in the days of Casablanca, Algiers, Oran, and Bizerte, were more cautious about comprising associations with those who had remained in France than even those who had boldly served in the F.F.N.F. from the first.

No doubt the leaders of the Navy, with vivid recollections of unpleasant experiences with political circles in Algiers, felt that they could better serve by confining themselves strictly to naval operations and technical matters in which they had been specially trained. This position was given point by the first act of the Commissioner of the Navy upon arriving in Paris, which was to appoint a commission to carry out a wholesale investigation of the French naval personnel who had remained in France during the armistice. And his appointee to head this commission was a retired officer, Vice

---

[5] On March 2, 1945, General de Gaulle mentioned this incident to the Consultative Assembly in these words: "At the moment when I arrived in Paris, there was handed me a message from a representative of Marshal Pétain. That representative had, by virtue of a written order dated August 11, 1944, full powers to seek with us 'a solution of a nature to avoid civil war.' I refused to meet the representative. Gentlemen, where is the civil war?"

Admiral Louis Sablé, who was recalled to active duty especially for the assignment.

Naturally, no admiral in service in France after November, 1942, was retained on the active list. Overseas, only Admiral Robert Battet and Admiral Louis Collinet, of the old circle, were retained. To have repudiated Admiral Decoux, the Governor General in Indochina, would have been madness at the time, but the circumstances under which he was temporarily continued in his post have already been described.

On September 5, 1944, the new Commissioner of the Navy addressed a letter to the Head of the Provisional Government, asking for the dismissal, without pension, of Admiral Robert, the former French High Commissioner in the Antilles, Admiral Esteva, the former Resident Governor General in Tunisia, and Admiral Platon, a former Cabinet Minister at Vichy, though the latter had already been dead for several weeks under the executioner's bullets of the Resistance. Then followed, in quick succession, orders either retiring or dismissing without pension Admirals Le Luc, Marquis, Gouton, Danbé, Paul Jardel, de Laborde, Abrial, Auphan, and Bléhaut. That these measures were without legality was proved when they were revoked by decrees of the Council of State, six or seven years later, when passions had somewhat quieted down.

"I have been without pity toward the leaders who showed themselves to be unworthy," stated Commissioner of the Navy Jacquinot in November, 1944, to a reporter of the newspaper, *Libération Soir*. Several months later, while addressing the National Assembly, Mr. Jacquinot's successor, Edmond Michelet, Minister of the Armed Forces, stated that he or his predecessor had eliminated 97 per cent of the flag officers of the Navy.[6]

That somewhat exaggerated figure was no doubt given in order to satisfy an ill-disposed public opinion. The significance of it is that a Minister of the Government could, without a voice raised in protest, declare that out of the 123 officers of flag rank in the Navy in 1939, only four or five were deemed worthy of being retained on the active list.

In addition to the flag officers, the Navy witnessed the departure of dozens of captains—some removed by Ministerial decision, others leaving the service voluntarily because of discouragement. Thus, at a time when the Navy was to be faced with the most difficult problems in Indochina and elsewhere, that service was losing an important percentage of its most experienced officers. Losing, in fact, three-quarters of the mature officers in the grade from which normally the leaders of the future would have been selected.

However, to the honor of the Navy, let it be said that the reunion which failed to materialize in the top echelons was often carried out spontane-

---

[6] *Official Journal,* April 4, 1946.

ously on the subordinate levels. Even while prison doors were closing on some of the most distinguished admirals of France, and a Ministerial decree was cancelling all promotions made in the Navy in France after November 8, 1942,[7] the two divisions were meeting amicably in the liberated ports, where the needs of the service brought about a quick mingling of officers from Metropolitan France with those from the empire. Admiral Thierry d'Argenlieu made it a point to praise the devoted officers who had protected the interests of France in the occupied ports. On his staff he had the former chief of the division most concerned with carrying out the clauses of the armistice—that is to say, an officer who for months had had to participate in constant negotiations with the Germans. And the new captain of the *Triomphant,* a former F.F.N.F. officer with a brilliant wartime record, especially requested, as his executive officer, an officer who had remained in Metropolitan France and who had never for a moment denied his past.

As quickly as the liberating forces swept past the residences of the purged admirals, these officers were arrested and arraigned. Not before a court-martial, which is the right of any service officer accused of dereliction of his military duty, but before a political High Court of Justice composed exclusively of civilians and politicians. On March 15, 1945, Admiral Esteva ran the gantlet of such a court and heard himself condemned to imprisonment for life. Then came in succession the trials of others high in military rank. General Dentz was condemned to death, but died in prison, of cold and privation, before the sentence could be carried out. Marshal Pétain was condemned to death. Various Ministers were condemned to imprisonment for life or slightly lesser terms. Even Weygand—Weygand, the irreproachable—after returning from incarceration by the Germans, went from one French prison to another until finally it was discovered that no true bill could be found against him.

After these sensations, the next spectacle promised to the public was the trial of those indicted for the scuttling of the Fleet at Toulon— Admirals de Laborde, Abrial, Marquis, and Auphan.

The first three of these were already under lock and key. But the warrant for the arrest of former Minister of the Navy Auphan could not be served because on September 9, when it was issued, he had gone to Paris to try to carry out the mission assigned him by Marshal Pétain. The admiral continued with his mission, feeling it more important than to answer indictments which had been brought against him without his even having a hear-

---

[7] An official order issued at Algiers and dated July 20, 1944, directed that no officer above the rank of commander be recalled to active duty except on specific authority of the Commissioner of the Navy in each individual case. Thus it was left to the discretion of the Commissioner to determine the conditions under which certain officers could be restored to the regular Navy.

ing. However, on October 20 he took advantage of a safe opportunity to communicate with Admiral Leahy, Chief of Staff to President Roosevelt.

Now that the French Government and the new naval regime had refused to listen to him, he tried to arrange for a meeting with the Commander in Chief of the Allied Armies in Europe, to whom he was accredited by the powers he held from Marshal Pétain. But Lieutenant Colonel Leonard H. Nason, U.S.A., brought back General Eisenhower's reply that the Government of General de Gaulle had been recognized by the United States, and that consequently he could have no contact with a fugitive from justice who was being sought in his own country.

Thus all doors were closed. The stage was set for the trial of the officers of the Toulon Fleet, which was set for the summer of 1946.

This presented the former Minister of the Navy with a difficult matter of conscience. An officer, particularly one who feels no guilt and who is responsible for actions taken by others, must not evade the course of justice. But could such a political trial—already being adjudged in a partisan press —be called a court of justice? The Keeper of the Seals, which is the technical title in France of the Minister of Justice, himself apparently did not think so. He had met the admiral several times in the Resistance in 1943 and 1944, and had been understanding; now, on the eve of the trials, he discreetly advised the admiral to evade a trial which could not qualify as a process of justice.

Thereupon the ex-Minister of the Navy made the decision not to present himself for trial. However, even at grave risk, he publicly gave his reasons why. When the case came up, on July 30, 1946, he sent to the President of the High Court of Justice, the Socialist Deputy Louis Noguères, a letter dated two days before, and of which he had sent a copy to the press. In this letter he defended the Navy and vindicated the actions of his subordinates until the moment of his resignation from the Government. He concluded with an emphatic statement:

> When the French wake up, they would never forgive me if I allowed the honor of the Navy—an honor never even questioned by the Germans—to be judged by a tribunal set up by a government in which there appears not only a deserter from the Navy, but also one who was a mutineer in the Black Sea.[8]

---

[8] The Deputy thus referred to as a "deserter" was Maurice Thorez, who deserted the colors in September, 1939, and fled to Russia until after the war. The "mutineer" was the Deputy Charles Tillon, a former petty officer of the Navy who had been serving on a ship in the French Black Sea Squadron in the early years of the Russian Revolution. In 1920, he had received a heavy sentence for having attempted to seize his commanding officer in order to turn the ship over to the Soviets. In 1946, Thorez was Vice President of the Council of Ministers, and Tillon was the Minister of Armaments.

At the time of the trial, Admiral de Laborde was prevented by a surgical operation from facing the court. Nor could Admirals Abrial and Marquis be tried, for, at the last moment, the Communist members of the High Court refused to sit—as a protest, they said, against verdicts which were becoming "too lenient." This attitude of vigilant rectitude, intended to appeal to the masses, naturally did not contribute to calm, judicious deliberation by the jury when the postponed trial finally began on August 12, 1946.

There was no justification at all for hailing Admiral Marquis before the court. The former Naval Commandant of Toulon had never exercised the slightest political function. If he were responsible for carrying out the scuttling of the ships of his command, this was a military act for which he was answerable only to his peers in a naval court-martial, as prescribed in the Military Code of Justice for the Navy. He had not handed over to the enemy one single weapon intact—quite differently from the Army generals in November, 1942, yet not one of these was ever prosecuted.

The case against Admiral Abrial was equally thin. He had been called out of retirement only eight days before the scuttling, and it was quite evident that the decision had not rested with him as to getting the Fleet under way at the time the Free Zone was invaded.

The man who had been Minister of the Navy at that time was the only one in a position to explain that point. Admiral Auphan claimed the privilege of doing so by submitting beforehand, to the lawyers of Marquis and de Laborde, a statement in his own handwriting in which he completely absolved the naval command of Toulon of any responsibility for the scuttling.

To try the ex-Minister of the Navy without his being present was, of course, a travesty of justice.[9] Nevertheless he was tried, *in absentia,* along with the other two—and, naturally, was given special attention. He was duly convicted and sentenced to hard labor for life, along with confiscation of all his property, both present and future. And, upon hearing the verdict, he was the person most astonished at not having been sentenced to death!

As for Admiral Abrial, the Court took into account the eminent services he had rendered at Dunkirk, and only sentenced him to ten years at hard labor. Admiral Marquis received the relatively minor punishment of five

[9] Translator's Note: I can confirm the ease with which I was able to get in touch after the war with Admiral Auphan a number of times in Paris, during his clandestine residence there. Apparently there were quite a few people who knew his whereabouts and who, in fact, frequently saw him. It would appear that if the authorities had seriously wanted to apprehend the admiral, they could have done so without any great difficulty. This leads to the conclusion that there were members of the Government who were afraid his testimony on a witness stand might place them themselves in an equivocal position.

years in prison and national degradation for life.[10]

Having recovered from his surgical operation, Admiral de Laborde faced the Court in his turn and heard himself sentenced to death—not on the charge of scuttling, from which he defended himself perfectly, but on indiscreet letters he had written to Admiral Platon relating to plans for the reconquest of the Chad from the Free French. However, he was not executed, and after two years in the prison of Riom he was given his freedom.[11]

Such summary justice did not appeal to Admiral Bléhaut, who, upon his return from the German prison with Marshal Pétain, had been arrested, and then provisionally released. He deemed it wiser to go to Switzerland and let himself be tried *in absentia.*

Admiral Robert received a sentence of ten years at hard labor, but the High Court itself was the first to recommend that the sentence not be carried out.

Admiral Le Luc, after several years of clandestine existence, was likewise sent to prison for two years, and served his term at the side of the former Chief of Police of Paris. Even Vice Admiral Régis Bérenger, the victor of Koh Chang, was dragged from one court of inquiry to another until finally, as a result of his protests, he secured a trial before a regular court-martial. Sitting on the court were the most respected leaders of the Navy of both the prewar and the postwar period.[12] Bérenger was triumphantly acquitted of the feeble charges which had been brought against him by the Court of Justice of Saigon.

Besides these, a number of officers of lesser rank were tried before various tribunals ranging from a simple purging committee to the Courts of Justice. Several sentences of death were pronounced and carried out, among them being the noted naval writer, Captain Paul Chack, accused of writing propaganda for the Germans, and Commander Joseph Lécussan.

---

[10] "*Indignité nationale,*" or national degradation, was a punishment imposed in France on those found guilty of collaborating with the Germans during the occupation.

[11] Admiral de Laborde, whose thirst for action was legendary in the Navy, could not reconcile himself to passive retirement. The main evidence against him was that he had begun a joint study, with the Germans, of the possibility of reconquering the Chad. Anything beyond the planning stage was never proved.

In Riom prison, with typical quarterdeck discipline he insisted on ruling with a rod of iron the other prisoners also sentenced to death—notably the well-known monarchist journalist, Charles Maurras.

[12] Among the distinguished officers sitting on the court were Admiral Nomy, the Chief of Naval Operations of the French Navy, and Admiral Durand-Viel, a former Chief of Naval Operations. Admiral Bérenger was blamed for certain actions carried out while he was Commandant of the Navy in Indochina after the Battle of Koh Chang—notably a study of a plan to reoccupy New Caledonia after hostilities began in the Pacific.

The years passed by, quickly for the rapidly changing Governments which tried in vain to put France back on her feet, but slowly and painfully for the countless prisoners, removed officials, and political exiles who had been the victims of the purge. The fiery passions of the postwar years, caught up in other problems, began to calm down.

Now, with a more sober perspective, it was realized that matters had not been as simple as they had seemed in the emotionally charged days of the liberation. In light of the difficulties which the country was facing, a union of the French—of *all* the French—seemed a necessity. The number of individual reprieves or general pardons increased, month by month—without, however, any modification of the principles underlying the trials. This fact sadly detracted from the significance of the remissions.

It was not possible to bring the dead back to life. But little by little, the condemned naval officers left their prisons, either through remitted sentences or through being placed on conditional liberty—acts of mercy which the Government did its best to conceal from the press and public opinion.

There remained, however, the cases of two—Admiral Bléhaut and Admiral Auphan. In trying them, the High Court of Justice, contrary to all principles of common law, had provided that sentences pronounced against those tried *in absentia* were final and enforceable even if they later presented themselves for trial. However, a law passed in 1953 revoked all that.

Under these changed conditions the two ex-Ministers of the Navy surrendered themselves to the authorities in January, 1955, and that same day were released on provisional liberty. Anxious that his surrender should not appear as a disavowal of his actions, Admiral Auphan had taken the precaution of writing the Attorney General beforehand, "An inquiry into my responsibilities from the point of view of the vague accusations under which I have been condemned *in absentia* would not have for me, or probably for the general public, the determination of the moral issues which would seem to be the very objective of justice."

Admiral Bléhaut was tried the following April, and was promptly and fully acquitted. It can thus be seen how times had changed, compared to the sentences handed out to the other admirals several years earlier.

Admiral Auphan was tried on July 19, 1955, in mid-summer when the public was more interested in vacations than in court actions. Not daring either to convict or to acquit, the High Court dodged the issue by finding him "partially responsible for the events of November, 1942," and sentencing him to five years in prison, and then suspending the sentence "on account of his attitude at that time." In the same manner it voided the punishment of "national degradation" for known "services rendered to the Resistance" during the German occupation.

Questionable as it may be whether the verdict recognized the full services rendered to the country and the attempt to reunite the French, at any rate it marked an end to the persecution which had befallen the Navy at the end of the war. All the Navy men who had been condemned by the High Court have had their property rights restored; the majority have been granted general amnesty. Admiral Auphan and Admiral Bléhaut are again carried on the Navy list in the retired flag officer section. But those who had lost their lives or their health in prison did not find them again, and broken careers were never reestablished.

Disturbing as the court-martials and dismissals of fighting senior officers was, the Navy can consider itself fortunate that the technical nature of the naval profession automatically protected it from wholesale incorporation into its ranks of poorly qualified individuals merely because these had achieved military rank in the Forces of the Resistance, as had happened in the Army. For though one can appoint himself a lieutenant or colonel in a partisan group without having to pass examination on technical subjects, he cannot thereby automatically endow himself with the technical qualifications for an officer of the deck or ship's engineer. The Navy limited itself to retaining on active duty those reserve officers coming from the merchant marine, as is often done in time of peace.

As for the radical gust that swept over France in 1944, it can be said that it grazed the Navy without actually touching it. The few officers who were won over by the Communist or Progressive Party rainbow soon left the Navy to enter politics. The others continue on in their profession.

CHAPTER 31

Conclusion

At the time when the Second World War began, the French Navy had been one of the four strongest navies in the world. When the German break-through on land occurred and the French armies were broken and scattered, the Navy still remained strong and intact. To the last moment it held the great ports and naval bases, which were finally taken only by assaults from the interior. It sacrificed ships and men to help evacuate from Dunkirk, Brest, and elsewhere the officers and men who eventually became an important part of the spearhead of the great amphibious effort that would liberate France.

Then came the armistice of 1940.

The decision to seek that armistice was made not by the Navy, but by the Civil Government, convinced that the Armies had no power left to fight, and that further resistance would only mean useless bloodshed and increased suffering for the civilian populace.

The one remaining bargaining piece that Government possessed was the Navy. And the neutralization of the Navy was the price the duly established leaders of the Government paid for the saving of countless lives, the continued existence of a French Government in at least a part of the country still unoccupied by the enemy—and the empire intact overseas, from which eventually would be launched the first operation in the liberation of Europe.

The negotiations at the armistice convention were not simply a list of conditions laid down by the conquerors and accepted by the conquered. The struggle across the convention table was as grimly contested as on the actual field of battle itself. The one and only thing the French negotiators had to fight with was the French Fleet.

What other resources, what other assistance, could France count on? None. Britain had lost practically all her land equipment, was frantically scraping up from everywhere the makeshift weapons with which to fight an invasion expected at any moment. The United States, despite the French Government's last appeals, would not, could not do anything. Russia was at that moment an accomplice, not an enemy, of Hitler.

Against the neutralization of the French Fleet, then, was balanced the occupation of the whole of France and a slave status for every French worker; a possible thrust by the whole might of the Axis into Egypt and Africa either through a sympathetic Spain or a conquered Turkey. And who could believe that Turkey could have long resisted the full assault of the power that later almost beat immense Russia to her knees.

There were sincere men even then who advocated removing the Fleet and the Government to Africa, and continuing the struggle from there. But a shift of the Government and the Armed Forces and the materials for the logistic support of those forces cannot be done at a moment's notice. It takes time, preparation—and there was no time, there had been no preparation.

The French Government exchanged the neutralization of the Fleet for the continuance of a viable country, an established government, an empire intact overseas—and the chance to fight again.

There were those, escaped from the crushing heel of the invader, who took the gamble—and desperate gamble it was—to set up a new resistance in England, the Free French under General de Gaulle. But these were, in the officer grades, only the smallest percentage of the whole officers' roster— only a few dozen, and these on an individual and personal basis. The great majority of the Navy, true to its traditional concept that the military should always be subordinate to the civilian authority, continued to carry out the orders they received from that authority. Only when the authorized representatives of that government, convinced that the time had come to throw off the shackles and reenter the war, decided to that effect, would the Navy take any such step.

That was the stand of the Navy—to carry out faithfully the conditions of the armistice the Government had thought best to sign, and to maintain the Fleet intact, ready as a powerful weapon when the Government called upon it. And in the meantime they would, as directed by their Government, defend that last remaining weapon of France against all comers.

That last was the plighted word given by the leaders of the Navy to Britain. But Britain did not heed it—and so came the tragedy of Mers-el-Kebir, and the unexpected Anglo-American attacks at Casablanca and elsewhere in November, 1942.

Those tragedies could have been avoided if the Allies had given the same credence to the French Navy's word that even the German did, and which that Navy proved fully valid when it sacrificed its Fleet at Toulon. In particular, if the Anglo-Americans had confided in the leaders of the French Navy before the landings, all the bloodshed could have been avoided; Darlan, as recognized representative of the established government of France, could have made his move one week sooner—and both the French Navy and France itself could have been spared the martyrdom and schism and partisanship that still affect their security today.

Even so, there could have been a reconciliation, a reunion in the Navy at any rate, had it not been for the interference of politics, For, fundamentally, those who had remained in England in 1940 to fight and those who remained in France to work and suffer with the country differed only in time and means on the question of resistance. Common to all was the firm determination to free France from the German invader.

But instead of reunion there were the courts-martial, the trials, the prison sentences, the dismissals. These left a heartburning, a bitterness, that will not be completely forgotten until a new generation replaces the old.

Meantime, what of the French Navy? What of it in the future?

At the beginning of the Second World War, the French Navy had a fleet of approximately 700,000 tons of combatant ships, of which 249 men-of-war, totalling 457,000 tons, were lost. To these casualties must be added 57,000 tons of auxiliary ships.

The French merchant marine, for its part, lost a total tonnage of 1,328,852, or almost one-half of it entire shipping.

In killed and missing, the Navy lost 8,358, of whom 361 were officers. The merchant marine lost over 1,500 men, of whom three-quarters were lost *after the armistice*.

On January 1, 1945, the complement of the French Navy was 4,532 officers and 74,600 petty officers and men, to whom must be added 941 French WAVES (S.F.F. in French, *or Services Féminins de la Flotte*). That was practically the figure at the time of Germany's surrender, as there had been no occasion for any increase in forces afloat.

Of the French fighting fleet, which had been the fourth largest in the world in 1939, there remained only two battleships, one of which was not completed, a few cruisers already pretty well worn out, a dozen submarines in almost the same condition, and a miscellaneous aggregation of destroyers, escort and patrol vessels, landing craft, and auxiliaries of all sorts and all derivations.

During the years immediately following the victory, the French Government retained the old traditional concept that the main enemy of France was—would always be—her neighbor on the other side of the Rhine. Just as in the days of the Czar, France contracted an alliance with Moscow. In order that the Second World War should really be "the last of all wars," it was held, there should be allowed no resurgence of militarism in Germany. And for these reasons, there was no reason to reconstruct a navy.

Hence it was that the Navy, without any but antiquated ships, and with practically no support from the public, had to fight the war in Indochina.

Now the political outlook of France, and of the entire world, has taken a completely different aspect—an aspect that anyone should have seen who did not forget the implacable ideological character of the Soviet Revolution. The points of contact between two hemispheres dedicated to radically differing ideologies have become points of dangerous friction. While the two great powers heading these ideologies compete with each other in a race of rockets, missiles, bombs, and other thermonuclear weapons, and at the same moment hope there will never be need to use them, subversive forces everywhere have exploited national partisanships, copying the Maquis and menacing the peace of the peoples of the globe.

In those countries which still strive to hold on to their spiritual liberty, the object of national defense is, first, to safeguard themselves from that menace, and then to assist other threatened nations to rid themselves of it. Such are the fundamental principles which led the United States to take the initiative in constituting defense bulwarks, such as NATO, SEATO,[1] etc. It is unthinkable that France will not participate in such endeavors in proportion to her means and her situation. But before asking the taxpayers to subscribe to a thing so costly and so generally misunderstood as a Navy, it is necessary to show them the risks for which they are invited to pay.

Within the next ten years or so, which is as far ahead as the human intelligence can at present project itself, the Asiatic countries, because of their prolific rate of population increase alone, are likely to present constantly mounting problems. Hence it would seem well to be prepared for a general war against the Soviet bloc, as well as localized conflicts like the wars in Korea or Israel, ranging all the way from colonial guerrilla warfare to assassination on the street corners, employing only conventional weapons, even to shotguns and kitchen knives.

Whatever the type of conflict, however, history teaches us one thing: that it has always been the sea which has played the decisive role in war, and that such will continue to be the case in the destiny that today binds the European, American, African, and Australian continents which form the prop of Western civilization.

It is conceivable that ultimately atomic explosions will contaminate the liquid mass of the oceans, as well as the earth which provides man with his food and the atmosphere which enables him to breathe. But on that day there will be no more problems that we now know—certainly no more

---

[1] NATO (North Atlantic Treaty Organization) and SEATO (Southeast Asia Treaty Organization) are collective security or defense systems for the North Atlantic and Southeast Asia areas, established on August 24, 1949, and September 8, 1954, respectively. NATO members include Belgium, Canada, Denmark, France, Iceland, Italy, Luxembourg, the Netherlands, Norway, Portugal, United Kingdom, United States, Greece, Turkey, and the German Federal Republic; SEATO members include Australia, France, New Zealand, Pakistan, the Philippines, Thailand, United Kingdom, and the United States.

politico-naval problems of the sort we are discussing. For humanity will have been reduced to a few surviving specimens, hiding in the depths of caves and living on pre-historic levels.

However, it is far from certain that man's madness will take him that far. It it doesn't, or if only nuclear weapons of limited force are used, or if a successful counterweapon is developed, which has always happened in the past, the sea will still retain its dominant strategic value. Fleets of war as well as merchant shipping will be as necessary to maintain contacts between the Allied countries as they will be to carry the war to the enemy. Thus once more will be met, but on a planetary level and with technical means infinitely advanced, the same problems as were encountered in the last war: defensive measures against submarines and planes and missiles; offensive measures against enemy raiders and, above all, against the territories and communications of the enemy forces.

On that assumption, the character of France's naval contribution, as well as the direction it will take, are already predicated. The main endeavor of France's seapower will be directed toward the Mediterranean and Africa. It is already provided for in the programs in progress: aerial and naval escorts of greater or less radius of action to protect shipping, and atomic-powered submarines to carry the war to the enemy. Neither France's means nor her position in the over-all strategic concept qualify her for the maintenance of the colossal carriers which presently constitute one of the principal reprisal weapons of the democracies.

But sober consideration impels one to believe that the Soviet strategy does not lead necessarily toward a Third World War. On the contrary, considering what has happened in the past few years, it would seem to be to the interest of the Communists to permit the present situation to deteriorate naturally, and to wait for the socialist germs to take effect in those countries where they have been planted. In the meantime they hasten the process by nurturing internal subversive movements or by bringing a discreet support to those disturbances which the general staffs are beginning to qualify as "revolutionary."

In that eventuality, which is rationally the most probable, the Navy has a role to fulfill. But in a country like France, that role goes beyond a simple naval participation in the physical tasks of providing supplies and of maintaining order. Hot or cold, modern war is first and foremost ideological. When the crisis reaches the personal point of killing or being killed, one must believe in something, one must feel that his actions are in agreement with the moral values which he believes to be those of his country and of humanity. And such moral strength comes only from a spirit of discipline, self-sacrifice, and devotion to country and to the people.

APPENDICES

APPENDIX A

FRENCH NAVY ON 1 JANUARY 1939

Type	In Commission	Under Construction[1]	Total
Battleships	7 (163,945 tons)	2 (70,000 tons)	9 (233,945 tons)
Aircraft Carriers	2 (32,146 tons)	1 (18,000 tons)	3 (50,146 tons)
Cruisers	19 (154,502 tons)		19 (154,502 tons)
Destroyers	71 (121,201 tons)	8 (14,176 tons)	79 (135,377 tons)
Submarines	76 (74,088 tons)	10 (9,194 tons)	86 (83,282 tons)
Totals	545,882 tons	111,370 tons	657,252 tons

[1] A certain number of ships authorized were not yet under construction.

ORDER OF BATTLE ON 1 SEPTEMBER 1939

Main Fleet

Under Orders of the Chief of Naval Operations

1st Squadron (Raiding Force, Brest)
  2 battleships (*Dunkerque, Strasbourg*); aircraft carrier (*Béarn*); 3 light cruisers; 8 super-destroyers.
2nd Squadron (Oran—Mers-el-Kebir)
  3 battleships (*Provence, Lorraine, Bretagne*); 9 fleet-destroyers.
3rd Squadron (Toulon)
  6 heavy cruisers; 9 super-destroyers.
5th Squadron
  2 cruisers at Dakar; 1 cruiser at Fort-de-France.
(Special ships and the overseas Naval Forces).

Under Orders of Admiral, North (English Channel and North Sea)

3 torpedo boats; 4 sloops; 4 submarines; 1 minelayer; submarine chasers and motor torpedo boats; 3 naval air squadrons; 1 infantry division along the coast.

Under Orders of Admiral, West (Atlantic)

2 old battleships (*Paris, Courbet*); 4 super-destroyers; 12 fleet-destroyers; 3 torpedo boats; 12 submarines; 16 sloops; 2 naval air squadrons.

389

Under Orders of Admiral, South (Mediterranean)

    (a) At Toulon: 2 super-destroyers; 3 torpedo boats; 4 sloops; 3 submarine chasers; 12 submarines; 9 naval air squadrons.

    (b) At Bizerte: *4th Squadron* (in time of war designated as the Light Attack Force).

        3 light cruisers; 8 super-destroyers; 4 torpedo boats; 3 sloops, 1 minelayer; 17 submarines; 3 naval air squadrons.

    (c) At Oran: 3 fleet-destroyers; 1 seaplane carrier; 1 submarine tender; 12 submarines.

    (d) At Morocco: 2 fleet-destroyers; 4 submarines; 1 naval air squadron.

Auxiliary Fleet
(Being Commissioned)

23 auxiliary cruisers; 70 patrol vessels; 344 minesweepers; 76 patrol boats; 2 hospital ships.

(Later, 8 trawlers ordered in England, equipped with asdic.)

St. Stephen's House, Westminster   London, 1 July 1940
(Westminster Underground Station)
Abbey 1384

By order of General de Gaulle, Vice Admiral Muselier assumes, on 1 July, command of the French Naval and Air Forces, determined to continue the fight, and addresses them as follows:

General Order No. 1

Flag and general officers, officers, warrant officers, petty officers and noncommissioned officers, seamen and airmen of the French armies of the Air and of the Sea,

Never has a more solemn hour nor a more opportune time struck to remind you that you must obey your superiors "in everything that they will command you, for the good of the service and for the success of the arms of France."

You are therefore released of all obligations to obey those who consent, on orders of the enemy, to hand over, without a fight, the ships of our Fleet, an act that stands alone in the annals of our glorious history.

I am issuing orders to French ships of war and of commerce and to the French Air Force to assemble without delay at the closest Allied or Free French base with a view to immediate operations against the enemy.

Everyone must understand that our enemies will always find, in the terms of the armistices signed under duress, a pretext to dismember France, after having totally occupied it, in order to have the Fleet, the Air Force, and the empire handed over to them and to utilize them against ourselves and against our Allies.

Only our action will deliver France by safeguarding the honor of our Flag. Our task will be facilitated by the French empire, even when provisionally separated from occupied France. The empire will understand, and it will do its duty by placing at our disposal its 70 million inhabitants and its infinite resources.

I assume full personal responsibility for the orders which I have just issued.

LONG LIVE FRANCE!

VICE ADMIRAL MUSELIER

APPENDIX C

To: Admiral Gensoul
From: Admiral Somerville

His Majesty's Goverment have commanded me to inform you as follows:

They agreed to the French Government approaching the German Government only on condition that if an armistice was concluded the French Fleet should be sent to British ports to prevent its falling into the hands of the enemy. The Council of Ministers declared on the 18th of June that before capitulating on land, the French Fleet would join up with the British Force or sink itself.

Whilst the Present French Government may consider that the terms of their armistice with Germany and Italy are reconcilable with these undertakings, H. M. Government finds it impossible from their previous experience to believe Germany and Italy will not at any moment that suits them seize French warships and use them against Britain and her Allies. Italian armistice prescribes that French ships should return to metropolitan ports, and under armistice France is required to yield up units for coast defense and minesweeping.

It is impossible for us, your comrades up till now, to allow your fine ships to fall into power of German or Italian enemy. We are determined to fight on until the end, and if we win, as we think we shall, we shall never forget that France was our Ally, that our interests are the same as hers, and that our common enemy is Germany. Should we conquer, we solemnly declare we shall restore the greatness and territory of France. For this purpose, we must be sure that the best ships of the French Navy will also not be used against us by the common foe. In these circumstances His Majesty's Government have instructed me to demand the French Fleet now at Mers--el-Kebir and Oran shall act in accordance with one of the following alternatives:

(a) Sail with us and continue to fight for victory against the Germans and Italians.

(b) Sail with reduced crews under our control to a British port. The reduced crews will be repatriated at the earliest moment. If either of these courses is adopted by you, we will restore your ships to France at the conclusion of the war or pay full compensation, if they are damaged meanwhile.

(c) Alternatively, if you feel bound to stipulate that your ships not be used against Germans or Italians since this would break the armistices, then sail them with us with reduced crews to some French port in the West Indies—Martinque, for instance—where they can be demilitarized to our satisfaction, or perhaps be entrusted to the United States and remain safe until the end of the war, the crews being repatriated.

If you refuse these fair offers, I must, with profound regret, require you to sink your ships within six hours.

Finally, failing the above, I have the orders of His Majesty's Government to use whatever force may be necessary to prevent your ships from falling into German or Italian hands.

APPENDIX D

(1) *Letter from Admiral Auphan to Grand Admiral Raeder*

Vichy, 11 November 1942

Rear Admiral Auphan
Secretary of the Navy
to
Grand Admiral Raeder

I do not have the honor of knowing you, but we are both members of the military profession and seamen, which is a sufficient introduction.

You are at the head of the German Navy, as I now am at the head of the French Navy, under the orders of the Marshal, Chief of State, Commander in Chief of the Armed Forces.

Patriots, each of us, you will certainly understand, as I do, the emotion which grips the French Navy in the circumstances existing today.

True to its agreements and to its given pledge, the French Navy fought fiercely, and without faltering, against the aggressors, who were your enemies and against who—I am speaking of the Americans—it harbored no hatred.

It did this out of respect for the armistice, for the sake of its honor.

Since Mers-el-Kebir and Dakar, some fifty ships of war sunk or damaged and thousands of dead or wounded are the price we paid for that fidelity.

Today, the bases of the armistice which safeguarded the independence of the Navy are impaired.

I earnestly request you to take into account our record since the armistice in order that the French Navy be respected, as well as the independence of the Marshal, for whom the Navy has fought.

There are things which we cannot do. But we can meet on the path of honor and of loyalty to our respective countries.

Please accept, Grand Admiral, the assurances of my high consideration.

Rear Admiral Auphan
Secretary of the Navy
Chief of Naval Operations of the Naval Forces
(Signed)   Auphan

394

(2) *Reply of Grand Admiral Raeder*

Paris, 12 November 1942

GRAND ADMIRAL RAEDER

to

REAR ADMIRAL AUPHAN

I thank you warmly for your letter and particularly appreciate the expression of patriotic sentiments on the part of a military man and a seaman.

You may rest assured, Admiral, that I understand all the better the sentiments which must under present circumstances animate the French Navy since I can appreciate the noble and courageous conduct of which the French Navy has given proof in the attacks it has been subjected to at Mers-el-Kebir, at Dakar, and now in that aggression in French Africa where it engaged itself to the utmost.

The German Navy values the heavy sacrifices which the French Navy has suffered in order to remain faithful to its treaties and to its honor.

Just as at the time of the armistice the German Command did not impose any demands which could reflect on the honor of the French Navy or of the French people, likewise in these new circumstances it does not intend to withdraw from the French Navy the respect the latter has merited by its attitude.

In accordance with the orders of the Führer, the German troops which have been sent to the Mediterranean coast must, with the French Army, undertake the defense of the French frontiers against all enemy attacks.

Up to the present the attitude of the French Navy justifies my conviction that it will not evade that task. The conduct of the leaders of the French Navy at Toulon—Admiral Marquis and Admiral de Laborde, to whom I request you transmit the high regard which I attach to their declarations—bears me out, as well as your letter, in that opinion.

It is for that reason that it was possible to entrust the defense of Toulon exclusively to the French Navy.

In the same way that I assure you that I have not contemplated restricting the French Navy and, in particular, its Fleet, allow me to point out to you that the Führer in his declaration pledged the complete liberty and independence of Marshal Pétain.

I express the hope that in the future our two Navies will carry out their common tasks in close and loyal cooperation.

Please accept, Admiral, the assurances of my high consideration.

(Signed) RAEDER, GRAND ADMIRAL

(3) *Note from French Admiralty to German Armistice Commission*

The engagement to defend Toulon against anyone cannot include offensive operations on the high seas in order to take part in hostilities between the Axis and its enemies, or to participate in common defense of those sections of the coast occupied by Axis troops.

(In accordance with Admiral Auphan's orders, this note was delivered on 14 November 1942, by Admiral Marquis, Commandant of the Toulon Naval District, to the local representatives of the German armistice commission.)

APPENDIX E

Algiers, 13 November 1942

Residents of French Africa,

The Marshal designated General Noguès as his Delegate in Africa on 10 November 1942, before the entry of German troops into the Free Zone, in the belief that I had been deprived of my liberty.

General Noguès came yesterday, 12 November, to Algiers. In complete liberty, in complete agreement with him and at his request, I assume the responsibility for French interests in Africa.

I have the support of the American authorities, with whom I count on insuring the defense of North Africa.

Every governor or resident remains at his post and insures, as in the past, the administration of his territory in accordance with the laws in force.

French and Moslems,

I rely on your complete discipline.

Each one to his post.

LONG LIVE THE MARSHAL, LONG LIVE FRANCE!

ADMIRAL OF THE FLEET DARLAN
(Signed)   Darlan

397

Index

Spitz, Lt. Comdr. Jean, 335
Sprague, Comdr. D. V., RN, 125
Stalin, Joseph, 21
Sticca, Lt. Comdr. Louis, 233
Stiesberg, Lt. Comdr. F. M., USN, 335
Stosskopf, Captain Jacques (EDO), 302, 311
Strasbourg, 13, 22, 30, 34, 97, 127, 131, 132, 133, 146, 255, 262, 263, 266, 267, 313, 315, 316, 337
Stülpnagel, General Karl H. von, GA, 186
Sturges, General R. G., BA, 205
Sub-Chaser No. 6, 56
Sub-Chaser No. 9, 56, 68
Sub-Chaser No. 41, 56
Suffren, 34, 272, 286, 290, 292, 366
Sullivan, Commodore William A., USN, 234
Sultane, 272, 290, 293
Supreme Allied War Council, 74, 75
Surcouf, 28, 90, 124, 125, 162, 168, 265
Surprise, 225, 226, 321, 324, 352
Suwanee, U.S.S., 230, 235
Suzanne René, 305
Syfret, Rear Admiral E. N., RN, 204, 205
Syria, attack on, 197

TA-36, 298
TA-37, 298
Tachin, Lieut, Marcel, 293
Tahure, 194, 195, 272, 356
Tanatside, H.M.S., 322
Tarbé de Saint-Hardouin, Jacques, 212, 275
Tarn, 187, 270
Tartu, 255, 266
Task Force, Center, 216
  Eastern, 216
  Western, 216, 229
Tautog, U.S.S., 356
Tempête, 272, 290, 296, 335, 347
Terraux, Rear Admiral Jules, 195
Terrible, 127, 133, 191, 272, 282, 287, 290, 293, 295, 296, 297, 298, 332, 334, 339, 348
Texas, U.S.S., 322, 334
Thames, H.M.S., 125
Thétis, 257, 267
Thierry d'Argenlieu, Lt. Comdr. Georges

(Admiral), 161, 182, 188, 192, 290, 304, 341, 365, 375
Thomburi, 196
Thorez, Maurice, 376
Tiens bon, 306
Tigre, 127, 133, 257, 264, 266, 290, 313, 347
Tillon, Charles, 376
Tirpitz, 163
Tonkin, reoccupied, 367
Tonnant, 236
Tornade, 225, 226
Toulon Fleet, talk of scuttling, 257, 258
  scuttling of, 262, 263, 264, 265, 266
Touraille, Lt. Comdr. Charles, 237, 350
Tourane, 360, 361
Tourville, 136, 272, 286, 290, 292, 368
Toussaint de Quièvrecourt, Comdr. Pierre, 182
Touzet du Vigier, Colonel Jean, 227
Tramontane, 225, 226
Trat, 195
Traub, Vice Admiral Marcel, 89
Trautmann, Comdr. Henri, 371
Trifels, 35
Triomphant, 50, 79, 159, 161, 168, 272, 290, 365, 368, 375
Trolley de Prévaux, Captain Jacques, 311
Trombe, 257, 264, 267, 290, 313, 347, 348
Troubridge, Commodore T. A., RN, 216, 226, 332
Tuck, S. Pinkney, 210
Tunisia, occupation by axis, 239
Tunisien, 335
Tur, Admiral Vittoria, IN, 312
Turquoise, 270
Tuscaloosa, U.S.S., 230, 233, 334
Typhon, 225, 226, 227

U-35, 90
U-41, 32
U-54, 32
U-55, 32
U-136, 161
U-156, 315
U-230, 335
U-371, 293
U-432, 164
U-444, 164